The Speeches
in Vergil's
Aeneid

THE SPEECHES
IN VERGIL'S
AENEID

GILBERT HIGHET

PRINCETON, NEW JERSEY
PRINCETON UNIVERSITY PRESS

Publication of this book has been aided by a grant from
the Louis A. Robb Fund of
Princeton University Press.

This book has been composed in Linotype Granjon

Printed in the United States of America
by Princeton University Press, Princeton, New Jersey

CONTENTS

v

CONTENTS

vii

ACKNOWLEDGMENTS

My gratitude goes to Professor Georg Luck of Bonn and Johns Hopkins, who was kind enough to read the entire book in draft form and to give me salutary criticism, and to the late Professor George Duckworth of Princeton, who discussed certain problems with me by letter. I have also to thank several scholars who helped me by answering enquiries: my Columbia colleagues Professors W. M. Calder III and Steele Commager; Professor Henry Rowell of Johns Hopkins; Professor Rudolf Pfeiffer, now of Munich; and Professor G. Widmann, head of the Tübingen University Library.

G. H.

Columbia University, New York
July 1971

The Speeches
in Vergil's
Aeneid

The symbol + joins two passages which should be considered as a unity. Thus, Dido's speech on her deathbed is denoted by *Aen.* 4.651-658 + 659-662.

The symbol ≈ placed between two quotations means that one is derived from, or closely parallels, the other. Thus, *Aen.* 4.366 ≈ *Buc.* 8.43 calls attention to the adaptation of "duris in cotibus" in the song of Damon as "duris . . . cautibus" in Dido's speech.

The symbol X between two citations shows that one contradicts the other.

CHAPTER ONE

INTRODUCTION

I N THE *Aeneid*, the speeches are one of the most important elements of Vergil's art. Through them he shows us the inmost hearts of his characters; recalls the past and forecasts the future; and expresses conflicts almost as violent as a duel in armor. They contain some of his most subtle and some of his most powerful achievements in style and meter. In several of them he deploys the devices of Greek rhetoric, highly developed, and yet, in his hands, neither unnatural nor ostentatious. By the skillful disposition of short and long speeches through the twelve books of his epic, he shows us the failure or success of a character, the growth of a determination, and the movement of a long and deadly struggle.

The speeches were studied by Roman critics and imitated by Roman writers as enthusiastically as the rest of the *Aeneid*. Quintilian often cites them to illustrate points of oratorical technique when we might expect him to quote a prose author.[1] But on the whole, unlike many of his successors, he is aware of the difference between prose oratory and poetic epic: *et poesis ab Homero et Vergilio tantum fastigium accepit et eloquentia a Demosthene atque Cicerone (Inst. 12.11.26)*; and he treats Vergil purely as a poet when discussing his literary merit *(Inst. 10.1.85-86)*. Later Roman authors, however, came to regard the entire *Aeneid* as a work of oratory, and Vergil himself as an orator. Early in the second century A.D., P. Annius Florus wrote a dialogue called *Vergilius orator an poeta*. It cannot now be judged, since nothing survives but part of the introduction. But the idea indicated by the title survived, and

---

[1] E.g. apostrophe *(Aen.* 3.56-57, *Inst.* 9.3.25), irony *(Aen.* 4.381 and 11.383-385, *Inst.* 9.2.48-49), a simple question *(Aen.* 1.369, *Inst.* 9.2.7), and a gesture of deprecation *(Aen.* 3.620 and 1.335, *Inst.* 11.3.70).

reappeared in the *Saturnalia* of Macrobius. In the fourth book of his *Saturnalia* one of the speakers sets out to prove that Vergil understood all the methods of exciting pathos known to rhetoric. To show how what he calls an *oratio pathetica* achieves its effects, he chooses Juno's second soliloquy (*Aen.* 7.293-322) and points out such features as initial exclamation ("heu stirpem inuisam!"), *breues interrogatiunculae*, hyperbole, irony, and so forth.[2] In Book Five, the symposiasts agree that Vergil should be styled an orator as much as a poet. A vague expression of admiration, we should think—except that one of them, Avienus, seriously inquires whether one would become a better orator by studying Vergil or Cicero. To this Eusebius replies that Vergil's genius embraces all forms of eloquence, Cicero's only one. He then classifies the Roman orators into four types, each with its own style: Cicero, rich; Sallust, curt; Fronto, dry; Pliny and Symmachus, full and flowing. When he declares, "Vnus omnino Vergilius inuenitur qui eloquentiam ex omni genere conflauerit," he has forgotten, or chooses to ignore, the fact that Cicero himself was proud of being able to speak in different styles and to maintain the manner proper to each type of subject. Cicero's ideal was the orator who could "parua summisse, modica temperate, magna grauiter dicere," as he says in *Orator* 101, where he proceeds to illustrate the ideal by three of his own speeches.[3] It is difficult to take Eusebius seriously when he proceeds (5.1.16) to distinguish styles of oratory which are "dispari moralitate diuersi," to assign one to Crassus and one to Antonius (the two chief speakers in Cicero's *De Oratore*, whose speeches

---

[2] "Nichts kläglicher und öder als die Behandlung, die Macrobius vom schulmässig rhetorischen Standpunkt dem virgilischen Pathos angedeihen lässt," says Heinze, p. 432 n. 1. St. Augustine tells how one of his exercises in rhetorical school was to rewrite Juno's first monologue (1.37-49) in prose as *uerba Iunonis irascentis*; but he implies that he thought it a poor sort of training (*Conf.* 1.17.27).

[3] For a discussion see L. Laurand, *Etudes sur le style des discours de Cicéron*, vol. 3 (Paris, 1936-1938, repr. Amsterdam, 1965), c. 4.

4

were not extant), and then to say that Vergil parallels them with the speech of Latinus to Turnus (*Aen*. 12.19-21) and a taunt of Aeneas to a doomed opponent (*Aen*. 10.599-600). Finally Eusebius declares that Vergil was better than all the ten Attic orators put together: at which one of his listeners rather ineffectually protests. This kind of thing was energetic propaganda for the national classic, and perhaps necessary in an age when culture was threatened, but it contributed nothing to the serious study of the speeches in the *Aeneid*.

In the same era, late in the fourth century A.D., one Tiberius Claudius Donatus wrote a continuous commentary on the *Aeneid* in which he treated the entire poem as oratory. Long before his time, professional teachers of rhetoric had been using the *Aeneid* as a manual by which to illustrate the principles of their art. The treatise of Donatus is the sole surviving example of this system.[4] It is not wholly misconceived. Donatus tries to interpret Vergil on a level higher than that of the *grammaticus*, the explainer of hard words, unusual genders, peculiar syntactical usages, and similar linguistic problems, whose questions and answers fill many a page of Servius. He himself says, "Si Maronis carmina conpetenter attenderis et eorum mentem congrue conprehenderis, inuenies in poeta rhetorem summum atque inde intelleges Vergilium non grammaticos, sed oratores praecipuos tradere debuisse."[5] However, he and his contemporaries believed oratory to be the central literary art. He treated the *Aeneid* therefore as an orator's masterpiece. He defines it (*prooem*., p. 2) as belonging to the *laudatiuum genus*, and explains it as something between a gigantic eulogy and a subtle speech for the defense: "purgata

---

[4] So says Georgii in his edition, vol. 1 (Leipzig, 1905) praef. vii. But see a brief analysis of Amata's speech (*Aen*. 7.359-372) into various types of *status* by the fifth-century scholar Grillius: *Commentum in Ciceronis Rhetorica*, ed. J. Martin (Paderborn, 1927) p. 66. There is a good introduction to Donatus by E. Wölfflin, "Die interpretationes Vergilianae des Cl. Donatus," *ALL* 15 (1908) 253-260.

[5] *Prooem*., p. 4.

persona (sc. Aeneae) quam propria defensione Vergilius tuebatur, quod ad oratoris officium pertinebat, diuersae partis, hoc est inimicae (sc. Iunonis), fuerat deformanda" (*prooem.*, p. 4). He does not regard the *Aeneid* as an imaginative poem which contains some speeches. He sees it as a single long speech delivered by Vergil. Furthermore, when he points out what he identifies as rhetorical devices used within the speeches of the epic, he does not make the basic distinction between a formal oration, in which the poet manifestly arranged the arguments according to the rules of art, and those rapid spontaneous utterances which would be suggested to any creative poet by the character and the situation. Thus, it is correct to analyze the opposing orations of Venus and Juno before the council of the gods (*Aen.* 10.18-95) as pieces of formal rhetoric. But when Andromache tells Aeneas how she was carried off by Pyrrhus as a concubine and then discarded (*Aen.* 3.321-329), it is quite inappropriate to treat her words as a quasi-legal speech in which she denies the implied charge of sexual immorality: "ecce egit oblique causam suam qualitate absoluta, . . . adserens non in facto esse crimen sed in uoluntate." This, like much of Donatus's work, is a sad example of dogged industry misdirected.[6] Of a similar Greek commentator, Spengel observes, "Vix credas hominem ita delirare, ut versus

[6] C. Hoppe, in *De Tib. Claudio Donato Aeneidos interprete* (Göttingen, 1891), gives examples of this man's carelessness, ignorance, and lack of critical acumen. When the Trojans turn their ships to the Libyan shore—*litora cursu / contendunt petere* (*Aen.* 1.157-158)—Donatus remarks that *contendunt* shows how difficult it is to walk quickly through water. On 5.270-272 he ignores *ordine debilis uno* and explains that, since all the oars were lost, Sergestus was pulling the ship by hand. One of the funniest of his misapplications of rhetorical theory is his comment on *Aen.* 4.367. Flaming with rage, Dido says that Aeneas was suckled by Hyrcanian tigresses. "Tractat poeta hoc loco pueris per alimoniam lactis etiam nutricum mores infundi, quod ipsum et Ciceroni placuisse manifestum est, qui in educatione futuri oratoris iubet praecipuas adhiberi mulieres." (Georgii suggests this is an allusion to *De Or.* 3.44-45; but it is a mistake for Quintilian 1.1.4-5, perhaps suggested by the mention of Laelia in both contexts.)

Homeri explicans artem rhetoricam docere sibi videatur" (3, praef., p. ix).

Some examples of this misplaced rhetorical subtlety can be found in the commentary of Servius. Naturally. Long before his day rhetoricians had gone through the entire epic, cutting it into sections suitable (in their view) for the teaching of oratory: "et Titianus et Caluus . . . themata omnia de Vergilio elicuerunt et deformarunt ad dicendi usum."[7] Servius himself is more of a grammarian, but brief remarks on rhetorical interpretation are not infrequent both in his commentary and in that of "Servius auctus." Some are appropriate enough in a superficial way—as when he calls Venus's coaxing speech to Vulcan (8.374-386) a *rhetorica suasio* and Anna's reply to Dido (4.31-53) a *suasoria omni parte plena*. Others are trivial or misconceived. For example, when Vergil describes the casualties of the first conflict between Trojans and Latins (7.531-539), why does he mention, first Almo, then many unnamed Italians, and then Galaesus, who attempted to make peace? Clearly because Almo was a brother of Silvia, whose pet stag was shot by Ascanius—so that the accidental injury done by the Trojans became a major wrong; and because Galaesus was a just man, not a hot-headed belligerent—so that the Trojans who killed him appeared to be ruthless marauders. But Servius explains it thus: "rhetorice uiles trudit in medium, nobiles uero primo et ultimo commemorat loco." He is thinking of the rhetorical device by which the more powerful arguments should be placed first and last, with the weaker between them—"in the Homeric manner," says Quintilian.[8] But is it really likely that Vergil had this pattern of persuasion in mind when he wrote his narrative of the unhappy combat? Surely this is to neglect deeper emotional values for the sake of neat external arrange-

---

[7] Servius on *Aen.* 10.18. Et uetanus et catulinus *F*. Servius possibly means Julius Titianus, a scholar and rhetorician contemporary with Fronto (*RE X*, 1.842-843, s.v. Iulius [512] Titianus).

[8] *Inst.* 5.12.14, alluding to *Il.* 4.297-300.

ment. Or again: one of the most moving moments in the epic is the appearance of Hector's ghost to Aeneas (2.289-295). The speech of the phantom is instant with urgency, heavy with doom. It is repugnant to the sense of poetry to have these few lines classified into arguments designed to persuade Aeneas, in spite of his undoubted courage, to take flight from his home; and yet Servius does so, saying that they form a *suasoria* employing the three main arguments—advantage ("eripe flammis"), necessity ("hostis habet muros"), and honor ("sacra suosque tibi commendat Troia penatis"). Eventually we come to distrust the common sense of scholiasts such as Servius, and the critical validity of rhetorical principles which can be so crudely misapplied.

Partly because of this distrust, modern scholars have paid less attention to the speeches in the *Aeneid* than to other aspects of Vergil's poetry. For example, in his long and careful article on Vergil in Pauly-Wissowa, Karl Büchner allots them no separate treatment.[9] Nor does Brooks Otis in *Virgil: A Study in Civilized Poetry* (Oxford, 1963), who devotes only five pages to the two great debates of Books Ten and Eleven.

One of the first modern critics to consider the speeches as a separate element in the *Aeneid* was J. Kvíčala, whose *Neue Beitraege zur Erklaerung der Aeneis* (Prague, 1881) contain the results of many years' careful and loving analysis of the poem. On the speeches his work was chiefly statistical. There are reasons for modifying some of his results,[10] but his keen eye for detail, his fine taste, and his tireless industry make him an admirable example for all Vergilians.

Eduard Norden remarked in the first appendix of his

[9] *RE* VIII A, 1 (1955) 1021-1264 and VIII A, 2 (1958) 1265-1486, published separately as *P. Vergilius Maro, der Dichter der Römer* (Stuttgart, 1959).
[10] See p. 304.

Antike Kunstprosa[11] that Vergil, with his delicate aesthetic sensibility, made a very limited use of "das Rhetorische"— which term, as the context shows, means both oratorical principles of structure and figures of speech and of thought. But later he came to believe that rhetoric was a most important adjunct of Vergil's art. In his edition of *Aeneid* 6 (Leipzig, 1903) he analyzed many of the speeches in that book along rhetorical lines. Here, as Richard Heinze was to point out, he sometimes went too far.[12] It is always tempting to apply the neat patterns of the rhetorical manuals to any extended speech, whether the author meant it to be a piece of oratory or not. Like others before and after him, Norden fell into this trap. When the sad ghosts of Palinurus and Deiphobus meet Aeneas in the underworld and describe the manner of their deaths (*Aen.* 6.347-371 and 509-530), is it even remotely likely that Vergil laid out their speeches in accordance with rhetorical schemata? Not in the slightest; and, as Norden applied them, the schemata do not fit.[13] Nevertheless Norden helped all students of Vergil by pointing out the exquisite symmetry underlying some of the great passages of the *Aeneid*: even though that symmetry was not always, or even frequently, rhetorical in inspiration.

Few scholars have written more wisely and sympathetically about Vergil's use of rhetoric than Richard Heinze. See in particular pp. 403-435 of *Virgils epische Technik*. Out of these pages, rich in learning and good sense, some central points emerge. One is that in the *Aeneid* the speeches are emphatically different in character from those of Homer: far more intense, more concentrated, less rambling, more carefully built and motivated. They contain many more arguments: for example, Latinus's address to Turnus (*Aen.* 12.19-45) is more

---

[11] First edition 1898; fifth edition reproduced from the second, Stuttgart, 1958. See section VIII of the book, p. 891.

[12] Heinze, pp. 424-425 n. 2.   [13] See pp. 107-108.

9

diplomatic and versatile than Priam's plea to Hector (*Il.* 22.38-76). Nevertheless, Heinze points out that (unlike Ovid and others) Vergil is usually careful to conceal the structural plan of his speeches. He knows the frontier between prose and poetry, and prefers to stress emotion rather than intellectual ingenuity. Both in this section and elsewhere in Heinze's book there are many illuminating remarks on the models (Homeric and other) which helped to inspire Vergil in composing his speeches. We can only wish that Heinze had gone further and given us a close analysis of them all.

When the second edition of Heinze's book came out, Wilhelm Kroll was moved to write a knowledgeable but slightly perverse review-article, "Die Originalität Vergils."[14] In this there is a suggestive critique of Vergil's speeches. The *Aeneid* is not, says Kroll, a set of declamations like the poetry of Ovid. Yet the study of rhetoric is obvious on every page; and Vergil's brilliant speeches constitute one of his chief claims to true originality. Kroll gives many examples of the poet's effective use of figures of speech and figures of thought which can properly be called rhetorical. From a sometimes captious critic who rather distrusted rhetoric, this is praise.

A Johns Hopkins thesis, *Aspects of the Speech in the Later Roman Epic*, was published by H. C. Lipscomb (Baltimore, 1909) and summarized by him under a slightly different title

[14] *NJbb* 21 (1908) 513-531. Kroll had already published an unfortunate essay, "Studien über die Komposition der Aeneis," *NJbb* Suppl. 27 (1902) 135-169, in which he described the epic as "planlos," and seriously asserted that inconsistencies between the facts of the narrative and their distortion in partisan speeches, or between different parts of a propaganda speech, proved Vergil's inefficiency. E.g., Sinon says that he went to war in his first youth (2.87) but claims to have "dulcis natos" (2.138). But these are both appeals for sympathy, some distance apart, and the listeners would not immediately detect their incongruence. In 7.52-80 Latinus is warned by omens and soothsayers not to give his daughter to Turnus; but, says Kroll, the speeches of Amata (7.365-372) and Allecto (7.423-424) "show that the facts are different." (On this general point see p. 285 below.) Kroll, by the way, did not believe Heinze, and refused to admit that the character of Aeneas changed in the course of the poem.

10

in *CW* 2 (1908-1909) 114-117. It is almost wholly statistical. It analyzes the length and frequency of the speeches in Vergil, Lucan, Valerius Flaccus, Statius, Silius Italicus, and Claudian; lists the different types of speaker in the different poems; compares the extent of dialogues and of grouped speeches (which become markedly fewer after the *Aeneid*); and examines the use of monologues. Although this is a dry little book, it contains many useful and some curious facts; and in spite of a few oversights[15] it deserves consideration in any study of the Roman epic poets.

Eduard Norden's practice of citing rhetorical manuals when analyzing Vergil was attacked with some subtlety (and perhaps a dash of anti-German rancor) by a young French scholar who later rose to eminence. This was Mlle. A. Guillemin in her doctoral dissertation at the University of Dijon: *Quelques injustices de la critique interne à l'égard de Virgile* (Chalon-sur-Saône, 1921). In her third chapter she asked whether the rhetorician Menander's rules might not have been inspired by the study of Vergil, rather than that (as Norden suggested) Vergil followed rules codified by Menander's predecessors.[16] She did admit that the tone of the *Aeneid* was "notably oratorical." She proposed that Vergil was following, not manuals of rhetoric, but the practice of Roman orators: in particular the pleas for sympathy, *commiserationes*, which marked the climaxes of some of Cicero's finest speeches, e.g. *Cael.* 79-80, *Mil.* 102-105, and *Mur.* 88-90. She also pointed to Vergil's use of

[15] E.g., he says that the longest speech in Roman epic appears in Statius. He is referring to Hypsipyle's narrative of the murder of the Lemnian men (*Theb.* 5.49-498). But that narrative recalls the recital of Aeneas both in its introduction, "immania uulnera, rector, / integrare iubes" ≈ *Aen.* 2.3, and in its close, "me praedonum manus . . . / . . . uestras . . . transmittit in oras" ≈ *Aen.* 3.715. Therefore Statius considered Aeneas's narrative to be a speech: it is of course far longer than Hypsipyle's. Lipscomb declares that the shortest speech is in Claudian, "ipse uenit" (*Bell. Goth.* 461), but excludes four one-word exclamations, "aquae!" (Stat. *Theb.* 4.805, 806), "mater!" (*Theb.* 9.350), and "Crenaee!" (*Theb.* 9.356).

[16] Menander does not mention Vergil; as a Greek, he cites Greek classics.

11

enthymemes ("une sorte d' *a-fortiori*") such as *Aen.* 1.39-48, 7.304-310, and 10.81-84, and to certain other usages borrowed from oratory, such as the exclamation "mene . . . !" (Cic. *Mil.* 102 and *Aen.* 1.37).

Writing at Tübingen in the depths of the depression after the First World War, Ernst Conrad produced a valuable thesis entitled *Untersuchungen zu der Technik der Reden in Vergils Aeneis* (1923). Suggested by Gundermann, supervised after his death by Weinreich, and submitted in typescript, it was never printed and never reviewed. A pity: because it is both learned and intelligent. It is an examination of twelve strongly emotional speeches—for instance, those of Euryalus's mother (9.481-497) and Pallas's father (11.152-181). Many parallels from literature and inscriptions are cited to illustrate them. Among other good observations, Conrad reminds us that, in order to appreciate a speech in Vergil, we must read it aloud—Vergil himself recited some of his poetry with great power and passion;[17] and that no two speeches in the epic follow precisely the same pattern, since each is rooted in its περίϲταϲιϲ.

In 1932 Karl Billmayer pushed the subject back to the fourth century with his Würzburg dissertation *Rhetorische Studien zu den Reden in Vergils Aeneis*. He began by assuming that all the speeches in the poem, without exception, were rhetorically constructed (because the "principles of form" were absolute and infrangible rules which not even a genius such as Vergil could transgress), that each of them necessarily fell into one of the three main classes of formal oratory (*deliberatiuum, demonstratiuum, iudiciale*), and furthermore that each could be divided into the sections specified for formal oratory by the youthful Cicero (*De Inu.* 1.14.19).[18] Since most of the speeches

---

[17] Servius on 4.323: dicitur autem ingenti adfectu hos uersus pronuntiasse, cum priuatim paucis praesentibus recitaret Augusto.

[18] In giving this scheme, Cicero is dealing mainly with legal speeches, as the context shows: see *De Inu.* 1.11.14-16, 13.17-19, 16.22.

in the poem will not respond to such analysis, this was a serious misconception. Billmayer made it worse by misapplying the rules: for example, by asserting that when the Penates reinterpret the oracle of Apollo (*Aen.* 3.161-171) their words are the solution of a controversy classifiable as a *constitutio incidens*. Many other such abuses of rhetorical theory disfigure this laborious but careless and wrongheaded little book.[19]

A brief but useful introduction to the subject was written by M. L. Clarke, "Rhetorical Influences in the *Aeneid*," *G & R* 18 (1949) 14-27. One suggestive sentence—"I reckon 2-3 rhetorical questions in each 100 lines of speech in the *Iliad*, 9-10 in the *Aeneid*"—is unfortunately not supported by detailed figures.

Georg Nikolaus Knauer's *Die Aeneis und Homer* (Göttingen, 1964) has put all classical scholars in his debt. Although it devotes no special section to the speeches of the *Aeneid*, it does demonstrate which of them had Homeric models, close or distant, partial or total; and it contains many penetrating comments on their technique and their interrelations. For example (pp. 325-326), Knauer points out that the opening words spoken by Jupiter at his final appearance in the epic, "*quae iam finis* erit, coniunx?" (12.793), recall the plea addressed by Venus to Jupiter at his first appearance: "*quem das finem, rex magne, laborum?*" (1.241); and that the same thought is echoed in Aeneas's encouraging speech to his exhausted comrades: "*dabit* deus his quoque *finem*" (1.199; cf. 1.223). That is only one of many subtle observations by which Knauer reveals unsuspected beauties and powers in Vergil's poetry.

Two works, both thorough and competent, which reached me as I was completing the first draft of this book, make scarcely any mention of the speeches in the *Aeneid* as worthy of study on their own account: K. Quinn's *Virgil's "Aeneid"*

---

[19] At least one entire paragraph dealing with Juno's speech in 10.63-95 has dropped out on p. 13, and smaller misprints are frequent.

(Ann Arbor, 1968) and R. D. Williams's *Virgil* (Oxford, 1967).

Thus there is a gap, even though it may be a small one, in Vergilian scholarship: a gap which it is hoped that this book will either fill, or encourage others to fill.

CHAPTER TWO

THE SPEECHES AND THEIR SPEAKERS

Definition

IT IS NOT altogether easy to define a "speech" in non-dramatic poetry. Still, the context and the phrasing usually show when Vergil intends his readers to imagine they are hearing the actual words of his characters, or their thoughts put into words unspoken. It is more difficult to determine whether a speech delivered in several sections separated by brief intervals is to be considered one speech or several; but it is by no means impossible.

The definition of "speech" proposed here is this. A speech is one or more sentences supposed to be the actual words of a character, framed together on one single occasion—either spoken aloud, or directly reported as being spoken, or shaped in the mind without utterance.

The speeches in the *Aeneid* are of many different types, and vary widely in length. By far the longest is the narrative of Aeneas (2.3–3.715). Because of its great size, scholars have sometimes refrained from listing and discussing it as a speech.[1] Yet it is clearly comparable to the narratives of Evander (8.185-275) and Diana (11.535-594). And it is more than a plain recital of facts. It contains passages of intense feeling in which Aeneas voices his inmost heart (2.431-434, 3.708-711) and even repeats his own passionate outcries (2.657-670). On the other hand, brief speeches are not to be neglected, for they can be intensely solemn (e.g. 6.620) or dramatically important (7.116). A few paragraphs, although perfectly coherent and well con-

---

[1] E.g., M. Schneidewin, "Statistisches zu Homeros und Vergilius," *NJbb* 129 (1884) p. 130, calls the narratives of Odysseus and Aeneas "nur zufällige einkleidungen der erzählung des dichters."

structed, are represented as being thoughts rather than spoken words: e.g., Juno broods over her hostility to Troy, *talia flammato secum . . . corde uolutans* (1.50). Still, these should rank as speeches, like the Homeric monologues in which a solitary hero addresses his own heart. Furthermore, throughout the poem many speeches are not spoken directly, but reported by persons who heard, or feigned to hear, them being delivered. Among these the most important are the narrative of Sinon reported by Aeneas (2.69-194) and the diplomatic response of Diomede reported by Venulus (11.252-293).[2]

Utterances and reflections couched in indirect speech are relatively rare, and seldom important: they are not counted in this analysis.[3] One unique sequence represents part of a choral song, which is given in direct speech after its opening has been summarized indirectly (8.293-302).

The unity of a speech can be established through the sense of dramatic necessity and continuity. For example, Sinon speaks four times to Priam and the Trojans (2.69-72, 77-104, 108-144, and 154-194). After each utterance he pauses. Nevertheless, the whole should be considered to be one speech: for several reasons. (1) Sinon delivers it on one single occasion to the same audience: *prosequitur* (2.107). (2) The three pauses in it are all occupied by questions, each leading on to the next stage: *hortamur fari quo sanguine cretus* (2.74), *ardemus scitari et quaerere causas* (2.105), "quo molem hanc immanis equi statuere?" (2.150). (3) Sinon has evidently planned it as a single effort of deception, a lie whose head and tail are connected like those of a snake. Thus it is best understood as resembling a messenger's narrative in Greek drama. Such narratives are often interrupted by questions and comments.[4] The essential difference is that almost all the mes-

---

[2] They are listed in Appendix 6.

[3] For a list, see Appendix 7.

[4] E.g., the herald's narrative in Aesch. *Agam.* 503-680, the guard's in Soph. *Ant.* 223-331, the messenger's in Eur. *Hipp.* 1153-1264.

sengers of Greek tragedy tell the truth as they understand it; while Sinon's narrative, so well articulated and so carefully detailed, is a lie.[5]

Unlike Homer, Vergil occasionally breaks a speech by parentheses and "stage-directions"—a practice in which he was followed by Ovid and other Latin poets. Such interruptions, however, do not make two speeches out of one. In a speech of the Sibyl he actually breaks a sentence:

> "at ramum hunc"—aperit ramum qui ueste latebat—
> "agnoscas."   (6.406-407)

He does the same in the oath of Latinus (12.206-211). The outcry of Aletes to Nisus and Euryalus is interrupted by a brief description of his gesture and his tears; still, his words constitute one speech and not two (9.247-250 + 252-256).[6] The command of Gyas to his steersman, although broken by a pause in which he waits for his orders to be obeyed, is a single speech (5.162-164 + 166) comparable to the triumphant cry of Iapyx (12.425 + 427-429). So is the final speech of Dido, which she breaks to kiss the bed on which she is to die (4.651-658 + 659-662).

The great genealogical prophecy of Anchises (6.756f.) does not, as is sometimes supposed, end with "debellare superbos" (6.853). The climax is still to come. The speech continues—as Vergil shows by *haec mirantibus addit* (6.854). Anchises points out M. Claudius Marcellus, signalizing him with "aspice," as before he pointed out Aeneas's son Silvius with "uides" (6.760), Romulus with "uiden?" (6.779), the Julian family and the Roman heroes with "aspice" (6.788), and the heroes of the early Republic with "aspice" (6.825). He describes him as greatest of all the Roman champions who lived before Augus-

---

[5] The only significant exception is the false account of Orestes' death in the chariot-race, given to Clytemnestra and Electra by the *paedagogus* in Soph. *El.* 680-763.

[6] So the plea of Eurydice in Statius, *Theb.* 6.138-176, although broken at 173, is still a single utterance, as is shown by "reddite" in 171 and 174.

tus: "uictorque uiros supereminet omnis" (6.856).[7] With his victories Marcellus outdid the achievement of Fabius Maximus. And he is the great example of the Roman principle of crushing arrogant resistance: for in his career as the Sword of Rome, "hic . . . sternet Poenos Gallumque rebellem" (6.858). With his rare feat of winning the *spolia opima* (6.859) the prophecy closes in triumph.

However, Anchises' somber evocation of young Marcellus's brief life and mournful death (6.868-886) is a different speech. It is initiated by a question from Aeneas, who did not speak during the prophecy; it is addressed to Aeneas personally in a tone of intimacy—contrast "o nate" in 868 with *mirantibus addit* in 854; and it is filled with totally different language and ethos.

If this analysis is correct, Anchises makes three different long speeches in Elysium, each with its own vocabulary, style, and feeling: one eschatological (6.722 + 724-751), the second oracular and paraenetic (6.756-853 + 855-859), and the last tragic (6.868-886).

Length

It is easy to count the number of complete lines which a speech contains, but more difficult to measure fractional lines at its beginning, inside it (if it is broken), and at its end. Vergil did not always make his characters speak in perfect blocks of symmetrically rounded hexameters. It would be mistaken to treat incomplete lines as though they were statistically equivalent to whole lines, or to treat all incomplete lines as equal to one another. For instance, after seeing the miraculous cure of Aeneas, Iapyx cries

arma citi properate uiro! quid statis? (12.425)

[7] This emphatic phrase makes it impossible to accept the analysis of F. Eggerding, "Parcere subiectis," *Gymnasium* 59 (1952) 31-52: he proposes that the pageant of heroes culminates in Fabius Maximus because of his

The rhythmical scope of this is different from that of other incomplete lines, such as Iulus's

$$\text{heus, etiam mensas consumimus?} \qquad (7.116)$$

and Aeneas's

$$\text{quo deinde ruis? quo proripis?} \qquad (5.741)$$

The differences are small, but they exist and should be taken into account. It seems reasonable to measure lines of verse in metrical feet. The cry of Iapyx comes to four entire feet plus a trochaic word occupying three-quarters of the fifth foot: this can be conveniently represented as nine-twelfths, i.e., three-quarters, of a line. Iulus's exclamation covers four feet, two-thirds of a line; and his father's three and a half feet, seven-twelfths of a line. (Extreme, and perhaps otiose, precision would demand that we distinguish between a trochaic word, covering three-quarters of a dactylic foot, and a long mono-syllable, representing an exact half; yet, as Horatio says, " 'twere to consider too curiously to consider so.") These then are the principles of measurement used in this analysis.

Numbers

On the basis of the above definitions there are 333 speeches in the *Aeneid*.[8] Some are set inside Vergil's narrative, while others are quoted within the context of other speeches. Most reported speeches naturally occur within Aeneas's recital of his adventures. If we count this recital as one single speech

---

magnanimous attitude at the capture of Tarentum, when he refused to treat the statues of the gods as booty (Livy 27.16.8).

[8] Appendix 1 gives all the speeches in sequence, book by book. Fingerle (pp. 68-69) counts 697 speeches in the *Iliad* and 672 in the *Odyssey*, adding (p. 79) that while there are more separate speeches in the *Iliad*, more of the *Odyssey* is occupied by direct speech: "die Ilias ist handlungsreicher, die Odyssee 'wortreicher.' "

19

and exclude numerically all the utterances reported within it (including his own) we have 290 speeches.

There are ninety speaking characters.[9]

On the average, there are about twenty-eight speeches per book. But certain books rise high above the average and others fall below it. Vergil cultivates variety in the ratio of speech to action, as in every other important structural principle. The sixth book, for example, contains little action and much talk. Nevertheless, only eight characters speak in it—four of them only once, and one twice; the speeches of the other three are vitally important.

Distribution by Books

Vergil conceived each book as an artistic unit, with its own special structural line. Therefore the character and the placing of the speeches at the opening and the close of individual books repay study. It is significant that the first voice heard in Book One (and heard twice in succession, if we consider the interior monologue to be equivalent to a speech) is that of Juno, and the last (also heard twice in succession) is that of Dido. Aeneas is surrounded by perils. In Book Four the first voice is that of Dido, and the last (when Dido can speak no more) that of the messenger of Juno. Throughout the book Aeneas says nothing directly until he is confronted by Dido and compelled to answer her (4.333-361): it is indeed this silence which is his dreadful error.[10] After that, in spite of persuasive attempts to make him speak (4.437-449), he opens his mouth only once, in a command to his men to awake and sail instantly (4.573-579).

The fifth book, describing the voyage of escape from Africa

---

[9] For a list, with the speeches made by each, see Appendix 4. Bassett (p. 78) says "There are about seventy-five speaking characters in the *Iliad*, and nearly as many in the *Odyssey*, if we include the Apologue and the tale of Proteus."

[10] See pp. 73-75.

to Italy, opens with a dialogue between Aeneas and his steers-man, and closes with Aeneas guiding his ship toward his future home, and sadly apostrophizing the helmsman, cast away and lost. In Book Six he is an instrument molded by higher forces. The book therefore starts, not with any word from him, but with three speeches by the Sibyl, two of them in a peremptory, even reproachful, tone; and its closing scenes are dominated by his father and teacher.

The Italian book, Seven, begins and ends with narrative. The voices heard in it are Italian—far outnumbering the single speeches of Iulus, Aeneas, and Ilioneus—or superhuman, those of Juno with the demon Allecto planning disaster. It finishes (if indeed it is complete as it stands)[11] with the noise of marching feet, the clatter of horses' hooves, the menacing advance of Turnus, and the paradoxical grace of Camilla. The Roman book, Eight, opens and closes with prophecies: the first, welcoming and reassuring, spoken by father Tiber; the last, foretelling the future of the whole enterprise, embodied without words in the magnificent vision of the shield.

Book Nine is a dreadful trial for the Trojans. Aeneas is ⬛⬛⬛ It starts with a Junonian summons to Turnus; the last ⬛⬛ speech in it is an appeal by a Trojan leader to his almost-defeated men (9.781-787); it ends with a description of Turnus saved, and purified from his sweat and blood, by the gently rolling Tiber. The book of battle, the tenth, is all conflict. It begins in heaven with an oratorical duel between the two divine antagonists, and closes with a combat between Aeneas and the most formidable opponent he has yet confronted in Italy. The last voice heard is that of Mezentius pleading that

[11] The muster of the Italians is no doubt complete by the end of Book Seven, and its ending is less abrupt than that of the catalogue of the Trojans and their allies in *Iliad* 2. Yet there is a marked gap in time and action between Book Seven and Book Eight; and at the beginning of Book Eight no connective appears, comparable to the opening words of Nine, Ten, and Eleven. Vergil may have intended a closing paragraph or two to round out Book Seven.

21

mercy be shown to his corpse. Stabbing him in the throat, Aeneas makes no reply.

After this victory, at the opening of the eleventh book, Aeneas is bold and resolute: he dominates the situation; the first four speeches are given by him. At the conclusion of Eleven there are no speeches, but the name is repeated three times in the same position in three adjoining lines, *Aeneas, Aeneas, Aenean*, as the hero moves toward the final conflict. Twelve opens with an extended conversation in which Turnus shows himself arrogantly confident, snubbing both the prudent king Latinus and the doting queen Amata. As the book ends, he is begging pitifully for mercy, which he does not receive.

The two long sections of Aeneas's narrative, Book Two and Book Three, both begin with impressive *exordia*. The former closes with an evocation of the dawn; the latter with an adieu from Aeneas to the dead Anchises. He has lost his wife, and the father who strengthened him: he is ready for a substitute love.

Grouping

From these general patterns, let us turn now to examine characters whose voices are heard in the *Aeneid*.

Vergil's poem is far more strictly concentrated on a few persons than the Homeric epics. As soon as the *Iliad* opens, a rich variety of voices sounds forth. Chryses pleads with the sons of Atreus. Agamemnon rebuffs him and he prays to Apollo. Achilles addresses Agamemnon and the assembly. Calchas explains the cause of the pestilence. Achilles quarrels with Agamemnon. Athena restrains him. Nestor makes a pacific proposal, but the dispute continues. Thetis tries to console her son and then pleads with Zeus. Hera taunts Zeus, and he silences her, and Hephaestus appeases them. They all speak eloquently and vividly. But Vergil affords to far fewer characters the opportunity to utter dramatic speech. He rarely allows his men and women room to display their personalities without materially advancing the plot, as Homer does with Nestor (*Il.* 1.254-284). Also, he is loth to report extensive interchanges between many different persons or divinities, while Homer delights in them. In the nineteenth book of the *Odyssey* the conversation is almost continuous.[12] Five characters speak: Telemachus thrice, Eurycleia four times, Melantho once, Penelope eleven times, and Odysseus no less than thirteen times: thirty-two speeches in all.[13] This point is made (with a slightly different reckoning—he says twenty-six speeches, perhaps omitting the tactical discussion in 19.1-46) by Bassett.[14] He follows Heinze (pp. 404-409), who analyzes the disparate techniques of Homer and Vergil in the grouping of speeches, emphasizing that Homer always aims at making each scene as vivid and all the characters in it as real as possible, even if the movement of the story is slowed down thereby. Vergil, on the other hand, omits all that his readers can imagine and supply: the steady pace of the narrative is his chief concern. Therefore he does not arrange his speeches in large groups so often and so copiously as Homer.[15] In the Homeric poems it is unusual for one character to address another without receiving a spoken reply, and conversations in which three or four people join are common. In Vergil, the reverse. Commands are issued, narratives are recounted, encouragements and challenges are uttered, often without a word of acknowledgment or reply. The hearer simply listens in silence; or obeys; or acts upon the advice offered; or shares, without speaking, the emotion of his companion.

Of the 333 speeches in the *Aeneid*, 135 are single utterances

---

[12] There is a brief pause at 19.47-64, but the principal character remains on stage. This book is just like a scene from a play.

[13] In addition, a suggested speech, 7-13; an earlier dialogue, 401-412; and two reported speeches, 141-147 and 546-550.

[14] Pp. 60-64: he adds statistics.

[15] See Appendix 3 for the speeches as they are distributed, singly, in couples, or in larger groups.

which receive no reply in words. True, eight of these are soliloquies, not intended to be heard, and a few of the others are apostrophes directed to the unhearing or the unfeeling; but all the rest are solo speeches, heard and accepted without comment.

Then there are 76 speeches set in pairs: usually an address or a question followed by a response, although there are other patterns. Occasionally the second speech is not a reply to the first but is inspired by it. So, when Iarbas prays to him, Jupiter (perhaps not unnaturally in view of his worshipper's insolent tone) vouchsafes no direct answer, but responds by sending Mercury on an admonitory mission (4.206-237).

Extended conversations between two characters are less common. Three speeches arranged in the A-B-A pattern occur twelve times. Four speeches set out like A-B-A-B, occur four times only: in three of these cases the speakers are openly or covertly hostile.[16] At two critical junctures Aeneas is engaged in dialogues where he is instructed and to some extent dominated by feminine advisers and guides. These interviews are particularly important: he and his mother exchange six speeches in 1.321-409, he and Deiphobe in 6.37-155. And the most momentous conversation in the entire epic is that which takes place between Aeneas and the soul of his father in Elysium, where he is taught the doctrine of metempsychosis and shown the future of his race in Italy (6.687-886): this is the only dialogue where eight speeches are distributed between two speakers.

In the *Aeneid* there are also some triangular colloquies involving three persons—like the scene between Hector, Paris, and Helen in *Il.* 6.326-368.[17] There are ten: in two of them one

16 Heinze (p. 405) says that "zweimalige Rede und Gegenrede" occur only in the first book, between Venus and Aeneas, and the ninth, between Nisus and Euryalus. But Jupiter and Juno each speak twice in 10.607-632; and there are more extensive exchanges elsewhere. See Appendix 4.

17 A. S. Pease was misled by Heinze, and perhaps by his own concentration on one book of the poem, into saying "It is in accord with Virgil's prac-

speaker is a god who comments in heaven unheard by human-
ity (Apollo in 9.641-644 and Jupiter in 10.467-472). The three
speakers thrice utter three speeches in all; in three other pas-
sages they speak four speeches; twice only, five speeches. On
two momentous occasions, the refusal of Anchises to leave
Troy (2.638-720) and the death of Pallas at the hands of Tur-
nus (10.441-495), there are six speeches in all.

The conference at which Nisus and Euryalus promise
Ascanius and Aletes to go out and find their leader (9.234-302)
embraces five speeches spoken by four different characters.
The most complex scene of all is the Latin debate (11.243-461)
at which five speakers—one absent but reported verbatim—
make six different orations. Just as Thucydides marks out
crises in his narrative by inserting a big oration or an energetic
debate, so Vergil (except in actual scenes of battle) draws our
attention to powerful moments, by marking them sometimes
with a single emotional speech, sometimes with an earnest and
complex conversation.

The Characters and Their Speeches

The principal speaker is Aeneas. His voice is heard sixty-
nine times.[18] Without counting the narrative in Books Two
and Three, he speaks forty-four times in the first six books,
but only twenty-five in the latter six. In all, he utters 1,958
lines, of which his narrative takes up 1,516.[19] His other speeches
amount in Books One to Six to 345 lines, and in Books Seven
through Twelve to 182 lines: a significant change of ratio.

In actual wordage the next most important speaker is
Evander, who has 249 lines, eight speeches altogether. He fills
the eighth book with the history of Latium and Etruria; but

---

tice . . . to confine his dialogues to only two speakers at a time." (*Aeneidos
Liber Quartus*, Cambridge, 1935, note on line 8, p. 93.)

[18] See pp. 327-329.

[19] Fractions of lines are here omitted (they are given in Appendixes 1 and
4) and figures are rounded off to the nearest integer.

after that he appears only once, uttering his lament for Pallas in Book Eleven.

The characters who, after Aeneas, dominate the greatest extent of the poem by their words are his father Anchises, his enemy Turnus, and his lover Dido. The three have very nearly the same number of lines, although the distribution, length, style, and matter of their speeches are very different.

Anchises speaks seventeen times, covering 235 lines in all: among others, he makes a unique didactic speech and a massive prophecy.

Turnus speaks on twenty-nine occasions, most important being his long strategic oration in the debate, his military address outside the Trojan fort, and his farewell to life. In all, he utters 233 lines.

Dido makes thirteen speeches—four in the first book and no less than nine in the fourth. Only three of these (a libation prayer, a request, and an order) are brief. The others are relatively long, carefully wrought, full of strong emotions. Her speeches amount to 231 lines.

Surely these figures are important. We know from Donatus's biography that Vergil planned his work in prose before starting to transform it into poetry; and we know from the analyses made by scholars working on different aspects of the epic that he was a master of construction and symmetry. Of course it would be far-fetched to suggest that he counted the verses which he allotted to his chief characters; yet he surely weighed their speeches and balanced them. That he should have written almost exactly the same number of lines for the three most active characters after Aeneas can scarcely be an accident.

Divinities appear less often in the *Aeneid* than in the *Iliad*, and speak less volubly. In the entire *Aeneid* there is only one assembly bringing in all the gods, whereas there are at least ten discussions or conversations among the deities in the *Iliad*.

After the five chief human personages, the most prominent

speakers are Venus the protector, Juno the persecutor, and Jupiter the monarch. With no less than five graceful speeches of entreaty (two addressed to Jupiter, one each to Amor, Neptune, and Vulcan) Venus speaks most of the divinities: eleven times, 216 lines. Juno speaks less copiously but more intensely: thirteen times, totalling 179 lines. Jupiter makes his most impressive speeches at the beginning of the epic and at its end: his voice is heard ten times altogether, for a total of 125 lines.

Neptune makes only two speeches (both in indirect opposition to his sister Juno) covering twenty-six lines. Apollo, although he is an important deity and a staunch protector of the Trojans, plays a surprisingly small part in the poem, and appears far less often than in the *Iliad*—although he is prominent in the description of Actium (*Aen.* 8.704-706). He speaks but fifteen lines, four short prophecies (one of them invented by Sinon).

Together with Anchises, the Sibyl Deiphobe dominates Book Six. She has thirteen utterances, the most striking of which are her oracle, her instructions for gaining admission to the other world, and her description of hell. She speaks 157 lines. Sinon's speech in Book Two covers 110 lines, broken into four sections. The feebleness of king Latinus is shown by the fact that, although he utters 111 lines and speaks six times, he remains silent from the seventh book (599) until well into the eleventh (302).

Subordinate characters in the *Aeneid* are painted very dimly as compared with those in Homer; there is no one like Eumaeus or Eurycleia. One reason for this is that they seldom speak. Aeneas's own wife Creusa utters only four lines before her death (2.675-678) and fourteen after it (2.776-789). The hero's constant companion, *fidus Achates*, speaks only four lines, in Book One (582-585): thereafter, though he is often present, he never makes another speech. Even the cattleman Philoetius in the *Odyssey*, who helps Odysseus in the fight

27

against the suitors, has more to say. The prophecy of Helenus covers eighty-nine lines, and Diana's biography of Camilla, sixty; the diplomatic orations of Ilioneus take up seventy-three lines in all, while Andromache has thirty-one.

Young people in the *Aeneid* say very little. The high-spirited Nisus talks most, with fifty-seven lines; but Pallas has only twenty-four, Camilla less than seventeen. Lavinia and Lausus, in spite of their importance in the plot, never speak at all. The voice of Ascanius is heard briefly for the first time in the fifth book, where he sounds like a young prince (5.670-673). During his father's absence, in the ninth book, he speaks four times, uttering forty-one lines in all. Thereafter we see him weeping (12.399) and in the farewell embrace of his father (12.433-434), but he speaks no more. He is no Telemachus.

Vergil gave at least one speech to many individual Trojans, striving to characterize each of them as vividly as Homer does the characters in the *Iliad* and *Odyssey*, although within a narrower compass. Thus in the *Aeneid* we hear the voices of Priam and Hecuba, Hector (loyal to Troy even after death) and Andromache (still remembering her husband and son), and Priam's other sons Polydorus, Helenus, and Deiphobus. However, only a few Greeks say anything: the treacherous Sinon, the brutal Pyrrhus, and the miserable Achaemenides. Helen does not speak. Odysseus, so eloquent in Homer, is silent in the *Aeneid*, although nearly always mentioned with hatred.[20] In the world of death Achilles is not identified, but

[20] The unique description of Odysseus as "infelix" in Aeneas's narrative (3.691) is surprising, coming from the man who elsewhere calls him "dirus" (2.261 and 2.762). It has simply been taken over from Achaemenides (3.613) and goes back to the *Odyssey*: ὄιζυρός, e.g. *Od.* 3.95, 5.105. The whole Achaemenides passage seems to have been written early and little revised. It is the closest of all Vergil's adaptations of Homer and contains fewest original touches; it does not advance the plot; and it contains one very weak invention, the idea that—although the Homeric Odysseus got his men out of the Cyclops' cave one by one (*Od.* 9.415-463)—the "immemores socii" forgot Achaemenides (*Aen.* 3.616-618) and he somehow escaped by himself but missed the ship. Even the name of the sailor is an unfortunate notion, for

he may be one of those who raise the frail, ghostly war-cry at the sight of the Trojan warrior.[21]

Aeneas

Through the speeches of Aeneas we see his character developing. If we read them carefully, we shall not be tempted to accuse him of being pompous, conventional, or unfeeling. His first speech is a cry of despair heard above the roar of a hurricane (1.94-101). His last is a furious shout of anger, spoken in the midst of a horrified crowd[22] before he plunges his sword into the heart of a suppliant (12.947-949). In the first, he wishes he were dead. In the last, he inflicts a cruel death on a helpless enemy. Between these two termini his spirit has changed. It has grown, at first firm, and then hard. Vergil emphasizes the complete transformation of his nature by using the same phrase, *soluuntur frigore membra*, of Aeneas in 1.92 and of his victim Turnus in 12.951.[23]

His second speech (1.198-207) is a brief but noble address,

---

its atmosphere is not Greece but Persia (Hdt. 1.125.3). Furthermore, it has an uncomfortable resemblance to the story of Sinon. In both episodes a solitary Greek throws himself on the Trojans' mercy, asking them to kill him rather than let him suffer; a Trojan elder reassures him and asks for his story, which he then relates. There are even coincidences of phrasing and thought: "qui sit fari, quo sanguine cretus, / hortamur" (3.608-609) ≈ "hortamur fari quo sanguine cretus" (2.74); and compare 3.614-615 with 2.86-87. See R. D. Williams's edition of Book Three, note on lines 588f. But some scholars read deep significance into the passage. A. G. McKay, "The Achaemenides episode," *Vergilius* 12 (1966) 31-38, proposes that Aeneas's kindness to the castaway symbolizes Augustus's sympathy for Greek culture and his diplomatic victory over Parthia; while Otis (pp. 263-264) says the episode "can . . . be understood only as a symbol of Anchises' death."

[21] *Aen.* 6.489-493 × *Il.* 18.215-231.

[22] The crowd's cry of horror can be heard in the vowels of 12.928-929:

> consurgunt gemitu Rutuli totusque remugit
> mons circum et uocem late nemora alta remittunt.

[23] Knauer, pp. 320-322, gives an acute analysis of the contexts and implications of the two speeches. Wlosok, p. 14 n. 3, interprets the repetition of the phrase as symbolizing the complete shift of hostile fortune from Juno's foe Aeneas to Juno's favorite Turnus.

with which he encourages his exhausted followers and conceals his own gloom:

spem uultu simulat, premit altum corde dolorem.

Aeneas is performing the first duty of a commander: strengthening his men with confidence in their purpose, encouraging them by reminding them of their past exploits, and uniting them in loyalty to himself. Never again do we see him in such hopeless agony as in his first speech; yet he is still subject to fits of gloom until he reaches Italy. He grieves (*secum*) for the loss of his men in the storm (1.220-222); he suffers, but conceals it, when preparing to leave Dido (4.438-449); and when his ships are set afire, he prays Jupiter either to save them or to kill him (5.687-692). Even after their miraculous rescue he is still *casu concussus acerbo* (5.700) because some of his own people have turned against him. Then, after a Trojan elder gives him advice (5.704-718) and his father in a nocturnal vision confirms it (5.722-740), he makes up his mind and announces a decision based on two foundations:

Iouis imperium et cari praecepta parentis.

(5.747)

Preparing to enter the other world he is firmly resolute:

non ulla laborum,
o uirgo, noua mi facies inopinaue surgit;
omnia praecepi atque animo mecum ante peregi.

(6.103-105)

Thenceforward, although sometimes anxious (8.18-30, 8.520-522) or grieved (11.39-58), he never falters.

How hard Aeneas becomes in the end, is shown by his final speech. The two preceding it are equally grim. His challenge to Turnus in 12.889-893 is a promise of death. His antepenultimate speech is even crueller: in 12.565-573 he summons the Trojans to storm the city of Latinus, and, unless its citizens surrender, to burn it to the ground as Troy was burnt. He has never spoken so violently as this before: now he sounds like vengeful Achilles (*Il.* 22.261-272) or savage Pyrrhus (*Aen.* 2.547-550). He opens the speech with two imperative lines remarkable for their vigorous rhythm and whiplash sound, ending, one with "hac stat," the other with "ito"; he utters a single sentence of drastic resolution; he passes on to a bitter rhetorical question introduced by the contemptuous "scilicet"; and ends in a burst of fury emphasized by explosive initial sounds:

ferte faces propere foedusque reposcite flammis!

These last three utterances of Aeneas in the epic are an angry order for the storming of a city, a dark threat of death, and a ruthless condemnation. So far has he come from his first cry of despair, in which he envied the dead.

However, his second speech in Book One is matched, in Book Twelve, by a more magnanimous speech. Beside his exhortation to his comrades (1.198-207) we may set his words of admonition and encouragement to his son (12.435-440). In them are embodied reminiscences of three Greek paladins. Hector prays that the baby Astyanax, when grown, may be judged a better warrior than his father (*Il.* 6.476-481). Odysseus, marching out with Telemachus to face the Ithacans, reminds him not to shame his fathers (*Od.* 24.506-509). Sophocles' Ajax says to his son Eurysaces (550-551):

ὦ παῖ, γένοιο πατρὸς εὐτυχέστερος,
τὰ δ' ἄλλ' ὅμοιος· καὶ γένοι' ἂν οὐ κακός.

In his adaptation Accius sharpened this antithesis (*Armorum Iudicium*, fr. X Ribbeck):

uirtuti sis par, dispar fortunis patris.[24]

---

[24] For a discussion of the place to be assigned this line see H. D. Jocelyn, "Ancient Scholarship and Vergil's Use of Republican Latin Poetry. II," *CQ* 15 (1965) 127-129, who proposes that Ajax is not committing suicide but, like Aeneas here, going out to win glory in battle.

31

Vergil defines it more broadly, so that it contains three leading themes of the *Aeneid*:

disce, puer, uirtutem ex me uerumque laborem,
fortunam ex aliis.

For the Romans, virtue and courage were best shown not by possessing good luck but by remaining steadfast in misfortune; the spectacle of this effort was the highest form of spiritual education; and the duty of a young man was to carry on the tradition of his ancestors. These grave sentences are the only words that Aeneas addresses to Ascanius throughout the entire poem. His son is often close to him—in the escape from Troy (2.723-724), at the royal hunt near Carthage (4.140-159), at the Sicilian games, and in the fateful picnic where the boy notices the Trojans eating their tables (7.112-117). Yet neither when Ascanius leads the Trojan Game (note 5.545-551) nor when he is freed from Troy-by-Tiber after the siege (10.604-605) does his father speak a single word to him until this climax, when he holds him, *fusis circum armis*, in an armored embrace.[25]

So then the earliest and latest speeches of Aeneas, at the opening and close of the poem, emphasize the change in his character from a desperate and almost suicidal wanderer to a determined and cruel fighter. "Once his blade has grown warm" with blood, Aeneas is compared in 10.565-570, not (like Homeric heroes) to a fierce animal, but to a dreadful monster, Aegaeon or Briareus, whom he saw in the underworld (6.287). Vergil makes this hideous creature more devilish by saying that he fought *against* Jove, not for him as in *Il.* 1.401-406 and Hes. *Theog.* 713-735. Aeneas never loses all humanity, or becomes absolutely implacable like Achilles at the Xanthus (*Il.*

---

[25] The speech has another reminiscence of earlier poetry: "cum matura adoleuerit aetas" (12.438) recalls Lucretius's description of the process by which mind and body grow together, *inde ubi robustis adoleuit uiribus aetas* (3.449), and evokes the following line: *consilium quoque maius et auctior est animi uis.* See also *Georg.* 2.362 and Hor. *Serm.* 1.9.34.

21.1-226). This is shown not only by his tears over Pallas (*Aen.* 11.39-58) but by his generous warning to young Lausus (*Aen.* 10.811-812) and his noble words and gesture after his opponent falls (10.821-832). Yet a few moments later he meets Mezentius's challenge with exultant ruthlessness (10.873-908). The change in his character and behavior is well analyzed by E. Klaggerud in *Aeneisstudien* (*SO* Suppl. 22, Oslo, 1968) who on p. 22 points out that in Book Two (595) Aeneas "rages" against the will of the gods and against destiny, while in Book Ten (545, 604, 802) he "rages" as the instrument of destiny, favored by the divinities, all save one.

The development of Aeneas's spirit comes out in his speeches, book by book. He speaks much less often in the second half of the epic than in the first, even if we exclude his narrative at the Carthaginian banquet. As the conflict moves toward its close, he says less and acts more.

This contrast emerges when we examine individual books in the second part of the poem. In the seventh he speaks once only (120-134), greeting the fulfillment of the prediction about eating tables. In Book Eight he prays once (71-78), greets Pallas (117-120), asks Evander to become his ally (127-151), and comments somberly on Venus's warning of war (532-540). From the ninth book he is absent altogether. In the tenth he makes no long speech, but utters ten brief challenges, commands, and prayers. The eleventh book opens with three long powerful speeches by Aeneas (14-28, 42-58, 108-119) and one brief farewell; thereafter his movements are reported (446, 511-514) and described (903-915), but he himself says nothing. In the twelfth book his longest utterance is his solemn vow before the duel (176-194). After that he speaks only briefly, trying to calm the tumult (313-317), bidding farewell to his son (435-440), ordering the assault on the city (565-573), challenging Turnus (889-893), and killing him (947-949).

In the first six books the pattern of Aeneas's speeches is quite

33

unlike that. He talks most of all in the sixth, with two long prayers (56-76, 103-123), a greeting to Dido (456-466), and nine short utterances, mostly prayers and questions, placed at significant points of his journey.[26] But after he greets his father in 695-698, he simply listens in respect and wondering awe, asking only two questions, one about reincarnation (719-721), the other about the sad ghost who is to be Marcellus (863-866).

Aeneas speaks least of all, during the first half of the epic, in Book Three, with two short speeches (85-89, 315-319) and two longer (359-368, 493-505)—only thirty-three lines in all. This is because Anchises as *pater familias* is in command during the Trojans' long search: at its opening (9), on the move to Crete (102-120), on the new voyage west (178-191), in the escape from the Strophades (263-267), in the crossing of the Adriatic (472-481, 525-543), and in the flight from Charybdis (554-569). It is Anchises who interprets oracles and omens (103-117, cf. 143-146, 178-189, 539-543) and prays for divine favor (263-266, 528-529); it is Anchises who is welcomed by the priest-king of Delos (80-82) and receives the suppliant enemy (610-611). Then, during the rapidly sketched tour of Sicily (682-706) he fades out of sight.[27] At Drepanum (707-713) he dies. Meanwhile Aeneas, young and vigorous, has been playing an active part, building cities (16-18, 132-137), request-

---

[26] On these questions Dante modelled the enquiries made by him and answered by Vergil, Beatrice, and others. A parallel appears in *Aen.* 6.560f. and *Inferno*, Canto 9: note "ipsa deum poenas docuit perque omnia duxit" and "vero è ch'altra fïata qua giú fui" (9.22) with the vision of the Erinyes.

[27] The opening of this passage (684-691) is unfinished. A hundred lines earlier, Anchises recognizes the roar of Charybdis ahead, and at his command the fleet veers to port (554-563). Thereafter the Trojans sail south to a harbor near Etna (now Catania), pick up Achaemenides, and take off in terror when the Cyclopes appear (682-683). By then they are many miles down the coast of Sicily. It is therefore pointless to bring in Scylla and Charybdis once again and mention "iussa Heleni" (684-686) as though the Trojans had not already seen the peril of Charybdis. Also, the phrasing of 684-686 is dislocated. "Retro" (686) must mean continuing the southward course set in 561-563, helped by the north wind (687), but would make satisfactory sense only if the fleet were now close to the straits of Messina, which it is not.

ing divine guidance (84-89, 358-368), and promising alliances for the future (500-505). But Anchises has held the *auctoritas*. This is demonstrated clearly at a highly important juncture, the first sighting of Italy (3.525-529). As soon as the promised land appears, it is Anchises who prays to the gods of sea and land, wind and weather, and offers them a libation, *stans celsa in puppi*. The phrase shows that he has regained much of his physical vigor.[28] It also contains a significant resonance. It is used twice again in the *Aeneid*: of Augustus leading his fleet into battle at Actium (8.680) and of Aeneas leading his fleet to the rescue of his son and his people (10.261). Anchises is therefore both father and monarch. Only after his death, is Aeneas himself called "father" (1.555, 3.716).

The fourth book is dominated not by Aeneas but by Dido, who speaks nine times, with remarkable range and energy. From the time of Mercury's fateful mission until her suicide, her voice is heard once in every fifty lines. In this book Aeneas speaks only twice: a formal address of self-exculpation (333-361) and a command to set sail (573-579). For the rest, he acts and suffers, but is not recorded as speaking. He is never heard saying any special words of love to Dido, as Paris does to Helen (*Il.* 3.438-446); nor is he ever seen embracing her, like Odysseus with Penelope (*Od.* 23.231-240).

In the second book (part of his narrative) he reports two of his own brief questions (281-286, 322) and a short summons to a resistance group (348-354). Once we hear him speak with the same bitter fury that shocks us many years and many hundreds of lines later, in the twelfth book: when he expresses vengeful hatred of Helen and determines to kill her (577-587).[29] Thereafter in this book he makes a wild speech of

---

[28] Similarly Odysseus' father Laertes is old and pathetic at his first appearance (*Od.* 24.226-231), but after he joins his son in a heroic enterprise he is full of new energy, and actually begins the final battle by killing an opponent (*Od.* 24.516-525).

[29] On the genuineness of the Helen episode see pp. 164-176.

desperation (657-670) followed by a calmer series of directions for escape from the doomed city (707-720) and nothing more.[30]

In the first book Aeneas speaks eight times, and in the fifth twelve times: the aggregates are sixty-three lines in the first, seventy-two lines in the fifth. The fifth, a book inspired by masculine energy and thankful rejoicing, is filled with his curt commands, but contains only two important speeches by him: the proclamation of the games (45-71) and the announcement of the foot-race (304-314), together with one deeply emotional prayer (687-692). His words are for the most part brisk, confident, imperatorial. However, in the first book he utters some of his most pathetic monologues: in despair (94-101), in longing (437), and in hope tinged with grief for the past (459-463). Thrice he speaks to his mother, twice in respectful ignorance (326-334, 372-385) and once in reproachful recognition (407-409). He gives his comrades cheer after the storm (198-207), and in Carthage he announces himself and expresses his gratitude to queen Dido with eloquent dignity (595-610).

Aeneas and his interlocutors

Vergil used his speeches to display the relations of his characters to one another. Aeneas is the sole hero. Therefore it is important to note whom he addresses, and when. His silences also are significant. Compared with Vergil's Aeneas, the several heroes of *Iliad* and *Odyssey* are free-spoken, with their arguments and their reminiscences and their reproaches and their vehement outbursts of anger and grief. Aeneas gives orders. He states his position. He prays; and in battle he challenges and threatens, although briefly. But he does not converse; and like a traditional Roman he says much less than he thinks.

He never speaks to Turnus until just before killing him

---

[30] Aeneas says that after losing Creusa he spoke in mad rage (745) and shouted her name again and again within Troy (768-770); but his words are not given directly.

(12.889-893 and 947-949). The two men have previously been face to face only once, during the oath-taking (12.161-215); but there Turnus is silent (12.219-221), and Aeneas, although mentioning his name in the oath (12.183), ignores him otherwise.

He makes only three speeches to Dido—in gratitude (1.595-610), in excuse (4.333-361), and in pitying love (6.456-466). Of course his account of Troy's fall and of his wanderings is addressed to her ("regina," 2.3), and we are told of other conversations between the couple (1.748-752, 4.74-79), but only the narrative and these three speeches are given in Aeneas's own words.

It is remarkable that he speaks so little and so coolly to his mother Venus: four times in all—twice without recognizing her (1.326-334 and 372-385), once with a reproach (1.407-409), and once with a perfunctory prayer (6.196-197). He invokes her once in an excited speech, with overtones of chagrin (2.664-667); but he never directly prays to her by name for help. When he might well have besought her assistance in discovering the golden bough, he merely exclaims (*forte*)[31] "si nunc se . . . ramus / ostendat!" (6.187-188). Immediately she sends her doves to guide him; but he does not thank her, speaks first to the birds, and adds rather brusquely "tuque, o, dubiis *ne defice* rebus, / diua parens" (6.194-197). He expresses no gratitude for the divinely made armor which she promised (8.534-536) and obtained for him with some anxiety and trouble, *haud animo nequiquam exterrita* (8.370), even though she brings it to him with a kiss (8.615). She protects him in battle (10.331-332), supports his forces (10.608-610), and heals his wound (12.411-431); yet he does not appear to notice, and certainly utters no word of gratitude. But he is usually punctilious about expressing his thanks for divine assistance (e.g. 8.71-

---

[31] Servius ad loc.: "uacat *forte*; et est uersus de his qui tibicines uocantur, quibus datur aliquid ad solam metri sustentationem . . . : nec enim possumus intellegere eum fortuitu rogasse." For an equally weak *forte* see 12.206; compare also 2.342, 6.171, and 11.552.

78). The association of Odysseus and Athena in the *Odyssey* is much closer and warmer than that of goddess mother and heroic son in the *Aeneid*: see, for instance, *Od.* 13.287-391. For Aeneas, the guidance which his father gives him is far more important than the occasional help of his mother. Apparently Vergil wished to erase the memory of Aphrodite carrying the Homeric Aeneas out of battle in her arms like a baby (*Il.* 5.311-317), to present him as a tougher and more successful warrior than the Aeneas of the *Iliad*, and to make the relation of father and son more important than that of son and mother.

As we have seen (p. 32), Aeneas addresses his son Ascanius only once. To his father, alive or dead, he speaks seven times, always in tones of deep affection and respect.[32] This is his closest and most durable relationship.

Most of his speeches are addressed to other Trojans. Some are directed to individuals.[33] Others are spoken to his comrades collectively.[34] Trojans and Sicilians together he addresses as contestants in the games in 5.304-314, 5.348-350, and 5.363-364; and Trojans and Etruscans and Arcadians together in 11.14-28.

Aeneas is cool to foreigners. We hear him speaking only five times to Greeks; and these are Evander[35] and his half-breed son Pallas.[36] Italians other than Turnus he addresses nine times. Only thrice does he manifest any kindness or pity

---

[32] See 2.657-663, 2.707-710 + 717-720; 5.80-83, 5.741-742; 6.695-698, 6.719-721, 6.863-866.

[33] Achates (1.459-463, 10.333-335); Hector's ghost (2.281-286); Panthus (2.322); Andromache (3.315-319); Helenus (3.359-368); Andromache and Helenus together with their subjects (3.493-505); Palinurus (5.26-31, 5.870-871, 6.341-346); Dares (5.465-467); Acestes, who is half Trojan (5.533-538); Epytides (5.548-551); and Deiphobus (6.500-508).

[34] See 1.198-207, 2.348-354, 4.573-576 (passing into a prayer), 5.45-71, 7.120-134 (beginning with a greeting to Italy and the Penates), 12.313-317, and 12.565-573.

[35] 8.127-151 and 8.532-540.

[36] 8.117-120; and after Pallas's death 11.42-58 and 96-98.

38

toward them.[37] The other speeches are all uttered in combat, just before or just after a slaying.[38] His Etruscan allies he speaks to only once, in a group including his own men (*omnis turba ducum*, 11.14-28). His negotiations for alliance with their leader Tarchon are recounted in oratio obliqua (10.149-153); and even when the forces are joined, Aeneas remains pointedly aloof (8.609-610).

To the gods, the pious hero prays eleven times.[39] In six supplications he addresses powers of whose identity he is uncertain,[40] or groups of deities.[41] There are five prayers to major divinities.[42]

He has only three monologues, all early in the poem (1.94-101, 1.437, 2.577-587).

In the final books of the *Odyssey*, Odysseus is still talking freely (*Od.* 23.183-204, 264-284; 24.244-279, etc.); and as the *Iliad* approaches its end, Achilles speaks at length (*Il.* 24.518-551, 560-570, 599-620, etc.); but as the close of the *Aeneid* impends, Aeneas turns into a silent warrior. The deep sensibility which he showed in recounting the fall of Troy and his search for a new home, the brisk energy with which he directed the games, the solemn wonder of his pilgrimage through the afterworld, and the quiet joy of his visit to Pallanteum—these disappear in Book Ten, when he starts fighting. Were it not for his sympathy for young Lausus (10.809-812 + 821-832), the humane tone of his address to the Latin suppliants (11.108-119), the restraint of his vow (12.176-194), and the nobility of his parting from Ascanius (12.435-440), he would appear to

[37] Lausus, 10.811-812 and 825-830; the Latin mission, 11.108-119.

[38] Magus, 10.531-534; Tarquitus, 10.557-560; Lucagus, 10.592-594; Liger, 10.599-600; Mezentius, 10.875-876 and 897-898.

[39] Sometimes he mingles a prayer with a speech whose main purpose is not worship: e.g. 4.576-579.

[40] 1.326-334, 4.576-579, and 6.187-188, a mere wish.

[41] 6.63-65, part of a longer prayer; 8.71-78, 12.176-194.

[42] Apollo, 3.85-89 and 6.56-62; Jupiter, 5.687-692; Venus, 6.196-197; Cybele, 10.252-255.

be a ruthless killer. His final words have a grim resonance far more somber than the conclusion of other epic poems, and more closely resembling the darkest of Greek tragedies.

Many readers have felt there was something lacking in Vergil's portrayal of Aeneas. As a hero he has been called cold; yet he is not cold: he has to fight a long struggle with his emotions. He has been described as stiff, because of his concentration on *pietas* and his apparent inability to relax; yet for a Roman, *pietas* was as central and important as "the word of the Lord" to a hero of the Old Testament. What is it that we miss in Aeneas? Partly it is physical clarity and vividness. We have no picture of his appearance, as we have of the Homeric heroes—thanks largely to the scene on the wall of Troy where Helen points them out to Priam and describes them so that we too can see them in their habit as they lived. Vergil seldom describes him in visually memorable terms, as Homer describes Hector dandling his baby son (*Il.* 6.466-474), Ajax striding over the ships with his huge pike (*Il.* 15.676-688), Achilles tormented by sleepless grief (*Il.* 24.3-13), and Odysseus dragged by the backwash like a struggling cuttlefish (*Od.* 5.428-435). Vergil gives few physical descriptions of his characters. We cannot, for instance, tell how Anchises was crippled. Homer would have told us in detail—that he halted on his right leg, and supported himself with a staff of tough oak-wood cut on the slopes of Ida. Achates, although so close to Aeneas, is never pictured; but we know exactly how the squire of Odysseus looked: Eurybates was round-shouldered, dark-skinned, and curly-haired (*Od.* 19.246).

But principally Aeneas lacks the sort of characterization that can only be conveyed through speech. The men and women of Homer and the heroes and heroines of Greek tragedy make long speeches in which they reveal the passions that dominate their souls. Aeneas makes one big speech, and one only: his narrative of the destruction of Troy and his wanderings. In that narrative, rich with suffering and vibrant with adventure, we can see the whole man laid bare. But outside this narrative, what are his important speeches? The longest is the least admirable: his speech of unwilling renunciation and icily controlled self-defense to Dido (4.333-361). The next is the address in which he celebrates the memory of his dead father and inaugurates the games: noble and sincere, but largely formal (5.45-71). Next to that is an even more formal oration, his diplomatic approach to Evander with its courtly genealogical detail (8.127-151). After that again come two earnest but elaborately phrased utterances: his prayer to Phoebus and the hostile gods and the Sibyl (6.56-76) and his request to be permitted to visit Anchises among the dead (6.103-123). This means that, outside the narrative in Books Two and Three, Aeneas does not reveal his whole heart in any of his long speeches. W. Y. Sellar[43] says "At no time has the character of Aeneas excited any strong human interest. . . . As compared with the hero of the Odyssey, Aeneas is altogether wanting in energy, spontaneity, intellectual resource, and insight." This is overstated, particularly in charging Aeneas with lack of energy; but it does mean that Vergil presents him as unsympathetic and cold. T. R. Glover[44] goes a little further into the problem. "We do not see the whole of Aeneas. . . . Achilles satisfies us, because at every point we feel that he is a man. . . . Aeneas does not so readily satisfy us, for his experience, though not improbable, . . . is not entirely interpreted to us. There remains something unintelligible about him."

Furthermore, Aeneas is aloof and alone. There is no one with whom he talks freely. The gulf between Aeneas and all his men is far wider than the distance between Achilles or Agamemnon and their followers, or between Odysseus and his servants. It is impossible to imagine Aeneas treating Achates

[43] W. Y. Sellar, *The Roman Poets of the Augustan Age: Virgil* (Oxford, 1877) p. 389.
[44] T. R. Glover, *Virgil* (London, 1912²), pp. 210-211.

or Epytides so warmly as Achilles treats Phoenix (*Il.* 9.607-619) or Odysseus the faithful Eumaeus and Philoetius (*Od.* 21.205-225). In fact he talks to Achates only twice: once in the shock of seeing the Trojan war depicted in a Carthaginian temple (1.459-463) and once giving an order on the battlefield, "suggere tela mihi!" (10.333-335). Aeneas has no Patroclus.[45]

The world of Aeneas as Vergil conceives it is not, like Homer's, aristocratic, nor, like that of Ennius and Livy, a combination of aristocracy and democracy. It is monarchic in the extreme. It is a curious conception: particularly curious because it is scarcely Roman. Although virtually a monarch, Augustus was far more sociable and far less lonely than Aeneas: he had Agrippa and Maecenas and a host of other friends.[46] So with nearly all the great Romans of the republic, for example Scipio Aemilianus: they had close attachments, and loved to relax in intimacy. Ennius praised such a states-man's friend,

> cui res audacter magnas paruasque iocumque
> eloqueretur, et unose[47] malaque et bona dictu
> euomeret si qui uellet tutoque locaret.

> (*Ann.* 239-241)

But nothing like this appears in the *Aeneid*: for two reasons. Vergil's own solitary retiring nature prevented him from fully understanding such affection and making it a theme of his poetry; and from earliest times he regarded Augustus as super-human, unlike ordinary mortals, a being who was able to rule

---

[45] Dido too is lonely. In trouble, Penelope has her attendants close to her and the old nurse comforts her (*Od.* 4.715-758). Dido has her sister and her husband's nurse with her and talks to them (*Aen.* 4.416-436, 478-498, 634-640), but apart from Anna's first reply (4.31-53) their voices are not heard.

[46] On his easy and affable manners, Suet. *D. Aug.* 53.3, 71.2-3; on his friends, Suet. *D. Aug.* 66; on his genial approach to Horace, Suet. *De Poetis* (ed. Rostagni, Turin, 1944/1964) pp. 113-116.

[47] et unose malaque *Vahlen*; et cuncta malaque, et cuncta malusque, et cunctam aliisque *codd.*

42

as god of earth, sea, or sky (*Georg.* 1.24-35). Contrast this with the deferential but far more natural attitude of Horace:

> cum tot sustineas et tanta negotia solus,
> res Italas armis tuteris, moribus ornes,
> legibus emendes, in publica commoda peccem
> si longo sermone morer tua tempora, Caesar.
>
> (*Ep.* 2.1.1-4)

Horace could not deify Augustus, who jested so gaily with him. But Vergil transferred to Augustus, the savior of the world, the adoration with which Lucretius had viewed the savior of man's soul. When Vergil's Tityrus cries

> erit ille mihi semper deus   (*Buc.* 1.7)

it is in the same exalted tone as the earlier master's

> deus ille fuit, deus, inclute Memmi   (Lucr. 5.8).

For Vergil both Augustus and his prototype Aeneas were more godlike than human; and a god, as we know from Aristotle, cannot have human friends.

Yet Vergil was fully capable of writing warmly dramatic speeches which revealed the whole heart—as the narrative of Aeneas and the speeches of Dido show. His refusal to allow Aeneas to speak freely must therefore be a deliberate choice. He made his hero as taciturn as a Spartan warrior, and (after many painful struggles) as thoughtful and silent as a Stoic sage. Did he not also wish to show him as one who, after almost unendurable losses and sufferings, had grown into the melancholy of middle age and the grave contemplation of approaching death?

Other characters

The disposition of the speeches given to the other chief characters can be more briefly treated.

Although the eight speeches of Evander occupy a good deal

43

of space, only half of them are personal: two addresses of welcome, a farewell, and a lament. The others (occupying over two-thirds of his total wordage) are mainly historical narratives, in which we sometimes seem to hear Vergil's voice rather than Evander's. Nevertheless, the old Arcadian king showing Aeneas the site of future Rome makes a pleasant parallel to Anchises showing his son the future race of Romans waiting for birth.

The character of Turnus is like his speeches: impetuous and strongly emotional, ranging widely between extremes of excitement and depression. His first speech (7.436-444) is haughtily contemptuous of an interlocutor who appears to be a weak old woman; his last (12.931-938) is a humble plea for mercy. Often he talks as arrogantly as Achilles. Thus he insults king Latinus in a brief speech (12.11-17) full of cold disdain, saying he is ready for the duel:

> fer sacra, pater, et concipe foedus.[48]

Imperatives so blunt as "fer" and "concipe" should not be addressed by a young man to one of his elders, or by a prince to a king—although Achilles under much greater tension speaks more harshly in *Il.* 24.560-570. When charged with poor generalship and personal cowardice, he bursts out into the longest oration of the entire poem, sixty-seven lines (11.378-444) full of violent energy. It is a good speech in a bad cause. Only twice more does he appear to advantage: once as a commander rallying his troops (9.128-158) and once when he accepts his approaching death (12.632-649); yet the former speech ends in over-confidence (see p. 88) and the latter is profound gloom.

The speeches of Anchises are discussed above (pp. 34-35). The first words attributed to any character in the poem con-

---

[48] The unnatural lengthening in "patēr" suggests that Turnus puts excessive and sarcastic emphasis on the word of respect. Similarly Latinus betrays something of his own feelings in his reply to the Trojans, 11.323: "considant, si tantus amōr."

vey the unspoken thoughts of Juno, ending in a vow of revenge (1.37-49). No sooner are the Trojans established in Italy than she renews her pledge with even intenser violence and determination (7.293-322); and hers is almost the last voice heard in heaven at the end of the epic, in a speech which shows she has not abated a whit of her original purpose, to destroy the Trojans (12.808-828). She speaks with such force and at such important junctures that her presence is felt almost all through the poem.

Venus speaks more frequently and fluently than Juno. Courtesans talk more than empresses. Her conversation in disguise with Aeneas and her plot with Love in the first book, together with her appearance as protector among the flames of Troy in the second, impress her character on the reader very early in the poem; and although her manner is gentle and cajoling, her will remains as strong as that of Juno. The debate in heaven (10.1-117) makes that quite clear.

The most eloquent character in the *Aeneid* is Dido. Her ten long speeches cover a wide range of emotion from regal graciousness to venomous hatred, from womanly tenderness to harsh self-loathing. From the hour when she learns Aeneas is deserting her (4.296-304) to the hour of her self-immolation, her voice fills the poem. Within less than four hundred lines Vergil creates a masterpiece of psychical analysis. In six speeches he displays all the phases of her passion: reproach turning into surrender (4.305-330), denunciation and rejection (365-387), appeals for mercy and pity (416-436), despair (534-552), fury, remorse, and imprecations (590-629), and at last the acceptance of death, together with a renewed assertion of love mingled with hatred (651-662) in a union which can issue only in death:

> sic, sic iuuat ire sub umbras.

The three most moving utterances in the *Aeneid* are not so much heroic as tragic. They are the last words of the queen

45

with Aeneas's sword at her breast (4.659-662), the last words of Aeneas plunging his steel into the heart of Turnus (12.947-949), and the apostrophe of Anchises to Marcellus, one of his "sons" still unborn but already doomed (6.868-886).

CHAPTER THREE

FORMAL SPEECHES

As we have seen, some critics in antiquity made the mistake of finding oratorical devices everywhere in Vergil and treating all his speeches as though he had composed them according to the rules of rhetoric. It is quite different nowadays. Some modern readers instinctively reject the idea that a poet ever uses his rhetorical training when writing an epic poem; others, deploring the excess of rhetorical display in Silver Age poets and admiring the subtlety of Vergil's art, tend to assume that he ignored or transcended the techniques he had learned in the school of rhetoric.

It is certain that Vergil, in the course of his thorough and wide-ranging education, was taught oratory. It was a regular discipline of higher education in his time.[1] A biography tells us that he actually spoke in a law-court, although only once because of his shyness.[2] An early poem written during his adolescence (*Catalepton* 5) expresses a thoughtful young student's lively disgust with the rhetoricians who have taught him only how to blow up balloons. He himself, he says in this biting farewell, is setting sail for another haven, the happy home of Epicurean philosophy. Even later, he never wholeheartedly admired the art of oratory, as so many of his successors did. Ovid and Seneca and Lucan could

[1] H. I. Marrou, *History of Education in Antiquity* (tr. G. Lamb, New York, 1956), part 3, chapter 6.
[2] *Vita Donati* (ed. Hardie, paras. 15-16). The Berne biography says he was a pupil of Epidius, the teacher of Octavius and Antony. Büchner (col. 1042) doubts the assertion, partly because it is unsupported, partly because Octavius was about seven years younger than Vergil. Yet although in the same school, they need not have attended the same class.

47

Enjoy their dear wit and gay rhetoric
That had so well been taught her dazzling fence.[3]

But Vergil distrusted it, doubtless because his training in philosophy emphasized the distinction between rhetoric and truth, and in particular because the Epicureans looked askance at the artifices of style. He despised the rhetorician's trick of combining big words and gaudy decorations with little true meaning—a habit through which, he says in a curious anticipation of St. Paul's description of the soul devoid of charity, they become *inane cymbalon iuuentutis*.[4] Still, many a young man of genius has cast off his teachers, without forgetting what they taught him. So it was with Vergil and rhetoric.

Among the speeches in the *Aeneid*, some, had they been made by real men in Vergil's own day, would have been rhetorically constructed. Such speeches are delivered on formal occasions, usually public, and are intended to achieve certain of the purposes which rhetoricians trained their pupils to accomplish. In composing these, Vergil employed the established techniques of rhetoric: for example, in the debates of Book Ten and Book Eleven. Other speeches, however, he conceived as spontaneous outbursts of emotion—soliloquies, threats, entreaties. In these it would be mistaken to look for a conventional rhetorical plan. Instead of the smooth flow of intellectually controlled eloquence, they display the tidal surge of emotion. It is not that they are incoherent: rather that they are shaped by the feelings of the speaker, with little or no relation to established schemata. Rhetorically arranged discourses fall into recognizable patterns; but every emotional speech in Vergil (even though it may use traditional themes) is strongly individualized.

[3] Milton, *Comus* 790-791.

[4] *Catalepton* 5.5 (inani *Mu*; in ani *B*; inanis *Ald. 1517*; inane *Heinsius*); χαλκὸς ἠχῶν ἢ κύμβαλον ἀλαλάζον, 1 Cor. xiii 1; and compare Socrates on the orators (Plato, *Prot.* 329a).

48

One of the admirers of Vergil, John Milton, used the same discernment when writing the speeches in *Paradise Lost*. Thus, in the debate of the fallen angels in Book Two, the speech of Moloch (51-105) has a perfectly clear rhetorical structure as a deliberative speech.

> My sentence is for open war.

This opening announcement is his proposal—the *exordium* being omitted as superfluous. Then he gives the arguments to support it. First, he asks whether the millions of fallen angels who are eager for combat must

> sit lingering here,
> Heaven's fugitives, and for their dwelling-place
> Accept this dark opprobrious den of shame,
> The prison of his tyranny who reigns
> By our delay?

This is the argument that war is more honorable than submission: the emotional words "opprobrious," "den," "shame," "tyranny" clearly indicate its character. Next comes the argument that the attack will be easy (lines 70-81)—a theme introduced by a typical anticipation of a possible opponent's objection:

> But perhaps
> The way seems difficult, and steep to scale
> With upright wing against a higher foe!
> Let such bethink them. . . .

Finally, the third of the chief traditional arguments, the argument from utility, is presented as a dilemma in lines 82-105: the fallen angels cannot possibly suffer more than they do now, and will either be utterly destroyed and freed from their miseries:

> happier far
> Than miserable to have eternal being!

or else be able to disturb heaven with perpetual inroads—
Which, if not victory, is yet revenge.

This is powerful and skillful oratory.

It would, however, be wrong to try to find such oratorical techniques in certain other speeches of *Paradise Lost*: for instance, in Eve's monologue (9.745-779) delivered while (already weakened by the tempter) she debates with herself whether or not to eat the forbidden fruit. Debates with herself: the phrase describes the speech, for it is a balancing of impulses and deterrents. She weighs the obvious value of the fruit (745-752) against God's prohibition (753-760); the threat of death (760-763) against the fact that the serpent has eaten and still lives (764-767); the denial of the fruit to human beings (767-768) against its accessibility to beasts (769-772); and lastly her ignorance (773-775) against the promise of knowledge (776-779). Although unschooled, this is logic; but it is not, in the formal sense, rhetoric.[5] A later speech by Eve, her farewell to Eden in 11.268-285, is neither logic nor rhetoric but a purely emotional lament.[6]

Political and Legalistic Speeches

The address of a statesman to an assembly, or an ambassador to a monarch, will usually be most effective if it employs the resources devised by great orators and codified by teachers of eloquence. To such speeches we turn first.

There are in the *Aeneid* ten political (or "deliberative") speeches, aimed at persuading an assembly or a potentate.[7] The usual (though not invariable) pattern of such speeches is this:

---

[5] Such, although longer and more emotional, are the monologues of some of Ovid's heroines: for example, the incestuous Byblis in *Met.* 9.474-516.

[6] See J. M. Major, "Milton's view of rhetoric," *Studies in Philology* 64 (1967) 685-711, who shows how, though deeply conscious of the power of oratory (*P.L.* 9.670-678), Milton came to distrust it as deceptive (*P.R.* 4.4-5) and artificial (*P.R.* 4.353-360).

[7] For a list see Appendix 2.

(1) an introduction, intended to win attention and sympathy, the *exordium*;

(2) a survey of the situation, including as many facts as are necessary to support the proposal the speaker intends to make: this is the *narratio*;

(3) the proposal, *propositio*, which may be single or double, or even (in complex situations) multiple;

(4) the presentation of reasons for adopting the proposal (*tractatio* or *argumentatio*), which is usually a demonstration that it is just, or profitable, or honorable, or necessary, or several of them at once;[8]

(5) a rebuttal of the opponent's arguments (*refutatio*); and

(6) a conclusion, *peroratio*.

There is a handy description of this type of speech in Volkmann's *Rhetorik*, pp. 294-299. But he omits one essential element: the *propositio*, namely, the advice which the speaker wishes his audience to accept, the statement of the policy he wants them to adopt.[9] For example, in Cicero's speech *De imperio Cn. Pompei* (which Volkmann takes as an illustration) the *propositio* occupies sections 49-50. This Volkmann calls "a recapitulation of the argument" and a transition to the rebuttal; but it is much more than that. It is the equivalent of a motion put to the assembly for its vote of approval, couched in terms which suggest its logical inevitability: "dubitatis, Quirites?" "quid exspectamus? cur non . . . commendamus?" Some ancient authorities and some modern critics omit the *propositio* from the analysis of political speeches, or are vague about its function.[10] Perhaps this is because in *legal* speeches,

---

[8] These general themes for argument, called τελικὰ κεφάλαια, were much elaborated by theorists, who subdivided them with hairsplitting ingenuity, and added others such as ῥᾴδιον, δυνατόν, νόμιμον. Cicero discusses them (with some naive psychological and ethical explanations) in *De Inu.* 2.156-176. Quintilian calls them *partes suadendi* (*Inst.* 3.8.22-35).

[9] Aristotle is the first to distinguish it: he calls it πρόθεcιc (*Rhet.* 3.13. 1414a35).

[10] E.g., Lausberg, para. 262, pp. 147-149.

51

which were more highly developed in antiquity and more closely analyzed, the corresponding element was less clearly defined and less commonly used. The charge that the accused was guilty or the assertion that he was innocent was diffused all through the speech. A *nuda propositio* such as "adulterium obicio" (Quint. 4.4.8) was uncommon. But in a political or diplomatic speech it was customary, and tactically almost inevitable, for the orator to put his proposal in compact, lucid, and succinct terms. This phase of a persuasive speech addressed to a ruler or to a decision-making assembly is usually marked by first-person verbs accepting personal responsibility for the advice ("moneo," "censeo") or enlisting the audience behind the speaker ("sic agamus"), or by second-person verbs urging a decision on one man ("pone animos et pulsus abi") or on an audience ("de salute uestra decernite"). So Demosthenes in the first *Philippic* (16): "First of all, *I say we must* fit out fifty warships and then be prepared to man them." So Cicero in the first *Catilinarian* (10): "Catilina, *perge* quo coepisti; *egredere* aliquando ex Vrbe; patent portae; *proficiscere!*" In the political orations of the *Aeneid* the proposals are all clear and definite, although they are not all simple: one speech has three, each presented in a different manner.

Ilioneus

Two such speeches are delivered by Ilioneus, the most eloquent of the Trojans after Aeneas. In his first (1.522-558) he asks Dido to protect the refugees and allow them to repair their ships before sailing away. He starts with a skillful *exordium* (522-523), which is a chain of arguments miniaturized:

> o regina, nouam cui condere Iuppiter urbem
> iustitiaque dedit gentis frenare superbas.

This touches no less than five points. Dido's rank, "regina," places upon her the responsibility for protecting suppliants. "Nouam urbem," which translates the name of her city,

Karthago, reminds her that cities are centers of higher civilization (cf. "quae . . . tam barbara . . . patria?" in 539-540). Jupiter favors only the magnanimous (cf. 543). Her city is founded on justice (cf. 544) and survives by controlling the savage tribes of north Africa (cf. 539-541).

Immediately after this *exordium*—because the danger is urgent—he puts forward his first proposal, "protect us!" (524-526).[11] He follows this with a narration of the facts, explaining who the Trojans are and how they reached Libya (527-538). Next come the arguments to support the proposal: an appeal to common humanity and divine justice (539-543) and a delicately phrased hint that Dido's kindness will be repaid and that the castaways have friends in Sicily to defend or to avenge them (the argument *utile*, 544-550). Then Ilioneus proceeds to a second proposal, which assumes that the first will be granted. He asks that the Trojans be permitted to repair their ships and sail away—to Italy if Aeneas lives, to Sicily if he is dead (551-558). There is no peroration: the Trojans supply its place with a shout of approval (559-560).

Approaching Latinus in 7.213-248, Ilioneus has a more difficult mission and makes a more complex speech. Since he is acting as the representative of Aeneas, who is far superior to Latinus in dignity, the *exordium* is merely a curt acknowledgment of the king's rank and ancestry: "rex, genus egregium Fauni." Then follows a long *narratio* (213-227) explaining why the Trojans have come to Italy. It is in the grand style. It glorifies the former might of Troy (217-218) and emphasizes the fact that the Trojans and Aeneas are descended from Jove.[12]

[11] This is the first time the reader has been told that Ilioneus and his comrades were attacked by Libyan tribesmen, while Aeneas and his men, landing in an uninhabited region, were not molested: Vergil likes to compress his narrative (Heinze, pp. 357-361).

[12] The name occurs thrice, "Ioue . . . Ioue . . . Iouis" (219-220), like the triumphant *Italiam: Italiam . . . Italiam* in 3.523-524, the pathetic triple repetition of *Eurydicen* in *Georg.* 4.525-527, and the earnest "nate" in 5.724, 725, 733.

It culminates in an evocation of the world-wide renown of the Trojan war (222-227):

> Quanta per Idaeos saeuis effusa Mycenis
> tempestas ierit campos, quibus actus uterque
> Europae atque Asiae fatis concurrerit orbis,
> audiit et si quem tellus extrema refuso
> summouet Oceano et si quem extenta plagarum
> quattuor in medio dirimit plaga solis iniqui.

This superbly modelled sentence, one of the most truly oratorical in the *Aeneid,* can stand beside the magnificent narrative proem of Book Three—which may, in an earlier stage of Vergil's composition, have been the opening of Aeneas's narrative.[13]

With this the following *propositio* makes a sharp contrast. In appearance it is modest and difficult to reject (229-230):

> dis sedem exiguam patriis litusque rogamus
> innocuum et cunctis undamque auramque patentem.

The humble adjectives "exiguam" and "innocuum" and the bland phrase "cunctis patentem" combine to suggest that the request will be easy to grant. As a matter of fact, the Trojans wish to settle down on Latinus' territory and build a city; but Ilioneus skillfully minimizes the implications by asking merely for "a home for the ancestral gods" together with "water and air." Commenting on this proposal, Donatus expresses much admiration for its dexterity. "Quid tam humanum," he says, "et tam simplex, morari uelle in litore, nullius molestiam pati, nullum onerari praesentia peregrini, uti aura, quam omnibus praestitit rerum natura communem, et habere aquae perennis copiam, quae nescit detrimenta, cum tollitur de sinu fontis

---

[13] This suggestion is made by W. H. Semple, *BRL* 38 (1955-1956) 228f. The paragraph 3.1-12 does not look like a continuation of the narrative of 2.796-804, but rather like the independent opening of a tale; and such phrases as "auguriis agimur diuum," "incerti quo fata ferant," are not consonant with 2.780-784.

aut de cursu fluminis rapitur?" (His remarks on the whole speech will repay reading.)

To support the request, Ilioneus argues that it will be requited (*utile*, 231-233), that it will bring honor to the Latins (234-238), and that, as being commanded by heaven, it is just and necessary (239-242).

The final line of the speech is incomplete. Vergil may have intended to add a peroration. However, the gifts which the ambassador presents to Latinus serve very well instead: a libation-bowl, representing religion, and rich regalia, symbols of power—the latter belonging to Aeneas's king, and the former to Aeneas's father (243-248). The implication is that the Trojans will revere Latinus as a monarch and love him as a father.

The most important formal orations in the *Aeneid* appear in Books Ten and Eleven.

Debate of the Latins and their allies

After the defeat of the Latin armies, king Latinus presides over a debate in council. It is initiated by the report of a speech addressed by Diomede to the Latin embassy (11.252-293). This marks the end of a long change in the relationship between Greeks and Trojans.[14] Diomede, the old enemy, refuses to renew hostilities, and adds a noble tribute to Aeneas as a patriot and warrior, the peer of Hector.

Venulus and the Latin mission were despatched to Diomede's city of Argyripa at the beginning of Book Eight. The speech which Venulus was to make—nowadays it would be a diplomatic note—is outlined in oratio obliqua (8.10-17). Short as it is, it follows the accepted patterns of a policy-making speech (with *exordium* and conclusion omitted): a proposal (*qui petat auxilium*), a statement of the situation (*Latio consistere Teucros*), and, as an argument supporting the request

---

[14] See pp. 173-174, 180.

for aid, a discreet allusion to Diomede's experience of the military prowess of the Trojans (8.15-17). (This is the simple argument *utile*: it is to the advantage of Diomede himself to crush the Trojan threat before it grows more powerful. As Donatus says, "ut, si inpetrationem non concederet, ex periculi sui contemplatione postulatis Diomedes adnueret.")

Diomede's reply (11.252-293) opens with a civil *exordium* (252-254): by alluding to the long Saturnian peace of Latinus's people, he implies that their request for aid in war is mistaken. Next comes one of Vergil's *tours de force*: a *narratio* (255-277) which sums up in twenty-three lines the *Nostoi* of the Greek heroes from Troy, culminating in the transformation of Diomede's own men into sea-birds and passing on to a reminiscence of his Trojan *aristeia*, when he wounded Aphrodite (*Il.* 5.311-354). Then Diomede makes his own proposal. He rejects the plea of the Latins (278-280) and recommends them to make peace and alliance with Aeneas (281-293). This is supported by the same argument as was used by Venulus, *utile*: it will be dangerous to fight against Aeneas (282-293). But Diomede also brings in honor (291-292), implying that it will be no shame to make a treaty with a hero so noble.

One danger of analyzing Vergil's speeches is that it makes us unconsciously put Florus's question "Vergilius orator an poeta?" and answer it "Orator," as though the dichotomy were legitimate. It is not. Vergil's oratory is part of his poetry, as is the oratory of Homer and Shakespeare and Milton and Racine. Even those speeches which are constructed in accordance with rhetorical precepts all contain memorable poetic phrases and rich imaginative effects which no contemporary orator would have dared. So here, Diomede's account of the fates of his comrades is oratorical in purpose and even in structure: the rapid summary of many different episodes is a *percursio*, and the passage contains two *praeteritiones*: "mitto" (256), and "referam?" (264). Yet, since it summarizes an entire epic poem, the *Nostoi*, it is also a feat of poetic skill, of the type admired by

56

the Alexandrians and practiced by Catullus and his friends;[15]
and it closes with the type of mythical transformation which
the Alexandrians enjoyed—although Vergil treats it more
seriously and with fewer physical details than his successor
Ovid (*Met.* 14.494-509). There is much poetry in the speech,
from its fine opening tricolon, "o fortunatae gentes, Saturnia
regna, / antiqui Ausonii," to its oracular close, "armis concur-
rant arma cauete!"

After the report of Diomede's message, king Latinus starts
the debate. His manner is gloomy, *haud laeta fronte*. After an
opening prayer (an anticipation of early Roman practice, says
Servius, adding, in one of his tantalizing asides, "ut sunt omnes
orationes Catonis et Gracchi") he begins with an *exordium ex
auditoribus*, addressed to the Latins, but containing (as Servius
points out, referring back to 7.596-597) the insinuation that
Turnus is to blame for the crisis, and the Latins too because
they followed him. Next, in his narrative (305-313), he covers
four salient facts: the Trojans are invincible; Diomede will not
bring aid; the kingdom is shattered; the Latin people have
done all they could, and can no more. Then two measured
and emphatic lines in closely similar rhythm (11.314-315)[16]
introduce a pair of alternative proposals, clearly marked by "si"
and "sin": (a) let us make a treaty with the Trojans and give
them land on which to settle down (316-323), or (b) if they
choose to migrate elsewhere, let us build them ships (324-329).
As insurance, a third proposition follows (330-334): mean-
while let us send a peace mission bearing gifts which symbolize
our surrender and our acceptance of Aeneas as a claimant to
regal power. A single line, reiterating the thought that the
situation is desperately urgent (335 ≈ 302-304), terminates the
speech.

---

[15] W. Kroll, *Studien zum Verständnis der römischen Literatur* (Stuttgart,
1964²), p. 240, n. 28, points to similar poetic epitomes in Catullus 64.338f.,
Culex 304f., and Ov. *Met.* 14.441f., 566f.

[16] The rhythm of line 314 is DSDSDS, and of line 315 DSDDDS; both
lines start with a similar unit, "nunc adeo," "expediam."

Now, speaking for the peace party, Drances continues the debate with a more complicated oration (11.343-375). Its complexity corresponds to the peculiar political situation. Two different men, with different characters and policies, divide authority uneasily between them. King Latinus virtually abdicated some time ago (7.577-622), but the return of Venulus' mission has caused him to emerge from seclusion and propose negotiations for peace. Turnus took command of the joint military forces of the Latins and the Rutulians (8.1-2), and now, defeated, he burns to continue fighting and redeem his losses. Since Latinus is a *roi fainéant* and Turnus, commanding the armed forces, holds most of the effective power, it would be easy for Turnus at this juncture to grasp the reins still more firmly and impose his own decision on the assembly. Therefore Drances sets out to divide the two rulers, distinguish their motives, and align the Latins firmly on the side of king Latinus. He wishes also to provoke Turnus to lose his temper, in order to contrast his hot-headed impulsive character with the mature wisdom of Latinus. Accordingly, he makes a double speech, addressed partly to Latinus and partly to Turnus.

In the *exordium* he first praises the king's wisdom directly (343-345) and then (346-351) attacks Turnus without naming him.[17] He blames him for intimidating the people, bringing on the recent disaster, and running away from the battlefield: the phrase "fugae fidens," alluding to Turnus's escape from the Trojan camp in 9.815-818, is an insinuation calculated to inflame the fiery young prince.

Now follows a dual *propositio*. The first, addressed to Latinus, accepts his suggestions and adds one more, the offer of Lavinia's hand to Aeneas (352-356). This is intended to enrage Turnus, and is worded as a skillful insult: Drances advises the

---

[17] Drances does not utter the name of Turnus until his direct face-to-face appeal in 11.362-363, when he effectively brackets the vocative between "pacem" and "pacis." Vergil's characters often avoid naming the persons whom they hate: see pp. 125-126, 135.

king "nec te ullius *uiolentia* uincat," and then, by describing
the wedding of Lavinia to Aeneas in such phrases as *"dignis*
hymenaeis" and *"egregio* genero," implies that Turnus is infe-
rior in rank and merit. In the second *propositio* Drances di-
rectly challenges Turnus and offers him two courses: either
(a) have pity on the Latins and make peace (357-367) or (b)
fight Aeneas alone in a duel (368-375). With both these alter-
natives the argument *honestum* is interwoven, as the emo-
tional phrases show: "miseros ciues," "supplex," "miserere
tuorum," "fama," and "patrii Martis." The total effect is to
make the Latins appear not as Turnus's allies but as his vic-
tims, and to taunt Turnus for being at once bold and cowardly.
(Good psychology, for this is how he appears in the climax
of the poem: contrast 12.87-106 with 12.219-221.) The speech
has no peroration, and ends in a broken line: Vergil may have
intended Turnus to cut it short with his eruption of fury.

Sometimes an orator may utter what he believes to be false,
and it can turn out to be true. In this powerful speech Drances
begs Turnus to have pity on the Latins and Rutulians, with
the phrase "miserere tuorum" (11.365)—although perhaps he
scarcely expects the prince to yield. Turnus rejects the plea with
disdain. Yet as the final crisis approaches, as his army is being
defeated and the city which he has tried to protect is being
stormed, a messenger rides to him crying the same desperate
words, "miserere tuorum!" (12.653).

The prince's reply, although forceful and passionate, is
not in the slightest degree incoherent. Heyne admired it great-
ly, saying: "nec quicquam in Graecis, multo minus in Ho-
mero, reperiri arbitror, quod ad artem declamatoriam propius
spectet."[18] Heinze (p. 426) declared that only this speech in
the *Aeneid* showed any tendency to stress its rhetorical struc-
ture, and he pointed to the emphatic dismissal of Drances in
410 and the triple arrangement of the proposals ("si," 411;

[18] Heyne's note on 11.376.

59

"sin," 419; "quod si," 434). In fact there are several other speeches in the poem which bear clear indications of their structure; but this one is certainly laid out with fine logic.

Like that of Drances, it is a combination of two speeches, with two purposes, two different addresses, and two different structural plans. The aims of Turnus are, first, to defend himself against the intolerable charge of cowardice and defeat; and, second, to persuade the council that the war should be prosecuted, with himself as leader.

It begins (11.378-409) with a rebuttal addressed to Drances. There is no *exordium* whatever: only the bare name "Drance." To begin with, Turnus refutes the accusation most painful to him, that of cowardice. In lines 378-391 he answers the sneer "fugae fidens" (351) by a comparison of himself and Drances as warriors, couched in a series of ironic challenges which culminates with "imus in aduersos—quid cessas?" This passage contains a quotation from the speech made by Venus at the Olympian council. Of course Turnus could not possibly know what the goddess said; nevertheless, she is the mother of his opponent Aeneas: so Vergil makes him use her rather exaggerated description of the horrors of the siege of New Troy, in the drastic phrase "inundant sanguine fossae" (11.382 ≈ 10.24).[19] Next, in 392-398, he replies to the suggestion that he was defeated: "pulsus ego?" takes up "pulsus abi" (366), and the seven lines constitute a brief narration of his exploits. Since the charge that he was beaten in battle rankles in his mind, he uses an outstandingly cruel epithet, calling Drances "foedissime"—a word never used elsewhere in the *Aeneid* of a human being, but applied once to the mischief-making Fama (4.195), once to the repulsive function of declaring war, which Latinus finds repugnant (7.619), and twice to the filth of the Harpies (3.216 and 244). Thirdly, in 399-405, Turnus rejects the proposal to make peace, quoting "nulla salus bello" from

---

[19] In the mouth of Turnus the verb "inundant" is intransitive, an exceedingly rare usage, on which Priscian comments.

362. He argues that the Trojans can be conquered now because they have been conquered before, and he ends with an ἀδύνατον about a river running backwards from the sea: the river Aufidus, suggested by the thought of Diomede, who had settled near it.[20] Fourthly, in 406-409, he refutes the charge of violent behavior, answering Drances' phrases "det libertatem fandi" (346), "uiolentia" (354), and "tantus terror" (357). Here there is an effect uncommonly subtle even for Vergil. When Drances began to speak, he said

> dicam equidem, licet arma mihi mortemque minetur.
>
> (11.348)

as though Turnus were raising an arm to threaten him. Now, during his reply, Turnus makes a real gesture, which we can almost see—

> numquam animam talem *dextra hac* (absiste moueri!) amittes—

and from which Drances flinches, or Turnus wishes the council to believe that he flinches. The threat of physical destruction being dismissed, the σύγκρισις ends: Drances is not even worth killing. Turnus's contempt for his opponent is shown in his syntax. The initial "uel" is colloquial, and belongs to the light style of Plautus and Cicero's conversational letters.[21]

---

[20] See H. V. Canter, "The figure ἀδύνατον in Greek and Latin poetry," *AJP* 51 (1930) 32-41. On p. 77 of *Le Thème de l'Adynaton dans la poésie grecque et latine* (Paris, 1936), E. Dutoit omits this instance of the figure, although on p. 139 he includes Statius's imitation of it (*Theb.* 7.553). R. D. Williams, in *CP* 61 (1966) 184-186, suggests that in mentioning the Aufidus Turnus is thinking of the kingdom of his own father Daunus. Line 11.404 (adapted from 2.197) should be excised. It is pointless to mention Achilles and Diomede, because Achilles is dead and Diomede has just refused to fight the Trojans. The relentless warrior-clan and the (initially) impetuous river are enough.

[21] "Vel" here is scarcely an archaism, as Quintilian says in 9.3.14 and as Szantyr suggests on p. 501 of his *Syntax*. It would be quite inappropriate for the impetuous youth to use an archaism in this context. "Vel" is careless

The phrase "artificis scelus" has provoked some discussion. It has been taken as nominative in apposition to the subject of "se fingit," i.e. Drances: if so, it would resemble Plautus's "scelus uiri Palaestrio" (*M.G.* 1434).[22] But when Vergil echoes himself, he usually keeps the syntax the same; and here "artificis scelus" echoes a phrase used in 2.125 of Ulysses by Sinon. The echo implies that, for Turnus, Drances is as skillful a liar as Ulysses. In Book Two the phrase is in the accusative. Here, therefore, it is likely to be in the accusative also—in apposition to the rest of the sentence ("cunning crime!") like *triste ministerium* in 6.223.[23] Surely also the brisk parenthesis "solitum tibi" in 11.383 is colloquial in tone.

Turnus's address to Latinus (11.410-444), although no less emotional, is in a quite different tone, and shows that he is not a barbarian but a civilized young prince. He opens with a respectful *exordium* (410) in which he calls Latinus "pater," just as Drances did in 356. Then he proceeds to examine the three strategic possibilities which confront the Latins and Rutulians. He answers each of them with a differently shaped reply.

To the proposal that peace should be made he says with bitter irony "oremus" (414). The alternative of continuing the war he voices in a question, "cur . . . deficimus?" (423-424). The proposal that he himself should fight a duel with Aeneas he meets with a calm asseveration, "ibo" (438).

---

and almost slangy, because in his excitement and contempt Turnus is talking informally. As parallels Szantyr cites Plautus, *M.G.* 59, and Cicero, *Fam.* 2.13.1 and 7.24.1.

[22] On this type of phrase see W. Havers, *Handbuch der erklärenden Syntax* (Heidelberg, 1931) para. 126, and J. Svennung, *Anredeformen* (Uppsala, 1956) p. 114. It is discussed by E. A. Hahn in *TAPhA* 84 (1953) 98-99. She proposes that "scelus uiri" is an instance of "partitive apposition": "a trait of the uir is scelus," and indeed he is *all* crime, like the man in Catullus 13.14 who will pray to be all nose.

[23] This parallel is cited by R. D. Williams, *CP* 61 (1966) 184-186.

Discussing the proposal to sue for peace (411-418), he gives a gentle reply to Latinus's gloomy picture of the situation (310-311 are answered by 412-413): it contains the argument *facile* (resistance is still within our power) and moves on to the argument that honor is at stake (death rather than surrender, 416-418). Next, he brings up the suggestion he himself favors: that war should be continued. He dares not propose this in terms blunt enough to shock his audience. Therefore he disguises it under two questions, both rhetorically exaggerated and both touching on the theme of honor (423-424):

cur *indecores* in limine primo
deficimus? cur ante tubam *tremor* occupat artus?

Then, listing the allies who are still on the Latin side although Diomede has refused his support, he stresses the argument *facile* (425-433). Finally, he takes up Drances' proposal that he should fight a duel with Aeneas. He accepts this as a possibility, supporting it by the argument that it will be honorable (note the ethical indicators "uirtus" and "gloria" in 444); and he counters Drances' final challenge "illum aspice contra / qui uocat" (374-375) with "solum Aeneas uocat; et uocet oro" (442). There is no peroration. Yet toward the end Turnus rises to heroic dignity with the sentence "uobis animam hanc soceroque Latino . . . deuoui" (440 + 442). Something of the Roman concept of *deuotio* is here retrojected into primitive Italy. The Decii made their self-sacrifice part of a ritual religious act.[24] But other Romans offered up their lives for their nation as part of a military operation, without religious sanctions: such was Q. Caedicius, who led a unit to a place where he expected himself and all his men to be annihilated by the Carthaginians, while the main Roman force had time to occupy key positions.[25]

[24] Wissowa s.v. *devotio*, RE V, 1.277-278.
[25] Cato frg. 83 in Peter HR Rel.

63

The debate does not continue with further arguments from both sides, leading to a vote, a decision, and an adjournment. At least, no later speakers are named, no speeches mentioned. The news that Aeneas is marching on the city (as he resolved to do in 11.17-21) throws the meeting into disorder. Warlike shouts, "arma . . . arma,"[26] come from the young men, sobs and murmurs from the old (11.453-454). In the same way a meeting of the Trojans is interrupted by the report that the Achaeans are marching on Troy (*Il.* 2.786-810); but there is no apparent dissension in the Trojan assembly. Hector instantly dissolves it and the men rush unanimously to arms. Here, on the other hand, Turnus seizes the initiative, quits the meeting before any vote can be taken, and wins his point by resuming command of the army (11.463-467). Latinus lacks the energy and authority to countermand Turnus's orders and to continue the debate in his absence: he disappears into the background (11.469-470) as he did before, when he dropped the reins of power (7.599-600). He makes a sorry contrast with old Priam, who remains active and exerts his full authority in a similar crisis toward the end of the *Iliad* (21.526-536). Drances is completely eliminated. He does not reappear in the epic: although doubtless he was the first to approach Aeneas after the slaying of Turnus, with eloquent phrases of congratulation.

This debate contains four speeches fully reported. All follow the "deliberative" scheme, although with many individual variations and subtleties. They are all clearly arranged, and all in different ways eloquent. The strangest and most decisive is that of Diomede. Wisdom and experience inform his closing words:

> coeant in foedera dextrae
> qua datur, ast armis concurrant arma cauete.

[26] See p. 179.

The weakest is the old king's address. Its despair is reflected in the heavy sigh after "spem . . . ponite" (308-309): a sigh made audible by the suspension of the process which would, if "ponite" and "spes" following it had been spoken in one breath, have altered the quantity of the final syllable in "ponite." The short phrases of 309 (verbs omitted as though in exhaustion) and 312-313 were evidently uttered slowly, with long pauses for gloomy reflection. Nevertheless, old and weak as Latinus is, he is not wholly incompetent. His proposals (316-334) are well thought out and couched in long balanced sentences: they end, as a king's should, with two imperatives. The speech of Drances is the cleverest. His aim throughout is described in the phrase *aggerat iras* (342), and he attains it:

$$\text{talibus exarsit dictis uiolentia Turni. (11.376)}$$

The reply of Turnus, furiously as it begins, shows him still governing his temper well enough to answer coherently and even convincingly. He is—although in the wrong—still master of the situation as the debate comes to its tumultuous and unsatisfactory end.

Debate in heaven

The other great debate of the *Aeneid* occurs in heaven (10.1-117). Besides Jupiter's initial and final addresses, only two speeches are reported, both skillful in the extreme.

Jupiter opens the council by rebuking the gods in general for disobeying his command by encouraging the war in Italy and joining in it.[27]

Venus immediately launches into an oration, addressed not to the assembly but to Jove himself (10.18-62). It is in the form

---

[27] Heinze, p. 297 n. 1, stresses the inconsistency of this with 1.263-264, and accounts for it as part of the disharmony between two concepts, both of which appealed to Vergil: one, to have Aeneas welcomed in a peaceful Italy; the other, to make him a conqueror forcing civilization on a primitive country by the sword.

of a "deliberative" or policy-making speech. But its ostensible purpose is different from its real intention. What Venus *asks* of Jupiter is that she may have permission—since Juno is determined to annihilate the Trojans—at least to save her young grandson Ascanius (10.46-47) and keep him, safe and harmless, in one of her sanctuaries. What she wants to *persuade* Jupiter to do is to condemn Juno's past conduct (she introduces a complete historical survey of Juno's acts of aggression) and to command her to stop persecuting Aeneas in the future. Such a speech, concealing its true aim beneath a substantially different proposal or presentation of facts, was called $c\chi\hat{\eta}\mu\alpha$ by the rhetorical writers.[28] Quintilian describes it in *Inst.* 9.2.65-99. There were three varieties: (1) the orator said less than he meant, a $c\chi\hat{\eta}\mu\alpha$ $\kappa\alpha\tau'$ $\check{\epsilon}\mu\phi\alpha\sigma\iota\nu$; (2) the orator said something different from his intention, a $c\chi\hat{\eta}\mu\alpha$ $\pi\lambda\acute{\alpha}\gamma\iota o\nu$; and (3) the orator, like Agamemnon in his disastrous speech to the Achaeans (*Il.* 2.110-141), said the exact reverse of what he intended, a $c\chi\hat{\eta}\mu\alpha$ $\grave{\epsilon}\nu\alpha\nu\tau\acute{\iota}o\nu$. The speech of Venus belongs to the second type: it is oblique, "ut quod aures offensurum erat si palam diceretur, id oblique et furtim subreperet."[29] In a monarchy, it is imprudent to attack the consort of the monarch directly. As Quintilian remarks (9.2.68), this type of speech is "multo ad agendum difficilior, cum personae potentes obstant."

As well as being angled, the speech of Venus contains distortions of fact. Vergil knows that the aim of oratory is not to inform but to persuade: therefore his orators use much *auxesis* and *meiosis*. A simple instance of this has been noticed above, in the Trojans' plea to Latinus (p. 54). So in this debate

---

[28] The material on this interesting rhetorical device is collected by Ernesti, *Graec.*, pp. 340-341, s.v. $c\chi\hat{\eta}\mu\alpha\tau\alpha$ and 341-343, s.v. $c\chi\eta\mu\alpha\tau\acute{\iota}\zeta\epsilon\iota\nu$; additional citations in Ernesti, *Lat.*, pp. 168-169, s.v. *figura*. There is a good discussion in Volkmann, pp. 111-123. It was the "scourge of Homer," Zoilus of Amphipolis, who confined the term $c\chi\hat{\eta}\mu\alpha$ to the device *quo aliud simulatur dici quam dicitur* (Quint. 9.1.14).

[29] Porcius Latro, quoted by the elder Seneca, *Controu.* 1. praef. 24.

Venus changes the four ships burnt in Sicily (5.699) to "exustas classis" (10.36).

In her *exordium* (10.18-19) she reminds Jove that, as father and supreme power of the universe, he ought to help her and can help her; and she bids for sympathy by adding that, but for him, she is alone and helpless. (This although the Trojans have been favored and aided by the god of Tiber river, 8.26-89; Vulcan, 8.370-453 + 534-536 + 612-614; Apollo, 9.638-663; and Jupiter himself, 9.630-631 and 799-805.)

Three points are stressed in Venus's narrative (20-30): the Rutulian and Latin attack on the Trojan camp; its helplessness in the absence of Aeneas; and the Latin request for assistance from Diomede. Thus she covers the events of Books Eight and Nine. The first sentence contains an exaggeration typical both of a skilled orator and of a wounded feminine spirit:

> cernis ut insultent Rutuli, Turnusque feratur
> per medios insignis equis tumidusque secundo
> Marte ruat?

Since Turnus has done most of his fighting on foot, especially his *aristeia* around and within the Trojan camp (9.559-562, 727-818), the statement that he was riding a chariot "per medios" appeared unreasonable to Otto Ribbeck, who excised it. But Servius correctly divined that Venus was exaggerating the effect of Turnus's first appearance in front of the Trojan camp, riding on a swift Thracian horse, surrounded by picked cavalry (9.47-50). Similarly Venus declares that Diomede is rising to attack the Trojans once more (10.28-29), although in fact he has already rejected the Latin offer of alliance and the disappointed embassy is returning (11.243-295). With plaintive impudence she even suggests that Diomede will again wound her with his spear as he did before Troy (*Il.* 5.330-342). In his three great female characters Vergil emphasizes the fact that women remember the past, and particularly recall personal slights and injuries. Men look forward.

Now Venus moves on to two arguments, both based on the theme of justice, which are ostensibly meant to support the proposal for which she is preparing the groundwork. The first (10.31-35) is phrased as a dilemma.[30] It is addressed directly to Jove. It asks whether he did or did not approve the migration of the Trojans to Italy. If he did, Juno's attack on them is contrary to his will and to destiny. Venus does not name the queen of heaven, but pointedly says "cur nunc tua *quisquam* / uertere iura potest?" The implication is that Jupiter should prohibit any further transgression of his clearly expressed orders. In the second argument also, Juno is not named (10.36-41). But Venus points her out more clearly by an allusion to Juno's threat "Acheronta mouebo" (7.312) as though she herself had heard it uttered ("manes / mouet," 10.39-40), and by naming Juno's accomplices Iris and Allecto. In a few trenchant phrases she summarizes the activities of Juno in Books Five (line 36), One (37-38), Nine (38), and Seven (39-41): the fire, storm, and war stirred up at Juno's bidding.[31]

Now she follows these preparatory arguments with her proposal (42-53). First she declares that she has abandoned all hope for a realm in which the Trojans may rule, and that she is ready to accept defeat because it is apparently the will of Jupiter. "Nil super *imperio* moueor," she says sadly (42), to remind Jupiter that in 1.279 he explicitly promised "*imperium*

---

[30] The word, common enough in modern languages, is quite rare in Greek. Its adjectival form appears in Hermogenes *De Inu.* 4 c. 6 as διλήμματον (sc. cχῆμα); Spengel 2, pp. 250-251. Cicero in his early *De Inu.* 1.45 tried calling it *complexio*, an unsatisfactory term which he later applied to the periodic sentence instead (*De Or.* 3.182). The best-known example is Dem. *De Cor.* 217; others are given by Volkmann p. 228.

[31] "Actam nubibus Irim" (10.38) might refer either to Iris's appearance in disguise among the Trojan women (5.604f.) or to her mission to Turnus (9.1-24). In her reply Juno takes it as referring to the mission to Turnus: for the entire context, 10.65-80, concerns the war in Italy.

sine fine dedi." She blames cruel Juno, and Juno alone, for the fact that the Trojans are homeless on the face of the earth.[32] Then, skimming lightly over the fate of Aeneas (48-49),[33] she asks for nothing but the life of the boy Ascanius—a prayer which she utters thrice (46-47, 50, 52-53). This, as the minimum possible request, she supports with two further arguments, both based on the theme *utile*. The first, indirectly aimed at Juno, appeals to her love of Carthage, and promises that Ascanius will be eliminated so that nothing may hinder the Carthaginian conquest of Italy.[34] This will assure Venus of the backing of those deities who foresee the Punic wars and intend to support Rome (see 10.11-14). The second argument (55-62) asks Jupiter whether, if this is to be their end, the Trojans have gained any chance of happiness by suffering so much and so long. Venus closes with the paradox (*utile et non possibile*) that it would be better for them to endure the Trojan war once again.

There is no peroration. Instead of it, we may easily imagine Venus, at the grievous words "casus Iliacos," bursting into glittering tears, as she did in her first appeal to Jupiter (1.227-229).[35]

Juno's answer to this oblique attack (10.63-95) is not the same type of speech. She will not stoop to persuade a group of inferior divinities, or her husband-brother, with counter-proposals and counter-arguments. Instead, *acta furore graui*, she

---

[32] J. Marouzeau, *Les Articulations de l'énoncé* (Paris, 1949) p. 181, points out the metrical emphasis on the "insidious epithet 'dura'" (10.45), separated from the noun it modifies and placed at the head of the line.

[33] "Sane" (48) is a word never before used in high poetry: it would seem to show that Venus is trying to sound offhand. See B. Axelson, *Unpoetische Wörter* (Lund, 1945) p. 93, who adds that the prosaic character of the word may account for the textual variant "procul."

[34] "Nihil urbibus inde / obstabit Tyriis," she says, as though there were many Tyrian cities at the moment, whereas even Carthage is only half-built. No doubt she is looking forward to the Carthaginian settlements in Spain.

[35] So with a tearful aposiopesis in Statius, *Theb.* 3.291.

turns directly on Venus with a speech of the forensic type: a rebuttal, justifying her conduct in a series of some fifteen angry rhetorical questions. These are the *interrogationes* not meant to be answered, which Quintilian discusses in 9.2.7: "quo usque tandem abutere, Catilina . . . ?"

Juno's *exordium* (*ab aduersariae persona*, Cic., *De Inu.* 1.16.22) is a reproach to Venus for starting the dispute. But it also reveals the driving psychical impulse which Juno cannot keep hidden: her pride, wounded by the judgment of Paris, which offended her beauty. "Obductum dolorem" (64) recalls the *saeui dolores* of 1.25 and the phrases which there follow. Indeed, the fury of Juno and the destructive ferocity of her speech and actions suggest that she is almost insane. Within the orderly system of the moral and physical universe, she is the chief source of storm and strife. She exults in evil.

Her *refutatio* is a survey of the events of the past twenty years or so. It is designed to show (a) that not Juno but Venus herself is responsible for some of the actions of which she complains (65-73 + 88-93): this is shifting the onus, called by the rhetoricians *remotio criminis*[36] or *translatio*[37] and μετάϲταϲιϲ;[38] and (b) that other acts done by Juno and Turnus are justified by the actions of Venus and Aeneas (74-84): this is *relatio criminis*[39] or ἀντέγκλημα.[40] Juno covers the events of Book Seven in lines 65-66; in 68-73 Aeneas's mission in Book Eight, and in 74-84 the siege in Book Nine; then, after a rude dismissal of two points in Venus's speech (85-87 ≈ 25 + 51-52), she reverts to the origins of the Trojan war (89-93).

The brief peroration (94-95) is all *indignatio*.[41] The violence and hostility of its phrasing are enhanced by its sound: it con-

---

[36] Cic. *De Inu.* 1.11.15.   [37] Quint. 7.4.13-14.
[38] Hermogenes, *Stat.* 2, p. 140 Spengel.
[39] Cic. *De Inu.* 1.11.15.
[40] Hermogenes, *Stat.* 2, pp. 139-140 Spengel; Quint. 7.4.8-9.
[41] Cic. *De Inu.* 1.53.100-54.105.

tains nine dentals, ten sibilants, and energetic alliteration on initial *l*. Its rhythm also is drastic. There is no strong caesura in line 95, only a weak caesura after "adsurgis," like the rushing wind of *Georg.* 1.357 and the runaway horses of *Georg.* 1.514; and the final three words of the line each occupy one foot, an unusual pattern which appears in other lines containing excited emphatic speech[42] or depicting violent action.[43]

In her speech Juno several times quotes the actual words of her opponent in order to rebut them (73 ≈ 38; 85 ≈ 25; 86 ≈ 50-51). She exaggerates and deforms the facts to a degree unusual even in passionate oratory. She depicts Aeneas as guided, not by oracles and prophecies and the will of ineluctable destiny, but rather "by the ravings of Cassandra" (10.68). She describes his leaving his camp as "puero summam belli credere" (70), in spite of his delegation of command to two senior officers (9.171-173 and 9.778-780). His acquisition of Etruscan allies is "Tyrrhenam fidem agitare" (71), although the Etruscans are in rebellion against Mezentius (8.478-495). Venus, not Cybele, is made responsible for transforming the Trojan ships into nymphs (83, cf. 9.77-122); and Aeneas's betrothal to Lavinia is "gremiis abducere pactas" (79). For Juno, Iulus's shooting of the pet stag (7.475-502) is "arua aliena iugo premere atque auertere praedas" (10.78). This last distortion (as Heinze points out) is of particular interest. In one version of the myth the Trojans actually did seize land from aborigines and drive off livestock—which occasioned the war.[44] Vergil does not adopt this version in the *Aeneid*, but, by putting it in the mouth of the great enemy of Troy, he shows knowledge of its existence and implicitly denies it.

The violence of Juno's phrasing is also remarkable. For instance, "Spartam expugnauit adulter" in 92: "expugnauit" suggests aggression and rapine, while "adulter" is not found in

---

[42] So 9.429, 12.582. [43] Cf. 1.101, 9.432, 12.528.

[44] Heinze, p. 247. See Cato (presumably the first Latin literary source of the story) in Peter, *HR Rel*, pp. 44-45; Livy 1.1.5; Dion. Hal. *Ant. Rom.* 1.57.

high poetry before this passage and the odes of Horace. Vergil uses it only twice, here and in Diomede's speech (11.268): for him the word is still—as it was for Cicero, *Cael.* 30—a *conuicium*.

Aeneas to Dido

There is one other formal speech of refutation and self-defense in the epic: the last words spoken by Aeneas to Dido in the world of life (4.333-361). This address has been much discussed. Some critics view it as a callous rejection of a devoted woman's love, made by a cold egoist. Others see it as a righteous man's priggishly formal self-exculpation. To others again it is an embarrassed endeavor to cloud the issue and obscure the facts. Otis suggests that its harsh tone is created by Aeneas's own feeling of guilt: "he should have avoided excuses and taken his share of the blame."[45] While sympathetic and basically correct, this comment does not go quite deep enough.

Three conflicting forces have been working on Aeneas: the power of God's command; his love; and his fear of Dido's ungovernable passions. All three appear in the important though unobtrusive paragraph of narrative (4.279-295) in which Vergil describes Aeneas's alarm at receiving the high behest of Jupiter (279-280 + 282); his warm affection for Dido (*dulcis*, 281; *optima*, 291; *tantos amores*, 292); and his reluctance to tell her the truth (283-284 + 291-294).

The first factor is overriding. A messenger from heaven could not possibly be disbelieved or disobeyed by Aeneas—any more than by the Aiantes and their followers in the *Iliad* (13.43-135) or by Priam (*Il.* 24.159-227). In the heroic age a summons from Olympus is unmistakable when delivered as directly as this; and, for the Roman mind, obedience to the will of God is the first virtue.

The pang of separation Aeneas feels deeply; but he hides

---

[45] Otis, p. 268. What was Dido's share of the blame?

his feelings. Vergil explicitly states that he obeyed the command of Jupiter by keeping his eyes unmoved, to conceal his passionate love (4.331-332). As Pöschl says, Aeneas is not an impassive Stoic, but a man who "experiences sorrow to the utmost," and who endeavors "to do what is necessary in spite of his great sensitivity."[46] But few will agree with Pöschl in the statement: "it is not so much the passion of his love that moves Aeneas. . . . Rather, he is moved by compassion for Dido's grief": a statement which he supports by saying *"cura* [in 4.332] does not originally signal passion or desire, but the sympathy with the beloved object."[47] On the contrary, *cura* in a context such as this, dealing with sexual love, means the pain of passion unfulfilled or frustrated: so it appears with great emphasis in the first line of Book Four, where it cannot conceivably mean "sympathy."[48] Aeneas is suffering just as much as Dido from thwarted love, and *curam sub corde premebat* (4.332) corresponds closely to *magno animum labefactus amore* (4.395).

It is the third factor in this painful equation which causes so much suffering. Because he was afraid of her, Aeneas concealed the truth from Dido. If, within the hour after receiving the command of Jove (who is emphatically styled *Omnipotens* in 4.206 and 4.220), while his awe and alarm were still fresh, he had gone to Dido and told the truth about the divine message, she might have shared his conviction of the ineluctable will of destiny and the irresistible power of God, and, although bitterly wounded, have accepted the inevitable. Although a demi-goddess and although in love, Calypso accepts her orders from Olympus forthwith and conveys them straight to her beloved Odysseus (*Od.* 5.116-170). During their dalliance with the Lemnian women, Hercules reproaches the Argonauts: im-

[46] Pöschl, p. 54. Contrast Lucan on Cato's remarriage, *B.C.* 2.350-391.

[47] Pöschl, p. 44 and n. 15 on p. 184.

[48] *Curae* are restless unsatisfied passion in Catullus 2.8-10; cf. *Aen.* 4.639 and 652, 6.474.

mediately, without any procrastination, they leave; Hypsipyle weeps and lets them go (*Argon.* 1.861-914). But Aeneas hesitates and temporizes. This is not heroic. None of the Homeric champions (unless, for special reasons, the wily Odysseus) would have hesitated before revealing to a wife, a lover, or a friend, an inevitable decision. Aeneas shrinks like a coward. And yet he has never disguised his purpose and his destiny. When telling Dido the story of his escape from Troy and his later wanderings, he made it perfectly clear that he was destined to reach a new country, Hesperia, where he would be king and have a queen. The words—repeated by himself at a crisis of his narrative—came from his own wife, protected and inspired by heaven:

> illic res laetae regnumque et regia coniunx
> parta tibi.   (2.783-784)

In spite of this—which Dido heard, and, as a woman, surely remembers—he refrains until too late from telling her the unavoidable truth. He hesitates. He issues orders which are impossible to fulfill without arousing suspicion: orders that his men shall prepare their ships for sailing, in silence and without revealing the reason for their activity. His hesitant reflections and his commands to his officers are given by Vergil in indirect speech (4.288-294), almost as though to indicate that they are less than frank.

This concealment is the first wrong with which Dido taxes him. It is the first charge which he endeavors to deny. His instructions to his crews were clear:

> classem aptent *taciti* sociosque ad litora cogant,
> arma parent, et quae rebus sit causa nouandis
> *dissimulent.*   (4.289-291)

Dido's accusation begins:

> *dissimulare* etiam sperasti, perfide, tantum
> posse nefas, *tacitusque* mea decedere terra?
>   (4.305-306)

74

His answer is:

> neque ego hanc *abscondere furto*
> speraui—ne finge—fugam.   (4.337-338)

To his hearer, and to nearly all readers, this must appear to be a barefaced lie. The only possible justification for it is that he *intended* to tell Dido, at some time after his preparations were nearly complete, in a tender moment, one of the *mollissima fandi tempora* (4.293-294); but that he had postponed doing so. No wonder, therefore, that this particular speech of Aeneas is so little admired, both as a revelation of character and as a piece of oratory. Apparently Vergil intended it to be inadequate; and it makes a bleak contrast with the last speech uttered by Odysseus to Calypso (*Od.* 5.215-224).

Nevertheless, the speech is skillfully composed, and merits examination in detail.

There is no *exordium*, except the title "regina," which Dido prizes, and which is intended to remind her of her own independent worth. The first sentence (4.333-336) is a frank admission[49] of Aeneas's debt to Dido ("promeritam" takes up "bene merui" from 317) and of their love—which he now describes as a thing of the past: gone, although not forgotten.[50]

Then in one phrase Aeneas moves from emotion to argument: "pro re pauca loquar." What does this mean? Not "de re."[51] One explanation gives "pro" its full force, "in defense of."[52] This makes Aeneas say, "I shall advance a few arguments in defense of the fact with which you charge me," namely, the fact that he is preparing to leave Carthage. Another explanation takes "pauca" and "pro" together, and interprets

---

[49] *Confessio nihil nocitura*, Quintilian 9.2.51, comparing Cicero, *Lig.* 2.

[50] Is it too fanciful to hear, in the unusual assonance "meminisse . . . Elissae," a hint of the obsessive magic of love, which works like a spell: "limus ut hic durescit et haec ut cera liquescit" (*Buc.* 8.80)?

[51] J. Svennung, *Orosiana* (Uppsala, 1922) pp. 38-41, shows that *pro* with a verb of speech was not used as equivalent to *de* until the late Empire.

[52] So Sall. *Iug.* 102.12: pauca pro delicto suo uerba facit.

"pro" as "in proportion to" or "in consideration of": so Cicero, *Clu.* 160: "pro Cluenti uoluntate nimium, pro rei dignitate parum, pro uestra prudentia satis dixisse uideor." According to this view, Aeneas says "I shall speak only briefly, in view of the situation"—which would not be improved by a long oration leading into a useless and painful debate.[53]

In favor of this second interpretation is the fact that Aeneas's speech is curt in tone, and concludes with two firm lines virtually cutting off all further discussion (360-361). Yet the first explanation seems to be supported by the logical sequence of his remarks: he begins (333-336) by dismissing the charge that he is ungrateful; and then he shows that he is compelled to quit Carthage: this is, as it were, a defense, *pro delicto suo*. Which is correct? The question is decided by line 333, which places *pauca* at the same place in the line as "pauca" in line 337, and therefore must give the word the same connotation. We should prefer the second interpretation—"I shall say little, in this difficult situation."

The word "pauca" has also aroused some discussion. The speech of Aeneas to Dido is not long, but it is not particularly short: in fact it is nearly three lines longer than Dido's speech of accusation. Conington, followed by Pease, suggests that the word implies the difficulty which Aeneas feels in speaking. Certainly it is not an easy speech to make; yet the pathetic lines 340-344 are fluent enough, and so is the description of the forces which press upon him, 351-359. A better explanation is advanced by A. L. Keith.[54] Here, as elsewhere, "pauca" is used

---

[53] Caesar, *B.G.* 5.8.1: ut . . . consilium pro tempore et pro re caperet; Cic. *Att.* 7.8.2: animaduerteram posse pro re nata te non incommode ad me . . . uenire.

[54] " 'Briefly speaking' in Vergil," *CW* 15 (1921-1922) 50-51. Keith adds that *multa* in Vergil can imply wild and unrestrained speaking rather than the fact that a speech lasts a long time: for instance, it is applied to Iarbas's thirteen-line prayer in 4.205; cf. 11.471 and 12.601. Note too the comment of Donatus on 8.154, about Evander's speech, introduced by *tum sic pauca refert*: "pauca debemus accipere, hoc est pauciora quam dici potuerunt."

76

relatively. It means that the speech is short in comparison with what the speaker might say if he could or if he chose. Thus Aeneas applies the word "breuiter" in 2.11 to a speech which will cover more than fifteen hundred lines; and Helenus in 3.377 before his long prophecy says he will reveal "pauca e multis." Heinze (p. 426), who often emphasizes the skill with which Vergil conceals the rhetorical structure of his speeches, notes that "pro re pauca loquar" stands out as an exception to this. He accounts for it by suggesting that Aeneas is about to lose his self-control—as is shown by the pathos of "dum memor ipse mei, dum spiritus hos regit artus" (336)—and then, in these four coldly logical words, pulls himself together. Yet perhaps this is too subtle. Lines 331-332 say unequivocally that Aeneas restrains himself with iron self-control imposed by God, *Iouis monitis.*

The heart of the speech is devoted to the theme that Aeneas *must* leave Carthage and sail to Italy. He argues this point for twenty-two lines (4.340-361). Once he opposes his passion for Dido to his longing for the new land, in a significant phrase: "hic *amor,* haec patria est," (4.347). He might easily have said "hic *domus,* haec patria est," as he is to do in 7.122; but he chooses to say "amor," to show Dido that he has given up his sexual infatuation under the pressure of a higher motive.

This section he begins with an outright rejection of Dido's two charges (4.337-339). He denies that he intended to leave Carthage secretly ("abscondere furto" X "dissimulare . . . tacitus," 305-306). He denies that he ever offered Dido marriage ("coniugis taedas" X "coniubia," 316).[55] His phrasing is not merely firm, but harsh. At the opening and close there are two blunt imperatives, "ne finge" (338) and "desine" (360).[56] In

[55] This direct denial the rhetoricians call ἔνςταςις (Hermog. *Inu.* 3.6, Spengel 2, pp. 209-210) or ἀνατροπή (Apsines 7, Spengel 1.2, pp. 268-269).

[56] The harsh tone of these imperatives is shown by the mood of the other passages in which they appear: "ne . . . finge" is said by Turnus to the false

77

360 "querelis" is a bitter word. Vergil uses it to describe the voices of frogs in *Georg.* 1.378 and (following Lucretius 2.358) of cattle in *Aen.* 8.215; but of speech only here and in the outburst of Juno, 10.94.

Thereafter Aeneas defends his conduct by justifying it.[57] His arguments are the strongest conceivable: the command of God (345-347 + 356-359) and his duty to his family (351-355). To these he adds an effective enthymeme. Dido herself migrated to found a new home (347-350), and therefore Aeneas's behavior in doing the same is just. More emotionally than logically, he asserts that he still regrets his lost home in Troy and is going to Italy against his will (340-344). The speech looks unfinished, and ends in a broken line. But the last ten words serve as a conclusion (restating the main point, Quint. 6.1.1-2), since they repeat Aeneas's chief argument ("sponte," 341 = "sponte," 361) and cut off all further discussion.

Vergil's orators often quote their opponents' words in order to refute them. Here Aeneas's "fugam" in 338 takes up Dido's "mene fugis?" from 314; and his "coniugis" in the same line replies to Dido's "conubia nostra" in 316. A more subtle echo is his "Italiam magnam" (345), which echoes the phrase "Hesperiam magnam" spoken by Dido in 1.569, with a deliberate alteration, as though Aeneas were remembering his first sight of the promised land in 3.521-524: in both passages the noun is repeated, "Italiam . . . Italiam."

The interplay of themes in this speech has been touched upon by T. Halter in *Form und Gehalt in Vergils Aeneis* (Munich, 1963) p. 117, n. 7. These themes are not rhetorical concepts, but emotional factors: Dido and Aeneas as a couple;

Calybe (7.438); and "desine" by the Sibyl in rebuke to Palinurus (6.376), by Mezentius in hatred to Aeneas (10.881), and in stern authority by Jupiter to Juno in 12.800.

[57] For the Greeks this is δικαιολογία κατ' ἀντίληψιν (Hermogenes, *Stat.* 1.2; Spengel 2.139); and for Quintilian (7.4.4) a defense under the rubric *qualitas absoluta: ipsum factum quod obicitur dicimus honestum esse.*

Troy and the Trojan destiny; and the command of God. Thus, lines 333-339 deal with the love of the ill-fated couple, while lines 360-361 express something of their newly-born hostility. Troy past is the subject of the pathetic sentence looking backward (340-344), and Troy future is represented by the warnings of Anchises and the hopes of Ascanius (351-355). The command of God fills lines 345-347 and 356-359. The central section of the speech, which sounds like a coldly logical enthymeme (347-350), is more than that: it places Aeneas and Dido in competition as founders of cities and carriers of a heroic destiny. Therefore, by implication, it frees Aeneas from enslavement to the love of a woman, the slavery in which he forgot his mission, "regni rerumque oblitus suarum" (*Aen.* 4.259-267).

Aeneas to Evander

Aeneas makes only one formal diplomatic speech. The first link between the Trojans and Dido was arranged not by Aeneas, but by Ilioneus in Book One; it was Ilioneus also who first negotiated with king Latinus in Book Seven. Only when making the difficult effort of suing for assistance from a Greek, does Aeneas himself speak in such a cause. Addressing Evander in 8.127-151, he opens with a polite *exordium* (127-128) and proceeds to a long and detailed narrative explaining what might seem incredible, the fact that he and his Greek host are kinsmen (129-145). This also serves as an argument based on the theme of justice: one kinsman should not repudiate another. On this fact and this argument, "his fretus" (8.143), Aeneas bases his request for aid. He adds another argument (*utile*): that the Arcadians and the Trojans have the same dangerous enemy, and that the Trojans will be valuable allies (146-149 + 150-151). It would not be fitting for Aeneas, either as a prince or as a suppliant, to detail his requests. Therefore his *propositio* is made with regal brevity: "accipe daque fidem" (8.150). There is no peroration.

79

Two important speeches of persuasion are made in private interviews. It might seem out of place to treat them as formal "deliberative" orations. Yet they both follow the accepted pattern for such speeches; and each of them is addressed to a monarch on a matter which, although personal, gravely affects public policy and national destiny. These are the speech in which Anna persuades Dido to struggle no longer against her love for Aeneas (4.31-53) and the speech in which Latinus tries to convince Turnus that he should join in making peace and abandon the proposed duel (12.19-45). They are not difficult to analyze.

Anna to Dido

Anna begins with an affectionate *exordium*, "o luce magis dilecta sorori"—which is to have a sad echo in 4.677-679 and 691-692. Her first proposal is made in the form of two questions which answer themselves (4.32-33): that Dido should abandon widowhood, admit the pleasures of love, and have children. (By mentioning children Anna shows that marriage, and not a secret liaison, is what she recommends. No one proposes that a queen should bear bastards.)

Then she proceeds to arguments. Dido has stressed her honor, and her devotion to her dead husband (4.24-29). Anna cannot suggest outright that her sister should abandon honor and devotion: so she concentrates the counter-argument in a single sentence, "do the dead care?" (4.34). Next she makes a comparison between Aeneas and all Dido's earlier suitors, pointing out that only he has inspired her with love. This is an argument seldom used in deliberative oratory, but appropriate here: τὸ ἡδύ, *iucundum*.[58] Because Dido is in love, Anna makes this argument longer and weightier than the argument about honor. But because Dido is a monarch and must think of her people's welfare, Anna emphasizes the third argument,

---

[58] For τὸ ἡδύ as one of the τελικὰ κεφάλαια see Anaximenes 1 (Spengel 1.2, p. 13). Rare, however, and reprehensible: Quint. 3.8.28-29.

τὸ cυμφέρον, *utile*, most strongly, and expands it in 39-49, concluding with two urgent exclamations carrying the potent phrases "coniugio tali" and "Punica gloria." She closes with a second *propositio* designed to lead to the fulfillment of the first: pray to heaven for help, and detain Aeneas in Carthage (50-54).

Latinus to Turnus

Anna has tried to calm and encourage her troubled sister. Latinus in 12.19-45 tries to calm and control the furious Turnus. His speech is therefore sober and rational in tone. It is suggested in part by the plea of Priam to Hector in *Iliad* 22.38-76, but is far less emotional. The *exordium* (19-21) combines a compliment with a warning, and instead of setting Turnus in opposition to Latinus, skillfully associates the two as allies.

> o praestans animi iuuenis, quantum *ipse* feroci
> uirtute exsuperas, tanto *me* impensius aequum est
> consulere atque omnis metuentem expendere casus.

Then comes a narrative of the general situation, and a recapitulation of the sad events of the previous five books (22-36). This is followed by the *propositio* (12.37-39). In substance, Latinus is persuading Turnus not to fight a duel with Aeneas. But he is not Turnus's father. Turnus is not bound to him by any ties of affection, and has misappropriated his regal authority; indeed, he has just addressed Latinus in terms of almost unforgivable rudeness (12.13, 12.15). Therefore Latinus cannot direct an undisguised plea to Turnus: he cannot say "μή μοι μίμνε, φίλον τέκοc, ἀνέρα τοῦτον!" Instead, he skillfully takes the responsibility on himself, and phrases it as a question to which the obvious answer is "Make peace." This is also a reminder that Latinus is after all Turnus's senior in rank and age, and that if he makes a decision ("cur non certamina *tollo*?") Turnus ought to accept it. Then follow two arguments supporting the proposal. One (40-42) is that the death

81

of Turnus would bring shame upon Latinus (the theme *honestum*), the other (43-45) that Turnus may be killed and leave his father bereaved and unprotected, i.e., that he ought to consider his family's welfare (the theme *utile*). This careful speech is preceded and followed by two examples of the *uiolentia Turni* (12.9-17 and 45-53; see p. 65), and has no effect on the turbulent youth except to make him so angry that he can scarcely speak (12.47).

Commanders' Speeches

There is an interesting variant of the policy-making or "deliberative" speech: the address spoken before or during a battle by a commander to his troops, or occasionally by a soldier to a group of his comrades. This type of speech has been less often discussed than it deserves. No doubt it was neglected by the Greek and Roman rhetoricians because it was not suitable to teach in school. When they dealt with warfare, they were apt to write a *suasoria* advising Alexander the Great not to embark on the Ocean (Seneca, *Suas.* 1) or Julius Caesar not to invade Germany (Quint. 3.8.19). Quintilian does not mention the commander's speech in his chapter dealing with deliberative oratory (3.8)—which indeed is one of the least satisfying parts of his book, and is concentrated on fictitious *suasoriae*. Later, however, he discusses its character (12.1.28):

> quid? non in bellis quoque idem ille uir quem instituimus, si sit ad proelium miles cohortandus, ex mediis sapientiae praeceptis orationem trahet? nam quomodo pugnam ineuntibus tot simul metus—laboris, dolorum, postremo mortis ipsius—exciderint, nisi in eorum locum pietas et fortitudo et honesti praesens imago successerit?

Yes; but in fact that is too lofty and philosophical for a fighting speech. No poet ever wrote better harangues for commanders than Shakespeare. King Hal's "Once more unto the breach, dear friends, once more" (*Henry V* 3.1) is rivalled by a less known but equally powerful and characteristic speech of Richard III (5.3.315-342), full of scorn for the opposing army of "bastard Bretons."

> Shall these enjoy our lands? lie with our wives?
> Ravish our daughters? Hark, I hear their drum.
> Fight, gentlemen of England! Fight, bold yeomen!
> Draw, archers, draw your arrows to the head!

These speeches and most of their prototypes in Greek and Latin contain no *sapientiae praecepta*, but instead stress the importance of the battle and stimulate the combative spirit of the troops.

For such a speech there seems to be no generic name in classical Greek: the verb παρακαλεῖν is sometimes used (e.g., Aesch. *Pers.* 380, Polyb. 1.60.5). In Latin it may be called a *cohortatio*. Ennius made Hannibal say to his army

> hostis qui feriet mihi erit Carthaginiensis,
> quisquis erit.   (*Ann.* 280-281)

Quoting this, Cicero (*Balb.* 51) declares that the poet "neque . . . Hannibalis illam magis cohortationem quam communem imperatoriam uoluit esse." Similarly, a speech made by a general to his troops at a critical moment is called a *cohortatio* by Nepos (*Hann.* 11.1) and Livy (28.19.9).[59]

The *Iliad* contains a large number of such speeches, although they are less carefully constructed than the generals' orations

---

[59] See also Caesar, *B.G.* 2.21.1-3 and 2.25.1. In Tac. *Ann.* 14.30 the word (in the plural) means little more than "shouts of encouragement." Cichorius in *RE* s.v. *adlocutio* warns his readers not to confuse the formal address of an emperor to his troops, the *adlocutio*, with the encouraging speech of a commander to his army, the *cohortatio*. Occasionally *cohortatio* occurs as a technical term of rhetoric, translating αὔξησις, the device of emphasizing the wrongs attributed to the opponent (*Rhet. Her.* 3.13.24, cf. Cic. *Part. Or.* 56 and 58).

in later epic and in history.[60] In the Trojan war they are made necessary by the weariness which afflicts both sides after nine years of fighting, and by the loose discipline of primitive armies with their great dependence on the heroism of individual warriors. Even gods often encourage human combatants with such speeches in the *Iliad*;[61] but in the *Aeneid*, although the major divinities watch the conflict,[62] Olympians address fighters only twice.[63]

Herodotus is un-Homeric in that he inserts only a few such speeches into his history; and these are small in scope. Before Marathon he reports an address by Miltiades, not to the soldiers, but to the polemarch Callimachus (6.109.3-6). Before Salamis he gives only two sentences in *oratio obliqua* spoken by Themistocles (8.83)—with which contrast Aeschylus, *Pers.* 402-405. Before Plataea the Persian commander makes a hybristic speech to three of the Thessalian Aleuadae (9.58); while after the first shock Pausanias the Spartan sends a message to the Athenians praising their courage and asking for their assistance (9.60).

Thucydides it was who introduced into history the practice of composing important speeches by commanders to their officers and troops on rhetorical lines, and of using them to mark critical battles.[64] Such is the speech of Archidamus at the

---

[60] Fingerle (pp. 82-108) counts forty-seven such speeches in the *Iliad*. He distinguishes them (pp. 102-109) from calls to battle addressed to an individual warrior by a comrade or a deity.

[61] E.g., 4.507-516, 14.135-152, 14.361-377.

[62] *Aen.* 10.464-473, 11.725-728, 12.792, 12.810-811.

[63] Cybele to the Trojans, 9.114-116; Apollo to Ascanius, 9.641-644.

[64] See R. C. Jebb, "The Speeches of Thucydides" in *Essays and Addresses* (Cambridge, 1907). He lists, on pp. 444-445, the twelve chief speeches of this kind, giving them as 2.11, 2.87, 2.89, 4.10, 4.92, 4.95, 4.126, 5.9, 6.68, 7.61-64, 7.66-68, and 7.77—together with 3.30, which, however, is a piece of strategic advice rather than a speech designed to encourage fighting troops. Jebb points out that these are imaginative compositions by Thucydides, and are sometimes rather improbable dramatically (e.g., the speeches supposed to be made by groups of officers, 2.86.6, 7.65.3).

Isthmus (παρῄνει τοιάδε, 2.10.3–11.9) and such is that of Demosthenes on Pylos (παρεκελεύcατο τοιάδε, 4.9.4–10.5). Sometimes the speech of one general is designed by Thucydides to sound like a reply to that of his opponent, although he could not possibly have heard it: e.g., Phormio's harangue in 2.89 before the battle of Naupactus counters that of the Spartan commanders in 2.87, and Pagondas in 4.92 is answered by Hippocrates in 4.95. The battle in Syracuse harbor is introduced with a pair of speeches, by Nicias (7.60.5–64.2) and by Gylippus and the Syracusan commanders (7.65.3–68.3), and then with a special appeal by Nicias to individual captains (7.69.2) like Agamemnon's ἐπιπώληcιc in *Il.* 4.223-421. Later historians followed Thucydides' example, and some wrote matched pairs of speeches before important conflicts: Polybius has two for Scipio and Hannibal before the Ticinus (3.62-64) which are imitated by Livy (21.40-44), and Calgacus and Agricola both speak at the Mons Graupius (Tac. *Agr.* 30-34).

The scheme of these orations is naturally simple. The *exordium* is brief. Sometimes the general remarks that it is scarcely necessary to exhort such valiant soldiers, or that he must say a few words to a new army (Livy 21.40.1-4). The proposal is clear: fight bravely! Most of the regular arguments may be employed: *utile* (you are defending hearth and home; retreat means certain death); *iustum* (our cause is righteous, the enemy are evildoers); *facile* (the foe are weak, we are strong and resolute); and of course *honestum* (death rather than dishonor). Skillful writers produced interesting variants to suit special situations, such as that of Catiline addressing his doomed army (Sall. *Cat.* 58).

Cohortationes are discussed by T. Burgess on pp. 209-214 of his *Epideictic Literature* (Chicago, 1902); but there is a much fuller and more valuable analysis by J. Albertus, *Die* παρακλητικοί *in der griechischen und romischen Litteratur*

85

(*Diss. phil. Argentoratenses selectae* 13, Strasburg, 1908).[65] In chapter 5 he lists seventy-five formal speeches of this kind in both Greek and Latin (excluding Procopius, who, he says, has no less than twenty-seven).

There are not many speeches by commanding officers in the *Aeneid*, far fewer than in the *Iliad*: nine in all.[66] Aeneas gives only two *cohortationes*, both early in the poem.[67] One is a speech made to the Trojans on the night of doom (*Aen.* 2.348-354). It is grim with despair: all our courage is vain; the guardian gods have departed; Troy is burning; we are sure to die. This is as somber as the words of Hector's ghost. Yet it would have been possible for Aeneas to give his comrades more positive encouragement. He might have said, This is our city, we know every inch of it; we are fighting to save our homes and families; we can still repel or kill the invaders; if not, make them pay dearly; revenge is half a victory. Ajax speaks more gallantly than this when the Achaeans are in similar straits (*Il.* 15.502-513 and 733-741). But apparently Vergil wishes to show that Aeneas was still immature at the intaking of Troy: his words lack the energy and élan of an experienced commander: he is not yet, as he will be, "Iliacis exercitus fatis."[68] Nevertheless, the final *epiphonema* is both a neat piece of rhetorical skill and a triumphant expression of heroic despair:

una salus uictis nullam sperare salutem.

"Nullam salutem" means "no survival (but rather death)"; "una salus" means "the one (and only) salvation," namely the

---

[65] The word παρακλητικός (says Albertus) does not appear in extant literature as equivalent to a noun until Aelius Aristides: e.g. *Or.* 50 Dindorf, Κατὰ τῶν ἐξορχουμένων, p. 569: ὡσπερεὶ Cαρδανάπαλλος τῆι κερκίδι τὴν κρόκην ὠθῶν ἧιδε τοὺς εἰς τὴν μάχην παρακλητικούς.

[66] For a list, see Appendix 2.

[67] Aeneas's words in 11.14-28 and 12.565-573 are not addresses of encouragement so much as decisive commands.

[68] Anchises to Aeneas, *Aen.* 3.182.

honor which comes with a gallant patriotic death.[69] The other *cohortatio* of Aeneas is a far finer speech, delivered after the calming of the tempest, in 1.198-207, reminding his men of the dangers they have survived and promising them a future bright with hope.

Turnus, in 10.279-284, makes a short address to his men, which is incomplete, but contains most of the traditional themes: wives and homes, ancestral glory, now is the time for a bold hand-to-hand attack. This speech, like that of Aeneas in 2.348-354, ends with a fine epigram, "audentis Fortuna iuuat"—which by the time of Seneca had acquired through forgery an ugly pendant, "piger ipse sibi obstat" (Sen. *Ep.* 94.28). A little later, Pallas rallies his men, unhorsed and retreating, with a speech on the theme "Fight or die here" (*Aen.* 10.369-378, modelled on the speech of Ajax defending the ships in *Il.* 15.733-741).

The most extensive and elaborate *cohortatio* in the epic is spoken by Turnus to his men at the moment when they are taken aback by the apparition and voice in heaven, and by the miraculous transformation of the Trojan ships into sea-nymphs (9.128-158). It is rather unusual in form; and the type of encouragement he gives his troops is not the conventional kind, since he must begin by destroying the effect of what seems like an earnest of heaven's favor to the enemy. There is no time for an *exordium*. He moves straight to the heart of the matter with four refutations: (1) the prodigy is not helpful to the Trojans, but damaging (128-133);[70] (2) their destiny, although fore-

---

[69] "Salut spirituel," says R. Allain in a perceptive essay, "Éloquence et poésie chez Virgile," *Revue Universitaire* 56 (1947) 219-225. The figure, not very common, contrasts two meanings of the same word. Rutilius Lupus 1.12 (Halm p. 8) calls it διαφορά, and adds as one example a line of Ennius (frg. inc. XLV) perhaps adapted from Euripides. Versifying his treatise, the *Carmen de figuris* 49 (Halm, p. 65) says "Si uerbum diuerse iteres, *distinctio* fiet." See Lausberg, paras. 660-662, pp. 333-335.

[70] This is the device of reinterpreting an omen which appears to be hostile to one's own cause, as Julius Caesar did: Suet. *D. Iul.* 59.

told by oracles, is not inevitable or irresistible (133-139); (3) they do not now deserve mercy because of their earlier sufferings (140-142)—this is a rather artificial reply to an imaginary objection, which the rhetoricians call ἐλέου ἐκβολή;[71] and (4) the Trojans are brave because protected by walls, but the walls of Troy did not save them (142-145).

After this, Turnus ought to issue a decisive call to action: an exhortation to fight, and to fight all the harder. Indeed he does call on his men to storm the Trojan camp (146-147), adding the argument *facile* (148-155). But then, instead of leading the charge in person, he remarks that it is getting rather late, and postpones the operation to next day (156-158). This is a serious blunder. A commander should always seize the favorable moment to attack. Vergil intended this to show Turnus's immaturity of character and his inadequacy as a tactician: contrast with it Aeneas's order for an immediate storming of the city of Latinus (12.565-573). Later, through the same weakness of temperament, Turnus makes another error, even more disastrous. At the news of Camilla's death he instantly abandons a well-prepared ambuscade, and loses his chance of catching Aeneas and the infantry in a Caudine Forks trap (11.522-531 + 896-902; cf. Livy 9.2). Finally, on the day before the crucial duel with Aeneas, he tries on his armor and visits his chariot-team; but when the fight begins he picks up the wrong sword *dum trepidat*, and in due course it breaks (12.735-741).

Knauer's collection of Homeric parallels to passages in the *Aeneid* shows that here, when Turnus tells his men to rest and have a meal, his command resembles those given by Hector to

[71] Hermogenes, *Progymn.* 6 fin. (Spengel 2, p. 11); Aphthonius, *Progymn.* 7 (Spengel 2, p. 35). "Nicht ganz zeitgemäss," says Heinze mildly (p. 433). Is it even remotely likely that a Rutulian soldier would suggest to Turnus that his army ought to go home, leaving the invading force established in its stronghold, because the Trojans had already suffered enough during the siege of Troy? This is the most intrusive piece of rhetoric in the whole *Aeneid*.

the almost-victorious Trojans in *Il.* 8.502-507 and 529-531.[72] Yet there are important differences.

Hector and his men, although outnumbered (*Il.* 8.56-57), have won a remarkable success, driving the Achaeans back inside their ramparts (8.213-216) and after a counter-attack defeating them once again (8.335-349). They hold the initiative. Turnus, on the other hand, has been attacking the Trojan camp (*Aen.* 9.47-76); but when the miracle metamorphoses the Trojan ships, his men are panic-stricken, *obstipuere animis*, and do no more fighting. Instead of converting their alarm into aggression, Turnus now permits them to relax. With their drinking and gambling (*Aen.* 9.164-167, 316-319, 334-338), the Rutulians are a sorry crew compared with the vigilant and hopeful Trojans of *Iliad* 8.553-565.

Furthermore, the timing is different. Hector was forced to halt the attacks of his men because darkness had come (*Il.* 8.485 + 500-501). But night has not yet fallen on the Rutulian army. Turnus says, "melior quoniam pars acta diei" (*Aen.* 9.156), which is very different from Hector's "κνέφας ἦλθε." Hector could not have fought on in the darkness. In the daylight, Turnus could have fought on, and did not. By making the two scenes like and yet unlike, Vergil shows that Turnus is an inexperienced and irresolute captain.

The other speeches made by commanders to their troops are short and need no analysis.

Praise and Blame

In an epic poem there is little occasion for speeches of the third type of formal oratory: "epideictic" or display orations of praise or blame, *laudationes* and *uituperationes*.[73] However,

---

[72] Knauer, pp. 270-273 and 407.

[73] See Quint. 3.7.1-2; he adds what is obvious, that both praise and blame incidentally enter into legal and political oratory. Sad that Caesar's vituperation of Cato (Quint. 3.7.28) is lost. Aphthonius 9 gives a vituperation directed

there is one long and carefully worked *uituperatio* addressed by Turnus's brother-in-law Numanus to the beleaguered Trojans (*Aen.* 9.598-620). It opens with the central theme of such speeches, τὸ αἰcχρόν ("non pudet?"), charging the Trojans with being cowards (598-599) and fools (600-602). The theme of *uituperatio gentis* is represented by the (dubious) identification of the horse-taming Trojans with the effeminate Phrygians (cf. Menander, *Aspis* 242). The main body of the speech is an effective contrast between the Italians (603-613) and the Trojans (614-620). The section praising the Italians is deftly set out as a survey of their vigorous lives from birth (603-604) through boyhood (605-606), youth and maturity (607-610), to old age (610-613). This is the traditional theme, praise of their ἐπιτηδεύceιc as contrasted with those of the Trojans. Line 616, introducing the idea that the Trojans are not men but women, is particularly dexterous, with the normal hexameter rhythm inverted into anapaestic units, and with two sneering internal echoes:

> et tu*ni*cae ma*ni*cas et habent redi*mi*cula *mi*trae.

The final four lines (617-620) are devoted to *uituperatio cultus*, ridiculing the Phrygian worship of Cybele, with its weird music and its castration ritual, as fit only for women and for effeminate men.

There is no oration of comparable length devoted to praise. However, Servius describes the closing lines of Anchises' speech in the underworld, "excudent alii . . ." (6.847-853), as *rhetoricus locus*. Norden therefore suggests that they form an encomium of Rome, following the pattern which is known from the late rhetorician Menander of Laodicea.[74] In Norden's view, this laudation is comparable to the eulogies of Rome by the second-century orator Aelius Aristides and the poets

---

against Philip of Macedon (Spengel 2, pp. 40-42). See also Lausberg, paras. 240, 245, and 376.

[74] Norden, pp. 335-337; Menander, c. 3, in Spengel 3, pp. 359-367.

Claudian and Rutilius Namatianus. He adds that it follows the rhetorical topic of a comparison between the diverse accomplishments of Greece (847-850) and Rome (851-853); and further (p. 337) that this comparison is set out as an antithetical enthymeme. A little earlier (on p. 320) Norden also describes the short paragraph exalting the city founded by Romulus (6.781-787) as an encomium of Rome, and remarks that one of the important themes of such an encomium, the ἐπιτηδεύσεις of the city, is postponed to the end of the speech, i.e., to 6.847-853. Norden writes so persuasively and cites so many valuable parallels that it is a little difficult to reject his main thesis; and of course it is true that in both these passages Vergil is eulogizing the city he loved. Yet surely it is erroneous to extract two separate paragraphs from a speech over a hundred lines long, and to analyze them as though they were an independent piece of oratory. Splendid the thoughts, memorable the words; but the two sections do not form a single artistic whole. The eulogy of Italy in *Georg.* 2.136-176—which (as Norden points out on p. 336) Servius also calls a rhetorical composition—is much longer and richer, far more clearly a unit distinct from the passages which precede and follow it.

Norden made an earlier attempt to analyze a small portion of Anchises' speech as though it were a separate work. In "Ein Panegyrikus auf Augustus in Vergils Aeneis," *RhM* 54 (1899) 466-482,[75] he proposed that *Aen.* 6.791-807 should be considered the earliest extant ἐγκώμιον βασιλέως in Latin, comparable to the panegyric of Augustus written by Varius Rufus (Hor. *Ep.* 1.16.25-29 and Porphyrio ad loc.). Its model, he conjectured, was a eulogy of Alexander the Great as world-conqueror. On pp. 322-323 of his edition of *Aeneid* 6 he repeated and reinforced this proposal. But the same objection still holds. This is not a speech, but part of a speech; and it is too closely connected with its context to be considered in detachment. Its opening words, "hic uir, hic est," continue the sequence "huc

[75] Now in *Kleine Schriften* (ed. B. Kytzler, Berlin, 1966) pp. 422-436.

... hanc ... hic" from lines 788-789, while its closing compari-son of Augustus to the benefactors Hercules and Dionysus whose victorious careers led them to heaven (801-805) moves straight into the paraenetic conclusion aimed at Aeneas, who is also destined for deification. Furthermore, as Verbockhaven points out,[76] this encomium does not follow the scheme set forth by Menander, and omits most of his subject-headings. Surely it is a noble compliment to Augustus; certainly it con-tains several themes suitable to the praise of a mighty mon-arch; but two or three τόποι do not make a brief passage of poetry into an independent oration.

If the speech of Anchises is to be rhetorically analyzed, it should be taken as a whole, from "Nunc age" (6.756) to "capta Quirino" (6.859). This Norden does on pp. 312-316 of his com-mentary, and here his analysis is far more convincing. Mod-elled on the scene in *Iliad* 3.161-244 where Helen on the wall of Troy tells Priam the names of the Greek heroes, and on Odysseus' account of the dead ladies he saw in the underworld (*Od.* 11.225-330), the speech has more movement, more variety, more power, and more spiritual significance than either. Nor-den correctly interprets it as a protreptic address.[77] Its purpose is to strengthen Aeneas's resolution by showing him the mag-nificent future for whose sake he will endure all the trials and dangers awaiting him in Italy. And beyond this, its aim is to teach the citizens of Rome their true mission. This purpose is clearly expressed in three passages. After the vision of Augus-tus (788-805) Anchises asks his son (806-807):

et *dubitamus* adhuc uirtutem extendere factis?
aut *metus* Ausonia prohibet consistere terra?

It is a strange and noble idea, to encourage Aeneas by the example of his centuries-younger descendant Augustus. Then

[76] V. Verbockhaven, "A propos de la Rhétorique dans Virgile," *Nova et Vetera* 2 (1913) 5-6.
[77] On protreptic argumentation see the first chapter of Anaximenes' *Rhet. ad Alexandrum*.

after the parade of republican warriors, Anchises gives the grand admonition to conquer, govern in peace, and rule the world (851-853). In a phrase perhaps inspired by Ennius, he says "tu, *Romane*, memento."[78] He speaks as though Aeneas were already in some sense a Roman; and beyond him he addresses the Romans yet unborn.

Not less significant than these two protreptic counsels is the warning that comes between them. Before the conquering soldiers (836-846) and after the early saviors of the republic (817-825) there appear two heroes whom Anchises does not name. Their armor is alike. They are kindred souls. And yet (says Anchises with sad foreboding) if and when they are born into earthly life, they will stir up terrible war with all the forces of east and west. By calling them "socer" and "gener" he identifies them clearly as Julius Caesar and Pompey the Great.[79] Calling them, with intense pathos, his children, he begs them not to turn their strength against their own country. Surely only Vergil, among all the poets of Rome, could have ventured to make one of his characters, even the most venerable, address the formidable Julius and the puissant Pompey as "pueri."[80] Then with passionate urgency he implores one of them, descended from a race divine, to be *the first* to cast away his weapons. "Sanguis meus!" he cries, to Caesar the descendant of Iulus.[81] Thus, at a climax of the *Aeneid*, the responsibility of the deified Julius Caesar for starting the civil war is admitted and condemned. By implication it is described as a crime,

[78] So Norden, p. 338, comparing what may be two other adaptations of the same Ennian touch: the mock-epic address "hunc tu, Romane, caueto" in Hor. *Serm*. 1.4.85, and (on p. 468) the grave vocative "Romane" in Hor. *Carm*. 3.6.2.

[79] "Socer generque, perdidistis omnia," wrote Catullus some thirty years earlier (29.24).

[80] The word is suggested by the speech in which Idaeus the herald stops the conflict between Hector and Ajax, saying "μηκέτι, παῖδε φίλω, πολεμίζετε" (*Il*. 7.279); but in old Anchises' mouth it has a tone of closer affection.

[81] The same phrase is spoken by Cacciaguida to his descendant Dante (who recalls this passage) in *Paradiso* 15.28.

comparable to fratricide (827) and matricide (833). This is Vergil at his noblest, most thoughtful, and most truly Roman.

The brief utterance which closes this great scene—the lament for young Marcellus (*Aen.* 6.868-886)—Norden describes as a funeral speech, built on the themes which were, or were becoming, traditional, and which were later described in a manual of epideictic oratory by the rhetor Menander.[82] Augustus himself spoke the last tribute to his son-in-law (Dio 53.30.5). Two allusions in Plutarch indicate that he mentioned the triumphator Marcellus,[83] as Anchises does; and Servius on Aen. 1.712 quotes him as saying of the young man *illum immaturae morti deuotum fuisse*, a thought which Vergil may be elaborating in "ostendent terris hunc tantum fata" (6.869). Furthermore, there is an explicit reference in 6.872-874 to the funeral procession and the interment of Marcellus in the mausoleum of Augustus. Norden therefore suggests that Vergil is here translating into poetry the essentials of Augustus's speech, and that Anchises' lament is the oldest extant Latin funeral oration constructed according to the rules of rhetoric.

However, there are several objections to this idea. Mlle. A. Guillemin remarks that the τόποι of Menander are really quite obvious, and would occur naturally to anyone making such a speech.[84] She proposes that Vergil may well have been more influenced by the funeral orations preserved in the archives of the great Roman families. F. De Ruyt corrects an overstatement of Mlle. Guillemin about the interpretation of lines 882-883, but agrees with her that Vergil did not need to use the clichés later tabulated by Menander, and earlier summarized by Cicero in *De Or.* 2.341-349.[85] As Cicero, speaking through

[82] Norden, pp. 341-346; Spengel 3, pp. 418-422.

[83] Plut. *Marcellus* 30.4; *Comparison of Pelopidas and Marcellus* 1.4.

[84] *Quelques injustices de la critique interne à l'égard de Virgile* (Chalon-sur-Saône, 1921) c. 3.

[85] "L'élégie [*sic*] de Marcellus dans l'Énéide: rhétorique ou lyrisme?" *LEC* 2 (1933) 138-144.

Antonius, observes, "Quis est qui nesciat quae sint in homine laudanda?" (*De Or.* 2.45).

Furthermore, there is one important central thought which it is unlikely that Augustus would voice on this occasion, and which looks like an idea of Vergil's own. Anchises says with great emphasis that no Roman youth will ever equal Marcellus (6.875-877):

> nec puer Iliaca quisquam de gente Latinos
> in tantum spe tollet auos, nec Romula quondam
> ullo se tantum tellus iactabit alumno.

This is a weighty comment on the problem of the succession to Augustus.[86] At his triple triumph in 29 B.C. (*Aen.* 8.714-719, Dio 51.21.5-9), Octavian in his chariot was flanked on the right by his nephew Marcellus and on the left by his stepson Tiberius (Suet. *Tib.* 6.4). Each was an heir presumptive to the dynastic power which Octavian was in process of establishing. The delicate balance between them represented a rivalry between the family of Octavian and his sister Octavia, mother of Marcellus, and that of his wife Livia: between the *gens Iulia* and the arrogant *gens Claudia.*[87] Gradually the balance tilted in favor of Marcellus. Augustus married him to his daughter Julia with splendid festivities, and granted him ten years' seniority in the *cursus honorum.* He was virtually heir apparent when he died in 23 B.C. At that time Tiberius was about nineteen years of age, the son of Augustus's consort. Surely he would be thought of as the natural heir to the principate. Yet, by these forceful negatives, "nec puer quisquam . . . nec . . . ullo . . . alumno," Vergil excludes Tiberius from consideration as a successor to Augustus, or at least as a successor worthy to be compared with Marcellus. Only a few hundred lines later (*Aen.* 7.706-

---

[86] See L. Pepe's article, "Virgilio e la questione dinastica," *GIF* 8 (1955) 359-371: he makes this point and elaborates it with keen insight.

[87] Tacitus characterized Tiberius by *uetere atque insita Claudiae familiae superbia* (*Ann.* 1.4).

709) Vergil brings forward Tiberius's putative ancestor Clausus[88] as a powerful enemy of Aeneas, the founder of the race.

The suggestion that in writing the little speech about Marcellus Vergil was using a rhetorical manual, or following a rhetorically constructed model, has not been widely accepted. Neither the structure nor the emotional tone of the lament, with its exclamatory apostrophes, resembles the pattern given by Menander; and the theme of consolation—so prominent in the scheme of a funeral eulogy—is not present. The ancestor of this beautiful speech is not formal prose oratory, but such poetry as the lamentations of the three women over Hector, at the end of the *Iliad*.[89]

---

[88] The patrician Claudii, to whom Tiberius belonged, claimed descent from the Sabine Clausus; the plebeian Claudii (including the Marcelli) did not.

[89] *Il*. 24.723-776. In rhetoric an intensely pathetic lament such as Anchises' requiem for Marcellus is called a monody. See Menander in Spengel 3, pp. 434-437: he remarks that a monody is more suitable for the death of a young man; Volkmann p. 360 cites a few late examples. "Monody" is the subtitle which Milton gave to *Lycidas*: "Lycidas is dead, dead ere his prime."

CHAPTER FOUR

INFORMAL SPEECHES

A
LTHOUGH rhetorical devices occur in them, most of the speeches in the *Aeneid* do not follow the patterns of formal oratory. They are arranged not in accordance with the schemes worked out by the experience of public speakers and the theorizing of teachers, but by their own inner logic, dictated by their functions in the poem and the nature and situation of those who utter them. Some are meant to convey factual information; some to challenge, question, or command; some to persuade or to respond to persuasion; and some to express an emotion or a chain of emotions.

Factual Speeches

Facts about the past are told in narratives. Facts about the present are set forth in what may be called descriptions. Facts about the future are predicted in prophecies.

Prophecies

The *Aeneid* contains nineteen prophecies and oracular utterances.[1] The most important for the plot are those given by Jupiter to Venus (1.257-296); Creusa to Aeneas (2.776-789); Apollo to the Trojans (3.94-98); the Penates (representing Apollo) to Aeneas (3.154-171); Celaeno to the Trojans (3.247-257); Helenus to Aeneas (3.374-462); the Sibyl to Aeneas (6.83-97); Anchises to Aeneas (6.756-859); Faunus to Latinus (7.96-101); Tiber to Aeneas (8.36-65); and Jupiter to Juno (12.830-840).

The placing of these predictions is significant. It shows that Vergil was writing not only an epic, but a Bible, for his nation.

---

[1] For a list, see Appendix 2.

The poem is framed between two forecasts of the future made by God Almighty. At the beginning, in 1.257-296, Jupiter tells Venus that Aeneas will build his city and reign in Italy; that he will be succeeded by Iulus and Iulus by the Alban kings, and they by Romulus the founder of Rome; and that at last Augustus will come, to bring Roman world-dominion and world peace.[2] At the end, in 12.830-840, Jupiter tells Juno that Troy and the Trojans will disappear, absorbed by the Latins: the peoples, mingling, will produce a new race. To Juno he says nothing of its future glories, remarking only that it will have an unequalled sense of duty and will honor Juno above all other nations. For this Juno cares little, but she is satisfied with the annihilation of the hated Trojans. In both these predictions the future is the same. For Juno, filled with destructive rancor, it is seen from the negative side ("subsident Teucri," 12.836). For Venus, inspired by maternal love, it is a promise of generation and regeneration to eternity.[3] She is *Aeneadum genetrix*, and her sons shall never perish from the earth.

Jupiter's first prediction falls into six sections: Aeneas (1.257-266); Ascanius (267-271); the Alban kings (272-274); Romulus (275-277); the power of Rome (278-285); Augustus and world peace (286-296). T. Halter, *Form und Gehalt in Vergils Aeneis* (Munich, 1963) pp. 13-29, demonstrates how skillfully

[2] That "Caesar . . . Iulius" in 286 + 288 is Octavian, and not (as Servius asserts) his adoptive father the dictator, is demonstrated (after Heyne) by E. Norden in an admirable study, "Vergils Aeneis im Lichte ihrer Zeit" (*Kleine Schriften*, ed. B. Kytzler, Berlin, 1966) pp. 386-387. Besides, the linkage of Augustus to Romulus (whose name he had thought of adopting) is too emphatic, here as in 6.777-805.

[3] This is one of the first passages in Latin literature where Rome is described as eternal and immortal. Before Vergil the belief was stated (with reservations about civil strife) by Cicero, *Rab.* 33, and in Vergil's own time by Livy (4.4.4, 5.7.10, 6.23.7, etc.). It was part of the tradition, for it is given as an oracle to Dardanus in Dion. Hal. *Ant.* 1.68.4. *Vrbs aeterna* appears first in Tibullus 2.5.23. See F. G. Moore, "On Urbs Aeterna and Urbs Sacra," *TAPhA* 25 (1894) 34-60, and W. Gernentz, *Laudes Romae* (Rostock, 1918) 40f.

they are interlinked.[4] Thus, Aeneas is paired with Octavian by parallels and oppositions:

feres ad sidera caeli / ... Aenean (259-260) ≈ hunc tu olim caelo . . . / accipies (289-290)
and
bellum ingens geret (263) × claudentur Belli portae (294)
to which we may add
mores . . . ponet (264) ≈ Fides et Vesta . . . / iura dabunt (292-293).

Subtle echoes of sound and parallelisms of syntax join the kingship of Ascanius and the future conquest of Greece by the descendants of Troy:

puer *A*scanius (267) ≈ domus *A*ssaraci (284)
uoluend*is* mens*ibus* (269) ≈ lustr*is* labent*ibus* (283)
imperio explebit (270) ≈ seruitio premet (285)
Longam *ui* muniet *A*lbam (271) ≈ *ui*ctis dominabitur *A*rgis (285).[5]

Jupiter's speech is forty lines in length. The sentence which stands exactly at its center (275-277) describes the central event of this many-centuried history, the foundation of Rome, toward which the suffering and effort of Troy led, and from which world peace and world dominion were to flow. Powerful alliteration adds emphasis to this affirmation. Jupiter's entire prophecy is an exemplification, in words and sounds and rhythms, of stability and order.

Midway between the initial and final predictions made by Jupiter lies the great revelation made by Anchises to Aeneas, through which the hero sees that Troy is to be transcended by

[4] Halter is keen on heptads, and wishes to make two sections out of the paragraph 278-285; but 283-285 do not differ from the preceding lines as the other sections differ from one another.
[5] For *uis* linked with *uincere* Halter (p. 110, n. 12) compares *inter alia* 2.452, 6.147-148, 11.401-402, 12.254 and 799.

something far greater and more perdurable (6.756-859).[6] In shape it is a forecast of the future, as the setting shows and as the tenses confirm: "ituras" (758), "surget" (762), "educet" (765), "uentura" (790), "aurea condet / saecula" (792-793), and so on to the closing evocation of victory over Rome's powerful enemies, Carthaginians and Gauls (857-859). In function, however, it is a protreptic speech, designed to kindle the heart of Aeneas with love of the glory that is to come (6.889).

Furthermore, it emphasizes and expands Jupiter's first prophecy. There Jupiter tells Venus that her son

> bellum ingens geret Italia *populosque ferocis*
> *contundet moresque* uiris *et moenia* ponet

—i.e. after warfare he will introduce civilization and urbanization (1.263-264). The phrase "rerum dominos gentemque togatam" (1.282) makes the same point: first, warriors conquering the world, then a nation wearing the garb of peace. This is now restated in Anchises' behest to the Roman race (6.851-853):

> tu regere imperio populos, Romane, memento
> (hae tibi erunt artes), *paci*que imponere *morem*,
> parcere subiectis et *debellare superbos*.[7]

On pp. 45-52 of his study cited on p. 98 above Halter suggests that one segment of this speech, lines 777-807, should be taken as a unit, and should be divided into seven paragraphs, as he proposes to divide Jupiter's prophecy in 1.257-296: because (p. 54) "in Inhalten, die konstitutiv durch das Strukturprinzip der Siebenzahl geformt sind, spricht Vergil von Geschehnissen oder Gehalten, deren Ursprung ihm als göttlich gilt." However, it is not possible to detach this part of Anchises' prophecy, grand though it is, from the rest. The first words, "*quin et* auo

---

[6] On the precise limits of this speech, see pp. 17-18.

[7] These observations are made by R. D. Williams in "The Opening Scenes of the *Aeneid*," *PVS* 5 (1965-1966) 14-23.

comitem sese Mauortius addet / Romulus," link it closely to the names and exploits of the Alban kings, and to Numitor in particular; and after the exhortation to courageous effort (806-807) it continues without a break by introducing Romulus's successor Numa (808-812) and the kings who followed. Why not take the entire apocalypse (after the introductory words, 756-759) as a unit? It divides itself very naturally into seven sections. But the order is not lineally chronological. On the contrary, it is twice interrupted.[8]

(1) The Alban kings: 760-776
(2) Romulus: 777-787
(3) Augustus: 788-807
(4) The Roman kings: 808-817
(5) The heroes of the early republic: 817-825
(6) Pompey and Julius Caesar: 826-835
(7) The heroes of the late republic: 836-853 + 855-859.

The sequence is broken once to introduce Augustus beside Romulus as the second founder of Rome,[9] and a second time to reproach Pompey and Caesar, mighty warriors, for turning their strength against their own country. Nevertheless, it is a powerful and well-balanced heptad.[10]

---

[8] J. Hubaux on p. 182 of an imaginative article, "Du songe de Scipion à la vision d'Énée," *Atti del I Congresso Internazionale di studi Ciceroniani* vol. II (Rome, 1961), proposes that the whole passage on Augustus is "out of place in the manuscripts" and ought to be the triumphal climax of Anchises' speech—presumably coming after "debellare superbos" in 6.853; while Ribbeck inserted Pompey and Caesar (6.826-835) after Augustus. But this is to discard Vergil's careful but unmechanical symmetry for a cruder and more obvious arrangement.

[9] Augusti cognomen assumpsit, . . . quibusdam censentibus Romulum appellari oportere quasi et ipsum conditorem Vrbis: Suet. *D. Aug.* 7.2.

[10] Norden, *Aeneis VI* (pp. 316, 319, 322, 326, 328, 334, and 338), divides it into eight segments; but he gives one entire section to the *"propositio"* (756-759) and one to the "epilogue" (847-853), takes all the republican heroes together in spite of the obvious break at "Camillum" (825), and gives the Marcelli a separate "episode" (854-886). He does, however, recognize that the elder Marcellus is linked with Romulus (778) and Cossus (841) as the third winner of the *spolia opima* (859)—which means that there is a climax, and a close, at line 859.

101

The predictions given to Aeneas are so arranged as to show his gradual awakening to the significance of his mission. On the night of Troy's fall Hector appears to him in a vision (2.268-297). The chief emphasis of Hector's speech is on the commands, "fuge . . . cape . . . quaere," which justify Aeneas's escape from Troy and implicitly rebut the charge that he was a deserter and a traitor; but in the last few words Hector tells him that he will found a city overseas. Some hours later the ghost of Creusa reveals that he will settle in the Evening Land, Hesperia, and reign as king with a royal consort (2.776-789). Soon after his wanderings begin, he receives an emphatic prophecy from Apollo, with the command "antiquam exquirite matrem" (3.94-98). After the settlement in Crete fails, the Penates (3.154-171) explain this command as pointing to Italy; and Celaeno the Harpy (3.247-257) confirms the prediction that the Trojans will reach Italy, but adds the grim forecast that hunger will make them eat their tables.[11] Then, at much length (3.374-462), Apollo's priest Helenus tells Aeneas exactly how he will recognize, upon the farther shore of Italy, the site of his future home; offers reassurance about the Harpy's prophecy; directs Aeneas how to avoid the worst dangers of the voyage; and describes the precautions, strategic and religious, which he must observe. He closes with directions to beg the Sibyl of Cumae for further revelations. In her turn, the Sibyl foretells war in Italy, and eventual victory through alliance with Greeks (6.83-97). The greatest of all the prophecies vouchsafed to Aeneas is the apocalypse of Anchises (6.756-859).

Thereafter he receives only two more glimpses into the future. One is the address made to him by the spirit of Tiber.[12]

---

[11] In 7.124-127 Aeneas says that Anchises gave him this forecast—doubtless in an earlier draft of the poem. This shows how successfully Vergil worked over his material, for the prophecy is far more effective when spoken by a famished Harpy to the feasting Trojans.

[12] As Servius remarks on 8.31, the Tiber is the *genius loci*, and one of the *ignota flumina* to whom Aeneas prayed in 7.135-138.

This is more than a friendly pronouncement. It gives Aeneas some important information. The Tiber confirms his recent interpretation of the omen of the tables (7.120-129); warns him to expect the prodigy of the white sow; and directs him to seek an alliance with Evander up river (8.36-65). This is the third time that a supernatural figure has been called upon to explain how Aeneas must win his wars in Italy. First, Helenus informs him that the Sibyl will describe the peoples of Italy and the wars which are to come, and advise him how to meet or avoid each particular trial (3.458-460); but the Sibyl vouchsafes him only a vague series of predictions (6.83-97). Then the narrative states that Anchises gives him a detailed briefing on the war (6.890-892); and now the Tiber explicitly tells him that he will win by acquiring the support of Evander. Apparently Vergil's basic plan was to make the wise prophetess reveal in dim outline the course of the war, while Anchises described what was to follow after its conclusion, the building of the Trojan city in Italy and the future of its people (5.737 = 6.756-859); and the prophecy of the Tiber was intended to explain in factual detail the oracularly obscure forecast of the Sibyl (6.96-97 = 8.51-56).[18] This is a pattern which Vergil has employed before. Apollo told Aeneas and the Trojans "Antiquam exquirite matrem" (3.96). Anchises interpreted the oracle, but wrongly (3.102-117); then the Penates gave the true interpretation and elucidated it in detail (3.154-171).

The last revelation given to Aeneas is the omen sent by his

---

[18] The brief summary in 6.890-892, attributed to Anchises, and going very ill with *his . . . prosequitur dictis,* is a variant (line 6.892 is virtually identical with 3.459, applied to the *Sibyl*) which Vergil would no doubt have discarded in his final editing. (So Norden, pp. 346-347, and Heinze, p. 360, n. 1.) It is appropriate that Anchises, who is an inhabitant of Elysium, almost godlike in wisdom, should make the far-reaching revelations of transmigration and immortality and the Roman fate, while the more immediate and local problems of campaigning are outlined by the Italian prophetess and explained by the Italian river-god.

mother in 8.520-540: the omen of impending war. Thenceforward he knows his destiny.

The inhabitants of Italy receive omens and prophecies which develop in the same way: at first vague, then gradually becoming more definite, and pointing to Aeneas as the man of destiny while foretelling the defeat of his opponents. Bees enter Latinus's palace and swarm on the sacred laurel: a foreign man will arrive and rule. Princess Lavinia's hair and robes and crown appear to catch fire at the altar, filling the palace with flame: she will become illustrious but will occasion a great war (7.59-80). In an incubation dream[14] Faunus tells Latinus that he must marry his daughter to a foreign husband and that their descendants will rule the world (7.96-101). Overborne by mob excitement, Latinus foresees the sufferings of his nation and the death of Turnus (7.594-599). Aeneas needs more troops than his own people and the small tribe of Arcadian settlers can provide: the Etruscans in rebellion have been warned (Evander tells him, 8.499-503) to await a foreign leader. Trumpets sound from heaven amid thunder and lightning; arms flash and clash in the clear sky. Aeneas recognizes the signal which Venus told him she would send, together with weapons

[14] Incubation was a Greek, not an Italic, method of enquiring into the future. See Heinze, p. 176 n. 2, and H. R. Steiner, *Der Traum in der Aeneis* (Berne, 1952), pp. 60-62. Faunus did indeed foretell the future, but he did so by speaking to a waking hearer; he was not a chthonic deity who had to be approached by a worshipper at night, in sleep, lying on bare earth covered with the fleeces of sacrificial animals (*Aen.* 7.85-95), nor had he anything to do with the subterranean powers of the grove of Albunea (7.82-84). Vergil wished to make the prophecy of Faunus more important than it would seem if it had merely been uttered by a disembodied voice (like the similar prophecy of Aius Locutius, which was disregarded: Livy 5.32.6-7, cf. 5.50.5): therefore he blended several different types of oracular enquiry and ritual. (However, both L. Deubner, *De incubatione* [Giessen, 1899], and Pley, s.v. *incubatio* in *RE* IX, 2.1256-1262, accept Vergil's description of the ritual, and Ovid's adaptation of it in *Fasti* 4.649-666, as genuine pieces of Italic tradition: I know not with what justification.)

made by her husband Vulcan.[15] Although he is certain of victory, he magnanimously describes it not as a glorious triumph for his own side, but rather as misery for the Laurentian people and punishment for Turnus (8.520-540).

Among these mighty schemes of prediction, one small prophecy stands out. Briefly phrased, it covers many centuries of history. Apollo addresses the victorious young Iulus after his victory with bow and arrow: "dis genite et geniture deos" (9.641-644). Here, what Anchises reveals at length to Aeneas in the sixth book is, for his son, compressed into a few sentences. They carry the same message: wars fought by Rome will be won, and will lead to world peace.

The parents of Aeneas also give a few interpretations of omens. Venus in disguise tells her son that the swans settling after attack by an eagle mean that his ships are in safe haven or heading for harbor (1.387-401). Anchises mistakes the "ancient mother" of Apollo's oracle as meaning Crete (3.103-117), but says correctly that the horses seen at the first landfall in Italy signify war with the hope of peace (3.539-543).

Descriptions

Several important speeches contain descriptions of facts unknown to the listener.[16] Two of these, during the battle books, report tactical situations, with a call to action. The nymph Cymodocea tells Aeneas that his ships have become sea-spirits, his son is beleaguered, and his allies are about to be attacked (10.228-245); and Saces announces to Turnus that the city of Latinus is hotly besieged (12.653-664). The former of these two speeches has an exquisitely evocative opening. As Aeneas sails through the moonlit Tyrrhenian sea, the nymphs appear and swim around him—as once the Nereids swam around the Argo (Ap. Rhod. 4.930-938). Cymodocea catches the stern of

[15] In the poem as it stands, Venus has made no such promise.
[16] See Appendix 2.

the flagship (like Thetis in *Argon.* 4.931), keeps pace with it
by oaring with her left hand, and addresses Aeneas because
she is *fandi doctissima.* She begins

> Vigilasne, deum gens,
> Aenea? uigila!

Now, Servius tells us that a similar summons was spoken to
the *rex sacrorum* on a certain day by the Vestal Virgins: they
said "Vigilasne, rex? uigila!" Thus, by the citation of a small
ritual formula, Vergil makes us see Aeneas with the nymphs
sprung from the ships he built, as a priest-king of Rome with
the inviolable priestesses; and behind that, far in the origins
of Italic religion, as a guardian father with his maiden daugh-
ters. But elsewhere (on *Aen.* 8.3) Servius says that, after war
was declared in Rome, the commanding general entered the
shrine of Mars, moved the sacred shields, and then shook the
spear held by the statue of the god, saying, "Mars, uigila!"
Aeneas is not only the priest-king, but the warrior whom Mars
will favor in the final conflict (12.179-180 + 187-188).

More impressive than these are the speeches which disclose
to Aeneas the supernatural forces hidden from mortal sight.
Venus tells him that the gods are overthrowing Troy, before
she reveals the awful spectacle (2.594-620); the Sibyl explains
the fate of the unburied dead (6.322-330) and the structure and
inhabitants of eternal hell (6.562-627); and in two linked
speeches (6.713-718, 722 + 724-751) Anchises expounds the
strange process of purgation and reincarnation. In words
fraught with religious awe (8.351-358) Evander suggests that
Jupiter the Cloud-Compeller lives on the Capitoline hill (thus
anticipating the dedication of the temple of Jupiter Tonans by
Augustus), and points out the citadels of Saturn and Janus.[17]

---

[17] Not the Janiculum across the Tiber (Livy 1.33.6), but one of the two
peaks of the Capitoline hill: see P. Grimal, "La colline de Janus," *REA* 24
(1945) 65-87.

Narratives

There are fourteen major narrative speeches recounting past events or explaining unusual situations, usually for the benefit of the reader as well as the characters who listen.[18] The most important is the tale of Aeneas's adventures, which virtually fills the second and third books. Inset within it are three others: two true and one false. The true stories are Andromache's recital of her sufferings since the fall of Troy and Achaemenides' account of the Cyclops. False from beginning to end is the narrative of Sinon.

Of these narratives, six enrich the background and intensify the emotion. Aeneas's plaintive tale, which is interrupted by his mother (1.372-385), Palinurus's story of his death (6.347-371),[19] and Deiphobus's description of his own treacherous slaughter (6.509-534) are like panels of a polyptych flanking the magnificent central saga told by Aeneas to Dido and her court. The sad stories of Andromache, Achaemenides, Deiphobus, and Palinurus also show that Aeneas, much as he has endured, has still been protected from the extremes of suffering, humiliation, and death.

In his enthusiasm for rhetorical structure, Norden unfor-

---

[18] Venus to Aeneas, 1.335-370; Aeneas to Venus, 1.372-385; Aeneas to Dido and the banqueters, 2.3-3.715; Sinon to the Trojans, 2.69-72 + 77-104 + 108-144 + 154-194; Andromache to Aeneas, 3.321-343; Achaemenides to the Trojans, 3.613-654; Dido's confession to Anna, 4.9-29; Palinurus to Aeneas, 6.347-371; Deiphobus to Aeneas, 6.509-534; Evander to Aeneas, 8.185-275 and 314-336 and 470-519; Venulus's report of his mission to Diomede, 11.243-295; Diana to Opis, 11.535-594. A complete list of the narrative and descriptive speeches appears in Appendix 2.

[19] Palinurus's story here is very unlike Vergil's description of his death in 5.835-871. Following a suggestion of Heinze (p. 146 n. 1), P. Jacob, "L'Episode de Palinure," *LEC* 20 (1952) 163-167, conjectures that in Vergil's first plan Palinurus was drowned in the storm off Africa (*Libyco cursu*, 6.338) like the steersman of Orontes (1.113-117, cf. 6.333-336); and that in Vergil's revision he had to be killed—not in a storm, because of Neptune's pledge (5.812-815 + 862-863), but after being cast overboard.

tunately misinterprets two of them. On p. 232 of his *Aeneis VI* he dissects Palinurus's speech into a prologue (347-348), narrative (349-362), and epilogue "in the form of a *commiseratio*" (363-371). He does not say that this is a formal oration; nor is it; but he does not fully grasp its purpose. The final section (363-371) is anything but an epilogue winding up the speech. It is shown by "oro" and by the imperatives "eripe," "inice," "require," "da," "tolle," to be a plea, and an earnest plea, following the narrative and justified by it. Similarly, on p. 265 Norden analyzes the speech made by the ghost of Deiphobus. Lines 511-512 he describes as a *propositio*. Now, a *propositio* is a statement of the policy which the speaker is trying to persuade his audience to adopt, or of the legal position which he is maintaining. But these two lines

> sed me fata mea et scelus exitiale Lacaenae
> his mersere malis; illa haec monimenta reliquit

are in fact the answer of Deiphobus to Aeneas's opening question (501-502): "haec monimenta" responds to "tam crudelis poenas."

Besides these Trojan and Greek narratives there are three Italian myths: Evander's stories of the overthrow of Cacus (8.185-275) and the founding of Latium (8.314-336) and Diana's biography of Camilla (11.535-594). They bear traces of their prosaic origin in the books of mythical lore from which Vergil adapted them. Evander's history of central Italy devotes a disproportionate amount of attention to such trifles as the origin of the name Tiber (8.330-332). It is natural for Diana to wish to avenge the death of her votaress (the name Camilla means *famula*, 11.558); yet it is scarcely convincing that a deity who has never appeared in the poem should suddenly intervene to relate a long saga about a doomed girl, and Vergil's justification, "neque enim nouus iste Dianae / uenit amor" (11.537-538), although graceful, is flimsy.[20]

[20] Heinze, p. 416.

108

Four narrative speeches there are which advance the plot. When Venus posing as a Carthaginian girl tells Aeneas the past history of Dido (1.335-370), she not only prepares him to meet a noble queen ruling a civilized nation, but touches his heart with sympathy for sufferings scarcely less bitter than his own and borne with like heroism.[21] Also, by appearing as a beautiful huntress, she prepares him to fall in love with Dido costumed for the hunt. Later, Evander's account of the rebellion of the Etruscans against Mezentius (8.470-519, especially 478-511) explains why a large body of native troops is prepared to join Aeneas, and convinces us that right lies on his side, against the cruel tyrant whom his own people consider a criminal worthy of death (8.494-495). Still later, in 11.243-295, Venulus announces that the mission on which he was dispatched in 8.9-17 has failed, and repeats the sapient speech of Diomede refusing alliance with the Latins and counselling peace with Aeneas. This comes at a crucial time. The Latin funeral pyres have burnt for three days. The dead have been committed to the earth. The living mourn, and curse Turnus, and call for him to fight alone if he is so eager for glory; others still champion his cause. Then the report of Venulus initiates a momentous debate, which ought prudentially to have led to negotiations for peace. When Turnus seizes the opportunity to quit the council before it can take any decision, he brings disaster on the Latins and death on himself.

Even more important is the speech of Dido to her sister in 4.9-29. It is a confession. It is a plea for advice and help. It is an effort to strengthen an already weakened resolution. Dido has evidently always imposed a queenly reserve upon herself, and has eschewed any display of feeling. Now her emotions have suddenly revived like a fire long smothered. The re-emergence of suppressed feelings has disturbed her soul, and has issued in terrifying dreams:

Anna soror, quae me suspensam insomnia terrent!

[21] Heinze, pp. 119-121.

109

Many readers have wondered what were the dreams that
alarmed Dido; and some have queried the meaning of the
word "insomnia." R. J. Getty did not manage to prove that it
means visions seen while the seer is awake, like those in Lucr.
5.1169-1170 and *Aen*. 5.722-723.[22] The word has been inter-
preted as meaning "sleeplessness," on the ground that *Aen*. 4.5
might mean "night denies all sleep" rather than "night gives
only troubled sleep."[23] But then Heyne's comment is apt:
"somnia possunt terrere, non vigilia." Evidently Vergil in-
tended the word "insomnia" to be parallel both in shape and
in meaning to ἐνύπνια, and to be a strange new Latin word
for "dreams." This is made quite clear and certain by the fact
that the word occurs only twice in the *Aeneid*, and in each case
Vergil is imitating a passage of Greek poetry dealing with
dreams. Dido's exclamation is modelled on Medea's "Δειλὴ
ἐγών, οἷόν με βαρεῖc ἐφόβηcαν ὄνειροι!" (Ap. Rhod. 3.636).
The narrative in *Aen*. 6.893-896 describing the two gates of
sleep, one giving egress to *ueris umbris* and the other letting
out *falsa insomnia*, is adapted from Penelope's speech, in which
are evoked δοιαὶ . . . πύλαι ἀμενηνῶν . . . ὀνείρων (*Od*. 19.562-
567). It is difficult to believe that Vergil could have imitated
two well-known speeches in Greek epic, using in both imita-
tions a Latin word apparently newly coined by himself, and
distorted the meaning of both originals. In fact, the word
somnia had acquired an unfavorable sense, "delusions," as in
Lucretius 3.1048:

> et uigilans stertis nec somnia cernere cessas.

Using this sense, Vergil himself says that the phantom Aeneas
resembles *quae sopitos deludunt somnia sensus* (10.642). Here

---

[22] "*Insomnia* in the lexica," *AJP* 54 (1933) 1-28.

[23] F. De Ruyt, "Note de vocabulaire virgilien: *somnia* et *insomnia*," *Lato-
mus* 5 (1946) 245-248, says "Didon se plaint simplement de n'avoir pu
dormir," and quotes Ov. *Trist*. 3.8.27 for *insomnia* meaning "sleeplessness";
but he fails to explain why the word should have, at its only other occurrence

he required a word with more serious connotations: so he coined *insomnia* on the model of Homer's ἐνύπνιον, or followed another poet who had done so.[24] Getty cites a passage in Livy (25.38.5) where the Roman officer L. Marcius Septimus says that he worries about the Scipios all day, dreams about them at night, and is sometimes awakened from sleep by the thought of their unavenged defeat: "praesto est enim acerba memoria, et Scipiones me ambo dies noctesque *curis insomnisque* agitant, et excitant saepe somno, neu se . . . neu rem publicam patiar inultam." Dido is suffering a typical invasion of her conscious mind by subliminal psychical forces. In this, the first stage, she has had disturbing dreams. Later she will have daytime anxiety (4.65-79); then fits of uncontrollable excitement (4.300-303); still later, sleeplessness (4.529-532); but not yet.

What then are the dreams of Dido? Penelope dreamed that her husband was lying by her side: this made her heart glad, and she wept only on finding it to be false (*Od.* 20.56-90). But Dido says that her dreams terrified her; now, in the following lines (4.10-14) she describes Aeneas with warmth and admiration: therefore she cannot have dreamed of him with terror. Since her emotions as a woman have been rekindled, and since she has known only one other man, her dreams must recall him, her husband Sychaeus. But apparently she has not dreamt of him as a loving husband, only as a warning ghost, a *turbida imago* like that later seen by Aeneas (4.353); and so indeed Sychaeus had appeared to her at an earlier crisis (1.353-359).

It has been suggested that Dido could not possibly have ig-

in the *Aeneid*, a different meaning, and a vague one at that—"impressions illusoires du dormeur" (*Aen.* 6.896).

[24] This point is made by A. Meillet, *Esquisse d'une histoire de la langue latine* (Paris, 1952⁶) 219-220. M. Leumann, *Lateinische Laut- und Formenlehre* (Munich, 1963) p. 210 para. 3, classifies *insomnium* formally with such compounds as *confinium, intermundia, postliminium*. The faithful Statius follows Vergil here, though not without some originality. The cry of a dying child comes to its mother's ears *qualia non totas peragunt insomnia uoces* (*Theb.* 5.543).

nored a warning by Sychaeus, and that therefore she dreamed of being married to Aeneas (like Medea in Ap. Rhod. 3.622f.) but was frightened by this revelation of her unconscious wishes. So says T. Kakridis, "Didonis insomnia," *Hermes* 45 (1910) 463-465. Yet is it true that Dido could not possibly have ignored such a warning? The god of love has already been endeavoring to "abolish Sychaeus" and to awaken her heart to a new love (1.719-722); and Aeneas ignores nightly warnings from his father Anchises—at least as strong an authority for him as Sychaeus for Dido—until a god comes to corroborate them (4.351-353). Both Aeneas and Dido had repressed desires, which the "inner censor" condemned but which the gods inflamed. Anna advised Dido to forget Sychaeus (4.32-34); and for a time she did. The elaborate rituals described in 4.56-64 show that she pushed him entirely out of her mind.

Now her excitement at meeting Aeneas breaks forth in five exclamations of admiration and sympathy ("heu, quibus ille / iactatus fatis!"). Then her deep uncertainty speaks, in a long grave careful five-line-long sentence (4.15-19) built on two brooding *if*-clauses.[25] The heart of her confession, the fact that she loves Aeneas—although she will not use the word "love"— is introduced by an appealing repetition of Anna's name (4.20-23). As she ends her speech, she turns away from her sister, inward to herself. It becomes a monologue: or rather a dialogue between her two selves, one dominated by *pudor*, the other consumed by the flames of passion. The conflict is so severe that she feels it may bring on her death. The last two lines of her speech end with the conflicting words "amores" and "sepulcro": after which Dido breaks down in tears, helpless. She hopes for advice to justify the decision for which she is emotionally prepared: her surrender to love, the love she knows is somehow linked with death.

[25] Here, as elsewhere in Dido's speeches, her emotions are reflected in the rhythm of her words: note the slow spondees and weighty monosyllables of "ne cui me uinclo," "si non pertaesum," "huic uni forsan."

Questions

Questions are frequent in the *Aeneid*: one scholar counts over three hundred.[26] Most of these, however, are not independent queries, but are small parts of longer speeches; and many of them are not genuine requests for information, but are unanswerable questions equivalent to passionate exclamations. (Such are the seven questions addressed by Euryalus's mother to her dead son in 9.481-492, and the long series which makes up Juno's rebuttal to Venus in 10.63-95; such are Aeneas's questions to Anchises and Venus in 2.657-667 and Creusa's question to him a moment later in 2.677-678.) Some questions are equivalent to commands: Mercury to Aeneas in 4.560-570, Turnus to his men in 9.51. Others explore a dilemma and point toward a solution: so Dido in 4.534-552 and Jupiter in 12.793-806. One curious group should be mentioned although it is not strictly relevant: questions uttered by the poet himself in the course of his narrative. Such is the incredulous "tantaene animis caelestibus irae?" (1.11) and such the summons to the Muses in 9.77-79, reminiscent of *Il.* 1.8.

There are in the *Aeneid* twenty independent speeches framed as questions.[27] Only four occupy more than four lines. The largest is the welcome addressed by Latinus to the Trojan embassy in 7.195-211. His interrogation occupies a few initial lines (7.195-198); the rest of the speech establishes a friendly relationship between Latins and Trojans, and prepares for the generous response which Latinus will give in 7.259-273. In 3.359-368 Aeneas questions Helenus about the future of his mission. This is a grave and formal inquiry. The address to Helenus occupies three lines (3.359-361) and is followed by a justification over five lines long (3.362-367): thereafter the question, one line and a half (3.367-368). Both these questions are long because Vergil wishes to emphasize the importance

26 A. L. Keith, "Observations on Vergil's Use of the Question," *CW* 16 (1922-1923) 210-211.
27 See Appendix 2.

113

of the answers which they will evoke. Helenus will reveal the course of the Trojans to Italy. Ilioneus will ask king Latinus for land on which the Trojans can settle.

In the world of the dead, Aeneas interrogates Palinurus and Deiphobus about the fates which overtook them. His questions are extensive, in order to allow his friends to be detailed in the description of their deaths, cruel and unrequited.

Emotional Speeches

So much for speeches of which the main content is factual. Many more speeches in the *Aeneid* are utterances of emotion and expressions of will; of friendship, love, and hate; of entreaty and command.

Greetings

There are remarkably few speeches of greeting.[28] We do not hear Aeneas greet Tarchon and the other commanders of the Etruscan forces at 8.597-607, or Latinus at 12.161-174. He does not greet the Sibyl. Characteristically, she does not greet him either, but begins by rebuking him for wasting his time.[29] Was Dante thinking of this when he made Beatrice rebuke him at her first meeting with him in the other world?

> Cosí la madre al figlio par superba,
>   com'ella parve a me; perché d'amaro
> sent'il sapor della pietade acerba.
>
> (*Purg.* 30.79-81)

Two greetings are exchanged by Aeneas and Dido when they first meet (1.595-610, 615-630) and two by Anchises and Aeneas in Elysium (6.687-694, 695-698); and in Sicily Aeneas greets the spirit of his father at the tomb (5.80-83). In Aeneas's opening speech to Dido there are two highly significant

---

[28] See Appendix 2.
[29] Compare her stern rebukes to Palinurus (6.373-376) and to Aeneas as he talks with Deiphobus (6.539).

phrases. He alludes to Dido's offer (which he overheard from the cloud)

uultis et his mecum pariter considere regnis?

(1.572)

by saying "urbe domo socias" (1.600). But here "socias" is a conative present (like *uellit* in 2.480), meaning "You *offer* to make us fellow-citizens."[30] The offer is implicitly rejected in Aeneas's closing words, "quae me cumque uocant terrae." This prepares for his defense in 4.340-361; and the preceding lines (1.607-609), declaring that he will never forget Dido's generosity, are to be echoed in that same speech (4.335-336).

The reply made by Dido is full of tact and charm. She establishes a link, however tenuous, between the Trojans and her own family (619-626): just so, at a later meeting, Aeneas will explain to Evander that they have an ancestor in common (8.134-142). She reminds him that she too is an exile—like Teucer, who spoke to her father about the courageous Trojans (619-621 + 625-626)—and that she has found a new home (628-629). She invites, not Aeneas alone, but all his men ("iuuenes," 627), to enjoy her hospitality, and she closes with a touching epigram, "non ignara mali miseris succurrere disco."

Farewells[31]

There are three farewells as the Trojans set sail from the little Troy-in-Greece. To Anchises as the leader, Helenus bids a respectful good-bye, containing a compliment to Aeneas (3.475-481); Andromache gives gifts to young Ascanius, who reminds her of her murdered son (3.486-491); and Aeneas says farewell to them both, with a promise of future friendship and alliance (3.493-505).[32] The speech of Creusa to Aeneas in

---

[30] Szantyr, *Lateinische Syntax und Stilistik* (Munich, 1965), p. 316.

[31] For a complete list see Appendix 2.

[32] This promise looks forward to the foundation, in the same region, of the city which commemorated Octavian's victory at Actium: Nicopolis. See

2.776-789 is a prophecy (with some explanatory narrative) but closes with a line of farewell. Deiphobus parts from Aeneas with the beautiful phrase "i, decus, i, nostrum" (6.544-546). To his son Pallas Evander utters a long farewell passing into a prayer (8.560-583), and Aeneas takes leave of Pallas's corpse with three sad lines (11.96-98). Camilla's brief good-bye to Acca is that of a soldier still thinking of the battle (11.823-827). In the last book Aeneas speaks a protreptic farewell to Ascanius (12.435-440; see p. 31). However, the final speech of Anchises to Aeneas is not reported: *his . . . prosequitur dictis* (6.897-898, evidently referring to the counsels given in 6.890-892). Dido leaves Aeneas with a curse (4.380-387); he does not bid her farewell, and they never see each other again alive. Nor, when dying, does she say farewell to her sister (4.685-692): her suffering has gone far beyond speech.

Threats and challenges

Threats, challenges, and taunts[33] are most frequent in the battle books, the ninth, tenth, and twelfth. One of the most striking is the last challenge of Aeneas to Turnus before the duel (12.889-893). For all its energy, it is but five lines long. In the *Aeneid* such utterances are fewer and briefer than the elaborate verbal combats of the *Iliad*.[34] The Homeric heroes can exchange taunts by shiploads, as the Homeric Aeneas says to Achilles (*Il.* 20.246-247): not so in the *Aeneid*.[35] However, the purpose of such verbal gestures is the same in both *Iliad*

W. W. Tarn in *CAH* 10, p. 113, and G. Bowersock, *Augustus and the Greek World* (Oxford, 1965), pp. 93-94.

[33] See Appendix 2.

[34] E.g., Ajax and Hector, *Il.* 7.226-243; Paris and Diomede, 11.380-395; Aeneas and Meriones, 16.616-625; Hector and Patroclus, 16.830-861; Achilles and Aeneas, 20.177-258.

[35] See A. L. Keith, "The Taunt in Homer and Vergil," *CJ* 19 (1923-1924) 554-560. Heinze also (p. 409) emphasizes the brevity of Vergil's challenges as compared with those of the *Iliad*.

and *Aeneid*—to throw the opponent off balance by ridicule and intimidation.[36] The most brutal of these flytings in the *Aeneid* is that in which a youth kills an old man, the dialogue of Priam and Pyrrhus (2.535-550). To the threats and challenges bandied in the *Iliad* between divinities in physical combat (*Il.* 21.383-501) there is nothing to correspond in the *Aeneid*. The Olympian debate in Book Ten is far more sophisticated. For all the grief and anger there expressed, it is impossible to imagine the Vergilian deities using names such as "dogfly" and "vixen," thrashing one another and throwing stones.

Prayers

There are twenty-nine prayers in the epic. Only five are of any considerable length and substance.[37]

Iarbas addresses Jupiter in tones remarkably sophisticated for an African tribal chief (4.206-218). His words are not so much a prayer as a challenge. He actually ventures to suggest that Jove the wielder of thunderbolts may not exist, and that thunder and lightning may be merely celestial sound and show. Here, anachronistically, he speaks in terms which recall Lucretius.[38] Thence he proceeds to a brief bitter vituperation of Dido and Aeneas. The Trojan hero is called

ille Paris cum semiuiro comitatu.

The hexameter, ending abnormally in two tetrasyllables, is intended to sound unnatural and weakly like an effeminate

[36] See J. J. Glück, "Reviling and Monomachy as Battle-preludes in Ancient Warfare," *AClass* 7 (1964) 25-31.

[37] For a list see Appendix 2.

[38] "Nubibus ignes" in the same position, Lucr. 2.214; "terrificant" in the same position, Lucr. 4.38, cf. 1.133; "murmure" of thunder, in the fifth foot, Lucr. 6.101 and 197; for the theme in general, Lucr. 5.1218-1221 and 6.387-422.

117

Phrygian; and effeminacy is imaged in the mincing alliteration on M:

> *M*aeonia *m*entu*m* *m*itra crine*m*que *m*adente*m*.[39]

Dido's final soliloquy passes into a prayer of execration (4.607-621), which is analyzed on pp. 178-179. At Cumae Aeneas supplicates his patron Phoebus and the hostile gods, coupling his invocation with a request to the Sibyl (6.56-65 + 65-76). He also utters eight briefer prayers.[40]

The scene of prayer in the final book is the most carefully developed and, except for Dido's curse, the most momentous. In 12.161-215 the leaders of the warring peoples meet to make a formal treaty: Latinus accompanied by Turnus, Aeneas with Ascanius. The ceremony is a religious rite, with sacrifice and libation, held at sunrise. It is curious that the actual basis of the treaty is not explicitly stated. Aeneas does not declare that he will fight a decisive duel with the representative of his opponents, Turnus; Latinus does not even mention the duel, save in the vague phrase "quo res cumque cadent" (12.203); and Turnus does not speak at all. Both sides have simply assumed that there will be a duel. What the treaty designs, and what both sides pray for, is peace, eternal peace (12.191, 202) between the two peoples—regardless of the outcome of the contest. Aeneas says that if Turnus wins, the "sons of Aeneas" will depart and live without thought of future aggression in Evander's city (i.e. the site of Rome, chosen by destiny); if he himself is victorious, he and his will be equal to the Latins, allies and friends. King Latinus will hold civil and military

---

[39] So the exquisite dancer in Horace, *Serm.* 1.9.24-25, "quis *m*embra *m*ouere / *m*ollius?"

[40] He prays to Venus disguised (1.326-334); to Thymbraean Apollo (3.85-89); to Mercury, if it is indeed Mercury (4.573-579; see p. 199); and to Jove (5.687-692); he utters an impromptu wish scarcely formal enough to be styled a prayer, but immediately answered (6.187-189); a summons to the doves and to Venus (6.194-197); a prayer to the Nymphs and the Tiber (8.71-78); and an invocation to Cybele (10.252-255).

power; and as for Aeneas, he says, "sacra deosque dabo" (12.192). This is not quite clear. At first reading it seems to imply that the Latins have no religious rituals and no gods, or only primitive and ignoble cults—like the Aztecs when the Spaniards landed—and that Aeneas will teach them a higher religion. Yet they seem to know the Olympian deities and to practice no barbarous ceremonies. But Aeneas has carried the gods of Troy to Italy, and here, discreetly, he declares he will establish them in his new home as objects of worship: he means the Penates, and Vesta, and perhaps the Palladium. What he says here is restated by Jupiter: "morem ritusque sacrorum / adiciam" (12.836-837). Vergil also implies that, of the three functions of a Roman king, Aeneas will assume only one, the nearest to heaven: he will be *rex sacrorum*, an august dignity.

Is it strange that Vergil made the terms of this treaty so broad, and that he omitted one of its fundamental elements, the duel and the regulations for the duel? The Romans were painfully punctilious about the formulae of treaties and rituals. Apparently Vergil found their legalistic exactitude narrowminded and unpoetic. He would not mock it, like Cicero (*Mur.* 25-28); but he ignored it. And he wished the concluding agreement in the *Aeneid* to be more magnanimous and far-reaching than that between Agamemnon and Achilles (*Il.* 19.238-275) or the oath of Agamemnon (*Il.* 3.276-291).

The two chiefs pray to different gods (at least in part) and in different terms, with very different implications.[41]

Aeneas and Latinus, like Agamemnon, invoke Jupiter and earth and sun. Agamemnon addresses Zeus first (*Il.* 3.276, 19.258); but Aeneas begins by invoking the sun and the earth, Latinus the earth, the sea, and the stars. Aeneas greets the sun because it is just rising and is the universal witness; the earth because he has struggled so long to win it. Latinus, descended

[41] For the following analysis I am largely indebted to F. I. Zeitlin, whose study appears in *AJP* 86 (1965) 337-362.

from the sun (12.162-164), ought to appeal to it, but instead calls on the stars, which sometimes mean heaven in general but more often connote night and darkness. Although this is a solemn treaty aimed at ensuring peace, Latinus has only somber forebodings about its outcome. After sun and earth, Aeneas calls to witness Jupiter, with Juno (called Saturnia as patroness of Italy, Saturn's realm) and Mars, god of war, here called father as the future ancestor of the Romans. But Latinus addresses "Latonae genus duplex"—Apollo and Diana, or sun and moon?—and Janus, the guardian of war's prison (*Aen.* 7.610), then the gods of the underworld, and finally Jove . . . as the deity who enforces treaties with the thunderbolt. Aeneas is confident, open-hearted even in his address to Juno ("iam melior, iam, diua, precor"), while Latinus is gloomy, anxious, weighed down by guilt. As the poem draws to its close, Aeneas stands in full sunlight while his opponents are shadowed by darkness.

There are four prayers by Anchises: to Jupiter (2.689-691); to the gods of Troy (2.701-704); to the gods generally (3.265-266); and to the divinities of sea, land, and weather (3.528-529). Apart from her execration, Dido is heard praying only once, in 1.731-735, to Jupiter, Bacchus, and "good Juno"; her words in 4.56-64 are not given. Nisus supplicates Diana as the Moon (9.404-409) and Ascanius almighty Jupiter (9.625-629). Turnus prays only twice, and then to minor deities: Iris, followed by an indiscriminate outpouring of entreaties, in 9.18-22, to Faunus and Earth in 12.777-779. Pallas prays once to Tiber (10.421-423) and once to his father's friend Hercules (10.460-463). Unbelieving Mezentius prays to no god, but to his own right hand and his spear (10.773-776). The cries of Turnus in 10.668-679 are too disorderly to be thought of as regular prayers, and the speech rather ranks as an excited apostrophe (p. 159).

The prayers in the *Aeneid* are remarkably varied and lively. Although many, and perhaps most, Roman prayers were rigidly codified,[42] and although Vergil knew much about Roman ritual, he was careful to avoid giving them the appearance of fixed formulae, which would make them repetitious and cold. They sound like spontaneous outpourings from the hearts of the worshippers.

Commands

A very large number of speeches in the *Aeneid* are in the form of commands.[43] Most are naturally brief: only fifteen are both long and important. Four of these are uttered by Aeneas himself: telling his household how to escape from Troy (2.707-720), proclaiming the festival prefiguring the Parentalia in honor of his father (5.45-71), directing his troops against the city of Latinus after the burial of the dead (11.14-28), and ordering the final assault (12.565-573). The tempest in Book One is quelled by Neptune's imperious dismissal of the winds ("maturate fugam," 1.132-141). At another crisis, the ghost of Anchises commands Aeneas to follow Nautes' advice (5.724-739). Dido gives elaborate instructions to Anna (4.478-498) and the Sibyl to Aeneas (6.125-155). Usually laconic (cf. 9.51 and 11.463-467), Turnus explains his tactics to Camilla at some length (11.508-519).

One speech of command has proved difficult to interpret: the speech in which Anchises orders Aeneas to say good-bye and escape with the rest of the family (2.638-649, or, more exactly, 635-649). It shows him as a stern old man whom age, infirmity, and suffering have made resolute in his determination to die. He has been living on borrowed time, "iam pridem inuisus diuis," and now he is calm and resigned. He speaks of himself as though he were lying on his deathbed: he urges the family

---

[42] See G. Appel, *De Romanorum precationibus, Religionsgeschichtliche Versuche* 7.2 (Giessen, 1909), for a complete list of Roman prayers and an analysis. I doubt if he is right in describing Aeneas's greetings in 5.80 and 7.120-121 as prayers, although of course "salue" in 8.301 is part of an invocation.

[43] A complete list is in Appendix 2.

121

to say farewell to him, as to a corpse which has just breathed its last (2.644). "Sic positum" means both "lying here without moving"[44] and thus "laid out for burial";[45] while "adfati" alludes to the ritual of saying farewell to a dying or dead man, as in 9.484.

The next sentence has caused some perplexity; and the manuscripts vary in their readings. Anchises says

> ipse manu mortem[46] inueniam; miserebitur hostis
> exuuiasque petet.

What does he mean? that he intends to kill himself? No. If we take his words to mean "I shall commit suicide," then the phrase "miserebitur hostis" is devoid of significance. Besides, it is wrong for a father to tell his son, "Go, leave me: I shall cut my throat after you have gone": it would be ethically improper and even cowardly. Another suggestion comes from R. G. Austin in his edition of Book Two: "Anchises will seek death in battle, as Priam tried to do." Priam, although old, had still enough strength to stand up to the enemy, and (however weakly) to cast a spear; but Anchises was a cripple, who had to be carried on Aeneas's shoulders. And even if he could take up arms, it would be unthinkable for him to tell his son "You run away: I shall stay and fight the Greeks." Servius gives a third explanation: he says "MORTEM autem ego manu hostis inueniam . . . MISEREBITUR HOSTIS affectu eius qui cupiebat interimi dixit, ut eum hostis quasi miseratus occideret," and he adds a reference to the ninth book—where the mother of Euryalus voices the same thought, that it would be merciful of Jupiter[47] to strike her dead (9.495-497). This is the best solu-

---

[44] Cf. 2.654: "sedibus haeret in isdem." *Positum sic* is used of a dead animal in Hor. *Serm.* 1.2.106, and Lucretius has *corpore posto* for an entombed corpse in 3.871.

[45] "Sic . . . posita" of Dido lying on her deathbed in 4.681.

[46] manum *PV?a?* morte *uel* morti *P¹*, morti *V*. Kvíčala, a good Vergilian, proposed "manens."

[47] Or of the enemy, 493-494: lines which are even more appropriate to this passage.

tion. Interpret Anchises' words as meaning "I shall wait here for the enemy to slay me," and the whole speech coheres and makes sense, although a grim sense.[48] Troy is being sacked. Every house will be looted and its inhabitants enslaved or killed. Anchises is too old and feeble to be worth enslaving, so the Greeks will kill him for the jewelry and the fine robe he wears—and this will be an act of mercy. It is a sort of reassurance to his family that he cares nothing about funeral rites; and that he will not live on, crippled and starving, in a ruined city, but die quickly. To readers of Vergil's own time, the spectacle of the old man prepared to die at the hand of the irresistible enemy would recall the fate of the Roman senators who refused to leave their city with the refugees when it lay at the mercy of the invading Gauls. *Turba seniorum* (says Livy, 5.41.1) *domos regressi aduentum hostium obstinato ad mortem animo exspectabant.* Those who had held curule office put on their most splendid ceremonial attire and sat in their ivory chairs. Their appearance and the majesty of their faces silenced the Gauls with reverential awe; and then, when one of them struck a Gaul for stroking his beard, *ab eo initium caedis ortum, ceteros in sedibus suis*[49] *trucidatos.* This is the death which Anchises envisages for himself; and like those Roman nobles, he cares nothing for the rites of decent burial in a city sacked and destroyed. At this point he is firmly determined to die, as later in Book Three he is energetic and resolute in commanding the Trojan fleet of refugees. It takes a miracle from heaven to convert him, but, once converted, he is indomitable. He is a real Roman paterfamilias.[50]

Of all the commands in the *Aeneid*, the most important are those given by the supreme ruler. First, Jupiter sends Mercury to Aeneas with peremptory orders to sail, in 4.223-237. Mer-

---

[48] On this interpretation "manu" means not "manu mea" but simply "ui."

[49] So Anchises *sedibus haeret in isdem*, 2.654.

[50] Heinze has a fine passage (pp. 55-57) showing that when Anchises receives the *auspicium maximum* he prefigures a Roman magistrate.

cury makes striking changes in Jupiter's wording. The Almighty, far-seeing, knew of the future hostility of Carthage to Rome, and said "qua spe *inimica* in gente moratur?" (4.235). Mercury knows less, and substitutes a phrase containing a contemptuous little echo, "qua spe Libycis *teris* otia *terris*" (4.271).[51] Jupiter asked "nec . . . respicit?" (4.236) and gave only one word to Ascanius (4.234). Mercury makes Aeneas's dereliction of duty toward his own son more urgent as a command, "Ascanium *surgentem* et *spes heredis* Iuli / respice" (4.274-275), followed by a fine expansion of Jupiter's "Romanas arces" (4.234) into "regnum Italiae Romanaque tellus" (4.275). He is the god of eloquence, *facundus nepos Atlantis*, and could not merely repeat the message verbatim. Later Jupiter directs the gods to maintain neutrality (10.6-15 and 104-113). At last, he utters to Juno the word which has been awaited for twelve books (12.806) : "ulterius temptare VETO."

Persuasions

Conflicts of will are manifested not only in physical strife but in words. A god, unless he be the ruling deity, cannot compel another god to obey: he must persuade by fair speech and promises, and he must make his commands acceptable even to subordinate divinities by offering reasons. A commander cannot kill all his recreant soldiers: he must use words to change their minds. Dido might have used force to keep Aeneas in Carthage, or (as she tells herself in 4.600-606) might have murdered him; but she preferred to entreat him. Informal speeches of persuasion used for such purposes are among the most momentous in the *Aeneid*.[52]

The two divine opponents each make several speeches of persuasion which are too subtle and personal to fall within rhetorical schemata, but on which Vergil lavishes effects of

---

[51] This is a παρήχησις like *Il.* 6.201: Hermog. *De inu.* 4.7 (Spengel 2, p. 251).
[52] For a list see Appendix 2.

style, sound, and rhythm. Both goddesses win their points, but it is Juno whose victory is the most final and satisfying.

Venus speaks persuasively to Jove in 1.229-253, to her son Love in 1.664-688, to Neptune for Aeneas's safe conduct in 5.781-798, and to Vulcan for the armor in 8.374-386. Her supple charm is felt in all these passages: for Jove, tears in her shining eyes (1.228); for Love the little tyrant, flattery (1.664-666) and affection;[53] for Neptune, a diplomatic reminder of Juno's encroachments on his dominion (5.789-792). The address in which she coaxes her husband to make weapons for the son begotten on her by a mortal lover is particularly graceful. During the war of Troy, she points out, she asked Vulcan for no favors (8.374-380)—in spite of her debt to the Trojans: a tactful allusion to her victory at the judgment of Paris. The name of her son Aeneas she does not mention until more than halfway through the speech. God's command (she continues) has now set him among the hostile Rutulians;[54] and so she begs for help (8.381-383). Vulcan has previously (she reminds him) yielded to the entreaties of other goddesses for their soldier sons. She ends with a picture of hostile cities sharpening their steel for her and her loved ones, and with an irresistible gesture:

> niueis hinc atque hinc diua lacertis
> cunctantem amplexu molli fouet.

The complaint of Venus to Jove (1.229-253) contains several touches of unusual subtlety. It would be highly undiplomatic for her to name Juno, sister and consort of Jupiter, as the persecutor of the Trojans. Therefore she asks "quae te sententia

---

[53] "Nate" in 1.664, emphatically repeated at the beginning of the next line, is the emotional word, whereas *filius* is merely descriptive. Anchises uses it three times in a more earnest speech of persuasion (5.724, 725, 733) and Mezentius twice (10.846 and 851). See Marouzeau, *Stylistique* p. 167.

[54] Still another of these persuasive exaggerations: Aeneas landed in Latium, not in Rutulian territory, which is southward across the Numicus.

uertit?" (1.237). The phrasing is remarkable. Apparently it blends two lines from Ennius:

quianam dictis nostris sententia flexa est?

(*Ann.* 259)

and

ingenium cui nulla malum sententia suadet

(*Ann.* 243).

"Quae te sententia uertit?" is a delicate way of asking "Cuius te consilium uertit?"—to which there is only one possible answer: "Iunonis." The peculiar turn of phrase is made acceptable by its archaic coloring and its allusiveness.[55] Behind the Ennian phraseology lies a more subtle allusion. After Thetis in the *Iliad* has persuaded Zeus to favor her son, it is Hera (= Juno) who provokes him with the question (*Il.* 1.540): "τίς δὴ αὖ τοι, δολομῆτα, θεῶν ϲυμφράϲϲατο βουλάϲ;" Even more diplomatically Venus says that the Trojan ships were destroyed "unius ob iram" (1.251). Both Venus and Jupiter well know who the One is. So does the reader, because on the first page of the poem Vergil says, in the same rhythm, that Aeneas suffered much on land and sea *Iunonis ob iram* (1.4).

Speeches such as this should not be fitted into rhetorical patterns. But recent studies have shown that Vergil sometimes gives them an exquisitely symmetrical structure.[56] Here the persuasion of Venus covers just over 24½ lines. Its chief thought—"quem das finem, rex magne, laborum?"—comes almost exactly in the center, at its thirteenth line. And the entire speech is built of four groups of lines, carrying four movements of thought thus balanced:

[55] Other Ennian echoes in Venus's speech are "hominumque deumque" (1.229, cf. *Ann.* 249); "prodimur" with the sense of destruction (1.252, cf. *Ann.* 428); and perhaps "finem laborum" (1.241, cf. *Ann.* 345).

[56] See in particular T. Halter, *Form und Gestalt in Vergils Aeneis* (Munich, 1963) and A. Wlosok, *Die Göttin Venus in Vergils Aeneis* (Heidelberg, 1967) to which I owe this analysis.

229-233	Sufferings of Aeneas	4½ lines
234-241	Jove's promise	8 lines
242-249	Antenor's escape	8 lines
250-253	Sufferings of Aeneas	4 lines.

In the *Iliad*, one hero will sometimes echo or comment on the words of another, although he could not have heard them. The poet intends both speeches to be present to our minds together; sometimes also he implies that they were delivered simultaneously in counterpoint. This observation is made by D. Lohmann,[57] who insists that analytical critics of Homer are wrong to consider the first of such speeches as a "model" and the second as an "imitation." The pair were designed together by the poet. Not infrequently Vergil uses the same device of echoing and allusion; but his verbal parallels are usually less emphatic, sometimes almost unnoticeable. So here it can be shown that Venus—without having heard it—is alluding to the hate-filled monologue of Juno (*Aen.* 1.37-49). There Juno reflected "Pallasne . . . potuit?" Here Venus pleads "Antenor potuit." There Juno thought of Greek ships wrecked "unius ob noxam," here echoed in a slightly different rhythm by Venus, "unius ob iram."[58]

The imperious will of Juno is early exerted upon Aeolus (1.65-75), who finds it irresistible, and suffers for yielding to it—as does Juturna at the end (12.142-159). These two speeches of persuasion are strongly characteristic. In the address to Aeolus Juno's spiteful hatred comes out in line 1.68:

Ilium in Italiam portans *uictosque* penates

which is followed by four harsh imperatives:

incute uim uentis submersasque *obrue* puppis
aut *age* diuersos et *dissice* corpora ponto.

---

[57] *Die Komposition der Reden in der Ilias* (Berlin, 1970) 161-169, 202-209.
[58] This is from Wlosok (cited above, n. 56) p. 57 n. 12.

Yet there is an alluring charm about the sinuous polysyllables describing the lovely nymph promised as Aeolus's bride:

> quarum quae forma *pulcherrima Deiopea*.

In Juno's speech to Juturna there is a piece of typical rancor. She avers that she has favored Juturna above all other local mistresses of her spouse—

> quaecumque Latinae
> magnanimi Iouis ingratum ascendere cubile—

a line which, as though to express the odiousness of the subject, has an unnatural rhythm, without a normal caesura. This speech also Juno ends with four hard imperatives: "accelera," "eripe," "cie," "excute."

Juno persuades Venus to help in arranging the union of Aeneas and Dido (4.93-104 + 115-127), and Venus, for her own motives, agrees. Juno cozens Jupiter to permit her to save Turnus (10.611-620 + 628-632). Finally, she contrives her most important persuasion near the end of the epic, in 12.808-828. Jupiter's severe veto (12.806) she meets *summisso uultu*, responding with a line composed of eight words, all except the last being light disyllables, making a patter of voluble dactyls:

> ista quidem quia nota mihi tua, magne, uoluntas.

Yet even so she cannot sustain her pose of submissiveness: grimly she adds that, were it not for Jupiter's prohibition, she would have descended to earth and would be fighting against the Trojans "flammis cincta"—not like a goddess, but like a Fury.[59] But then, with a further pretense of yielding, she shifts the responsibility for the mysterious bowshot which wounded Aeneas (12.318-323) from herself to Juturna, in spite of the broad mandate she gave her: contrast her words in 12.152-153 and 156-159 with her oath in 12.813-817. Having thus softened

---

[59] Descriptions of human furies embattled, in Italy, Livy 7.17.3; in Britain, Tac. *Ann.* 14.30.1.

Jupiter's heart, she begs him to destroy the Trojans, to obliterate their language, costume, national identity, and name. Lines 12.819-828 are among the most serious and weighty in the *Aeneid*, constructed with firm regular caesurae, strong alliteration, and urgent anaphorae ("pro," "pro"; "cum iam," "cum iam"; "sit," "sint," "sit"). The rhythm reflects Juno's emotions. Grave and controlled at first, she begins with a line containing five spondees, slow and measured: the first spondaic foot being one single word, heavily emphatic:[60]

illud te, nulla fati quod lege tenetur. . . .

She maintains a predominantly slow pace, with a high proportion of spondees, until the last line.[61] Then her passion runs away ("occidit, occideritque sinas") in a rapid verse with an initial one-word dactyl[62] followed by two more dactyls. This line ends with the last word Juno is to speak in the poem, the word which to her is the most hateful of all:

occidit, occideritque sinas cum nomine Troia!

Is it possible that Vergil intended the odd phrase "cum nomine" to be not only hateful but obscene? Cicero twice states that the Romans avoided saying *cum nobis* because it sounded like an obscenity.[63] See *Orator* 154, and a detailed discussion of unintentionally shocking words and combinations of syllables,

[60] "Spondeischer Versanfang mit darauffolgender Diaerese ein für den Rhythmus stark retardierendes Moment bildet": Norden, *Aeneis VI*, Anhang VIII, p. 435.

[61] The pattern in lines 819-828 is this: SSSSDS, DSSSDS, SDSSDS, SSSSDS, DDSSDS, SDDSDS, SSDSDS, DSSSDS, SDDSDS, and finally DDDSDS.

[62] When the initial one-word dactyl is a verb, it is usually energetic. Within this context in Book Twelve see, for instance, *deserit*, 683; *proluit*, 686; *deserit*, 698; *frangitur*, 732; and the fierce *immolat*, 949. This is a favorite device of Vergil's in scenes of violent action: in one page of the fight between Hercules and Cacus (8.236-267) he has *impulit, aduocat, euomit, non tulit, corripit,* and *panditur*.

[63] In fact, J. Marouzeau, *Les Articulations de l'énoncé* (Paris, 1949) pp. 48-49, points out that it was obligatory to put *cum* after the personal pronouns.

129

in *Fam.* 9.22. When he wrote that letter Cicero was working on the *Paradoxa Stoicorum*: it is part of a discussion with the Stoic Paetus. The Stoics held that a word, if correctly applied to the thing it connoted, could not possibly be objectionable; but Cicero points out that an apparently innocent word or conjunction of syllables may evoke an obscene meaning. The letter and the topic are exhaustively analyzed by W. Wendt in *Ciceros Brief an Paetus IX 22* (Giessen, 1929); see also M. Demmel, *Cicero und Paetus* (Cologne, 1962), pp. 219-245. Wendt shows that in practice the purist Caesar usually avoids *cum + no* and *cum + nu*, as well as ambivalent words such as *bini* and *tumeo*. Quintilian backs up Cicero's statement, asserting that the Romans would not say *cum notis hominibus loqui* so as to avoid *praefanda* (*Inst.* 8.3.45). Now, Vergil's ear was more sensitive and his taste more delicate than Cicero's. Is it possible that, if *cum nomine* sounded obscene, he would have overlooked the fact? Vergil never treats Juno with anything but revulsion and hatred: for him she is a devil, and devils can speak foully. It is curious to note that the obscene word which the phrase suggests is twice used in passages of contemporary poetry dealing with the Trojan war: Horace, *Serm.* 1.3. 107-108, and *Priapea* 68.9-10.

Servius on 2.27 remarks that "Dori*ca ca*stra" makes a *cacemphaton*: that is, it not only produces an ugly little jingle like "ad nu*men men*tis" (Lucr. 3.144) but also shapes an obscene word.[64] Quintilian makes the matter very clear: "uitia ... quae imperitis quoque ad reprehensionem notabilia uidentur, id est quae, commissis inter se uerbis duobus, ex ultima prioris ac prima sequentis syllaba *deforme aliquod nomen* efficiunt" (9.4.33). Now, Vergil was far from being *imperitus* in subtle effects of sound and significance. Did he therefore intend this obscenity to stigmatize the detestable invading force of Greeks, here and in its repetition (6.88)? And did he

---

[64] R. G. Austin's note on this line deals only with the sound-effect, and is corrected by G. Luck in *Gnomon* 37 (1965) 53.

intensify this ugliness in "*Achaica ca*stra" (2.462)? The poet who could imitate the sound of steel scratching on flint (*silici scintillam ex*cudit A*ch*ates, 1.174) is not likely to have been deaf to this coarser sound-effect.

J. S. Th. Hanssen, "Remarks on Euphony-Cacophony and the Language of Vergil," *SO* 22 (1942), deals with *cacemphaton* only on pp. 105-106. There he observes, "If a collocation of words really is cacemphaton, then it must be impossible to use it; even the occasional occurrence must be taken as a proof that no cacemphaton is heard. Would Vergil have written *cum nomine* (12.828), *cum nocte* (7.427), and *secum nostrae* (4.662) if there was any chance of cacemphaton? The ancient commentators who elsewhere eagerly note the cacemphaton have overlooked these places, which would be the worst of all." Yet in 4.662 the true reading is "nostrae secum," which gives the maximum metrical emphasis to "nostrae . . . mortis." In 7.427 there is small chance that readers would note a *double entente* (and yet it is in a Junonian context). As for 12.828 (the passage under discussion), it is not *impossible* to use *cacemphaton*, any more than it is impossible to employ in an epic poem words which are alien to the traditional epic style, as Vergil sometimes does.[65] But if it is used, the poet must have a special purpose—like Shakespeare, when he made his noblest prince utter *cacemphata*.[66]

The will of Juno is inflexible. Jupiter yields to her persuasion. At last she has won her victory. In a few brief mortal years Troy will have ceased to exist. Long desired and long deferred, her revenge will be complete.[67]

[65] See pp. 223-224.

[66] *Hamlet* 3.2.120-129, 260-265.

[67] The final dialogue of Jupiter and Juno (*Aen.* 12.791-842) is analysed with great, perhaps excessive, ingenuity by T. Halter (cited on page 98) pp. 78-93. He breaks it into twenty-six segments, the center being Juno's long-awaited "et nunc cedo equidem pugnasque exosa relinquo" (12.818):

131

No other divinities make long speeches of persuasion, except the disguised Iris inciting the Trojan women to burn their ships (5.623-640) and Allecto to Turnus, almost as much commanding as persuading (7.421-434).

Half-maddened by Allecto's poison,[68] Amata endeavors to convince Latinus to reject the alliance with Aeneas (7.359-372); and then, before the catastrophe which she has helped to cause, attempts to coax Turnus not to fight the duel (12.56-63). Brief though it is, the speech of Laocoon to the Trojans is an important dissuasion (2.42-49), ending in a memorable *epiphonema*:

quidquid id est, timeo Danaos et dona ferentis.[69]

The address of Palinurus to Aeneas in the underworld (6.347-371) is a response to questioning, and a narrative of facts unknown to the questioner; but at the end it passes into a persuasion (363-371). This plea has several features in common with the twenty-eighth lyric in Horace's first book, the "Archytas ode." Both are spoken to living men by the ghosts of sailors cast up on the coast of Italy and still unburied. There is even a verbal resemblance. Horace's sailor says "me . . . Notus obruit undis" (*Carm.* 1.28.21-22); and just before meeting Palinurus Aeneas sees two other drowned comrades, *quos . . . obruit Auster* (*Aen.* 6.335-336). Possibly both these poetic speeches, within different stylistic frames, are suggested by the Greek epigrams in which a dead sailor addresses a living seafarer,[70] or discusses his burial.[71] In position and proportion, the story told by Palinurus (lines 347-362) is comparable to the Horatian sailor's sermon on death (lines 1-22). Palinurus

---

"die entscheidende Peripetie des ganzen Liedes"; and he underlines some remarkable parallelisms throughout the scene, asking whether such effects can be the result of pure chance.

[68] Yet notice the curiously bitter phrase *solito matrum de more* (7.357).

[69] " 'Quidquid id est' n'est pas très élégant," says Marouzeau (*Stylistique,* p. 111); true, but it expresses anxiety and excitement.

[70] E.g., Leonidas of Tarentum, *AP* 7.264 and 266.

[71] E.g., Callimachus, *AP* 7.277; Diocles of Carystus, *AP* 7.393.

then utters a formal request ("quod te," 363), as does the sailor in Horace ("at tu, nauta," 23). Both ask for the formal ritual of burial. But the ghost in Horace is materialistic, negative, minatory, while the ghost in Vergil beseeches help which he is confident will be vouchsafed. In Horace the speaker appeals to his hearer's hope of safe voyages and much profit (25-29), while Vergil's Palinurus invokes "caeli iucundum lumen et auras." In Horace the words are cold:

> neglegis immeritis nocituram
> postmodo te natis fraudem committere?

In Vergil they are warm:

> per genitorem oro, per spes surgentis Iuli.

In Horace a stranger summons a stranger to do the least that should be done, saying "iniecto ter puluere curras." In Vergil a comrade pleads with a comrade to release him from half-death, to make a special journey and bury his corpse, or (if his divine birth makes it possible) to break the rule segregating the unburied dead (6.327-330) and carry him across the Styx. Vergil had a heart softer than Horace.

The chief informal speeches of persuasion are those in the fourth book. Dido utters two. Only one is spoken to Aeneas face to face: a queen will not deign more. The other is addressed to him through Anna as an intermediary.

The first of these (4.305-330) is a subtly modulated speech in which strong passions struggle with one another.[72] Foremost is love. Even when Dido hates Aeneas and curses him, she still loves him: "miseratus *amantem* est?" (4.370); "extremum . . . munus *amanti*" (4.429); "me soluat *amantem*" (4.479). She loves him even when she kills herself—using his

---

[72] For a sensitive analysis of the effects of sound and rhythm in this speech see J. Soubiran, "Passion de Didon: métrique de Virgile," *Pallas* 10 (1961) 31-54.

sword, with her lips pressed to the bed where they had slept together, and with his effigy lying beside her. It is only after death, reunited with her husband, that she utterly rejects Aeneas (6.467-474). Therefore, although this speech begins with a hiss of hatred and a scornful epithet—

> dissimulare etiam[73] sperasti, perfide, tantum
> posse nefas?—

Dido soon changes to a gentler reproach, the reproach of a loving woman, "crudelis" (311); and then to a name of kindness, "hospes" (323), a substitute for the word she longs to use but cannot, "coniunx" (324). She had told herself that she was his wife (*coniugium uocat*, 4.172). Therefore in this speech she enumerates every element of a woman's married happiness: "amor" (307), "data dextera" (307, 314), "conubia, hymenaeos" (316), "domus" (318), and "suboles" (328). Although she begins with violent emotion (300-304) and is still hissing with fury in the third and fourth sentences (309-313), thereafter she bursts into tears and grasps the hand of Aeneas (314); and at the end she is helpless with shock and grief ("moribundam," 323). Within less than thirty lines she has passed through a wide range of the varying emotions with which a woman confronts an unfaithful lover.

Her agitation is reflected in the pulse of the hexameters, as Soubiran (above, n. 72) has shown. Of the six lines in the long sentence which forms her central plea to Aeneas (314-319), three have abnormal endings. Only twenty-nine lines in all Vergil's poetry have a final monosyllable preceded by an iambic

---

[73] This particular elision, "dissimular(e) etiam," is unusual. Eight times in the *Aeneid* the final short vowel of an initial pentasyllabic word ($- \smile \smile - \smile$) is swallowed up by the first vowel of a following anapaestic word. Five of these phrases describe abrupt astonishment, in the pattern *obstipuere animis* (2.120, 5.404, 7.447, 8.530, 9.123); one an emergency tactical move (9.469); and one the energy of Dido's curse (4.625). See A. Siedow, *De elisionis aphaeresis hiatus usu in hexametris Latinis ab Ennii usque ad Ovidii tempora* (Greifswald, 1911) pp. 71-76.

word, like "tuam te" (314); the tetrasyllabic ending "hymen-
aeos" (316) is rare; and so is the ending in two disyllables,
"tibi quicquam" (317). The initial one-word spondees "oro"
(319) and "saltem" (327) are also uncommon, and weigh
down the rhythm (see p. 129, n. 60).

Next to her love for Aeneas, Dido's strongest passion is her
pride. Vergil displays it in many subtle touches. For instance:
from the moment that she realizes Aeneas is turning away
from her, she never once addresses him by name or speaks of
him by name. To his face she calls him "perfide" (305, 366),
"crudelis" (311), and "improbe" (386); in his absence, some-
times "uir" (423, 495, 498); once, in humiliation, "hostis super-
bus" (424); once, in angry contempt, "aduena" (591); once,
thinking of his son by another woman, "pater" (605); twice
"caput" (613 and 640); sometimes merely "hic" (591) and
"ille" (421); and twice in one line (479) she uses oblique cases
of the pronoun is—which are usually below the level of epic
poetry.[74] Even on her deathbed she still does not speak his
name, but, with the thought of Trojan treachery ("Laomedon-
teae periuria gentis," 542), calls him "Dardanus" (662). The
sole exception to this is the touching sentence in which she
mentions the son she hoped for: "paruulus Aeneas" (329).

Her pride comes out in every one of her speeches. She
speaks as a monarch ("mea terra," 4.306, and see 373-374, 591,
597), as a woman much wooed but disdainful of her suitors

[74] See M. Hélin, "Le pronom 'is' chez Virgile," REL 5 (1927) 60-68.
Szantyr on p. 186 says it is almost wholly avoided by Lucan, and appears
only twice in Horace's lyrics: Carm. 3.11.18 ("sicher unecht") and 4.8.18.
Bentley in a vigorous note on the former of these passages points out that
Vergil never employs eius, and declares that it would debase the majesty of
epic poetry. In Vergil is cannot be called undignified (see 8.321), but it is not
common; isque is more frequent. The oblique cases of the pronoun are rare:
eum 7.757, 8.33, 8.576, 11.12, and eumque 5.239; eo 10.101; eius and ei
never. On Aen. 4.479 R. G. Austin suggests that Dido uses the pronouns here
not because she hates Aeneas, but "to seem casual and to put her sister off
the scent"; yet this scarcely accounts for her determined avoidance of the
name elsewhere.

(534-536), and as a heroine aspiring to immortality (322, 653-656). In certain constraints which appear in her entreaty to Aeneas, her pride is very marked. She begins with five reproachful questions, which are in fact arguments addressed to Aeneas's honor (305-308), self-interest (309-313), and love (314). Then she utters her main plea, in a long sentence which contains no less than seven appeals (314-319). Six of these are: her grief at the thought of being deserted by him (314), his pledge (314), her helplessness (315), their half-realized marriage (316),[75] her hospitality to him (317), and the ruin his departure will inflict on the life they have been building together ("domus labentis," 318). But she is too proud to state the seventh outright: the fact that he had found her a beautiful and lovable woman. She can only make herself say "si . . . fuit . . . tibi quicquam / dulce meum." And then, after all these appeals, she cannot bring herself to utter the essential word "Mane!" She says only, with a hesitant hyperbaton, "istam . . . exue mentem." Then follow two more appeals stressing her hopelessness and loneliness: an appeal to his honor (320-326) and an appeal to the love they have shared (327-330). This she phrases with the utmost delicacy, saying that she might have been able to endure the separation if she had had a little son to remind her of his lost father. She has not. She has nothing.

Pride and love: the two passions strive together throughout the speech. Heinze (p. 425) divides it into an *indignatio* (305-313) and a *miseratio* (314-330).[76] Formally this is correct: the

---

[75] In 4.316 both "nostra" and "inceptos" should be taken ἀπὸ κοινοῦ with both the nouns. This figure, commoner in Vergil than sometimes supposed, is discussed by T. Düring, *De Vergilii sermone epico* (Göttingen, 1905) c. 3, with solutions to some problems such as *Aen.* 3.659 and 5.326. With 4.316 compare 2.422 and 535, 8.57 and 588. See also F. Leo, "Analecta Plautina: De figuris sermonis I," *Ausgew. Kl. Schriften* I (ed. E. Fraenkel, Rome, 1960) pp. 71-74, and examples given later in the same study.

[76] Heinze also points out that Dido's later pleas refer to the past (315-318), the present (320-323), and the future (324-326); and that the mention

indignatio is the expression of injured pride, for she was a queen before she was a lover, and the *miseratio* is the voice of wounded love. Yet Vergil interweaves the emotions more subtly than that scheme suggests. "Noster amor" (307) and "moritura" (308) are appeals to tenderness; "qua sola sidera adibam / fama prior" (322-323) is the voice of pride, to be echoed later (654) in the hour of death.

Later Dido addresses a final message of persuasion to Aeneas—this time indirectly, through Anna, and asking for much less (4.416-436). Formerly she begged him to stay for ever. She did not take his quest for Italy seriously: she had hoped for marriage with him, and children. Now she hopes only that he will stay for a little: a month or two (430) to make the separation less abrupt (433-434). Yet she has known from the first that, when he left her, she would die (308, 323, 385, 415). As she finishes giving her message to Anna, she realizes this again. Her realization is expressed in one of Vergil's most deeply moving sentences (435-436):

> extremam hanc oro ueniam (miserere sororis)
> quam mihi cum dederit cumulatam morte remittam.

The sounds in these two lines are strange. There are twelve *M*'s: six are initial or medial, and six are final, therefore probably nasalized.[77] Within two lines there are no less than three combinations of final *M* and initial *M*. This cannot be accidental: surely it is meant to suggest the sound of speech half-stifled by sobs.

Although beautiful, this final sentence is difficult: Pöschl (p. 195 n. 43) says it "remains unexplained." Certainly "extremam hanc ueniam" is elucidated by "extremum hoc . . .

---

of the future naturally evokes the concluding thought, Dido's childlessness. This division is typical of the *ethopoeia* or *sermocinatio*: Aphthon. *Progymn.* 11 (Spengel 2, p. 45, 11.17-19) and Nicolaus Soph. *Progymn.* 11 (Spengel 3, p. 490, 11.6-7).

[77] W. S. Allen, *Vox Latina* (Cambridge, 1965), pp. 30-31.

munus" (429), which the following lines show means a few weeks' delay. But how can Dido repay this favor, and how can her repayment be increased in value by her death, "cumulatam morte"?

Vergil often quotes his own poetry, and in the love-passages of the *Aeneid* he sometimes quotes his own love-poems. Here he is alluding to his poem about the lover who determined to commit suicide when his sweetheart married another man: *Bucolics* 8 (which Dido has already cited to Aeneas in 4.365-367). Bidding farewell to the woods and declaring that he will leap from a cliff into the sea, Damon cries (60):

extremum hoc munus morientis habeto.

The rejected lover's death is his last gift to his beloved: he is doing her a kindness by disappearing from life as though he had never existed. So here Dido begs for a favor (a brief delay) and promises to return the favor with the addition, or interest, of her death. Returning the favor must mean some kindness Dido proposes to do for Aeneas—and that can only be giving him free permission to sail away without reproach, after spending the period of leave-taking with her. Adding interest must mean that she will kill herself—so that he will not have any guilty sense that he ought to return to her, as though she were an Ariadne left weeping on the shore. The full pathos of this plea has sometimes been overlooked. For instance, Heinze (p. 135 n. 1) asserts that Dido does *not* expect to die at this point: he says Vergil would have expressed the sense more clearly if he had written "cumulatam uel morte remittam," *und wäre es mit meinem Leben.* But this cannot be reconciled with "moribundam" (323) and *moritura* (415).

Aeneas does not reply. But later, in a moving scene, he addresses a speech of persuasion to the ghost of Dido (6.450-476). In the myrtle grove where the souls of those who have died through love wander unquiet, he attempts in vain to assure her that he had not willed his departure and had not believed it would result in her death. Norden (*Aeneis VI*, p. 253) points out some eloquent echoes of Book Four in this speech. "Infelix Dido" (6.456) recalls Dido's apostrophe to herself (4.596); "hunc tantum . . . ferre dolorem" (6.464) resembles "hunc . . . tantum sperare dolorem" (4.419); and "quem fugis?" (6.466) echoes "mene fugis?" (4.314). The emphatic central line (6.460) with its powerful opening molossus

> inuitus, regina, tuo de litore cessi

restates the final words of Aeneas's refutation, "Italiam non sponte sequor" (4.361). Furthermore, his insistence on the irresistible divine command, "iussa deum . . . imperiis egere suis" (6.461-463), looks back to "iussere" in 4.346 and "interpres diuum . . . mandata . . . detulit" in 4.356-358. But his refutation in Book Four was rhetorically arranged, and sounded legalistic. Here there is no rhetoric. Aeneas's opening words mingle surprise and sorrow. The heart of his speech is a passionately sincere declaration that he obeyed God's command in leaving Dido, and did so against his own will. Then comes a touching and quite non-oratorical conclusion: "siste gradum . . . quem fugis?" But even while he speaks to her, Dido's somber figure is turning away. At this he breaks down. For almost the last time in the poem, he weeps: *prosequitur lacrimis longe*.[78] Those who do not see and understand these bitter tears do not fully comprehend the character of Aeneas. *Piangea*, says Dante of another heartbroken lover, *sí, che di pietade / io venni men cosi com'io morisse*.[79]

Responses to persuasion

To Aeneas's plea Dido returns no answer: she gazes at the ground with bleak disdain and rock-hard hatred. There are, however, fourteen speeches of some length in the *Aeneid*

---

[78] He weeps once more, for Pallas, in 11.41.
[79] *Inferno* 5.140-141.

which are replies, positive or negative, to persuasion.[80] Most of them are notable for their tact, all for their aptness to the characters who utter them.

There is much charm in Dido's response (1.562-578) to the diplomatic address of Ilioneus. She could scarcely be more generous—explaining why some of the Trojans had met with a hostile reception (563-564), acknowledging their fame (565-566) without admitting the implication that Carthage is a remote and rude frontier settlement (567-568, answering 539-540), and promising protection and supplies (569-571). She goes further. She offers her visitors a share of the city, in the open-hearted phrase "urbem quam statuo uestra est." Yet these words can also mean "You will take possession of Carthage," as the Romans were later to do.[81] This is one of the amphibologies which are so strikingly effective in Vergil and have so often puzzled his critics.[82] And when Dido wishes the king Aeneas himself were present (575-576), it is possible to divine that, after her long loneliness, she is unconsciously ready to give him her love.

On a similar mission to Latinus, Ilioneus receives an almost equally cordial reply. In 7.259-273 the king grants the Trojans more than they have requested, and, as is right for a gentle old monarch, both opens and closes his speech with a prayer.[83]

Evander also replies with genuine warmth to Aeneas's proposal of an alliance between Trojans and Arcadians (8.154-174). He does not think of discussing terms and balancing the contributions of the two peoples and drawing up draft agree-

[80] For a full list see Appendix 2.

[81] So E. Fraenkel, who points to the echo of the phrase in 4.655: *Glotta* 34 (1954) 157-159.

[82] See Pöschl, pp. 83-85.

[83] Halter, pp. 72-77, subdivides Latinus's speech into no less than nine small segments. In fact it has not nine, but three clear divisions: Latinus accepts the Trojans' pleas and gifts (259-262), makes a warm gesture of reciprocal friendship (263-266), and proposes an additional link between the peoples (267-273).

ments. The alliance is at once accepted, and will be generously realized on the morrow (8.169-171). Before even mentioning it, he gazes at Aeneas and welcomes him with real affection: recalling how, a generation ago, he met Aeneas's father Anchises (then young and handsome enough to bewitch Venus herself) and became his friend (8.154-168). The speech recalls the welcome of Telemachus by Helen and Menelaus (*Od.* 4.137-182), but it is warmer. Evander loved the father as a friend, and now loves the son almost as a son.

In 11.108-119 *bonus Aeneas* himself responds to the pleas of the Latins by giving a justification of his conduct to them and reproaching Latinus and Turnus. This is not only a response: it is itself a persuasion. It is answered by Drances (11.124-131) with flatteries, the most deferential in the entire *Aeneid*—praising Aeneas to the sky and declaring that the Latins will enjoy carrying stones to build his city. Short as it is, this suave response perfectly reflects the character of Drances as we are to see it displayed in the debate of Book Eleven. He employs an oratorical trick by alluding to the actual words of Aeneas: Aeneas's "fata" (11.112) is taken up in "fatalis moles" (11.130). The speech also foreshadows the tactics he is to use at the debate, strongly supporting king Latinus and endeavoring to isolate Turnus: thus, "te . . . Latino / iungemus regi" (11.128-129) is realized in "natam egregio genero . . . / des, pater, et pacem hanc aeterno foedere iungas" (355-356); while the contemptuous "quaerat sibi foedera Turnus" (129) is restated in 371-373 as "scilicet ut Turno contingat regia coniunx, / nos . . . sternamur campis."

Some have believed that Drances—unwarlike, not nobly born, skilled in political maneuver, and a master of both invective and blandishment—was modelled on Cicero. Macrobius (6.2.33) says that "o fama ingens, ingentior armis" (*Aen.* 11.124) is adapted from an epigram in Cicero's *Cato*, the lost eulogy of Cato the younger. Yet the epigram, as he quotes it,

141

is not very close to Vergil's neat antithetical phrasing: *contingebat in eo . . . ut maiora omnia re quam fama uiderentur.* Apart from that, however, Vergil's view of Cicero compels reflection. He treats Cato the younger with respect (*Aen.* 8.670, and cf. 1.148-153, on which see p. 283). He places Cicero's opponent Catiline in hell (8.667-669). But he never mentions the name of Cicero; and, by saying in his comparison of Greek and Roman achievements, "alii . . . / orabunt causas melius" (6.847-849), he withholds tribute to Cicero's eloquence. Fraenkel suggests that Vergil must have admired the harmony and grandeur of Cicero's prose, and that one of his most important advances on the poetic technique of Lucretius and Catullus was to write long complex periods full of hypotaxes—an art which he learned from Cicero.[84] This may well be true. Yet it is difficult not to see, in Vergil's silence, something like hostility to the man and his policies. We know that Vergil's first patron, Asinius Pollio, loathed Cicero: he was *infestissimus famae Ciceronis* (Seneca, *Suas.* 6.14), and his hatred invaded his own history of the civil war, for (says the old rhetor, *Suas.* 6.24) *Ciceronis mortem solus ex omnibus maligne narrat.* As for Augustus himself, when he came on one of his family reading Cicero, the boy was terrified and tried to hide the book; and although the Princeps spoke generously of Cicero ("λόγιος ἀνήρ, ὦ παῖ, λόγιος καὶ φιλόπατρις," Plut. *Cic.* 49.3), nevertheless the boy expected a rebuke and evidently believed Augustus to be inimical to Cicero even after death.[85]

One scholar has gone further. This is F. Olivier, in "Virgile et Cicéron," pp. 199-213 of his *Essais* (Lausanne, 1963). On p. 211 he says emphatically, "*Virgile détestait Cicéron.*" He com-

---

[84] "Vergil und Cicero," *Atti e Memorie della r. Accademia Virgiliana di Mantova* 19 (1926) 217-227; and see Norden, *Aeneis VI*, Anhang II.

[85] Horace also, although in *Serm.* 2.1 he addresses Cicero's friend Gaius Trebatius Testa in terms of respect, never mentions the name of Cicero throughout his poems.

pares Vergil's account of Drances' parentage (*Aen.* 11.340-341)—

> genus huic materna superbum
> nobilitas dabat, incertum de patre ferebat

—with Plutarch's description (*Cic.* 1.1) of Cicero's: his mother Helvia nobly born, περὶ δὲ τοῦ πατρὸς οὐδὲν ἦν πυθέςθαι μέτριον, some associating him with a fuller's shop, others tracing his family back to a Volscian king. Cicero was indeed despised as a *nouus homo*: the invective of Q. Fufius Calenus in Dio 46.1-28 (which evidently contains contemporary material) attacks his birth and upbringing as ignoble. From the same invective (Dio 46.18.6) Olivier extracts the charge that Cicero committed incest with his daughter. Then he points to one notable sinner punished in hell (*Aen.* 6.623) who

> thalamum inuasit natae uetitosque hymenaeos.

This might have been merely a generalization like the earlier groups of malefactors in lines 608-614 (says Olivier), were it not that it is placed next to the characterization of Mark Antony, who

> fixit leges pretio atque refixit.

The charge of incest which Cicero himself levelled at Catiline (*Oratio in toga candida*, frg. 20 Puccioni; see also Plutarch, *Cic.* 10.2) and at one of his minor victims (*Clu.* 199, cf. *Or.* 107) was turned against him by his enemies while he lived, and, Olivier suggests, by Vergil after his death. It is not easy to accept this repulsive suggestion. Yet it is true that Vergil does damn Mark Antony (and perhaps Curio) in the same paragraph. Furthermore, the sin of incest with a daughter seems a weak conclusion to the long list of crimes punished by eternal damnation, a list which begins with the storming of heaven by the Titans and the blasphemy of a king against

Jupiter—weak, unless it has some particular application which would give it more weight. Vergil wrote on many different levels of meaning.

The reply of Neptune to Venus's plea on behalf of Aeneas (5.800-815) is, as befits a senior divinity, proud. He reminds her that she is a comparative newcomer to Olympus, and was in fact born in his own dominions (800-801), and that he himself—in spite of his grudge against Troy—once saved Aeneas in a dangerous duel with Achilles, when Venus herself did not intervene (5.803-811 ≈ *Il.* 20.75-339). Then, granting her request, he nevertheless takes one Trojan life as a sacrifice to his power.

The biggest speech made by Ascanius is his enthusiastic reply (9.257-280) to Nisus' proposal for a nocturnal mission to Aeneas. Simple though it is, it reveals his character. The first six lines (257-262) with their emphatic oath show that, although mature beyond his years (311), he is still dependent upon his father (257). He swears by the Penates, to whom Aeneas is devoted,

> Assaracique larem et canae penetralia Vestae
>
> (9.259)

—a line which, with the substitution of "Pergameumque" for "Assaracique," echoes an act of worship performed by Aeneas after a vision of *his* father (5.744). Next he promises the two scouts their rewards. Because he is young, the rewards are extravagant. He offers, at once, two silver cups and a pair of tripods and two talents of gold and a wine-bowl. Further, he vows that, if and when the Trojans are victorious, he and his father will give the scouts Turnus's war-horse, shield, and helmet, twelve male and female prisoners (the men with their weapons), and the royal domain of king Latinus. For a similar mission in the *Iliad* (10.204-217) Nestor promises that a volun-

144

teer shall receive a ewe and a lamb from each captain, together with invitations to banquets. The lavish gifts offered by Ascanius rather resemble the presents tendered to Achilles by Agamemnon through the embassy (*Il.* 9.121-130). Finally, Ascanius turns to Euryalus with a special pledge of personal affection (275-280); when Euryalus requests that his mother be cared for, Ascanius vows she will be treated like his own mother Creusa (9.297, 302).

The final utterance of a major divinity in the *Aeneid* comes from Jupiter (12.830-840). It is couched in the form of a prophecy, with a number of oracular future tenses, and it corresponds to Jupiter's initial prophecy to Venus;[86] but in effect it is also a response to Juno's persuasion. Beginning with an allusion to her indomitable Saturnian nature,[87] Jove goes on to say that she has won her long struggle. He is beaten. He surrenders, saying with a smile "me uictusque uolensque remitto." This is a concession unexpected enough from the Roman Jupiter, and impossible for the Zeus of the *Iliad*, who vaunts his own invincibility, and silences Hera with a fierce snub, telling her to go to hell (*Il.* 8.444-483). Juno is victorious. "We have heard from Jupiter's lips how the union of the two peoples will take shape," says Heinze (p. 437); but it will be an unequal union, made on terms laid down by the enemy Juno. The Trojans will cease to exist as Trojans. Their descendants will be loyal worshippers of the goddess who hounded the Trojans to extinction.

---

[86] See p. 98.

[87] There is a discussion of this by C. W. Amerasinghe, "Saturnia Iuno," *G & R* 22 (1953) 61-69. (But he should not say that only Juno and Jupiter were born of Saturn: see *Aen.* 5.799.) See also L. A. MacKay, "Saturnia Iuno," *G & R* 3 (1956) 59-60, and W. S. Anderson, "Juno and Saturn in the *Aeneid*," *Studies in Philology* 55 (1958) 519-532: an ingenious essay which diagnoses, but does not wholly explain, some contradictions in Vergil's view of Saturn and Saturnian descent. If Vergil believed that Saturn's name was cognate with the root of *satur* (pp. 522-524), why are Juno's passions *insa-*

All these are affirmative replies to persuasion. However, in five important speeches, a plea is rejected. Aeneas and Turnus refuse the opportunity of escaping from death; Jupiter resists both Juno and Cybele; and Dido rebuffs Aeneas.

Only in very few speeches, and those early in the poem, does Aeneas display the turmoil of excitement. Such is his cry of despair at his father's refusal to leave Troy (2.657-670). It expresses the fury of frustration, and shows Aeneas as still unsure of his destiny. His kinsman Hector commanded him to flee, his mother Venus guided him through flames and foes to save his family; but now his father refuses to be rescued. Aeneas is still a fighter; and he can break this impasse only by putting his armor on again and going out to meet death in battle. His desperation appears in the words which evoke the imminent slaughter of Anchises (2.661-663) and his reproach to Venus for leading him to his home, only to see its destruction (2.664-667).[88] Apart from certain prayers directed to several deities, this is the only speech in which Aeneas addresses several different hearers ("genitor," "alma parens," "uiri"): the fact betokens his extreme excitement.

The refusal spoken by Turnus in response to the persuasion of Juturna (12.632-649) is his last long speech. It shows his character gaining stronger and deeper tones as he faces death. Addressing his sister first (632-636), he nobly refrains from reproaching her. Indeed, he expresses sympathy for her sufferings—caused (although Turnus does not know it, 634-635) by

---

tiable (5.608 and 781, 7.298)? If she loves the old peaceful Italy (pp. 520-522), why does she prefer Carthage and fear Italy (*Aen.* 1.12-18)?

[88] The impetuous speech will not pause at the close of line 665, but, with "utque," an unusually light final word, hurries on into the next line. "Hodie" in 670 "non tempus significat, sed iracundam eloquentiam ac stomachum": so Donatus on Ter. *Ad.* 215. "Numquam hodie" is an emphatic negative in Naevius, *Equus Troianus*, Pl. *Pers.* 219, Hor. *Serm.* 2.7.21, Verg. *Buc.* 3.49. See J. B. Hofmann, *Lateinische Umgangssprache* (Heidelberg, 1951[8]), §47, pp. 41-42.

Juno's intervention. Then his speech moves into a soliloquy on the inevitability of death.[89] The questions in 637-646 are addressed more to himself than to the listening Juturna.[90] It is as though, aware of his doom, he were withdrawing into himself; at last he turns away from the world of life and prays that the spirits of the dead may welcome him (646-649), saying

> sancta ad uos anima atque istius inscia culpae
> descendam magnorum haud umquam indignus auorum.

The metrical irregularity of this is one of Vergil's most daring experiments. Although nominative, "anima" must be spoken with a long final *A*, which suggests a heavy sigh and a long pause at the caesura. The line ends with three final words each occupying one foot, to show decision and emphasis.[91] The soul of Turnus is a stranger to cowardice, "ístius ínscia cúlpae." The echo in the last line, "magnorum . . . auorum," is like a groan of resignation.

To a provocative speech by Jupiter, Juno replies with a brief persuasion (10.611-620) containing the same $c\chi\tilde{\eta}\mu a$ as that which Venus used at the council of the gods (10.42-53; see p. 66). "Let Turnus perish," she says submissively, "since you will it so." Jupiter responds (10.622-627) by permitting her to rescue her champion for the time being, but rejects the implied persuasion by warning her—in an angry final phrase containing two emphatic *P*'s and five sibilants—to go no further. "*Spes pascis inanis*" reduces Juno to tears.

Jupiter speaks more graciously to his mother Cybele in rejecting her request (9.83-92) that Aeneas's ships, built from

[89] When Nero asked the praetorian guard to join him in fleeing from Rome, one called out "Vsque adeone mori miserum est?" (Suet. *Nero* 47.2).

[90] The peculiar word-order in "uidi oculos ante ipse meos" conveys extreme energy and emphasis. It combines what Marouzeau calls the "interposition" of "ante" (*Les Articulations*, pp. 57-63) and an unusual position for "ipse," which Norden (*Aeneis VI*, p. 227) considers a Hellenism.

[91] See p. 71.

147

the trees of her sacred grove, should be permitted to sail the seas unendangered by storm or other perils. In reply (94-103) he tells her that such immunity is impossible for any god to grant, but compensates for his refusal by promising that those ships which reach harbor in Italy shall be transformed into sea-goddesses. This speech marks another of the essential differences between Vergil's gods and those of Homer. It is difficult to think of the Iliadic Zeus as acknowledging any limitations whatever on his power; while in the *Odyssey* (3.231) Athena says

$$\dot{\rho}\epsilon\hat{\iota}\alpha\ \theta\epsilon\dot{o}c\ \gamma'\ \dot{\epsilon}\theta\dot{\epsilon}\lambda\omega\nu\ \kappa\alpha\grave{\iota}\ \tau\eta\lambda\dot{o}\theta\epsilon\nu\ \ddot{\alpha}\nu\delta\rho\alpha\ c\alpha\dot{\omega}c\alpha\iota.$$

When examined more closely the idea is a little artificial. If not Jupiter, then surely Neptune possessed the power to guarantee safety from sea-perils to any ships he favored. And Donatus is exaggerating when he says that Cybele asks "ut nauibus decernatur *aeternitas*"; Jupiter exaggerates too:

> mortaline manu factae *immortale* carinae
> *fas* habeant?

By far the most violent of all replies to persuasion in the *Aeneid* is Dido's rejection of Aeneas's self-defense in 4.365-387. It is a spontaneous outbreak of passionate rage. Indeed, it contains several self-contradictions which show that she is too angry to think coherently. She appeals to the justice of the gods (371-372, 382) and yet ridicules Aeneas's claim to be guided by Apollo and Mercury. Immediately after refuting him, she declares "neque dicta refello" (380). Unprompted and even incoherent as it may seem, the speech is carefully worked and full of psychical truth.

The opening sentence contains the double insult of bastardy (like that of Priam to Pyrrhus in 2.540) and treachery. Still, it carries an overtone of love remembered, in an echo of Vergil's

148

own poetry. Traitor, cries Dido, you are not the son of Venus and the Trojan,

> sed *duris* genuit te *cautibus* horrens
> Caucasus, Hyrcanaeque admorunt ubera tigres.

So in one of Vergil's love-poems the despairing Damon says (*Buc.* 8.43-45):

> nunc scio quid sit Amor: *duris* in *cotibus*[92] illum
> aut Tmaros aut Rhodope aut extremi Garamantes
> nec generis nostri puerum nec sanguinis edunt.

The allusion is explicit, and carries a double meaning. Damon cries that Love is not a being with a sympathetic human heart, but a strange creature born among savages in a savage clime. By making Dido echo Damon's words Vergil shows that, for her, Aeneas is still love personified, but marked by all Love's power and cruelty.

After this double-edged insult Dido turns away from Aeneas

---

[92] Note the change from *cotibus* in pastoral to *cautibus* in epic. The medial vowel-sound –o– in such words was felt to be more countrified and plebeian than –au–: thus the rabble-rousing tribune changed his name from the aristocratic Claudius to the "popular" Clodius. Propertius writes *cotibus* in 1.3.4, but the more refined Tibullus has *cautes* in 2.4.9. See W. S. Allen, *Vox Latina* (Cambridge, 1965) pp. 60-61; R. G. Kent, *The Sounds of Latin* (Baltimore, 1945³) para. 41; and J. Marouzeau, *Stylistique*, pp. 5-6. Elegant as it may sound, *cautes* is artificial. M. Leumann, in "Die lateinische Dichtersprache" (*Kleine Schriften*, Zurich, 1959) p. 142 n. 2, says: "*cotes* 'Felsenriffe' bietet die Überlieferung Enn. ann. 421 *de co(n)tibus celsis*, Cic. Tusc. 4, 33, Caes. Gall. 3, 13, 9 β (*cautes* α), Verg. ecl. ge. Prop. Curt. (4 Stellen); sonst stet seit Vergils Aeneis nur die Form *cautes*. Wenn man in *cotes* 'Riffe' eine übertragene Verwendung von *cos cotis* 'Wetzstein' anerkennt, so ist *cautes* als hyperurbane Form zum poetischen Wort geworden. Man fragt sich freilich, wie Vergil dazu kam, von *cotes* zu *cautes* überzugehen." But the same change was adopted by Tibullus, who died before the *Aeneid* was published. Evidently it was part of a general trend, which continued for some time. Thus Vespasian was criticized by a man called Florus for pronouncing *plaustra* as *plostra*; next day he greeted the man as Flaurus (Suet. *D. Vesp.* 22).

and speaks of him as though he were absent—or as though he were an accused man being denounced to a listening audience. From line 369 to the beginning of line 380 Aeneas is not "you" but "he." The body of the speech (368-380) is composed of three reproaches. The first (368-370) is aimed at Aeneas's enforced coldness of demeanor: "num lumina flexit?" ≈ *immota tenebat / lumina* (331-332). The second (371-375) accuses him of thanklessness. In spite of his expression of gratitude in 333-336, Dido now details and exaggerates what she only hinted at in "si bene quid de te merui" (317). She hurls back at him a thought voiced in his very first speech to her. Then (1.598-600) he said

> nos, reliquias Danaum, terraeque marisque
> omnibus exhaustos iam casibus, omnium *egenos,*
> *urbe domo socias.*

Now she retorts

> eiectum litore, *egentem*
> excepi et *regni* demens *in parte locaui.*

Thirdly, she rejects with contempt his central plea, the command of heaven. At this point she is in a cold frenzy of rage: frenzied, she says herself ("heu furiis incensa feror!" 376), but cold, because she retains her intellectual control. Although its structure is unobtrusive, this is a finely constructed dramatic harangue. The passage in which Dido turns away from Aeneas to denounce him contains three main sections, each following the same pattern: an indignant, exclamation or exclamatory question, followed by an expanding tricolon,[93] thus (368-370):

> nam quid dissimulo aut quae me ad maiora reseruo?

leading into

---

[93] On this figure see E. Lindholm, *Stilistische Studien. Zur Erweiterung der Satzglieder im Lateinischen* (Lund, 1931).

num fletu ingemuit nostro? num lumina flexit?
num lacrimas uictus dedit aut miseratus amantem est?

Next, after an appeal to heaven, Dido cries (373-375):

nusquam tuta fides!

followed by "eiectum . . . excepi, regni . . . locaui, amissam
classem . . . reduxi." And then, even more passionately,

heu furiis incensa feror!

moving into "nunc . . . nunc . . . nunc . . . per auras."[94]
To add force to her rejection of Aeneas's argument Dido
quotes his own words. "Nunc . . . nunc . . . nunc . . ." (376-
377) answers and hammers down his "sed nunc . . . nunc
etiam" (345, 356). Her "augur Apollo" (376) is a variant of
his "Gryneus Apollo" (345).[95] "Lyciae sortes" (377) is his
phrase (346) in a different rhythmical shape; and his "interpres
diuum Ioue missus ab ipso / . . . celeris mandata per auras /
detulit" (356-358) she repeats in a disparate rhythm (377-378):

Ioue missus ab ipso
interpres diuum fert horrida iussa per auras.[96]

This phrase is the third in a remarkable series of echoes. In
4.226 Jupiter commands Mercury: "celeris defer mea dicta per

[94] This analysis is made by O. Maar, *Pathos und Pathosrede in dem Dido-
buch von Vergils Aeneis* (Vienna, 1953, microfilm) p. 147. According to it,
"heu furiis incensa feror!" begins a new section (as in Sabbadini's text) and
ought not to be placed between parentheses and tacked on to the previous
utterance (as in Mynors' edition).

[95] "Augur Apollo" and "augur . . . Phoebus" are dignified and worshipful
in Hor. *Carm.* 1.2.32 and *Carm. Saec.* 61-62. Yet it is difficult to think that
Dido is speaking respectfully in calling Apollo an augur. The only other
persons to whom the word "augur" is applied in the *Aeneid* are dishonor-
able enemies—Rhamnes, killed when drunk (9.324-328) and Tolumnius, who
starts the fight at the oath-taking and is killed (12.258-269 + 460-461).

[96] Surely the jingles of sound and rhythm are meant to be scornful: "augur
Apollo," "missus ab ipso"; "missus ab ipso," "iussa per auras."

auras." Mercury in addressing Aeneas (4.270) makes this more respectful: "ipse haec ferre iubet celeris mandata per auras." Then, to Dido, Aeneas quotes Mercury's words (4.357-358): "celeris mandata per auras / detulit." In reply, Dido distorts them with a harsh adjective (4.378): "fert horrida iussa per auras." Even Aeneas's proud "Italiam" followed by "quaerere regna" (345 + 350) is challenged by her in line 381:

i, sequere *Italiam* uentis, *pete regna* per undas!

The notion that the gods send messages to mankind, she rejects in a sentence which curiously blends Epicurean belief in the untroubled serenity of the divine beings with a fury that spits like Medea:[97]

*s*cilicet i*s s*uperi*s* labor e*s*t, ea cura quieto*s s*ollicitat.

This heavy alliteration on *S* (cf. Juno in 10.94-95) carries on from line 379 almost to the close of the speech: "sequere," "spero," "supplicia," "scopulis," "saepe," "sequar," "seduxerit." Dido concludes her denunciation with an abrupt dismissal (381) and a string of curses (382-387) emphasized by a succession of verbs standing emphatically at the beginning of their clauses: "i," "sequere," "pete," "spero," "sequar," "dabis," "audiam."[98] The power of her love, which she still feels intensely, is transformed into the desire for vengeance and the awareness of approaching death.

---

[97] Soubiran (cited on p. 133) points out metrical anomalies which show Dido's agitation. The dactylic second foot composed of a single word, "frigida" (385), occurs only eleven times in all Vergil's work, thrice in the speeches of Dido. The elision of the final *-am* in the cretic "audiam" before a short initial vowel (4.387) is also rare, and occurs in passages describing great excitement: so Anna in 4.684 and Aeneas in 12.569. Alliteration on sibilants in Euripides' *Medea* 476-477.

[98] J. Marouzeau, *L'Ordre des mots* II, *Le Verbe* (Paris, 1938) stresses on pp. 49-82 the fact that to place the verb at the beginning of the sentence in Latin is exceptional and strongly emphatic. He gives many examples, but few if any in which the effect is repeated so often as in this passage.

Apostrophes

Some of the most moving speeches in the *Aeneid* are imme-
diate utterances of pure emotion. Among them are apostrophes
addressed to the dying or the dead.[99]

In the ninth book young Euryalus is killed, leaving behind
the widowed mother who has followed him lovingly for years.
His head is stuck on a spear and carried past the Trojan fort.
Seeing it, she shrieks: her shrieks can be heard in the unusual
rhythm and vowel-spread of *femineo ululatu*, in which the
hiatus comes like a gasp of agony.[100] Then she breaks into a
tirade of grief and despair (9.481-497). This is far less re-
strained and far closer to insanity than its chief extant model,
the lament of Andromache after seeing Hector's body dragged
behind his slayer's chariot (*Il.* 22.477-514). Partly this is be-
cause the situations are different. Andromache has heard
Hecuba's cries of horror: she has a premonition of her hus-
band's death. But the old mother of Euryalus has not even
known that her son has been risking his life outside the walls
(9.287-289), far less that he has been killed and mutilated,
until the moment when she sees his head upon the spear.
Therefore her speech is hysterical with shock, it contains far
more exclamations and exclamatory questions than that of
Andromache, and—instead of dying away into pathos like
Andromache's—it rises to a peak of frenzy at the end, so that
she has to be carried away screaming. Her speech is one of
complete despair and suicidal misery. Andromache is far more
rational. Indeed, more than half of her speech is taken up with
a description of the future unhappiness of her son Astyanax
as an orphan friendless and outcast. Even this, although pa-
thetic, seems a little forced: for if Troy had not fallen (*Il.*

---

[99] For a list, see Appendix 2.

[100] Vergil does this plangent sound-effect once elsewhere, to evoke the
shrieks of the Carthaginian women at the suicide of their queen (4.667). It
is hard to believe that Marouzeau (*Stylistique*, p. 41) describes it adequately
by saying "[Virgile] *s'amuse* . . . à faire dans le pied pénultième un hiatus."

153

22.487) Astyanax would still have been the grandson of the king and one of the royal family. It is not easy to imagine him begging for scraps from Hector's friends and being pushed away from the table by another boy (491-498).

The outcry of Euryalus's mother also contains reminiscences of the speeches Hecuba makes to Hector before and after he is slain (*Il.* 22.82-89, 431-436). Her question "potuisti relinquere solam?" (*Aen.* 9.482) may reflect Hecuba's τί νυ βείομαι / cεῦ ἀποτεθνηῶτοc; (*Il.* 22.431-432). Her harsh reproach, "crudelis" (9.483), is like Hecuba's cχέτλιοc (*Il.* 22.86); and her incessant care for him "noctes . . . diesque" (9.488) echoes Hecuba's νύκταc τε καὶ ἦμαρ. Hecuba also complains that she will be unable to mourn her son on his bier (*Il.* 22.86-87); the mother of Euryalus says that she could not close his eyes or wash his wounds (*Aen.* 9.486-487). But there is a closer model than Hecuba. This is the lament of Electra over the supposed ashes of Orestes in Soph. *El.* 1126-1170: Electra grieves that she was prevented from washing the dear corpse and giving it the last rites (*El.* 1138-1140 ≈ *Aen.* 9.486-489).[101] She speaks of the little heap of dust which alone remains of Orestes, as Euryalus's mother of the pitiful head (*El.* 1141-1142 ≈ *Aen.* 9.490-492). Finally, like the old Trojan woman, Electra prays for death (*El.* 1165-1170 ≈ *Aen.* 9.493-497).

Although vehement, the speech is not incoherent. Indeed, it might almost be a consolation reversed. In a consolation, the speaker praises the dead and speaks of comfort and hope for the living. Here the bereaved mother reproaches the dead son (*Aen.* 9.481-492) and implores death for herself (493-497). In this her words reach a painful climax. While reading speeches in the *Aeneid* we should do well to remember that the poet

---

[101] There is also an echo (brought out by Macrobius, 6.2.21) of Ennius's Meropa when told that her son has been killed in a strange land: lines 9.486-487 resemble Ennius, *Cresphontes* frg. VIII:

neque terram iniicere neque cruenta conuestire corpora
mihi licuit neque miserae lauere lacrimis salsum sanguinem.

(There are minor textual variants.)

154

means us to visualize and to hear the actions and sounds accompanying them. Thus Neptune's famous aposiopesis in 1.135 is not simply an unfinished sentence interrupted by an intrusive thought. At "quos ego—!" we are intended to see him (in a pose well known from sculpture) raising his mighty trident over his recreant subjects' heads. Next instant he would bring it down upon them, but that he remembers the storm is still raging. So here, the old woman first stretches out her hands towards all that remains of her son, his gory head ("hoc . . . hoc," 491-492). Then she points to her own breast and cries to the Rutulians to pierce her with their spears ("figite me!"). Lastly, turning her face up to the sky, she prays to Jupiter to strike her dead with his thunderbolt. Her screams as she is carried away mingle with the sobs of the crowd (500-502), but are instantly followed by the blast of the trumpet, and that again by the shout of battle (503-504).

The apostrophes of Aeneas and Evander to the dead Pallas (11.42-58 and 11.152-181) are more controlled, although not less sorrowful. Both praise the dead youth for his courage. Aeneas voices his pity for Pallas (42-48) and for his father (49-55), closing with regret for a lost future: the young man would have been an elder brother for Ascanius after Aeneas's own death. As he concludes, Aeneas is under the pressure of deep emotion. The ejaculation "ei mihi!" he has used only once before: when he recalled his dreadful vision of Hector's ghost (2.274).[102] And the rhythm of line 57—

optabis nato funus pater. ei mihi, quantum

—reflects his anguish.[103] Here we should imagine Aeneas weeping bitterly.

---

[102] Turnus will use it in 12.620 when he hears the noise of disaster from the city of Latinus.

[103] See R. Lucot, "Ponctuation bucolique, accent et émotion dans l' 'Enéide,' " *REL* 43 (1965) 261-274, who shows that the bucolic diaeresis, when followed by the unusual line-ending $-/\smile\ \smile/--$, expresses emotional

Evander begins with a reproach to his son (152-158) but in milder terms than the mother of Euryalus. After speaking of his own misery (158-163) he absolves Aeneas of responsibility for the death, consoles himself by reflecting on the glory won by Pallas, and ends with a call for vengeance on Turnus (175-181)—a call which foreshadows the end of Book Twelve, "Pallas te immolat."[104]

Two briefer apostrophes, spoken by Anna to Dido (4.675-685) and by Mezentius to Lausus (10.846-856) similarly open with reproaches. Anna rebukes her dying sister for deceiving her instead of inviting her to share the same fate. Then she cries (4.680-681)

> his etiam struxi manibus patriosque uocaui
> uoce deos, sic te ut posita crudelis abessem?

Does "crudelis" refer to Anna herself, or to Dido? Some scholars believe she is blaming herself: they cite Silius Italicus, who imitates the passage in *Pun.* 13.655-657, "cur / ulla fuere adeo quibus a te *saeuus* abessem / momenta?" But consider that all the other sentences are reproaches to Dido, culminating in "extinxti te meque . . . urbemque tuam"; that it is more pathetic for Anna to express her grief in a continuous complaint than to stop for a moment and blame herself instead; and that in a similar apostrophe the mother of Euryalus uses the same word, "crudelis," to address her dead son: the conclusion is clear.

Mezentius, on the other hand, bitterly reproaches himself and himself alone, with the harsh antithesis, "morte tua uiuens." Both speeches end—as do those of Evander and

---

stress. So again, Aeneas to his mother in 1.328, Dido captivated by Aeneas in 4.13, Jupiter in anger at 10.9.

[104] Heinze (p. 425) detects another arrangement of ideas: Evander thinks first of the past, then of the present, next of the future, and last of a prospective consolation. This sequence is one of the schemes of an *ethopoeia* (see p. 137): it may be present here, but it is less natural than the movement of thought from one person to another.

Euryalus's mother—by foreshadowing the speaker's imminent death.

Apostrophizing her doomed brother beset by the Fury, Juturna in 12.871 makes the same gestures of grief as Anna in 4.673; they are described in the same words:

> unguibus ora soror foedans et pectora pugnis.

She complains of her helplessness, which is voiced in ten unanswerable questions. She does not, however, rebuke Turnus or herself. Instead, she reproaches Jupiter (12.878-880) for giving her immortal life in exchange for her virginity—an immortal life which will now, after the death of her brother, be a hell to which death is far preferable (880-884). She complains that she recognizes "iussa superba / magnanimi Iouis" (877-878). The adjective is applied only once more to Jupiter in the *Aeneid*, and then it occurs in the same context, in the same case, and in the same position in the line. Juno (12.143-144) says she prefers Juturna to all

> quaecumque Latinae
> magnanimi Iouis ingratum ascendere cubile.

Juno's sneering "magnanimi" is now repeated by Juturna; and with her question to Jove "haec pro uirginitate reponit?" she recalls Juno's biting phrase "*ingratum* cubile." Her last words, a prayer for death, resemble her brother's invocation to the Manes (12.646-649) and echo his cry to the earth to open and swallow him up (10.675-676).

Soliloquies

The complex human soul often speaks to itself. In monologues the poet's knowledge of character and his power to convey the intricacies of thought and emotion have their fullest scope.

Few as they are, the soliloquies of the *Aeneid* are among Vergil's most striking contributions to epic poetry. There is

157

nothing quite like them in the *Iliad* and the *Odyssey*: no monologue which displays such intense emotion ranging so widely.[105] His inspirations for them came, in part, from Euripidean tragedy; from Hellenistic poetry (there are some fine soliloquies in Apollonius); and from the poetry of Catullus and his friends.[106]

They are more full of violent and sustained emotion than those in the Homeric poems, which—although they often begin with a rueful exclamation, ὤ μοι or ὤ πόποι—often contain a logical appraisal of a difficult situation, weighing various courses of action against one another: e.g. *Od.* 5.356-364, 408-423, 465-473. In particular, Vergil completely eschews one of Homer's favorite themes in monologue: the debate of a hero with himself whether he should face the foe or take to flight (e.g. Agenor in *Il.* 21.553-570). Turnus has no doubt that he must and will fight Aeneas (*Aen.* 12.632-649), and of course Aeneas himself never falters after battle has been joined. Vergil knew that Rome had been built by inflexible will-power, and he can scarcely have admired the passage in the *Iliad* where Hector, in a long and thoughtful monologue (22.99-130) considers whether he should flee from Achilles or perhaps treat with him, determines steadfastly to fight, and then (22.136-144), before even striking a blow, runs away. When in a similar situation Turnus takes to flight, it is after a fierce duel during which his sword has broken in his hand (12.710-741), and he does not utter a word.

Vergil's soliloquies are more complicated than those of Homer. They contain more psychical material, and their point of view shifts more often. Thus, Menelaus in *Il.* 17.91-105 con-

---

[105] See Heinze (pp. 427-430) on *Monolog*, with some valuable comparisons between Vergil's monologues and the soliloquies in Homer.

[106] Heinze, p. 429 n. 1, suggested that Vergil also drew from post-Euripidean tragedy, a suggestion which he repeated in *Ovids elegische Erzählung* (*SB Leipzig* 71, 1919, 7) pp. 123-124; but we have scarcely enough evidence to test the idea.

templates (a) the shame of abandoning Patroclus and the spoils of victory, and (b) the danger of facing the Trojans all alone: so (c) he determines to find Ajax and fight with his support. Compared with this calm internal debate, the monologue of Turnus (*Aen.* 10.668-679) is an outburst of frenzy. It begins with an unjustified accusation against Jupiter, rushes on through eight despairing questions, and closes with a plea to the winds to dash Turnus on the rocks. Again, Poseidon sees Odysseus sailing toward the Phaeacians' land, makes an angry comment on the hero's good fortune, and determines to damage it—all in five lines (*Od.* 5.286-290). But Juno (*Aen.* 1.37-49) sees the Trojans sailing toward Italy, and utters thirteen lines, setting herself to oppose the fates, comparing herself with Pallas Athena, proclaiming her queenly rank, recalling her long conflict with Troy, and ending with the thought that though divine she will lose all her worshippers if this humiliation continues. (Her second monologue in a similar situation, 7.293-322, is even longer, more varied, more wrathful, and more eloquent.)

There are eight soliloquies in the *Aeneid*, some uttered aloud, and some represented as streams of thought unspoken.[107] Aeneas has three, early in the poem: 1.94-101, 2.577-587, and the brief exclamation 1.437, which has the same shape as the opening of the first: "o fortunati!" ≈ "o . . . beati!" There are two (the two just mentioned) attributed to Juno. The first (1.37-49) she thinks, *flammato corde uolutans*. The second (7.293-322), more violent, she speaks with a gesture of rage, *quassans caput*.[108] Dido has three: 4.534-552 is thought

[107] There is a list in Appendix 2. In a useful analysis, "Die Monologe in den Homerischen Epen," *Phil* 63 (1904) 12-30, C. Hentze lists eleven in the *Iliad* and ten in the *Odyssey*. Odysseus utters seven in the *Odyssey* and one in the *Iliad*; Achilles has four, Hector two, Zeus and Poseidon two each, Menelaus, Agenor, and Penelope one each. Their distribution is curious and significant.

[108] It has been suggested that this is the threatening gesture of the head

in her mind; 4.590-629 and her dying words, 4.651-662, are spoken aloud.

All these soliloquies have striking features in common. The speakers are invaded by almost unbearably violent emotion: *flammato corde* (1.50); *soluuntur frigore membra* (1.92); *furiata mente* (2.588); *magno irarum fluctuat aestu* (4.532); *flauentis abscissa comas* (4.590); *effera, furibunda* (4.642, 646); *acri fixa dolore* (7.291). Their emotion breaks out into incredulous questions ("quo feror? unde abii?") or exclamations of anger, envy, despair ("o terque quaterque beati!" "heu stirpem inuisam!"). The impulse of the soliloquy is a realization of frustration and defeat. Sometimes this is expressed in a comparison of the speaker with others. So Juno reflects "Pallasne ... potuit? ... ast ego ..." (1.39-40 + 46) and cries "Mars ... ualuit? ... ast ego ..." (7.304-305 + 308). The speaker may see no possible escape from his predicament, and wish for death or determine on death: so Aeneas in his opening monologue, so Dido in 4.534-552, "en, quid ago? ... quin morere." Or else the speaker may find another way out. Then the monologue ends with a resolution—unspoken, as in Juno's first tirade, or else clearly expressed. Aeneas determines to take vengeance on Helen (2.585-587), Dido utters a prayer for heaven-sent revenge on Aeneas, and a command to her people to pursue the Trojans and their descendants with hatred (4.607-629), and Juno, though thwarted of her main purpose, resolves to destroy both the Trojans and the Latins (7.313-316).

---

like an angry animal about to butt (Hor. *Serm.* 1.5.58-60), but that is too grotesque for the queen of heaven. The gesture is the resentful headshake of Poseidon in a similar context (*Od.* 5.285). C. Sittl, *Die Gebärden der Griechen und Römer* (Leipzig, 1890) p. 83, proposes that its essential meaning is negation—as it surely is in *Aen.* 12.894. "Der Betrübte schüttelt, wie der Ratlose, den Kopf, indem er denkt: 'Ist es möglich, dass es so kam?,' oder er bewegt ihn energischer, um die traurigen Gedanken wegzustossen." He cites Plaut. *Trin.* 1169-1170. In the *Iliad*, however, Zeus shakes his head to express quite a different emotion, pity: *Il.* 17.200 and 442.

Juno

The initial meditation of Juno (1.37-49) expresses her predominant qualities of character: her indomitable will (37-39), her refusal to be outdone by any rival (39-45), and her pride in her queenship and her descent from Saturn (46-49). Vergil sometimes displays an unshakable determination through a steady repetition of rhythmical elements. Here the first four lines of her soliloquy all end with four tetrasyllables and four disyllables, the four tetrasyllables being all present infinitives: "desistere uictam," "auertere regem," "exurere classem," "summergere ponto." Noting the effect of homoeoteleuton, Marouzeau suggests that it is an involuntary error of taste,[109] but in such a highly wrought speech it is surely deliberate. Later Juno describes the doom of Ajax with savage gusto expressed through harsh sound-effects:[110]

> illum exspirantem transfixo pectore flammas
> turbine corripuit scopuloque infixit acuto.

Violent phrasing such as this betrays one of her most persistent characteristics, her love of conflict and destruction for their own sake (cf. 7.620-622 and 12.810-812).[111]

Juno's outburst at the beginning of action in Italy (7.293-322) is far longer and more violent. In the first she said "una cum gente tot annos / bella gero" (1.47-48), but here she cries "infelix . . . / uincor ab Aenea!" (7.309-310).[112] The first was followed by a storm at sea. The second issues in fury, war, and suffering for thousands of people. Not only does this speech show all her accustomed traits accentuated, but it contains a survey of the previous seventeen years, from the attack on Troy

---

[109] *Stylistique*, pp. 51-52.   [110] Ibid., pp. 28-29.

[111] Pöschl (pp. 16-18) is good on the fundamental difference between Juno as the spirit of disorder and Jupiter as the god of order and sanity and justice.

[112] Heinze (p. 182 n. 1). Fraenkel, *Kleine Beiträge* 2.150, emphasizes the parallel structure of the two speeches and the greater intensity of the second.

(294) and its fall (295-297) through the long sea-wanderings (299-303) to the arrival in Italy (303). As soon as she speaks the name of Aeneas, long postponed (310), she moves into a new intensity of rage. Something like snarling can be heard in an exceptionally long line with three elisions of final nasalized *M* (7.310-311):

> quod si mea numina non sunt
> magna satis, dubit*em* haud
> equid*em* implorare quod usqu*am* est.

This is followed by the deadly antithesis which allies her with hell rather than heaven:

> flectere si nequeo superos, Acheronta mouebo.

Accepting a disagreeable inevitability with "esto,"[113] she determines nevertheless to do as much harm as possible. Although she is the deity presiding over marriage, she distorts the words appropriate to a wedding so as to give them a sinister meaning: "gener atque socer" (which, as in 6.830-831, would remind Roman readers of the civil war), "dotabere, uirgo," "pronuba," "iugalis," "taedae." Finally, threatening Lavinia with the doom of Hecuba, she snarls and hisses in a slow spondee-filled line with two *GN*'s[114] and seven sibilants (7.320):

> Ci*ss*ei*s* prae*gn*a*s* i*gn*i*s* eni*x*a iugali*s*.

Sprung from the same emotion, uttered in similar situations, the two soliloquies follow similar patterns. First, an angry realization of defeat (1.37-38, 7.293-297). Next, a comment on

---

113 "Esto" is a favorite word of Juno, who uses it in three powerful speeches: here (7.313), counter-attacking Venus (10.67), and persuading Jupiter (12.821). The only other speaker to use it is Anna (4.35).

114 *GN* was not pronounced *G-N*, but with a velar nasal sound "like the *ngn* of hangnail" (Allen, p. 23, cited above, n. 92). The Romans felt the sound to be hard and disagreeable: *syllabae, ut ait Varro, aliae sunt . . . durae, ut ignotus* (Diomedes, *Ars Gramm.* 2, Keil I p. 428).

the cause and character of the defeat, quite brief in Book One ("quippe uetor fatis," 1.39) but in Book Seven a long reflection on the Trojan will to survive (7.297-304). Then an enthymeme, comparing Juno's own power with that of lesser deities who avenged themselves on defiant warriors (1.39-48, 7.304-310). The first soliloquy ends with a negative question (will anyone now worship me?) which is equivalent to a strong assertion of Juno's resolve to reverse the situation (1.48-49); while the second moves into threats of destruction against all those mortals who have thwarted Juno's will (7.313-322). The monologue of Book Seven is more energetic than that of Book One, because Vergil intended the second half of his epic to be a *maius opus* (7.45).[115] It also marks a change in Juno's attitude to the Trojans and their mission. In Book One, she said with apparent contempt, "quippe uetor fatis" (1.39), as though she did not believe that destiny was a serious obstacle to her. But by the time the Trojans have landed in Italy she has been compelled to admit the power of their fate. Now perforce she will accept the decrees of destiny, but try to delay their fulfillment, and wreak her personal vengeance on those whom they favor (7.310-322). The word "fatis," prominent in 1.39 (before the penthemimeral caesura), reappears in 7.314 even more prominently, centered between the penthemimeral and hephthemimeral caesurae. The essential difference between the two monologues is that the second ends *crescendo*, with a resolution for immediate and far-reaching action.

It has been suggested that the powerful emotion of these monologues of Juno differentiates them from their prototype, the speech of Poseidon on sighting Odysseus (*Od.* 5.286-290), and brings them closer to the prologues spoken by gods in Greek tragedy.[116] Yet if these were in Vergil's mind, he has far outdone them in energy and passion. Contrast these tirades of

---

[115] The idea and its execution are discussed by W. H. Alexander in "*Maius Opus (Aeneid* 7-12)," *Univ. Cal. Pub. Class. Phil.* 14.5 (1951) 193-214.

[116] Heinze, pp. 428-429.

Juno with the calm tone of Hermes (Eur. *Ion* 1-81), or Poseidon (Eur. *Troad.* 1-47), or Aphrodite (Eur. *Hipp.* 1-57), who gives her name, narrates the background of the drama, and ends by introducing the hero to the audience.

Aeneas

There is one remarkable monologue spoken by Aeneas himself and reported by him in his description of the fall of Troy (2.577-587). Sole survivor of the group defending Priam's palace (2.445-468 + 559-566), he sees Helen hiding in the temple of Vesta, to escape the hatred of the Trojans and the anger of the Greeks. She is a fiend, who has brought destruction to both nations, "communis Erinys" (2.573). His rage blazes up. He breaks out into angry self-questioning: shall Helen, after all this fire and slaughter, return home in triumph with the Trojan women as slaves? No! Although it is an inglorious deed to kill a woman, yet it is a just retribution and a sweet revenge. As he rages, his mother Venus appears, calms him, reminds him of his duty to save his family, and shows him that the gods themselves, and not Helen or Paris, are annihilating Troy (2.589-631).

The style of this speech is as powerful and its psychology as cogent as any of the other monologues. It begins—like those of Juno—with the realization that an enemy is about to escape vengeance and survive victorious; it ends, like them, in a resolution to take action. It is the most violent speech that Aeneas makes throughout the epic, closer to madness than his cry of despair in 1.94-101 and wilder than the cruelty of 12.565-573 and 12.947-949. Aeneas himself acknowledges this: "exarsere ignes animo" (2.575), "furiata mente ferebar" (2.588). It is his moment of utmost desperation. After a resistance of ten years Troy has fallen; he has seen Priam butchered on the household altar; he is alone in the blazing ruins. It is a speech worthy of the moment.

Nevertheless, it is not in any of the early manuscripts of the

164

poem. The text of the *Aeneid*, as it has come down in them, runs straight through without a gap from 2.565-566, describing the mass suicide of the defenders of the palace, to 2.589, the epiphany of Venus. But Servius, in his biography of Vergil preceding his commentary, quotes 567-588, states that they "are known to have been removed," and discusses them on the same footing as the four lines preceding *Arma uirumque cano*, ascribing the deletion of both passages to Tucca and Varius, who edited the poem after Vergil's death. Later, on "ignibus aegra dedere" (2.566), Servius auctus says quite clearly, with no "ferunt" or other qualification, "post hunc uersum hi uersus fuerunt qui a Tucca et Vario obliti sunt," and proceeds to quote them in full—but not to comment on them, which suggests that they had not been part of the traditional text and had not received an accretion of scholia.[117]

Recently, however, R. T. Bruère has given reasons for believing that they were known within their context during the first century A.D.[118] Lucan often imitated and tried to outdo important scenes in Vergil. When he was writing the tenth book of his *Civil War*, about Julius Caesar's sojourn in Egypt, he not only compared Cleopatra with Helen of Troy but adapted a number of striking phrases from this speech. Aeneas calls Helen "Troiae et patriae communis Erinys" (*Aen.* 2.573); Lucan also links the rival powers, calling Cleopatra "dedecus Aegypti, Latii feralis Erinys" (*B.C.* 10.59). Is Helen (asks Aeneas in *Aen.* 2.577-578) to return home safely?

> partoque ibit regina triumpho?

[117] H. T. Rowell conjectures that Servius lifted both the discussion and the lines from the Vergilian commentary of Donatus: see his "The Ancient Evidence of the Helen Episode in *Aeneid* II," *The Classical Tradition* (ed. L. Wallach, Ithaca, N.Y., 1966) pp. 210-221. A number of discoveries of almost-forgotten Latin poetry were made in the fourth century (see P. Wessner, "Lucan, Statius und Juvenal bei den römischen Grammatikern," *PhW* 49 [1929] 296-303 + 328-335) and it is possible that Donatus disinterred both these lines and the putative proem, *Ille ego*.

[118] "The Helen Episode in *Aeneid* 2 and Lucan," *CP* 59 (1964) 267-268.

In *B.C.* 10.65 Lucan speaks of Cleopatra as victorious over Rome,

Caesare captiuo Pharios ductura triumphos.

Such agreements of word, rhythm, and meaning are too striking to be accidental.[119] Lucan evidently knew the monologue of Aeneas. Later in Book Ten he made further adaptations not only from it but from its immediate context. When Caesar is besieged in the Ptolemies' palace, he hides in its recesses (*B.C.* 10.458-460)

ceu . . . captis femina muris,
quaerit tuta domus, spem uitae in limine clauso
ponit et incerto lustrat uagus atria cursu.

Here Caesar is like Helen when Aeneas catches sight of her (*Aen.* 2.567-568)

limina Vestae
seruantem et tacitam secreta in sede latentem.

But he also recalls another fugitive within doomed Troy, Priam's son Polites, who in flight from Pyrrhus (*Aen.* 2.528)

porticibus longis fugit et uacua atria lustrat.

And Caesar is determined, even if defeated, to avenge himself by killing young Ptolemy, as Aeneas determines to avenge the defeat of Troy by killing Helen. Aeneas cries "sumpsisse merentis / laudabor poenas" (*Aen.* 2.585-586); and Caesar takes the child-king everywhere with him (*B.C.* 10.462)

sumpturus poenas et grata piacula morti.

Therefore in the first century A.D. the passage was believed, by a good poet and a keen student of Vergil, to be by Vergil; and in the fourth it was believed by scholars to have been written by Vergil and excised by his editors. This indicates

---

[119] Bruère also compares *Aen.* 2.577-580 and *B.C.* 10.60-61.

that Vergil wrote the lines, and somehow showed in his manu-
script that he was not satisfied with them and had not defi-
nitely made them a part of the poem.

In the received text of the *Aeneid* several passages are still
obviously provisional, incomplete, or incongruous. Such is *Aen.*
8.268-272, where the sequence of time and logic between lines
267 and 273 is broken. Such is 10.721-729, where at least one
stage in the simile is omitted, and one line is no more than a
fragment.[120] There are a number of unfinished sections: for
instance, the final deliverance of the Trojans from the siege
deserves more than eleven words (10.604-605), and surely there
is a gap in time and action between 8.85 and 8.86.

In the tenth book a battle episode (328-344) is unfinished.
Aeneas is confronted by a group of seven brothers, the sons of
Phorcus. They throw seven spears at him, some of which are
deflected by his helmet and shield, others by Venus. The hero
calls on Achates to supply him with spears. He kills one
brother. He maims a second. A third hurls a spear back at
him, misses, and grazes Achates' thigh—and there, at 10.344,
the sequence breaks off. It seems clear that Vergil intended
Aeneas to be stirred to hotter battle-rage by the wound in-
flicted on his squire, to kill this third brother, and then to dis-
pose of the rest: each, no doubt, in a different way, as Clausus
kills two groups of three brothers *per uarios casus* (10.350-352);
but he did not complete the passage. Certainly it should not
end, as it does, with a minor defeat imposed on the Trojan
side. It was suggested by an incident in the Patrocleia in which
two sons of Nestor kill two Lycian brothers (*Il.* 16.317-329).
But, as often, Vergil wished to outdo Homer.[121] In the *Iliad*

---

[120] *Conspexit, gaudet hians, comas arrexit* are all preliminary to the leap
of the lion, which is omitted, although the leap (= *sic ruit*) is the key of
the simile. The word *haeret* describes a stage *after* the leap, when he has
struck down his prey and (in a pose familiar from the plastic arts) crouches
upon it to devour it.

[121] In Homer the stone hurled by Hector could hardly be lifted onto a

two Greeks kill two brothers who are their foes: so Aeneas alone must kill seven brothers fighting against him.

More gaps and inconsistencies and divergences from the developing scheme of the *Aeneid* exist within the poem than any modern reader can detect. All that we are told of Vergil's method of composing and revising confirms what we see throughout the epic, and makes it likely that the passage containing Aeneas's monologue is his work—although incomplete, and discarded by himself as unsuitable to the advancing plan of the poem. Some scholars have accepted it; others have rejected it without question. Sabbadini ad loc. says succinctly "Hos versus vere Vergilianos puto, a poeta ipso deletos, qui morte impeditus est quominus alios in eorum locum sufficeret." Heinze (pp. 45-51) declares that there is not the slightest doubt that they are not by Vergil, but that they fill a gap Vergil left in the poem. There was, he thinks, a passage in which Vergil described Aeneas, shaken by witnessing the death of Priam, deciding either to kill himself, or (more probably) to seek death by attacking Pyrrhus and the triumphant Greeks; and Vergil excised this because it merely repeated, without intensifying, the emotions of lines 316-317. Norden (*Aeneis VI*, pp. 261-262 and 454.3) also describes them as an interpolation, dismissing as ignoramuses those who try to defend them: sad fate of philology, he reflects, that such problems provide "einen Tummelplatz für Dilettanten." R. G. Austin has examined the question in a sane and thorough article, "Virgil, *Aeneid* 2.567-88," *CQ* 11 (1961) 185-198, with a copious bibliography, and again in his edition of *Aeneid* 2 (Oxford, 1964) pp. 217-228, and gives what seem to me sound reasons for accepting the lines as genuinely Vergilian—although experimental, although

---

wagon by *two* men of the poet's time (*Il.* 12.445-449). Jason in the *Argonautica* (3.1365-1367) casts one which *four* men could not have raised even a little. In Vergil (12.899-900) Turnus throws one which *twelve* picked men could scarcely lift.

imperfect, and although not part of Vergil's scheme of the poem as he left it at his death.

Six destructive criticisms of the passage have been advanced.

First, it is not in the traditional text and is unknown to ancient scholars, apart from Servius (doubtless following Donatus): they never quote from it or discuss it. True; but the statements in Servius offer a reason why this should be so.

Secondly, it is ethically unworthy of Aeneas to think of killing a woman.[122] True; but this is the point of the monologue. It expresses a conflict. Aeneas speaks while he hesitates. He himself says it would be an inglorious deed; but he has just seen the brutal slaughter of an old man, and he is hot for vengeance. In *Odyssey* 22.435-473 Telemachus takes a far crueller and more leisurely, more cold-blooded revenge on helpless women: a passage which Vergil knew well. The murder of Helen is discussed in similar terms by Pylades in Euripides' *Orestes* 1132-1152; and in Euripides' *Helen* (71-77) Teucer no sooner sees Helen than he thinks of killing her. It is unworthy of Aeneas; but at this moment it is credible. But surely he would not kill Helen at an altar after seeing Priam butchered at his household altar? and surely not at the altar of Vesta, the divinity whom Hector entrusted to his protection (2.296-297)?[123] Yet Aeneas would think it a vile profanation that the adulterous woman who had destroyed so many homes should even venture within the sanctuary of the patroness of hearth and home.

Thirdly, it is inappropriate that Aeneas, in narrating his adventures, should repeat a monologue of his own: he does not do so elsewhere in Book Two and Book Three, nor does his model in this part of the epic, Odysseus relating his exploits in *Od*. 9-12 (except for his brief cry of despair in *Od*. 12.371-373). Heinze advances this objection (pp. 46-47), saying that the

---

[122] This is one of the two reasons why, according to Servius auctus on 2.592, the lines were excised: "turpe est uiro forti contra feminam irasci." But did Varius and Tucca work on such principles?

[123] So Heinze, p. 46.

speech sounds "unnatürlich und frostig." But, as repeated by Aeneas in the course of his narrative, it sounds no more unnatural than his outburst in 2.657-670, with its apostrophe to Venus, its melodramatic "reddite me Danais!", and its prefatory exclamation, "nam quod consilium aut quae iam fortuna dabatur?"

Fourthly, the style and meter of the passage are said to be unlike those of the authentic *Aeneid*. This objection is well traversed by R. G. Austin (cited on p. 168); but we might take one example and go a little further. The hostile critics object to "sceleratas sumere poenas" (576), saying that it is an impossible phrase and cannot mean "poenas sceleris sumere." To begin with, a forger usually tries to make his work acceptable by avoiding anything startling or questionable; and this is certainly startling. Then again, it is one of Vergil's favorite figures, hypallage, which he uses frequently and daringly: e.g. *tepidaque recentem / caede locum* (9.455-456) and *uim deum infernam* (12.199). It is not too far removed from "poenam scelerato ex sanguine sumit" (12.949); and the description of hell gate (6.563) as "sceleratum limen," i.e. "limen sceleratorum," makes it easier to accept. A little later in the same passage Aeneas calls the same act "sumpsisse merentis / . . . poenas." Austin seems right in suggesting that both phrases are bold experiments by Vergil along the same lines ("criminal punishment," "deserving punishment") and that in his final version he would have suppressed one at least. It is very unlikely that a forger would have ventured on such a daring extension of thought and language—twice. A third experiment of the same type is "feminea poena" (584) for "punishment inflicted on a woman."

As against this objection, there are several stylistic figures in the passage which are peculiarly Vergilian and appear elsewhere in the *Aeneid*. For example, the three indignant questions in the future perfect tense, "occiderit? . . . arserit? . . . sudarit?" are like Dido's furious "inluserit?" (4.591) and the reproaches of Mnestheus, "ediderit? . . . miserit?" (9.785).

"Coniugium . . . uidebit?" (579) reappears in Diomede's speech (11.270), "coniugium optatum . . . uiderem?" The hatred which hisses out in lines 585-587 is as violently expressed in multiple sibilants as that of Dido in 4.603-606.[124] Thinking of what she could have done in revenge, Dido utters four verbs all of the same form: "tulissem . . . implessem . . exstinxem . . . dedissem." Thinking here of what he will achieve by executing Helen, Aeneas utters four verbs all of the same form: "exstinxisse . . . sumpisse . . . explesse . . . satiasse."[125]

A further Vergilian characteristic is the adaptation of interesting or vigorous words and phrases from earlier poets.[126] Here "patriae communis Erinys" (573) echoes Πριαμίδαισιν . . . Ἐρινύς from Aeschylus, *Agamemnon* 747-749. The word "praemetuens" (which Norden, p. 262, calls un-Vergilian) is used by Lucretius in a fine passage about conscience (3.1019)— which Vergil knew, because he adapted "mens sibi conscia factis" (1018) in his own "mens sibi conscia recti" (*Aen.* 1.604). The phrase "sudarit sanguine litus" is suggested by a metaphor in one of Ennius's tragedies about the Trojan war, *Hectoris Lytra* (frg. IX): "terra sudat sanguine."

The metrical objections put forward by Norden and others are not very serious. For example, Norden (*Aeneis VI* p. 454) points out that Vergil does not often elide the last syllable of a spondaic word between the second and third feet, but that this effect occurs thrice in the passage under discussion ("Troiae et," 573; "turba et," 580; "†famam et," 587). This objection has been countered (see p. 187 of Austin's article, cited on p. 168); but in any case it is a mistake to believe that Vergil's rhythms are homogeneous throughout the epic. It would not be difficult to select several important passages from the most carefully finished books of the *Aeneid*, and to show that they contained several rhythmical usages employed in a

---

[124] Cf. also Juno in 10.94-95.

[125] Both speakers use "exstinguere"; "implessem" and "explesse," closely similar verbs, are both syncopated.

[126] See ch. 5 below.

ratio quite different from the average. Highly wrought passages in Vergil usually stand away from the norm: each has its special ethos, style, and pulse.

On pp. 30-38 of his *Neue Beitraege zur Erklaerung der Aeneis* (Prague, 1881) Johann Kvíčala defends this passage on several grounds which other scholars have advanced, but adds one which has less often been noted. The subtle alliteration, he says, is typically Vergilian:

*s*eruantem et tacitam *s*ecreta in *s*ede latentem (568)

et *D*anaum *p*oenam et *d*eserti coniugis iras

*p*raemetuens (572-573)

ulcisci *p*atriam et *s*celeratas *s*umere *p*oenas. (576)

A fifth objection is that this passage is inconsistent with the context. Before it begins, in 2.564-566, Aeneas is alone on the roof of Priam's palace; from there, later, he can see the gods destroying the city, walls, gates, and citadel (2.604-618 + 624-631); and from there he will descend (2.632) to make his way home under divine protection. But in this section when he utters the soliloquy Aeneas is not standing on the palace roof. He is on the ground, roaming through the streets, and looking into the dark temple, where he sees Helen by the light of the flames (2.567-570). (It will not do to suggest that he catches sight of her from the roof—since she was hiding within the shrine, and since he describes himself as "wandering," just as Creusa later strayed, *errauit*, in the dark streets, 2.739.) All this is true. Yet if we take the poem as it stands, without this passage, then the remaining context is still inconsistent with itself and demands something resembling this episode. In 2.559-566 Aeneas is standing alone in shock and horror, *thinking of his home and family* (560-563). In 2.589-600, the lines which follow immediately in the received text, Venus holds him back, apparently from some violent action ("continuit," 593), and rebukes him for *not thinking of his home and family* (596-600); and she goes on to explain that Troy is not being de-

172

stroyed by *the hateful Helen* ("inuisa") and the guilty Paris, but by the gods (601-603). Her restraint of Aeneas, her reproaches, and her explanation are quite superfluous, and indeed misplaced, for a man in the state of mind described in 2.559-564, who is thinking of nothing but returning home to save his family. Therefore the context desiderates some incident in which (after seeing the slaughter of Priam, 581) Aeneas *forgot his family* and broke out into a fit of violence somehow connected with *the hateful Helen*: some incident, in fact, such as his discovery of Helen in the temple, which leads him to call her hateful ("inuisa," 574), and the fit of rage which follows.[127]

Finally, it is objected that this passage is inconsistent with Book Six. There (6.509-530) Deiphobus tells Aeneas that, after hiding his weapons, Helen admitted her husband Menelaus together with Ulysses to his house, where they mutilated and then killed him. The implication is (6.526-527) that this guaranteed Helen's safety: therefore she would have no need to hide in the temple of Vesta. This is correct. The two episodes are incompatible—just as the death of Palinurus in the safe waters of the Tyrrhenian Sea (5.835-861) is incompatible with his own narrative of being cast overboard in a tempest on the passage to Africa, "Libyco cursu" (6.337-362: see p. 107). It was partly because of this glaring inconsistency that Varius and Tucca excised the passage, or else followed Vergil's own indication that the passage had been superseded. In the inconsistency lies the solution of the problem of authorship.

One of the main themes of the first part of the *Aeneid* is bitter hatred for Greece and the Greeks. It appears again and again, in small phrases like Laocoon's warning "timeo Danaos" (2.49), Aeneas's dedication (3.288)

AENEAS HAEC DE DANAIS VICTORIBVS ARMA,

[127] Heinze (pp. 49-50) suggests that Venus appeared in order to restrain Aeneas from killing himself like his comrades (565-566) or from seeking death at the hands of the enemy as he proposed to do later (2.668-670). But of such a purpose and such an emotion there is no trace whatever in the text;

and Helenus's warning against the "evil Greeks" (3.398); and in important episodes like the lie of Sinon (2.69-194) and the forecast of Roman conquests in Hellas *avenging* Troy (6.836-840). Now, Helen, who brought on the war by yielding to her passion and yet survived it to live happily with her husband—how was she regarded by the Trojans? There are divergent views of this in the Homeric poems. *Iliad* 3.146-165 shows us the Trojan elders saying that it is no shame for Trojans and Achaeans to suffer for such a woman, although they wish she would go home; and Priam declares she is not to blame. Yet in her lament for Hector she implies that she was often reproached by Hecuba and the rest of Priam's family (*Il.* 24.768-772) and made to feel a stranger. Even so, she is not excluded from the funeral rites. In the *Odyssey* her position is more equivocal. She herself declares that she recognized Odysseus disguised in Troy, did not betray him, and rejoiced when he killed many Trojans and escaped (*Od.* 4.235-264). But a moment or two later, Menelaus recalls how she almost succeeded in wrecking the stratagem of the Wooden Horse by walking round it and calling on the Achaean princes in the voices of their wives: Odysseus restrained them from replying, but the plot was very nearly exposed (*Od.* 4.265-289). Therefore, a few hours before the fall of Troy, Helen was assisting the Trojan cause against the Greeks, and (Menelaus remarks thoughtfully) escorted by handsome Deiphobus.

Vergil will have none of this ambivalent attitude. Helen caused the destruction of Troy, and survived. Therefore she is evil, wholly evil—as she appears in Greek tragedy so often.[128] Impossible to omit her from the *Aeneid*. He wrote one episode

---

and it is rendered unlikely by the emphasis with which Aeneas says that he *now* thought of his family (560-563), i.e., that he must *now* fight no more, but survive to save them.

[128] Ἑλέναc, ἔλανδροc, ἐλέπτολιc (Aesch. *Agam.* 689-690); this is the vengeful spirit that moves Euripides' Hecuba (*Hec.* 265-270, *Tro.* 122-137. 890-894), Andromache (*Androm.* 103-110, *Tro.* 766-773), and the Trojan women (*Hec.* 942-952).

showing how a heroic Trojan prince detested and condemned her. He wrote another showing—through her own deeds, not through the thoughts of an enemy—how evil she was. In the first episode, that of Book Two, Helen is passive; Aeneas wishes simply to punish her for her past acts and the doom she has brought on Troy. In the second, that of Book Six, she is active, and executes a triple deed of treachery: first leading the Trojan women in a dance of victory, "falsa gaudia," which helped to abolish suspicion of the Wooden Horse and kept the city off guard; then signalling to the Greek fleet from the citadel; and finally, in exchange for her own safety, arranging for the death of her consort Deiphobus. In the *Aeneid* this is a treacherous and brutal murder, because Helen has hidden Deiphobus's sword and he is outnumbered (6.523-529); but in Homer the attack on Deiphobus's house is described as the most desperate fight Odysseus ever had (*Od.* 8.516-520). Both the Helen episodes were partly suggested to Vergil by the vengeance taken on the maidservants of Odysseus and on Melanthius in *Od.* 22.435-477. Aeneas thinks of punishing Helen's treachery by death, as the maids were punished; and Deiphobus, like Melanthius, was savagely mutilated. There are also similarities of wording in the two passages. Aeneas says that at the sight of Helen he burned with eagerness *"sceleratas sumere poenas"* (2.576); on meeting Deiphobus (6.501) he asks "quis tam crudelis optauit *sumere poenas?*" and Deiphobus in his reply speaks of *"scelus exitiale"* (6.511). In both one and the other Vergil uses the word "Lacaena" (2.601 and 6.511, never elsewhere in the *Aeneid*) and the ironic "scilicet" (2.577, 6.526). It is possible also to hear an echo of the sibilants of 2.585-587 in Deiphobus's "nimium meminisse necesse est" (6.514).

The two passages, then, were both written by Vergil in order to introduce, and to condemn, Helen. The second, briefer, more bitter, more concentrated, more effective, was chosen by Vergil to represent his view of Helen's part in the destruction

175

of Troy and to correct the ambivalence of the Homeric poems. Having chosen it, he excised the first; but when he died, he had still not rewritten the context where it stood, in such a way as to conceal all traces of its previous existence.

Dido

The soliloquies of Dido contain some of the finest poetry in the *Aeneid*. They help to make her its most memorable figure. There is no one else who utters his or her inmost soul with such frankness and such pathos.

Her midnight monologue in 4.534-552 is, as it were, a rejoinder to her opening address to Anna (which was half a soliloquy) in 4.9-29. That was inspired by terrifying dreams; this is accompanied by torturing sleeplessness. Heinze (p. 138) remarks that it is not presented as a monologue, but as Dido's unspoken thoughts. However, several Homeric monologues consist of a hero's address to his own heart: e.g. *Il.* 17.91-105, where it is unlikely that Menelaus speaks the words aloud.[129] Close scrutiny suggests that Dido's soliloquy begins as a flood of interior musings (*corde uolutat*, 533) but ends in actual speech (*rumpebat pectore questus*, 553).[130] The resolute line 547 with which she concludes her search for a solution—

> quin morere ut merita es, ferroque auerte dolorem

—can hardly be conceived as passing silently through Dido's mind. Surely she speaks it aloud, as a sentence of death pronounced upon her guilty self. And the plaintive reproach to her absent sister which follows, "tu . . . tu," sounds as though it were actually spoken, and with tears.

The core of the soliloquy is a series of nine unanswerable

---

[129] So C. Hentze (cited above, n. 107). Note ὅρμαινε, *Il.* 17.106.

[130] R. G. Austin on 4.553 interprets *rumpebat pectore questus* as "kept pouring out these grievings within her heart"; but the other occurrences of *rumpo* + *pectore* with a noun connoting speech refer to audible, indeed loud, utterance: Celaeno, 3.246, and Turnus, 11.377.

questions elaborating the hopeless dilemma in which fate has placed her. To these questions there is no solution, except one. Dido must end her life, which has become unendurable. The last word of the monologue, the name of her husband Sychaeus, surely brings on a passion of remorseful weeping: even in death she can scarcely face the husband she has betrayed. This scene contains one of Vergil's most poignant contrasts. On his ship, Aeneas sleeps peacefully, all preparations made for departure to a new life. Sleepless, Dido wails in the extreme of torment: nothing is left for her but shame, ending in self-destruction.

A few hours later dawn shows her an empty harbor. Aeneas has gone. Beating her breast and tearing her hair, she breaks out into a tirade of Junonian fury and hatred (4.590-629). But it is even more complex than the speeches of Juno. It moves through five different emotional moods. The first three are expressions of raging hostility, raging but impotent. Thereafter, realizing that she is powerless, she turns from vain remorse and frustrated impulses to a formidable set of curses couched in the form of prayers and commands.[131]

First comes an outburst of regal fury (590-594). Her dignity as a queen has been outraged by Aeneas's departure.[132] She shouts orders to her subjects, bidding them to overtake and destroy him. But she is alone in her room: the orders are unheard.[133]

---

[131] The speech is an exception to the principle stated by Heinze (p. 415): "die [virgilische] Rede ist der Ausdruck eines einzigen Affekts, eines Vorsatzes oder Gedankenganges."

[132] The *Aeneid* is full of *peripeteiai*. One of the most important is the joy which Turnus takes in despoiling the corpse of Pallas (10.495-500), to be followed by the doom which Vergil forecasts for him (10.501-505). One of the smallest but not the least significant is Dido's imperative to Aeneas, "i!" (4.381), to be followed by her outcry "pro Iuppiter, ibit / hic?" (4.590-591).

[133] She must be alone: it is inadmissible to imagine her as uttering this tirade in the presence of a group of attendants—in spite of Maar (cited in n. 94 above) p. 19: "eine einsame Stellung der Sprecherin ist in diesem Fall unwahrscheinlich."

Then she feels that she is going mad (595-599). Nothing can be more terrifying than such an eruption of psychical energy, which threatens to destroy the very identity of the sufferer:

quid loquor? aut ubi sum? quae mentem insania mutat?

With a dire effort (marked by slow spondees) she masters herself:

infelix Dido, nunc te facta impia tangunt?

and reproaches first herself, and then, with bitter contempt, Aeneas.

Next, another outbreak of anger, this time darkened by remorse: a sequence of seven lines (600-606) in which she wishes she had acted like the cruel heroines of tragedy—Medea, who dismembered her brother and scattered his limbs on the waves, and Procne, who gave her false husband his own son's flesh to eat. She goes even beyond this, telling herself with the violence of frustration that she ought to have burned the entire Trojan fleet, murdered Aeneas and Ascanius and all their people, and thrown herself triumphant in death on the flames consuming their corpses. Deadly hatred is voiced in these lines, filled with furious alliteration on *F* and *S*. Passion can scarcely go further and remain articulate.[134]

Now once again she pauses, as the change in rhythm and the emphatic new beginning at 607 show. In an imprecation (607-621) opening with four slow solemn lines and containing a strange half-magical rhyme—

et *Di*rae ultrices *et di* morientis Elissae

—she pronounces a series of curses on Aeneas. These curses are in fact to be fulfilled. She prays that, if he does reach Italy, he may be harassed by war (612-615)—as in Book Seven; be separated from his son and constrained to beg for help (616-

---

[134] Two of Shakespeare's heroes in similar situations become incoherent and feel the approach of madness: *Othello* 4.1.35-45, *King Lear*, 2.4.274-289.

178

617)—as in Book Eight; see his own men killed (617-618)—as in Books Ten to Twelve; and, after peace is made, enjoy no long reign, but die soon, to lie unburied in the sand. This was indeed his fate. He was killed three years after his landing in Italy (*Aen.* 1.265-266) and his body was lost in the river Numicus (Livy 1.2.6).

After praying to the gods to punish Aeneas, Dido turns to her own people (622-629). In a final mandate spoken with the majesty of a dying monarch ("cineri nostro," 623; "nostris ex ossibus," 625) she commands the Carthaginians to hate the Trojans and their descendants, and invokes a future avenger who will harry them with fire and sword. The penultimate sentence calls for total hostility:

litora litoribus contraria,[135] fluctibus undas
imprecor, arma armis.

In that last phrase we can hear the very clash of weapons. *Arma*, the first word in the poem, is one of the commonest words in the *Aeneid*. In several important passages it is doubled, as here and in Diomede's warning "armis concurrant arma cauete" (11.293). The straightforward "arma, arma!" is a war-cry, "To arms!" "Out swords!", and apparently echoes an actual shout.[136] Turnus when inflamed with the lust for battle (7.460)

arma amens fremit, arma toro tectisque requirit.

---

[135] Cf. 1.13: *Karthago, Italiam contra.*

[136] This is pointed out by E. Fraenkel, *JRS* 35 (1945) 1-14, following W. Schulze, *Kleine Schriften* (Göttingen, 1933) 2, pp. 163-164. (There was a similar war-cry in old German. Grimm's *Deutsches Wörterbuch* 13 [ed. K. von Bahder] quotes "wâfen, herre, wâfen" from *Kudrun* 1360, 3, and gives many other citations for "waffen! waffen!") Horace alludes to the war-cry in *Carm.* 1.35.15: *ad arma cessantes, ad arma.* In Ovid (Met. 12.241) the drunken Centaurs *omnes uno ore "arma, arma" loquuntur.* Statius produces several variations: e.g. "Arma, arma, uiri, tuque . . . arma para!" (*Theb.* 3.348-350) and *Arcades arma fremunt, armis defendere regem* (*Theb.* 6.618); see also 7.135 and 11.305-306.

Later, at the news that Aeneas is marching on the Latin city (11.453),

> arma manu trepidi poscunt, fremit arma iuuentus.

At the end of Dido's speech, the hypermetric syllable in "nepotesque" hangs in the air like the echo of a scream, as though her rage were spilling over all bounds of normal speech, and as though she wished to convey the long duration of her ardent hate. Only here in the *Aeneid*, and in the conclusion of a boastful speech by Turnus, is the hypermetric syllable syntactically disjoined from the following line, in which metrically it is swallowed up. The effect is like a grim chord prolonged beyond expectation or endurance.[137] Dido's command was fulfilled a thousand years later, when Hannibal swore at the altars of Baal and Tanit (the Punic name for the supreme goddess corresponding to Juno) to take vengeance upon Rome. This speech contains an essential part of one of the chief themes of the *Aeneid*: the conflict of Rome (or of Troy surviving in Rome) with Carthage. Beginning in enmity, the struggle of Troy and Greece closes in reconciliation through Evander's and Diomede's noble gestures toward Aeneas. Beginning in friendship turned to love, the hatred of Junonian Carthage for Trojan Rome will never be reconciled, and will be extinguished only with the annihilation of one of the two enemies.

A speech of such power and importance as this must be, in spite of its passionate impetus, orderly. Its order is not that of rhetoric, but of emotion, and is as clear to analysis as the different movements of a piece of music. Dido concentrates on four different individuals and groups: herself and her lover; the gods and her people.

---

[137] In 7.470 Turnus finishes a speech (in oratio obliqua, perhaps a draft which Vergil meant to work up) by saying *se satis ambobus Teucrisque uenire Latinisque. / haec ubi dicta dedit. . . .* In other hypermetrical lines the sense runs on continuously, e.g. *magna ossa lacertosque / exuit* (5.422-423); *cadentique / imminet adsimilis* (6.602-603); *tecta Latinorum / ardua* (7.160-161).

First (4.590-594), Aeneas. He has actually gone, and gone unmolested. The insult to her pride is still incredible: the fact is worse than her imaginings.

Second (595-606), Dido. A queen cannot be taken and then cast away. Not to have revenged herself on the man who outraged her womanhood and her pride is unforgivable. The lines, 600-606, in which she speaks like a soldier thinking over a difficult battle, are a threat to Aeneas, retrojected into the past and now presented as a rebuke to her own cowardice ("quem metui moritura?") as though that were the motive which prevented her from attacking Aeneas and the Trojan ships.

Third (607-621), an address to the divinities: the sun, Juno (who is invoked in an entire line, as an accomplice), Hecate the witch-goddess, and the Furies. Avenge me, Dido cries, saying that she asks this with her blood, even more effective than with the dying breath.

And fourth (622-629), in the future, the Carthaginians, the people of the new city which she created, must remember their duty of hatred and revenge. Her command extends to the descendants of her citizens and so on endlessly: "pugnent ipsique nepotesque. . . ." The people will live, but she must not. And she plans immediately for her death, hating the very light of day.

Dido's final speech, *nouissima uerba* (4.651-662), is her most beautiful.[138] We do not leave her cursing and raving, we do not see her ride off like Medea in a chariot with corpses at her feet. Instead, her charm and her nobility appear in her farewell to the garments and weapon of Aeneas, "so dear while God and fate allowed" (651). She lies down on the bed—"the marriage bed," as once she called it, "in which her life was ruined" (4.496-497). Beside her is the effigy of Aeneas, wearing his own clothes (4.507-508, 648). She kisses the bed at the mo-

---

[138] It is analyzed by E. Conrad in c. 3 of his *Untersuchungen*, from which I borrow a few points.

ment when she stabs herself, using his sword, to show that it was he who killed her (4.646-647, 663-665).

The speech begins with one of the echo-effects of which Vergil was a master: "meque his exsoluite curis" (4.652) recalls both in rhythm and in vocabulary the first words spoken by Dido to the Trojans (1.562):

soluite corde metum, Teucri, secludite curas.[139]

Its rhythm is exceptionally solemn. (It was often set to elegiac music by composers of the baroque era.) Of its opening eight lines, no less than six begin with slow weighty spondaic words, "dulces," "uixi," "et nunc," (which coalesce), "urbem," "felix," "numquam."[140] In five of these lines Vergil deliberately repeats the same rhythm as far as the first caesura. "Dulces exuuiae" (651) gives the pattern --/-◡◡/- followed in 653, 654, 657, and 658. Such repetition of the same rhythm is rare, if not unique, in the *Aeneid*.[141] It shows that, although profoundly sad, Dido is in full control of her mind and emotions.

After the farewell (651-652), the next four lines (653-656) are like the epitaph of a monarch, three of the four closing with a verb in the perfect tense of achievement and finality.[142] Although a woman, Dido has the will-power of a man. She says "Vixi," as though her career had come to a satisfactory close and as though her glory as a ruler were assured: this in order to blot out the thought that her life has been ruined, ending in an ἄωρος θάνατος. In the same spirit spoke Q. Caecilius Metellus Pius Scipio. Stabbing himself rather

---

139 This is observed by O. Maar on p. 159 of his study cited in n. 94 above.

140 This is highly unusual. See Norden, *Aeneis VI*, Anhang VIII, on spondaic words in the first foot. Since it is followed by a punctuation pause, "felix" is the slowest of all these openings. It marks what Dido might have been, rather than "infelix Dido" (in the poet's voice, 1.749, 4.68, 4.450; in her own, 4.596; and last in that of Aeneas, 6.456).

141 For another example see p. 161.

142 Conrad (cited above, n. 138) actually calls the speech a paramythetic encomium, and breaks it down perhaps rather hypercritically.

than live as Caesar's subject, he replied, when his captors asked where the general was, "Imperator bene se habet."[143] For the same reason she does not mention the fact that she is childless, although she spoke of it to Aeneas in 4.327-330. Instead of children, she has produced a city. Only a successful ruler could say "urbem praeclaram statui, mea moenia uidi." Her proud nature, which will not brook injustice, emerges in the declaration "ulta uirum poenas inimico a fratre recepi" (656).[144] And here she recalls Augustus himself, who emphasized in his survey of his career that he had avenged the murder of his father Julius (*Mon. Anc.* 1.2). She adds that her destiny after death is secure: "magna mei sub terras ibit imago" (654). She expects therefore to be heroized as the founder of a city. So Romulus after becoming Quirinus appeared *pulcher et humano maior* (Ov. *Fast.* 2.503).[145] For a moment (with an echo of the grieving nurse in Euripides' *Medea*) she gazes back at her lost happiness. Then, forgetting that she has hoped and prayed for vengeance, she says "moriemur inultae." The phrase carries a powerful resonance from a sentence in Aeneas's narrative. Among the flames of Troy, refusing to stay and see his family butchered or enslaved, he called for weapons so as to die in the streets fighting (2.670):

> numquam omnes hodie moriemur inulti!

Like Aeneas, Dido now faces death in desperation; but she cannot take a life for a life. Unavenged, she cries "moriamur!" With the somber final words "omina mortis" she stabs herself.

[143] Livy, *Per.* 114; Val. Max. 3.2.13.

[144] Kvíčala on pp. 207-210 of his book (cited on p. 172) athetizes this line on the ground that Dido did not take adequate revenge on her brother, but merely fled carrying the treasure with her. But Dido is making the best of her sad life: this is one more example of unconscious exaggeration on the part of a speaker emotionally moved.

[145] The Persians repelled from Delphi by miracles saw two local heroes pursuing them, μέζονας ἢ κατὰ ἀνθρώπων φύσιν ἐόντας (Hdt. 8.38). Creusa, after being taken into the retinue of the goddess Cybele, showed herself to Aeneas as a "nota maior imago" (2.773).

Deeply moving though this is, Vergil adds one even more plangent note of suffering. With the blade in her body, Dido cannot die. The wound grates within her breast. She lies writhing like a sacrificial animal struck and not killed. She can speak no more; but she still suffers. Vergil expresses the extreme of agony in a sentence which can scarcely be read without tears:

> oculis errantibus alto
> quaesiuit caelo lucem, ingemuitque reperta.[146]

When the rainbow messenger brings her death at last, it is a miraculous gift from the divinity whose cruelty is only once and only then tinged with mercy.

[146] The last words of Racine's Phaedra, surely inspired by this scene, rival the pathos of Dido:

> Et la mort, à mes yeux dérobant la clarté,
> Rend au jour, qu'ils souillaient, toute sa pureté.

CHAPTER FIVE

THE SPEECHES AND
THEIR MODELS

VERGIL's poetry is rich in echoes. He defines a situation by quoting a few words from another poet; and he brings into his later work phrases and even sentences from his earlier poems. His exclamation, *Improbe Amor!* (*Aen.* 4.412) is touching in its context, but it is more touching as it recalls Cχέτλι' Έρως from the scene in which Medea commits a dreadful crime for the sake of love (Ap. Rhod. 4.445); still more, perhaps, as it echoes Vergil's own shepherd contemplating suicide in *Buc.* 8.49-50, and saying "improbus ille puer." From a poem which Vergil loved, there is a fainter echo. In Catullus 64 Ariadne falls in love with Theseus when she first sees him, like Dido with Aeneas. Catullus then (64.95) apostrophizes the god with amazement at his power:

> sancte puer, curis hominum qui gaudia misces!

Sometimes again Vergil shows that an event is not what its participants believe, by introducing verbal allusions to another event with a different outcome. In Book Nine an Italian warrior taunts the besieged Trojans with the sneer that they prefer soft living to warfare and hardship (9.614-616). Obviously this is false, since the Trojans are experienced warriors, and have endured much on their journey to Italy. Now, the challenger uses some of the words and ideas of Menelaus in the *Iliad* (13.636-639); but there Menelaus is gloomily reflecting that the Trojans really prefer battle to soft living; and in the *Aeneid*, a few moments later, the Italian warrior is struck dead by a Trojan weapon.

In particular Vergil remodels scenes and speeches from ear-

185

lier poetry in order more subtly to define the characters of his men and women and gods. Thus, when we first meet Dido, she is a lonely figure, wholly a queen, but in secret longing for a husband equal to her, a lover and a consort. This is adumbrated in the gentleness and warmth of her words and demeanor in the first book; but it is emphasized by the resemblance of her speeches to those made by Hypsipyle to Jason and by Circe to Odysseus.[1] As her tragic destiny develops, new aspects of her character emerge. This is shown in many ways: but not least in the similarity between her later speeches and the utterances of such heroines as Euripides' Medea and Alcestis.

No single prototype will explain any important character in Vergil. The poet himself grew and changed, becoming not happier but greater. So did his poems and his characters. The young dilettante who sang sportively about Tityrus was transformed into the seer who combined epic, tragedy, and philosophical mysticism, and who evoked Rome

> Bearing on shoulders immense,
> Atlanteän, the load,
> Wellnigh not to be borne,
> Of the too vast orb of her fate.[2]

In this way his Aeneas grows: not against his will, indeed, but against the warmest impulses of his heart. The change appears in all Aeneas's actions: even in such small matters as the words used (like stage-directions in a drama) to describe his manner as he speaks. But it is also echoed in the speeches made by Aeneas. He is always a hero. At first, however, he is a despairing hero; at last a hard cruel hero; and the change is shown by the varying resonances of Homeric and other speeches which Vergil intends his readers to recall.

> Amat poeta quae legit immutata aliqua parte uel personis
> ipsis <uel> uerbis proferre.
>   —Servius auctus on *Aen.* 3.10.

---

[1] See pp. 218-219.   [2] Arnold, "Heine's Grave," 93-96.

Vergil does not always use his models once only. Sometimes a striking scene in Homer or a powerful utterance in tragedy will appear in two or more different contexts of the *Aeneid*. Thus, Pyrrhus drags Priam to the altar, saying, "nunc morere" (*Aen.* 2.550); Mezentius uses the same phrase to Orodes (*Aen.* 10.743). The model for both is Achilles' τέθναθι spoken to the dead Hector (*Il.* 22.365). The two Vergilian situations differ. Pyrrhus echoes his father because Priam has just declared that he is no son of Achilles. Mezentius's victim Orodes has forecast the approaching death of his killer, as Hector did to Achilles, and is met with the same brusque dismissal. Both speeches are even more cruel in Vergil than their model in Homer: for they are spoken to the living, while Hector in the *Iliad* is already dead (καὶ τεθνηῶτα). So, too, the last plea uttered by Hector before his death, the plea that his corpse be returned to his people in exchange for a ransom (*Il.* 22. 338-343), is echoed partly by Magus in the *Aeneid*, who offers a ransom for his *life* (Aen. 10.524-529), and partly by Turnus, who begs, not for a ransom but for the sake of humanity, that he *or his corpse* be returned to his people (*Aen.* 12.931-938).

Aeneas

The first part of the *Aeneid* is largely modelled on the *Odyssey*, the second on the *Iliad*: exile, search, temptation in the first, arrival, combat, and victory in the second.[3] Aeneas's temperament changes with the movement of his destiny. The change appears in his actions. It is reflected (as we have seen in chapter 2 and chapter 3) in the tone of his speeches. But it is also quite as clearly reflected in the models on which Vergil chooses to mold his hero's speeches and the situations where they are uttered.

Aeneas begins by speaking like Odysseus. He ends by speaking like Achilles. At first, almost completely hopeless. At the

[3] Full details of the plan in Knauer, and exposition in Otis.

end, almost wholly ruthless. The opening speech (*Aen.* 1.94-101) is chiefly modelled on a despairing cry of Odysseus (*Od.* 5.299-312). The situations of the two heroes are similar. Odysseus has sailed safely for seventeen days after his deliverance from Calypso's island and is in sight of the land of the Phaeacians when Poseidon rouses a hurricane to destroy his craft. Aeneas has crossed the Adriatic, coasted round the dangerous gulf of Tarentum, avoided Scylla and Charybdis, escaped the Cyclops, rounded Sicily, and is just losing sight of its western tip on his voyage to Italy, the last lap, when Juno persuades Aeolus to rouse a hurricane to destroy his fleet. To die when approaching a safe haven, and to die an ignoble death choked by water instead of winning glory in battle, is most bitter. Each hero envies his comrades who died on the plains of Troy: they are τρισμάκαρες καὶ τετράκις, "terque quaterque beati." Each wishes he had died in one of his hardest fights—Odysseus over the body of Achilles, and Aeneas confronting Diomede at the time when his opponent overmatched not only men but gods (*Il.* 5.166-351, cf. 846-863).

The final speech of Aeneas, condemning Turnus to die (*Aen.* 12.947-949), is modelled on the words of Achilles to the dying Hector (*Il.* 22.331-336). Again the situations are similar. After long preparation and many postponements, the enemies meet in a duel to the death. Hector, defending the city, faces Achilles boldly (*Il.* 22.90-130), then runs from him in terror, turns to face him, and is speared (*Il.* 22.306-329). Turnus, defending the city, faces Aeneas boldly (*Aen.* 12.681-727), then runs from him in terror, turns to face him, and is speared (*Aen.* 12.919-929). Hector and Turnus both beg for mercy (although Hector is dying and Turnus is not). Achilles and Aeneas both refuse, and claim the death of the foe as requital for the slaying of a friend. Hector and Turnus die, and their souls fly with a groan into the darkness.

Two pairs of scenes, similar in outline and in important features. But the differences within each pair are significant.

188

The outcry of Odysseus in the storm is almost twice as long as that of Aeneas: fourteen lines, compared with just over seven. It embodies both a reminiscence of Calypso's prophecy (*Od.* 5.300-302 ≈ 206-210) and a comment on the tempest which does little more than restate the facts given in the narrative (5.303-305 ≈ 291-296)—although incidentally it shows that Odysseus is unaware of Poseidon's responsibility for his disaster. It opens with a dramatic question:

Ὤ μοι ἐγὼ δειλός, τί νύ μοι μήκιστα γένηται;

It contains two exclamations:

τρισμάκαρες Δαναοὶ καὶ τετράκις, οἳ τότ᾽ ὄλοντο
Τροίηι ἐν εὐρείηι, χάριν Ἀτρείδηισι φέροντες.
ὡς δὴ ἐγώ γ᾽ ὄφελον θανέειν καὶ πότμον ἐπισπεῖν
ἤματι τῶι ὅτε μοι πλεῖστοι χαλκήρεα δοῦρα
Τρῶες ἐπέρριψαν περὶ Πηλείωνι θανόντι.

Most of it, however, is couched in simple declarative sentences, two of them making the same statement in the same form (305 ≈ 312).

The speech of Aeneas is composed of three exclamations, less reflective and more emotional than Odysseus' appraisal of the situation, and more carefully wrought.[4] In spite of its apparent spontaneity, it is built of triplets: three exclamations, the last longer than the others (*Aen.* 1.94-96, 96-97, 97-101); three *ubi* clauses in the same proportion (99, 99-100, 100-101); and, in the final line, three κόμματα in a similar ratio, "scuta uirum," "galeas," "fortia corpora." The sound-effects are striking also, with strong alliteration on *O* in 94-97 and on *O* and *S* in 99-101. The complaint of Odysseus ends in a gloomy statement:

νῦν δέ με λευγαλέωι θανάτωι εἵμαρτο ἁλῶναι.

---

[4] A penetrating if sometimes over-subtle analysis of this speech is given by E. Conrad in c. 1 of his Tübingen dissertation.

But Aeneas is cut off while his exclamations are still increasing in vehemence, by the roar of the storm.[5]

The μακαρισμός comes in the middle of Odysseus' speech, but it is the first utterance of Aeneas, and is therefore more striking. Both men call their dead comrades blessed. Odysseus, who did not want to go to war in the first place, bitterly comments that the Danaans died "to do a favor for the sons of Atreus" (*Od.* 5.307).[6] Aeneas says the Trojans were happy who died "in the sight of their fathers" to defend the city (*Aen.* 1.94-96). A favorite theme of Vergil: Trojans are nobler, being patriots, not aggressors. Odysseus reflects that, instead of going to feed the fishes, he would have been buried with honor as a hero (*Od.* 5.311). Aeneas, more generous of heart, does not speak of honorable burial: he thinks only of a glorious death (*Aen.* 1.97-98). He does not mention the cremation of Hector (*Il.* 24.782-804) and the divine rescue of Sarpedon's body (*Il.* 16.676-683), and thinks rather of the corpses lying slaughtered on the plain (Hector, *Il.* 22.367-375; Sarpedon, 16.638-640) or weltering in the waves of the river (*Il.* 21.114-221). Even so, to have died there would have been better.

Vergil does not employ one model and one alone for speeches, scenes, or characters. So here, "ante ora patrum Troiae sub moenibus altis" (*Aen.* 1.95) recalls a line in a simile from *Od.* 8.524—

ὅς τε ἑῆc πρόcθεν πόλιοc λαῶν τε πέcῃcιν

—but with overtones. That simile enhances a description of Odysseus weeping as he remembers the Trojan war: therefore

---

[5] Fluctus intervenit qui uocem loquentis obcluderet; esset enim uitium poetae, si finitis querellis Aeneae fluctum faceret superuenisse . . . ergo sit "talia iactanti," hoc est adhuc loquenti, intervenit uis fluctuum nec siuit Aenean explicare quae uoluit. ceterum si complesset, diceret felices qui in Troia perierunt, se infelicem qui esset periturus in fluctibus. (Donatus on *Aen.* 1.101.)

[6] The same phrase is used in the same tone by Pandarus of Hector (*Il.* 5.211) and by Achilles of Agamemnon (*Il.* 9.613).

in this echo there is redoubled sorrow for the past. The last three lines of Aeneas's short speech

> saeuus ubi Aeacidae telo iacet Hector, ubi ingens
> Sarpedon, ubi tot Simois correpta sub undis
> scuta uirum galeasque et fortia corpora uoluit

are modelled on a sentence spoken by Nestor in *Od.* 3.109-112:

> ἔνθα μὲν Αἴας κεῖται Ἀρήιος, ἔνθα δ' Ἀχιλλεύς,
> ἔνθα δὲ Πάτροκλος, θεόφιν μήστωρ ἀτάλαντος,
> ἔνθα δ' ἐμὸς φίλος υἱός, ἅμα κρατερὸς καὶ ἀμύμων,
> Ἀντίλοχος, πέρι μὲν θείειν ταχὺς ἠδὲ μαχητής.

The theme, remembrance of dead comrades who are named, is the same; "saeuus" resembles Ἀρήιος and "ingens" κρατερός, though the Latin adjectives are slightly more intense; and the anaphora of "ubi" echoes Nestor's repetition of ἔνθα. Then further, the description of Simois rolling shields and helmets recalls a narrative passage in *Il.* 12.22-23. (In one of the many significant echoes of the *Aeneid* within the *Aeneid*, the phrase will be spoken once more by Aeneas, in a different mood, as he prepares for war, 8.538-539.) But there is another prototype for the speech of Aeneas in the storm. Achilles, beset by the river in *Il.* 21.272-283, groans, looks up to heaven, and wishes he had been killed in battle by Hector instead of drowning like a swineherd boy. His eulogy of his opponent Hector (*Il.* 21.279-280), blended with a tribute to Diomede spoken by Helenus to Aeneas and Hector (*Il.* 6.98), is echoed here in Aeneas's praise of Diomede (*Aen.* 1.96-97). Later in the *Aeneid* Diomede will more than repay it (*Aen.* 11.281-293).

It is clear, therefore, that Vergil when introducing Aeneas wished to present him in a situation comparable to that of Homer's Odysseus, but with a character somewhat more chivalrous and Achillean.[7]

---

[7] In the view of Conrad (n. 4 above) the opening monologue of Aeneas is so dramatic that it may have been inspired by Greek tragedy: for instance,

The last speech of Aeneas (*Aen.* 12.947-949) is briefer than its counterpart, the speech of Achilles to Hector (*Il.* 22.345-354), but it is loftier in tone; while the speech of his opponent Turnus is less noble than its Homeric model. With Achilles' spear in his throat, Hector knows he is a dying man. He makes only one plea, that Achilles accept a ransom for his corpse rather than allow dogs to eat it (*Il.* 22.338-343). Achilles refuses. Calling Hector himself a dog, he says he wishes he could cut up and eat the corpse raw, and declares dogs and birds will devour it even if Priam offers its weight in gold as ransom. With Aeneas's spear in his thigh, Turnus is disabled but not dying. Unlike Hector, he can still hope for life. He abases himself more deeply than Hector: I deserved this, he says, I am beaten, all have seen me beg for mercy, Lavinia is your wife (*Aen.* 12.930-938). He does not plead for life and life alone; but he does ask for his life as the first alternative:

> *me*, seu corpus spoliatum lumine mauis,
> *redde meis.*

And his final words, "ulterius ne tende odiis," mean simply "hanc animam serues." Less brutal than Achilles, Aeneas hesitates and almost consents (12.940-941)—until he sees that Turnus is wearing the baldric which he stripped from Pallas's corpse with an ill-omened word of hatred for the Trojan prince (10.494-495, cf. 501-505). Then and only then Aeneas is filled once more with fury. His anger is more ethical than the iron-hearted wrath of Achilles (*Il.* 22.356-357). To him, Turnus is a criminal.[8] It is Pallas, he cries, who now takes vengeance on

---

by the speeches of Orestes and Electra on Agamemnon (Aesch. *Cho.* 345-353, 363-371) and that of Peleus on Neoptolemus in Eur. *Andr.* 1182-1183. However, the careful structure of the speech appears to me not to resemble these passages, and although their thought parallels Vergil's, the situations do not.

[8] "Scelerato ex sanguine," 12.949. *Sceleratus* is a harsh word; Aeneas uses it in connection with Helen (2.576) and with the murderous Thracians (3.60, cf. 3.42). It is also applied to hell-gate (6.563), to the madness of war (7.461), to Laocoon considered as a blasphemer (2.231), and by Turnus in his fury to the Trojans (9.137).

you: you are a victim to appease his wronged spirit. Achilles merely watches Hector die; but with a final gesture more drastic than that of Achilles, Aeneas plunges his sword into his helpless enemy's heart.

This method of adaptation can be observed in many of Vergil's speeches which are based on Homer, and in particular in the speeches given to Aeneas. Although intentionally reminiscent of the original situation and the original Homeric words, they are usually compressed, made more emotional, and sometimes ennobled. For all their vigor and directness, Homer's heroes sometimes appeared to Vergil as barbarous or naive. He makes this judgment clear by his technique of modifying or omitting some of Homer's effects. It is savage enough for Aeneas to stab a wounded opponent, but can we possibly imagine him saying he wished he could slice Turnus's flesh up and eat it, or dragging Turnus's corpse behind his chariot?

Another example. After long wanderings Odysseus is welcomed by a hospitable monarch. A minstrel sings two tales of Odysseus' own adventures in the Trojan war. During the songs Odysseus weeps (*Od.* 8.72-95) as bitterly as a woman (*Od.* 8.485-534). This theme appears in the *Aeneid* in two different guises. Entering Carthage in concealment, Aeneas sees paintings of the Trojan war. Alone with his friend he weeps, groaning most bitterly when he sees, not an exploit of his own, but the ransoming of Hector's corpse by king Priam (*Aen.* 1.450-493, especially 485-487). Later, welcomed by a hospitable monarch, he is invited to relate the story of the fall of Troy. He declares the story gives him unutterable pain (*Aen.* 2.3, cf. 1.597) and asks whether even the cruellest Greeks would not weep at such a tale (*Aen.* 2.6-8); but he will not shed tears. So again, landing in his home but not recognizing it, Odysseus strikes his thighs and laments in a long monologue of self-pity, abusing his Phaeacian hosts and πόλλ' ὀλοφυρόμενος (*Od.* 13.187-221). Aeneas, landing in his future home but not

193

recognizing it, is, in spite of his lack of supplies, silently happy (*Aen.* 7.25-36 + 107-111). Flexible, garrulous, frank, Homer's heroes give utterance to every emotion as it possesses them. Aeneas always says less than he feels, and often remains silent when a Greek would be talking. Indeed, it is worth comparing the speeches of Aeneas as a warrior in the *Aeneid* with the speeches of Aeneas as a warrior in the *Iliad*. In all the scenes of fighting from Book Ten to Book Twelve of the *Aeneid* he never speaks more than a few sentences to any opponent. In the *Iliad* the Homeric Aeneas fights a duel with Achilles. The center of the episode covers about two hundred lines (*Il.* 20.156-352). Of these, Achilles' challenge occupies twenty-one, and Aeneas's reply no less than fifty-nine, including his own complete genealogy and an account of his great-great-great-grandfather's stud of horses. Outside the narrative in Dido's palace, Vergil's Aeneas never makes any such long and voluble speeches. Of course the conventions of oral poetry and the special interest of Homer's audiences in ancestral history differentiate such episodes in the *Iliad* from anything in Vergil; yet there is something dissimilar in the character of the two peoples, which comes out in this contrast. Vergil evidently agreed with the Homeric Aeneas in his comment on garrulity (*Il.* 20.248-249):

στρεπτὴ δὲ γλῶσσ' ἐστὶ βροτῶν, πολέες δ' ἔνι μῦθοι
παντοῖοι, ἐπέων δὲ πολὺς νομὸς ἔνθα καὶ ἔνθα.

Aeneas, then, begins by resembling Odysseus in his speeches and ends by resembling Achilles. Between the first book of the poem and the last he occupies a number of situations similar to those champions, and also from time to time delivers speeches which remind the reader of other heroic figures, and other scenes in epic and drama.

His address encouraging his storm-tossed comrades (*Aen.*

194

1.198-207) is principally suggested by Odysseus' speech to his men as they approach Charybdis (*Od.* 12.208-221). Both captains tell their men that they have seen trouble before, name previous dangers escaped (Κύκλωψ ≈ "Cyclopia saxa"), and forecast that they will emerge from this plight too. Odysseus speaks with some caution (τῶνδε μνήcεcθαι ὀίω). Aeneas is a little more encouraging: "forsan et haec olim meminisse *iuuabit*," he says, with some resemblance to Eumaeus's words in *Od.* 15.400 and to a famous line in Euripides' *Andromeda*.[9] Odysseus then issues specific orders for facing the emergency (*Od.* 12.213-221), looking no further beyond it. But Aeneas (*Aen.* 1.204-207) reminds his men of their future home, a new Troy, and happiness to be earned by endurance. Here his speech shows striking coincidences with the words of Teucer in Horace, *Carm.* 1.7.25-32. Teucer says "o ... peiora ... passi," and Aeneas "o passi grauiora" (both resembling κύντερον ἄλλο ποτ' ἔτλης in *Od.* 20.18). Apollo promised Teucer "tellure noua Salamina futuram," and destiny tells the Trojans that in Latium "fas regna resurgere Troiae."[10] (This theme, the theme of eternity imaged in the recurrent processes of nature, has a long history, and goes back at least as far as the *Certamen Homeri et Hesiodi*, lines 266-268 Allen.)

[9] Frg. 133 Nauck, cited by Macrobius 7.2.9; see his earlier comments in *Sat.* 5.11.5-8. The line reads ἀλλ' ἡδύ τοι cωθέντα μεμνῆcθαι πόνων.

[10] On this speech Knauer (p. 374) also cites *Od.* 10.174-177: this, however, is parallel to Aeneas's speech only in the broad affirmation "we shall not die yet" and in the situation: both commanders bring food to their men, although Aeneas characteristically does not mention it. Knauer adds *Od.* 10.189-197, which, with the utter despair of lines 192-193, seems quite different from Aeneas's inspiriting words. Servius auctus declares the whole passage is borrowed from Naevius's *Punic War*; but he gives no quotation to illustrate this and may be merely copying a list of Vergil's *furta*. Cartault (p. 149) compares "durate" with τλῆτε, φίλοι in *Il.* 2.299. The situation is different; still, it *is* Odysseus who says these words, in a crisis, to encourage the troops.

For the narrative of Aeneas in *Aeneid* 2-3, the model is of course the narrative of Odysseus in *Odyssey* 9-12.[11] The two begin in the same way: *Aen.* 2.3-13 ≈ *Od.* 9.2-15. Knauer (p. 378) notes that the sadness of Aeneas's *exordium*

Infandum, regina, iubes renouare dolorem

is inspired by the earlier remarks of Odysseus to Arete (*Od.* 7.241-243):

'Αργαλέον, βασίλεια, διηνεκέως ἀγορεῦσαι
κήδε᾽, ἐπεί μοι πολλὰ δόσαν θεοὶ οὐρανίωνες·
τοῦτο δέ τοι ἐρέω ὅ μ᾽ ἀνείρεαι ἠδὲ μεταλλᾷς.

There are other Odyssean touches, such as *Aen.* 2.8-11 ≈ *Od.* 11.330-331 + 379-384.

The models for Aeneas's own speeches within his narrative are very diverse, because he is shown in so many different critical situations. His greeting to the ghost of Hector (*Aen.* 2.281-286) is partly inspired by Achilles' words to the ghost of Patroclus (*Il.* 23.94-98); but the amazement and horror in it come rather from an address to Hector's ghost or his mutilated corpse (perhaps prophetically uttered by Cassandra) in Ennius's tragedy *Alexander* (frg. VIII):

o lux Troiae, germane Hector,
quid ita cum tuo lacerato corpore
miser . . . ?

Aeneas's exclamation as he recalls its appearance, "ei mihi, qualis erat!" (2.274) is also from Ennius (*Ann.* 7).

Although it is part of his continuous narrative, his apostrophe to his fatherland in 2.241-242 carries as much emotion as a passionate speech:

o patria, o diuum domus Ilium et incluta bello
moenia Dardanidum!

[11] S. E. Bassett, in *The Poetry of Homer* (Berkeley, 1938) p. 73, makes a curious comment. "Vergil inserts his Apologue in a love story, to which it contributes nothing. If both the questions of Dido . . . and the narrative it-

This is adapted from one of Andromache's lyrical laments in Ennius (*Andromacha Aechmalotis* frg. IX):

o pater, o patria, o Priami domus![12]

—together with a fragment of the *Annals*, "diuum domus," and the adjective "incluta," which Ennius applied to Rome herself (*Ann.* 575 and 502).

In extant Greek poetry there are no models for the "forlorn hope" speech made by Aeneas to the group of Trojans whom he collects for the counter-attack (*Aen.* 2.348-354). Even during the Trojan attack on the ships in *Iliad* 13-15, no Greek warrior speaks of death as certain, and only Agamemnon thinks of quitting the beach-head (*Il.* 14.65-81). Macrobius (5.22.7) suggests that Aeneas's words "excessere omnes adytis arisque relictis / di" (351-352) are adapted from Eur. *Tro.* 25; but although the event is basically the same in both epic and tragedy, it is seen from different points of view. In Euripides, Poseidon[13] says he is leaving Ilium and his altars because he has been worsted by Hera and Athena: "λείπω τὸ κλεινὸν Ἴλιον βωμούς τ᾽ ἐμούς." But Vergil's Aeneas declares that *all* the πολιοῦχοι θεοί have departed: a more powerful picture,

---

[12] J. Endt, "Der Gebrauch der Apostrophe bei den lateinischen Epikern," *WS* 27 (1905) 116, points out that the apostrophe to one's home is a device found in Greek tragedy. Soph. *O.T.* 1089 is not quite relevant; but "ὦ κλεινὰ Cαλαμίc" in *Ajax* 596 is. Plautus parodies Andromache's apostrophe in *Bacch.* 933. H. D. Jocelyn, "Ancient Scholarship and Virgil's Use of Republican Latin Poetry. II," *CQ* 15 (1965) 140-143, shows that Servius sometimes distorted the verses of earlier poets used by Vergil; he warns scholars to be wary of such comments as Servius's remarks on 2.241 and 2.274, and suggests that both "ei mihi!" and "o pater . . ." may come from Ennius's *Alexander*.

[13] Macrobius (followed by Cartault, p. 221) gives the speech to Apollo. In 3.9, citing *Aen.* 2.351-352, he talks about the ritual of *euocatio* by which the gods of a besieged city were summoned to desert it; but the concept is not relevant, since the Greeks have uttered no such summons (the theft of the Palladium is different) and in any case it is a purely Roman ceremony.

perhaps suggested by a narrative in the epic tradition, say among the cyclic poems. (A scholiast on Aesch. *Sept.* 310 mentions a tragedy by Sophocles called Ξοανηφόροι in which the gods carried their images out of Troy, knowing that it was being captured: a strange vision, unattested elsewhere.) The somber phrase "urbi / incensae" (*Aen.* 2.352-353) is recalled by Aeneas from the announcement of Panthus, "incensa . . . in urbe" (2.327). The beginning of Aeneas's final summons to self-sacrifice, "una salus uictis," may have been inspired by a line in one of Catullus's poems of bitter suffering (76.15):

una salus haec est, hoc est tibi peruincendum.[14]

The furious soliloquy of Aeneas on seeing Helen (*Aen.* 2.577-587) is unlike anything in Homer, and is based on Greek tragic poetry. (For a discussion of its authenticity and a review of some parallels in drama, see pp. 164-176.

In despair at Anchises' refusal to leave his home, Aeneas determines to die fighting bravely if hopelessly, like Hector alone before Achilles (*Aen.* 2.668-670 ≈ *Il.* 22.300-305). His desperate phrase "patet isti ianua leto" (2.661) is a reminiscence of Lucretius (*haec rebus erit pars ianua leti*, 1.1112)— and an apt one, since Lucretius is thinking of the dissolution of the universe.

In Book Four Aeneas addresses Dido in his own defense (*Aen.* 4.333-361). Superficially his speech is comparable to that of Odysseus to Calypso (*Od.* 5.215-224); but, since he is speaking to an equal and not to an immortal goddess, it is calmer and less apologetic. Its opening (*Aen.* 4.333-336) recalls two of Jason's speeches in the *Argonautica*: his expression of thanks to Hypsipyle (1.836-837) and his assurance to Medea of eternal gratitude (3.1079-1082). The earnest line 336, "dum memor ipse mei, dum spiritus hos regit artus," is modelled on two declarations made by Achilles, one to Phoenix (*Il.* 9.609-610)

---

[14] A commander in Livy says "una est salus erumpere hinc atque abire" (7.35.9); but that is more prosaic, and the situation is more hopeful.

198

and one remembering Patroclus (*Il.* 22.387-388). Then in *Aen.* 4.340-344 there is a distant echo of Telemachus wishing for the all but impossible (*Od.* 16.148-149). Affirming that he will not abandon his mission in order to share Dido's realm (*Aen.* 4.345-350) Aeneas speaks in the same way as Jason to Hypsipyle (*Argon.* 1.839-841) although with greater intensity; and he mentions the impressive visitor from heaven (*Aen.* 4.356-359) with the same emphasis as Priam speaking of Iris in *Il.* 24.220-224.

Cutting the cable and commanding his men both to fall to the oars and to set full sail (*Aen.* 4.573-574), Aeneas is like Odysseus—not as he departs from Circe sailing with a fair wind (*Od.* 11.1-12) but rather as he and his men row hastily away from the blinded Cyclops (*Od.* 9.469-472); he also resembles Jason, cutting the cables and encouraging his men to row homeward after he has won the Fleece, while the Colchians rush threateningly after him (Ap. Rhod. 4.190-211). He tells his men of the god he saw in sleep (*Aen.* 4.554-559 + 574-576) in terms like those which Agamemnon uses of the dream messenger sent by Zeus (*Il.* 2.56-71). There is something a little strange about this. Vergil says that the divine visitor was *like* Mercury (*Aen.* 4.558-559) and that the *shape* of the god returned (*Aen.* 4.556). Aeneas knows that the messenger was a god (4.574) and tells both his men and the deity that it was the god's second visit ("iterum," 576 and 577): therefore he assumes that it was Mercury who came to him as he slept aboard his ship. Why, then, does he address the god merely as "sancte deorum, / quisquis es" (576-577) and why does Vergil remind his readers of the deceitful vision sent by Zeus to Agamemnon? Servius gives three explanations: one mystical (there were three divinities called Mercury), one diplomatic (the messenger, coming from Jupiter, did not need to be closely identified: cf. Turnus in 9.22), and one dramatic ("non plane nouit esse Mercurium"). H. R. Steiner, *Der Traum in der Aeneis* (Berne, 1952) pp. 51-53, conjectures that the iden-

199

tity of the apparition was intentionally left a little vague. This is not because it visited Aeneas in a dream. The Penates were clearly recognizable to him in a dream (3.148-152 + 173-174) and Tiber appeared in person (*deus ipse*, 8.31). But it was not necessary for Mercury himself to make a portentous journey from heaven, as he did in 4.238-278, because this time the message given to Aeneas was not wholly true. The god's warning was exaggerated. There is no hint in the narrative that Dido had already considered attacking the Trojan fleet (566-568). She thinks of it after the ships sail (592-594); she blames herself for not doing so (600-606); but she had not even attempted. Why then does the dream come to Aeneas at all, when he intended to sail in a few hours? The dream (Steiner suggests) was devised by Vergil in order to make Aeneas quit Carthage abruptly, without seeing Dido again and attempting to bid her farewell, thus initiating another painful interview in which he could scarcely have appeared to advantage; and for this reason Vergil made the apparition a little less definite than the many veridical visions. Vergil knew Lucretius well; and I have wondered whether the dream was not a projection of Mercury, like the *simulacra* of the gods which in Epicurean doctrine come to mankind from the *intermundia* (Lucr. 5.1169-1182 and 6.76-77).

In the fifth book, for a time, Aeneas resembles Achilles. Both preside at games held in honor of one they loved, now dead. Both distribute prizes generously and settle disputes. Neither competes: they remain above the contest. (Before the chariot-race Achilles says that if he entered he would certainly win, *Il.* 23.274-278: a remark inconceivable for Aeneas.) In his brief speech to the defeated Trojan boxer Dares (5.465-467) Aeneas says "infelix, quae tanta animum dementia cepit?" This is one of Vergil's own phrases: he applied it to Corydon in *Buc.* 2.69, Pasiphae in *Buc.* 6.47, and Orpheus in *Georg.* 4.488; but here it can scarcely be meant to recall any of these figures. It does, however, resemble the rebukes addressed by Agamemnon to

Menelaus and by Poseidon to the Homeric Aeneas when they propose to duel with stronger men (*Il.* 7.109-114, 20.332-336): note "dementia" ≈ ἀφραίνειc, "uiris alias" ≈ ἀμείνονι φωτί and cεῦ κρείccων. Later, after fortune shows her changed face and the fleet has been set afire, Aeneas prays for help to Jupiter in the tones, not of Achilles, but of wise Nestor at the moment when Apollo breaks down the wall around the Greek ships (*Aen.* 5.687-692 ≈ *Il.* 15.372-376). The Lord hears his prayer, and (as for Nestor) thunders assent.

The sixth book takes Aeneas to the realm of the dead. Here again he mainly resembles Odysseus. First, however, he prays to Apollo, reminding him of a prophecy made by his kinsman Hector, which Apollo later fulfilled (*Aen.* 6.57-58 ≈ *Il.* 22.359-360). Then he asks the Sibyl to ensure his settlement in Latium (*Aen.* 6.65-68) as Odysseus begs Circe to send him home (*Od.* 10.483-486). But Aeneas prays her of his own will to permit him to visit the world of death and see his father (*Aen.* 6.106-123), whereas Odysseus, told by Circe that he must go to the dwelling of Hades, weeps and grovels (*Od.* 10.487-498).[15] Aeneas is much firmer than this. Indeed, the opening of his speech (103-105) is remarkably like a sentence spoken by the fettered Titan in Aeschylus (*P.V.* 101-103):

> non ulla laborum,
> o uirgo, noua mi facies inopinaue surgit:
> omnia praecepi atque animo mecum ante peregi.

> πάντα προυξεπίcταμαι
> cκεθρῶc τὰ μέλλοντ᾽, οὐδέ μοι ποταίνιον
> πῆμ᾽ οὐδὲν ἥξει.

Among the dead Aeneas greets Palinurus as Odysseus greeted Elpenor, although he does not (like Odysseus) make

---

[15] Later, it is Tiresias that Odysseus asks how his mother's silent ghost may speak with him (*Od.* 11.140-144); but this is less important than the general description of the journey to the underworld, and the parallel of Aeneas with the Sibyl to Odysseus with Circe is more emphatic.

a grim joke: *Aen.* 6.341-346 ≈ *Od.* 11.57-58. To the soul of Dido he speaks gently, as Odysseus to the soul of Ajax, and is likewise met by silence and pride and inextinguishable hatred (*Aen.* 6.456-466 ≈ *Od.* 11.553-562). Norden (*Aeneis VI*, pp. 247-249) points out that his speech is colored with reminiscences of Alexandrian erotic poetry. The most remarkable echo, however, is the central line:

inuitus, regina, tuo de litore cessi.[16]

This is an adaptation, with small changes, from line 39 of Catullus 66, itself a free translation of Callimachus's *Coma Berenices*.[17] In Catullus a lock of hair cut from a woman's head as a gage of love speaks from heaven, where it has become a constellation, and says to her:

inuita, o regina, tuo de uertice cessi.

That declaration, although solemn in manner, is playful. The Vergilian echo of it on the lips of a lover to a woman who killed herself after losing him seems to our minds to strike a false note. Doubtless Vergil's ear was haunted by the cadence,[18] and he thought of the general context of the line: separation, and love remembered in an after-life.[19] In a sensitive article entitled "Vergil's Debt to Catullus," *AC* 1 (1958) p. 59, R.E.H. Westendoerp-Boerma points to another adaptation in which Vergil borrowed a cadence from Catullus but changed its playful tone to one of tragic pathos. The girls singing the bridal song in Catullus 62.24 declare that for a girl her wedding is like rape and enslavement—"quid faciunt hostes capta crudelius

---

[16] Austin in his edition of Book Two points out the rhythmical resemblance of this line to 2.3: "infandum, regina, iubes renouare dolorem."

[17] Norden observes that in Catullus the line is followed, in Vergil preceded, by a lover's oath.

[18] Vergil improved the sound by changing Catullus's slightly cacophonous –*ce cessi*.

[19] A. Thornton in *AUMLA* 17 (1962) 77-79 suggests a further implication: Aeneas is destined, like the Lock, to be translated "ad sidera caeli" (*Aen.* 1.259-260).

urbe?"—and are answered by the young men, who say that the wedding is heavenly happiness. But Aeneas, desperate after the loss of his wife, madly cries (*Aen.* 2.746)

> quid in euersa uidi crudelius urbe?

On p. 60 the same scholar brings out a third such echo. Catullus hails the Argonauts with enthusiastic admiration (64.23-23b):

> heroes, saluete, deum genus![20] o bona matrum
> progenies, saluete iter<um . . .

In deep affection and melancholy yearning, Aeneas greets his father (5.80-81):

> salue, sancte parens, iterum; saluete, recepti
> nequiquam cineres.

Later in the underworld Aeneas hails Deiphobus and hears the ghastly tale of his murder, as Odysseus does with Agamemnon (*Aen.* 6.500-508 ≈ *Od.* 11.397-403); but his greeting to his comrade is warmer than that of Odysseus to his overlord. The fine adjective "armipotens" (500) stresses the courage of Deiphobus (and therefore the indignity of his mutilations): Lucretius in an emphatic passage (1.33) applies it to Mars; Vergil also to Mars (*Aen.* 9.717), to Minerva (2.425, 11.483), and in this book to Achilles (6.839). Aeneas tells how, after building a cenotaph, he called Deiphobus's name thrice, as Odysseus did for his comrades slain by the Cicones (*Aen.* 6.506 ≈ *Od.* 9.65). Afterwards, meeting his father, he tries to embrace him, as Odysseus to embrace his mother; but the spirit melts like air or dream (*Aen.* 6.695-702 ≈ *Od.* 11.204-214). His plea to Anchises, "teque amplexu ne subtrahe nostro" (*Aen.* 6.698), is a warmer version of his earlier plea to Dido (6.465), "teque aspectu ne subtrahe nostro." His phrase about the young phantom-soul of Marcellus, "nox atra caput tristi circumuolat

---

[20] Madvig proposed *deum gens* here; Vergil uses "deum gens" of Aeneas in an Argonautical context, *Aen.* 10.228.

umbra" (6.866), comes originally from the seer who saw the suitors of Penelope as doomed (*Od.* 20.351-352):

$$\nu\nu\kappa\tau\grave{\iota} \ \mu\grave{\epsilon}\nu \ \acute{\upsilon}\mu\acute{\epsilon}\omega\nu$$
$$\epsilon\grave{\iota}\lambda\acute{\upsilon}\alpha\tau\alpha\iota \ \kappa\epsilon\phi\alpha\lambda\alpha\acute{\iota} \ \tau\epsilon \ \pi\rho\acute{o}c\omega\pi\acute{\alpha} \ \tau\epsilon. \ . \ . \ .$$

Yet the wording recalls Aeneas's own description of the Trojan warriors facing death in the fallen city (*Aen.* 2.360):

nox atra caua circumuolat umbra.

In the seventh and eighth books Aeneas speaks seldom, and in the ninth not at all. His prayer to Tiber and the nymphs in 8.71-78 is built on Odysseus' prayers to the kindly river in *Od.* 5.445-450 and to the nymphs of Ithaca in *Od.* 13.356-360: one saves the hero's life, the others welcome him to his home.[21] The invocation to the river is a verbal reminiscence of Ennius (*Ann.* 54):

teque, pater Tiberine, tuo cum flumine sancto.[22]

Vergil keeps the old-fashioned "cum," but elaborates "pater Tiberine" into "Thybri . . . genitor."

Aeneas's diplomatic speech to Evander (8.127-151) is only remotely akin to Telemachus's address to Nestor in *Od.* 3.79-101, but its rich genealogical detail recalls the speech made by the Homeric Aeneas to Achilles, *Il.* 20.200-241. The fine phrase "accipe daque fidem" comes from a speech in Ennius, apparently uttered by Aeneas himself to a prospective ally, the king of Alba (*Ann.* 32). Because he is talking of old far-off things, he uses another Ennian phrase: "ut Grai perhibent" (8.135) reflects *Ann.* 148, "uento quem perhibent Graium genus aera lingua." Cartault (p. 641) points out in "sed mea me uirtus" (8.131) a reminiscence, perhaps unconscious, of Lucretius's address to Memmius (1.140): "sed tua me uirtus. . . ."

---

[21] Jason in the *Argonautica* 4.1305-1336 is helped by local nymphs, and thanks them briefly.

[22] Spoken by Aeneas himself (so Norden, *Ennius und Vergilius*, Berlin, 1915, pp. 161-162) or by Ilia (so Vahlen).

The tenth book, where the fighting flares up, contains a cluster of brief speeches by Aeneas (see p. 33 above). Where they have Homeric models, they are adapted from speeches made by combatants in the *Iliad*—although the disparity in context and atmosphere is sometimes considerable. After the nymph Cymodocea tells him she and her sisters are his ships transformed by Cybele, he prays to the mother-goddess to continue her favor to the Trojans as they enter the war (*Aen.* 10.252-255). In the fateful sixteenth book of the *Iliad* (233-248) Achilles prays Dodonaean Zeus to help Patroclus as he enters the war. The Homeric prayer seems to have suggested the prayer of Aeneas (Knauer, p. 311 n. 2 and p. 414). The divinities are both ancient and venerable; both prayers are set at the opening of a crucial, though not final, conflict. On p. 297 Knauer also refers to Achilles' words at the close of his tirade to Patroclus, when he wishes that all the Trojans might die and all the Argives too—all except Patroclus and Achilles himself (*Il.* 16.97-100); but surely this is far removed from Aeneas's sober "adsis pede, diua, secundo." The few phrases uttered by Aeneas before stabbing Magus in the throat (*Aen.* 10.531-534) and after beheading Tarquitus (*Aen.* 10.557-560) are compressed excerpts from the two long speeches of Achilles to Priam's son Lycaon (*Il.* 21.99-113 and 122-135).[23] All three victims are killed in the same way, with a sword-blow in the neck. Vergil follows his model a little too closely when he makes his hero say (559-560) that Tarquitus, unburied, will be eaten by fishes. Achilles has indeed thrown Lycaon's body into the Scamander, but Aeneas is fighting in the middle of a plain with chariots wheeling all around. A little later, he hits the charioteer Lucagus with a throwing-spear, and says he jumped out of the chariot to escape (*Aen.* 10.592-594). This is a briefer and less farcical version of Patroclus' taunt that Cebriones might do well diving for oysters (*Il.* 16.745-750). At

---

[23] "Pallante perempto" (10.533) also recalls Achilles' words to Hector, Πατροκλῆ' ἐξεναρίζων (*Il.* 22.331).

the end of the book, driving Mezentius to death, Aeneas echoes Achilles challenging Hector (*Aen.* 10.876 ≈ *Il.* 20.429) and Sarpedon chiding Hector for cowardice (*Aen.* 10.897-898 ≈ *Il.* 5.472).

In Book Eleven Aeneas grows even more like the Greek champion of the *Iliad*. Standing beside the trophy bearing the bloodstained armor of Mezentius, he addresses his commanders as Achilles addresses the Argives after slaying Hector (*Aen.* 11.14-28 ≈ *Il.* 22.378-394): here is our victory; now we must attack the city; but first let us bury the dead. The phrase "non uirtutis egentem" (11.27) is from Ennius (*Ann.* 599), and the last line, describing Pallas' early death, is touchingly quoted from the description of the souls of dead children in *Aen.* 6.429. Next, he apostrophizes the corpse of Pallas (*Aen.* 11.42-58) as Achilles laments over the corpse of Patroclus (*Il.* 18.324-342). Each recalls the promises he made to the dead man's father and reflects on the defeat of human hopes. But there the resemblance between the speeches ends. Achilles goes on to declare that although he too must die at Troy, meanwhile he will avenge Patroclus by killing Hector in battle and cutting the throats of twelve Trojan prisoners. Aeneas says nothing of himself or of revenge, but pities the old father, praises the dead youth's courage,[24] and thinks of the loss his death will mean to Italy and to his own successor Ascanius. The affectionate phrase "miserande puer" (11.42) was uttered once before by Aeneas, over the body of Lausus (10.825), and before that by Anchises, contemplating the spirit of Marcellus (6.882). E. R. Curtius[25] points out that for the Romans *puerilis* was a word of disapproval, but that Vergil used the word *puer* with affection (*Buc.* 4.60) and even with respect ("uenerande

---

[24] Here "at" (*Aen.* 11.55) introduces a thought of consolation, as ἀλλά often does: cf. Archilochus *Eleg.* 7 (*Anth. Lyr. Graec.* 3, ed. Diehl-Beutler, 1952).

[25] *Kritische Essays zur europäischen Literatur* (Berne, 1963³) pp. 18-19.

puer," *Aen.* 9.276). In lines 45-46 Vergil incorporates an echo
of the love-poem he often quotes:

at non haec quondam blanda promissa dedisti
uoce mihi.   (Cat. 64.139-140)

The verse describing Evander's farewell to Aeneas (11.47)

mitteret in magnum imperium metuensque moneret

has a dense alliteration on *M*, and contains a curious phrase
which is also applied by Anchises to Numa in 6.812: curious,
in that it is really an exaggeration to describe either the little
city of Numa or the still unbuilt city of Aeneas as "magnum
imperium." The heavy homoeoptoton made Norden (*Aeneis
VI*, p. 327) suggest that the phrase was borrowed from Ennius.
This may well be true: cf. *magnus Titanu'* (*Ann.* 28, ci.
Merula), *magnis dis* (*Ann.* 201), *magnis animis* (*Ann.* 515),
and *templum magnum* (*Ann.* 541). If so, it had impressive
overtones for Vergil's Roman readers. There is an echo of
Greek tragedy in "nil iam caelestibus ullis / debentem" (*Aen.*
11.51-52), which may well come from Sophocles, *Ant.* 1072-
1073:

ὧν οὔτε coὶ μέτεcτιν οὔτε τοῖc ἄνω
θεοῖcιν.

The courage of Pallas is enhanced by the closing exclamation,
"quantum / praesidium, Ausonia, . . . perdis!"—which distant-
ly recalls the apostrophe of Ennius's Romans to the dead
Romulus (*Ann.* 112):

qualem te patriae custodem di genuerunt!

The last farewell of Aeneas to Pallas (*Aen.* 11.96-98) resem-
bles the last farewell of Achilles kindling Patroclus's pyre (*Il.*
23.179-183); but it incorporates a tender reminiscence of Catul-
lus's farewell to his brother, "in perpetuum . . . aue atque uale"
(101.10), and does not mention the human sacrifices to the

207

spirit of the dead.[26] Gilbert Murray had a theory that the Homeric poems were originally full of references to customs which to the later Greeks appeared barbaric (such as poisoning arrows) and that a process of "expurgation" had cut most of them out of the text.[27] Certainly Vergil's method in adapting Homeric material within the *Aeneid* involved, among other changes, something like expurgation of barbarity. In this same episode there is another instance of Vergil's care to modify a piece of Homeric cruelty. In the *Iliad*, after Achilles has killed Hector he strips the body. Then the sons of the Achaeans stand over it and utter words of triumph, and stab it every one (*Il.* 22.367-375). In the *Aeneid*, with his last breath, Mezentius begs Aeneas to protect his corpse from the bitter hatred of the other Etruscans (*Aen.* 10.903-906). Next day, as Aeneas is constructing the trophy, we are specifically told that (although Aeneas killed him with a stab in the throat) Mezentius's cuirass was pierced in twelve places (*Aen.* 11.9-10). The implication is clear: he was stabbed after death by one warrior from each of the twelve Etruscan cities, so that they might symbolically take part in the death of the tyrant.[28] But the

[26] Achilles captures twelve Trojans in *Il.* 21.26-32, promises them to Patroclus's ghost in *Il.* 23.19-23, and butchers them in *Il.* 23.175-182, telling the ghost as he does so. Aeneas captures eight Italians (four sons of each of two fathers) in *Aen.* 10.517-520, and sends them off to be sacrificed in Pallanteum at the cremation of Pallas (*Aen.* 11.81-82), but never speaks of them. S. E. Bassett (cited above, n. 11) pp. 203-206, has a persuasive defense of Achilles' behavior in this point.

[27] G.G.A. Murray, *The Rise of the Greek Epic* (Oxford, 1934⁴) ch. 5.

[28] Cf. Joshua x. 15-26. After the victory at Gibeon, the king of Jerusalem and four other kings were found hiding in a cave. Joshua "called for all the men of Israel, and said unto the captains of the men of war which went with him, Come near, put your feet upon the necks of these kings. And they came near, and put their feet upon the necks of them. And Joshua said unto them, Fear not, nor be dismayed, be strong and of good courage: for thus shall the Lord do to all your enemies against whom ye fight. And afterward Joshua smote them, and slew them, and hanged them on five trees." Com-

action is not described by Vergil: only its result, and that very briefly.

In the final book Aeneas speaks seldom but forcibly. His oath in 12.176-194 resembles two oaths sworn by Agamemnon in the *Iliad* (see pp. 119-120); and his farewell to Ascanius (12.435-440, discussed above, p. 31) draws on the *Iliad*, the *Odyssey*, Greek and Roman tragedy, and Roman epic. When he commands an immediate attack on the city of Latinus (*Aen.* 12.565-573), his words are reminiscent of Achilles' speech over Hector's body (*Il.* 22.378-394, especially 381-384), but there is a hard ring in them like the voice of a Roman general, "Iuppiter hac stat" (Ennius, *Ann.* 258); while his imperious phrase

ni frenum accipere et uicti parere fatentur

(12.568)

ominously recalls Allecto exhorting Turnus to attack king Latinus,

ni dare coniugium et dicto parere fatetur.

(7.433)

For his terminal challenge to Turnus, the menacing words in which he tells his foe to change shape, fly up into the sky, or hide in the interior of the earth (12.889-893), no close parallel has been discovered. It goes beyond Achilles' challenge to Hector in *Il.* 22.261-272, although "contrahe quidquid / siue animis siue arte uales" is an elaboration of παντοίης ἀρετῆς μιμνήσκεο, κτλ. But there is a dark resemblance to a remark made by Turnus's patron Juno. In 7.309, speaking of her efforts to thwart Aeneas, she says "memet in omnia uerti." Now Aeneas, facing Turnus, tells him "uerte omnis tete in facies." The emphatic pronominal forms "memet" and "tete" emphasize the similarity.

---

pare also the killing of Neoptolemus by the Delphians in Eur. *Androm.* 1149-1155: τίς οὐ cίδηρον προσφέρει, τίς οὐ πέτρον;

The words Aeneas speaks before the death-blow (12.947-949), based on the speech of Achilles after spearing Hector (*Il.* 22.331-336), complete his final resemblance to the fiercest of the Homeric heroes.

Turnus

Turnus is a man of action. In combat he talks little. Also, he is subject to fits of depression when he scarcely speaks (e.g. *Aen.* 12.219-221). He makes only six speeches of any size and weight.

His chief oration is delivered at the debate of the Latins in Book Eleven. For the debate itself, the model is the council called by Agamemnon in *Iliad* 2. Both are initiated by a serious setback: the Achaeans have lost the support of Achilles, the Latins are denied that of Diomede. Both are opened by a discouraging proposal to cut short the war, uttered by the monarch (*Aen.* 11.302-335 ≈ *Il.* 2.110-141). In both, a spiteful and loquacious orator attacks one of the princes and provokes a violent reply (*Aen.* 11.336-409 ≈ *Il.* 2.211-269). Both end in the resumption of hostilities (*Aen.* 11.445f. ≈ *Il.* 2.381f.).

Turnus's speech has a skillful structure (analyzed on pp. 59-63 above). It is based on several Homeric models. He begins (11.378-409) with a rebuttal of Drances' charges against him. This is elaborated from a warning of Iris (disguised as Polites) to Priam and the Trojans in *Il.* 2.796-797. It states the basic antithesis between words and war: "copia fandi" × "bella"; "uerbis" × "hostem"; "eloquio" × "tropaeis"; "uentosa lingua" × "pedibus fugacibus." The contemptuous tone is suggested by Odysseus' reproof to Thersites (*Il.* 2.246-269). Vergil has prepared this by making Drances hate Turnus as Thersites hated Achilles and Odysseus and Agamemnon (*Aen.* 11.122-123 + 336-337 ≈ *Il.* 2.220-222), although he paints him as less of a clown and more of a serious politician. Odysseus silences Thersites by striking him with the speakers' sceptre and threatening to strip him and thrash him if he offends again (*Il.* 2.258-269). This is beneath the dignity of the Latin assembly. The two central ideas of Turnus's attack on Drances—that Drances is a coward, and that he deserves a blow from Turnus's sword—are put more bluntly in the last sentences of Hector's retort to Polydamas in *Il.* 12.244-250. Something of Hector's threat and something of Odysseus' blow, both are contained in the intimidating gesture of Turnus (*Aen.* 11.408-409; see above, p. 61). His rejoinder to Drances contains other Homeric echoes. Lines 384-386 are an inversion of Nestor's encouragement to Diomede (*Il.* 8.152-156); there are overtones of the rebuke addressed to Antenor by Paris in *Il.* 7.357-364 ("demens," *Aen.* 11.399 ≈ θεοὶ φρένας ὤλεσαν, *Il.* 7.360).

After this rebuttal Turnus discusses the alternative proposals before the meeting: to make peace—which he denounces as cowardice, saying death would be better, in accents reminiscent of the Homeric Diomede (*Aen.* 11.416-418 ≈ *Il.* 8.146-150)—or to continue to fight, which he recommends, as Hector does in responding to Polydamas (*Aen.* 11.419-433 ≈ *Il.* 18.285-309). In this part of his speech he is more optimistic than Hector, although scarcely more valiant. Hector admits that Troy, once rich, is now poor (*Il.* 18.288-292), whereas Turnus enumerates the resources and allies of the Latins (*Aen.* 11.419-420 + 429-433), saying they are still amply sufficient for the struggle. Hector argues that the fortune of war may favor either side (*Il.* 18.309). So does Turnus (*Aen.* 11.425-427) in phrasing adapted from a passage in Ennius's *Annals* 287-289 dealing with the hard effort of the Hannibalic war:

multa dies in bello conficit unus; . . .
et rursus multae fortunae forte recumbunt:
haudquaquam quemquam semper Fortuna secuta est.

To conclude, Turnus signifies that he is willing to fight a decisive duel with Aeneas (*Aen.* 11.434-444). Here he sounds partly like Paris challenged by Menelaus, although bolder (*Il.* 3.67-75), and partly like Hector determining to face Achilles (*Il.* 18.305-309 + 20.371-372, with which compare *Aen.* 11.438-440: καὶ εἰ ≈ "licet"). Thus in one speech Vergil has blended elements from several different Homeric debates, and has given Turnus the lineaments now of Odysseus and now of Paris, but chiefly of Hector.

It is Hector also whom Turnus most often resembles in his other important speeches. Less lovable and more complicated, he is nevertheless placed in Hector's position, as a defender counter-attacking the invaders of his country, and he reacts in ways which are significantly similar or dissimilar.

His first words in the poem are a snub to "Calybe," whom he dismisses, telling her that wars are men's work (*Aen.* 7.436-444). With the same maxim Hector dismisses Andromache in *Il.* 6.490-493.[29] But what a difference! the loving husband affectionately sending his wife home, the arrogant youth contemptuously mocking the old crone! The little scene is apparently modelled on an episode in Callimachus's *Hymn to Demeter* 42-64. A goddess disguised as a priestess gives a warning to a mortal; he makes an insulting reply; she changes to her true shape (γείνατο δ᾽ ἁ θεύc) and upbraids him.

After the miraculous metamorphosis of the Trojan fleet he makes a long harangue to encourage his men (*Aen.* 9.128-158). It blends thoughts from two speeches of Hector, one delivered while he is pursuing Diomede and Nestor and hears Zeus thunder thrice to encourage him (*Il.* 8.173-183) and the second some hours later, after night interrupts the battle (*Il.* 8.497-541). Still, there are important differences, which are discussed above on pp. 88-89. The speech also contains a brief echo of Achilles addressing the embassy (*Aen.* 9.136-139 ≈ *Il.* 9.340-343). As Cartault points out (p. 694), Turnus appears to have read the *Aeneid*, for he quotes it several times in this

---

[29] The same thought in different contexts: Zeus to Aphrodite, *Il.* 5.428, and Telemachus to Penelope, *Od.* 21.350-353.

discourse: "non mille carinis" (9.148) ≈ "non mille carinae" (2.198); "caeca condemur in aluo" (9.152) ≈ "nota conduntur in aluo" (2.401); and, a more impressive citation,

> at non uiderunt moenia Troiae
> Neptuni fabricata manu considere in ignis?
>
> (9.144-145)
>
> tum uero omne mihi uisum considere in ignis
> Ilium et ex imo uerti Neptunia Troia.
>
> (2.624-625)

One line in the speech, attested by the whole manuscript tradition, "Palladii caesis late[30] custodibus arcis" (9.151) is, with one word changed, repeated from 2.166. Some editors have excised it. Being one of several such repetitions in this speech, it should be kept in the text. The others contain little variations (e.g. "Neptunia" ≈ "Neptuni fabricata manu"), and here the variation "late," well supported, should be preferred. Turnus's "maria inuia Teucris" (9.130) is reminiscent of Helenus's prophecy (3.381-383): "Italiam . . . / longa procul longis uia diuidit inuia terris." Cartault (p. 694) remarks that the harsh phrase "exscindere gentem" (9.137) "reproduit mécaniquement la fin d'hexamètre, IV, 425, Troianam exscindere gentem." This is far from being a mechanical repetition: it is a meaningful echo. The phrase occurs only twice in the *Aeneid*: here, and in a sentence in which Dido mentions the Greek oath to "root out the race" of Troy (4.425).[31] It is a mistake to assume that Vergil's effects are not carefully planned.

In despair as he is borne away from battle on the Etruscan

---

[30] late *FRbr, Tib.*: summae *MPω.*

[31] Vergil uses the active verb *exscindere* again in two equally energetic sentences: the gods themselves could not uproot hell (6.553), and Juno plans to uproot both Trojans and Latins (7.316). He employs the passive no less forcibly, of the destruction of Troy (2.177) and of the destruction of the Latin city (12.643): would Cartault have called that also "répétition mécanique"? Statius, although often imitative, knew the flavor of Latin words: he uses "exscindere gentem" in a context of extreme violence (*Theb.* 4.670).

ship, Turnus shouts a passionate apostrophe to Jupiter asking why he deserves such a humiliation, and to the winds begging them to wreck the ship (*Aen.* 10.668-679). It has been suggested that the model for this speech is Achilles' outcry when attacked by the river Scamander (*Il.* 21.273-283). Yet Achilles hopes for life, not death—or a noble death rather than drowning; Turnus prays for shipwreck. Achilles thinks of his own safety, Turnus of his hard-pressed comrades. Achilles is engaged in an exhausting conflict, while Turnus raves because he is kept from fighting. In fact, there is no close Homeric parallel for this speech in its situation. Several paladins of the *Iliad* are miraculously snatched out of battle by gods who wish to preserve them, and set down in safety. They never complain or protest. Paris says there will be another day, and goes to bed with Helen (*Il.* 3.437-447). Aeneas is rescued by Aphrodite (*Il.* 5.311-317) and then by Apollo, who takes him away and substitutes a phantom for his body (*Il.* 5.343-346 + 431-453); but when he returns he makes no comment (*Il.* 5.512-518). Later, carried through the air by Poseidon and warned not to fight Achilles, he still says nothing (*Il.* 20.318-340). Hector is somehow excluded from the battle by Zeus, and accepts the divine command (*Il.* 11.163-164 + 195-209). Later he is concealed by mist from the eyes of Achilles, and next appears standing outside the Scaean Gate, apparently quite unmoved (*Il.* 20.441-454 + 22.5-6). The closest parallel for Turnus in this situation is Achilles cut off from the fray and weeping for his lost honor (*Il.* 1.348-356); yet there is no Homeric speech so frantic in its tone. Diomede's address to Nestor (*Il.* 8.146-150), which Turnus echoes (*Aen.* 10.675-676 ≈ *Il.* 8.150),[32] is, although gloomy, much calmer and more controlled.

Turnus makes one of his finest speeches in anticipation of death (*Aen.* 12.632-649). It begins as a reply to his sister Juturna disguised as his charioteer—echoing Diomede to Athena (*Il.* 5.815). It passes into a series of questions and

[32] Also Agamemnon to Menelaus, *Il.* 4.182.

complaints which are addressed to himself as much as to her, and ends with an invocation to the spirits of the dead. Similarly Hector, awaiting Achilles outside Troy, hears his father and mother beg him to take refuge inside the walls. He does not answer them, but communes with himself (*Il.* 22.99-130). First he considers the disgrace of flight: this is Turnus's chief concern, and he recalls the taunts of Drances, as Hector the warnings of Polydamas. Hector thinks of avoiding combat by offering surrender and retribution, but dismisses the idea (*Il.* 22.111-125). Turnus merely glances at this thought and instantly rejects it (*Aen.* 12.645). But Hector closes by telling himself it will be a fair fight, whose outcome Zeus will decide. Turnus concludes with the certainty of death: death with honor. He is less confident than Hector. And in his final plea to Aeneas for mercy—suggested by the words of both Hector and Priam to Achilles (*Aen.* 12.931-938 ≈ *Il.* 22.338-343 + 24.486-487)—he abandons his determination and begs for his life. Not so Hector, who grimly forecasts the death of his foe (*Il.* 22.356-360). Turnus is a weaker figure, less nobly tragic.

The shorter utterances of Turnus are modelled on brief speeches made in debate or combat by heroes of the *Iliad*. Both their resemblances to their models and their differences from them repay analysis. He hails Iris (*Aen.* 9.18-22) more eloquently than Achilles in *Il.* 18.182 + 188-195. His war-cry in *Aen.* 9.51-52 is too short and asymmetrical to have a Homeric counterpart; but his situation and his excitement resemble those of Hector driving his chariot up to the Achaean wall in *Il.* 15.343-355: note *fremitu horrisono* ≈ ἠχῆι θεσπεσίηι. His gesture of hurling a spear toward the foe is not mere useless exhibitionism. It prefigures a Roman custom dating to the time of the kings, and described by Livy 1.32. Before the Romans began operations of war, an envoy formally asked the prospective enemy for satisfaction of Rome's grievances. If it was not forthcoming, a priest from the college of *fetiales* carried a bloodstained spear to the frontier, recited the formal declaration of war, and threw the spear into the enemy's territory.[33] Turnus is much less formal, more impetuous. Still, his gesture is a Roman gesture—as when he hoisted the red *uexillum* on the citadel as a signal for war (*Aen.* 8.1-2).

Challenging Pandarus (*Aen.* 9.741-742 + 747-748), he likens himself to Achilles:[34] his challenge echoes the threat of Achilles to Hector (*Il.* 22.268-271), as does his earlier taunt to Lycus (*Aen.* 9.560-561): "euadere" and "effugies" ≈ ὑπάλυξις; "uirtus" ≈ ἀρετή. When summoning his men to resist the Trojans and their allies on the beach (*Aen.* 10.279-284), he speaks in the accents of Achilles to the Myrmidons (*Aen.* 10.279 ≈ *Il.* 16.207-208), of Patroclus to Meriones (*Aen.* 10.280 ≈ *Il.* 16.630), and of Nestor rallying his comrades as the Trojans attack the Greek ships (*Il.* 15.661-666). He ends vigorously with "audentis Fortuna iuuat," which is close to Ennius's "fortibus est fortuna uiris data" (*Ann.* 257) and closer still to *fortis Fortuna adiuuat*, a proverb used by Terence, *Phormio* 203, and cited by Cicero, *Tusc.* 2.4.11. As he drives forward to meet Pallas (*Aen.* 10.441-443) he sounds like Sarpedon facing Patroclus (*Il.* 16.423-425), but more confident, and as cruel as Pyrrhus (*Aen.* 2.526-532); while his words before launching his fatal spear are like Diomede's mockery of Paris (*Aen.* 10.481 ≈ *Il.* 11.391-392) though more brief. For his speech over the body of Pallas (*Aen.* 10.491-495) it is hard to find a parallel, since a Homeric hero normally does not send a victim's corpse back to his kinsmen.

When he shouts a challenge to Aeneas, Turnus resembles Achilles calling to Hector (*Aen.* 10.649 ≈ *Il.* 20.429). His foe "Aeneas" here is a fleeing phantom made of cloud, and a moment later in the *Iliad* Apollo shrouds Hector in thick mist.

---

[33] G. Wissowa, *Religion und Kultus der Römer* (Munich, 1902) pp. 478-479. Octavian himself went through the ritual (at the temple of Bellona, not at the frontier) when declaring war on Cleopatra in 32 B.C.: see Dio 50.4.5.

[34] In 6.89-90 the Sibyl predicts the appearance of another Achilles in Italy.

The long debate of the Latins and Rutulians is terminated by Turnus' call to arms (*Aen.* 11.459-461) as the Trojan assembly is broken up by Hector (although his actual words are not given, *Il.* 2.807-810). However, since methods of warfare in the *Iliad* are primitive, there can be no Homeric prototype for Turnus's complex strategic dispositions in *Aen.* 11.463-467 and 508-519. Cavalry engagements and tactical surprise are unknown to Homer's warriors.

During his conversation with Latinus (*Aen.* 12.11-17 + 48-53) Turnus expresses sentiments like those of Paris to Hector (*Il.* 3.59-75); but he is far more arrogant. When he insults Latinus by saying that his subjects should be content to sit and watch while he himself risks his life, "*sedeant* spectentque Latini" (*Aen.* 12.15), he is repeating, and, by addressing it directly to their monarch, aggravating a taunt he has already uttered, "pacem laudate *sedentes*" (*Aen.* 11.460). No hero in the *Iliad* addresses a much older man with such bitter asperity, except Achilles berating his enemy Priam (*Il.* 24.560-570).

After Hecuba begs Hector to avoid battle, he makes no reply (*Il.* 22.82-92). When Amata makes a similar plea, Turnus throws her three curt lines (*Aen.* 12.72-74) recalling the words of Jason to his mother Alcimede (*Argon.* 1.295-297 + 304) and more distantly those of Priam to Hecuba (*Il.* 24.218-219).

No one in the *Iliad* invokes his spear and urges it to help him in killing his enemy, as Turnus does in *Aen.* 12.95-100.[35] His taunt to the dying son of Dolon (*Aen.* 12.359-361) has no exact Homeric model; perhaps the closest parallel is the Trojan Agenor's boast when facing Achilles (*Il.* 21.583-589: "petisti" ≈ ἔολπας). His exclamation of alarm at hearing the outcries from the city (*Aen.* 12.620-621) is primarily inspired by the

---

[35] Homer makes both Hector and Achilles call on their horses to help them in the fray (*Il.* 8.185-197, 19.400-403); Turnus visits his horses but does not speak to them (*Aen.* 12.81-86). Mezentius invokes his right hand and his spear in *Aen.* 10.773-774. The pathetic apostrophe of Philoctetes to his bow— "φρένας εἴ τινας ἔχεις"—in Soph. *Phil.* 1128-1139 is quite unlike Turnus's speech in feeling and in pattern: a connection is not probable.

soliloquy of Achilles hearing the clamor of retreat after Patroclus's death (*Il.* 18.6-14); but Vergil gives Turnus words ("quid tanto turbantur moenia luctu?") which recall the awakening of Aeneas at the capture of Troy ("diuerso interea miscentur moenia luctu," 2.298). When Turnus tells Juturna he is resolved to face death (*Aen.* 12.676-680), he echoes Hector saying that the gods have summoned him to perish (*Il.* 22.297-305). In the last few moments of his life he speaks of the enmity of Jupiter, as Hector of Zeus and Apollo before his last charge (*Aen.* 12.894-895 ≈ *Il.* 22.300-303).

Dido

Dido makes thirteen speeches, ten of them long and important. Her great utterances have many resonances from earlier literature. Since so much of the best Greek and early Latin poetry has been lost, we can scarcely hope to trace all their inspirations; but in the main they are drawn from epic combined with tragedy.

Welcoming the Trojan embassy in *Aen.* 1.562-578, she sounds somewhat like Alcinous addressing Odysseus in *Od.* 7.309-328. Both monarchs promise safe-conduct out of their dominions; both express the wish that their guests would stay and settle down.[36] But Dido is less confident than the king of the Phaeacians. She speaks with downcast gaze, *uultum demissa*. This has been called a false note.[37] But it is a natural reaction to the harsh questions put to her by Ilioneus (1.539-540), "Quod genus hoc hominum? quaeue hunc *tam barbara* morem / permittit patria?" and accompanies the apologetic words with which she begins (1.563-568).[38] Furthermore, it is intended to recall another queen who, by offering hospitality,

---

[36] Pelasgus gives the Danaids a similar reassurance and a similar invitation in Aeschylus, *Suppl.* 954-965.
[37] Heinze (p. 138 and n. 2), on whom see Hügi, p. 88.
[38] So J. Kvíčala, *Vergil-Studien* (Prague, 1878) pp. 143-145.

delayed a hero on his mission. Hypsipyle turns her eyes away from Jason's, blushing as she speaks (*Argon.* 1.790-792); and the terms in which she invites Jason to settle in Lemnos (*Argon.* 1.827-831) are echoed in Dido's offer to the Trojan embassy (*Aen.* 1.572-574).[39]

When Aeneas appears out of the cloud, Dido significantly addresses him in phrases of wonder and admiration (*Aen.* 1.615-630) which faintly recall those of Circe kneeling before Odysseus (*Od.* 10.325-335). True, her speech is far more dignified than that of the wily enchantress; yet Vergil wishes us to remember that Circe invited Odysseus to her bed. Dido's last sentence, "non ignara mali miseris succurrere disco," resembles the reminiscent speech of Menelaus at the arrival of Telemachus (*Od.* 4.33-35) as well as the generous words of Theseus to Oedipus (Soph. *O.C.* 560-568). At the banquet she speaks like Alcinous, pouring a libation to Zeus patron of suppliants (*Aen.* 1.731-735 ≈ *Od.* 7.179-181) and then questioning the guest about Troy and his wanderings (*Aen.* 1.750-756 ≈ *Od.* 8.572-586). There is also, it would seem, a reminiscence of Naevius's *Punic War*, of which one fragment (frg. 23 Strzelecki) may apply to Dido:

> blande et docte percontat Aenea quo pacto
> Troiam urbem liquerit.

With *blande* compare Venus's "tenet Dido blandisque moratur / uocibus" (*Aen.* 1.670-671); with *docte*, Dido's own protest (1.565-568) and the paintings in Juno's temple (1.456-493).[40]

Her first speech in Book Four (9-29), reflecting on her infatuation with Aeneas, echoes the words of several women. A

[39] Dido's heroic verse "uirtutesque uirosque aut tanti incendia belli" (566) is adapted from a melancholy pentameter of Catullus (68.90), *Troia uirum et uirtutum omnium acerba cinis.*

[40] So L. Strzelecki, *De Naeviano Belli Punici carmine: Nakładem Polskiej Akademji Umiejetności: Rozprawy Wydziartu Filologicznego* T. LXV, nr. 2 (Cracow, 1935), pp. 12-14.

maiden, Nausicaa, tells her attendants that Odysseus would make a good husband (*Od.* 6.239-246). Another, Medea, dreams of a heroic newcomer as her choice in love, and wishes for death before dishonor (*Argon.* 3.636 + 690-691 + 798-801). A wife describes her love for a man forbidden to her, and, cursing infidelity, resolves on death: Phaedra in Euripides' *Hipp.* 373-430. (When Anna endeavors to reassure Dido in *Aen.* 4.31-53, she distantly resembles Phaedra's nurse, *Hipp.* 433-481; but her speech is both more intimate and more ethical. Her "posce deos ueniam" is far removed from the cynical realism of the nurse in *Hipp.* 459-481 + 490-497—which is the sort of thing that earned Euripides the reputation of misogynist.) There are other echoes: several from Catullus 64. Dido's "quis nouus hic nostris successit sedibus hospes?" points to the deserted Ariadne's complaint in Catullus 64.171-176, "utinam ne . . . hic . . . in nostris requiesset sedibus hospes!" In line 4.16 "uinclo . . . iugali" recalls *taedas . . . iugalis* in Cat. 64.302; while "sparsos fraterna caede penatis" (4.21) is adapted from "respergas sanguine" (Cat. 64.230) and *fraterno sanguine fratres* (Cat. 64.399); "ueteris uestigia flammae" in 4.23 echoes Catullus 64.295, *ueteris uestigia poenae.* Dido's final death-wish (*Aen.* 4.24-27) is as intense as Hector's wish to die before seeing Andromache enslaved (*Il.* 6.464-465), more passionate than Penelope's prayer for death in *Od.* 18.202-205. (Yet immediately after Penelope speaks, she appears before her suitors, more beautiful and more desirable than ever: *Od.* 18.190-196 + 206-213.)

To Aeneas Dido addresses two powerful speeches of reproachful entreaty (*Aen.* 4.305-330) and hateful denunciation (4.365-387). The chief models for both are Medea's invectives against Jason in Euripides' tragedy (465-626), Medea's tirade in the *Argonautica* (4.355-390), and the Ariadne episode in Catullus 64.52-264.[41]

[41] Knauer (pp. 212-214) suggests a functional resemblance between these two speeches of Dido and the addresses of Calypso to Hermes (*Od.* 5.118-

Even beyond the speeches there are close connections be-
tween the tale of Dido and the monodrama of Ariadne. See a
perceptive essay by P. Oksala, "Das Aufblühen des römischen
Epos: Berührungen zwischen der Ariadne-Episode Catulls
und der Dido-Geschichte Vergils," *Arctos* n.s. 3 (1962) 167-197,
from which I borrow a number of points. On pp. 175-195
Oksala points to a number of small but cumulatively striking
resemblances between situations and phrases in Vergil's narra-
tive and Catullus' description of Ariadne's woes: for example,
Catullus's apostrophe to Cupid and Venus (64.97-99):

> *qualibus* incensam iactastis mente puellam
> fluctibus, in flauo saepe hospite suspirantem!
> *quantos* illa tulit languenti corde timores!

and Vergil's apostrophe to Dido (*Aen.* 4.408-409):

> *quis* tibi tum, Dido, cernenti talia sensus,
> *quos*ue dabas gemitus!

Before confronting Aeneas, Dido raged through Carthage like
a bacchante (*Aen.* 4.300-303); deserted Ariadne let her head-
dress and garments fall, and looked like a statue of a bac-
chante (Cat. 64.60-67). Theseus struck down the Minotaur as
an invincible storm uproots an oak (Cat. 64.105-111); but
Aeneas resisted the pleas and tears of Dido as a powerful oak
resists a storm (*Aen.* 4.441-449). For a more remote, yet still
unmistakable similarity, compare the first appearance of Dido
to Aeneas, *qualis in Eurotae ripis . . . / exercet Diana choros*
(*Aen.* 1.498-499), with the first appearance of Theseus to the
maiden Ariadne perfumed and flowerlike, *quales Eurotae
progignunt flumina myrtus* (Cat. 64.89). Looking at the
poems on a larger scale, Oksala proposes that Dido, commit-
ting suicide after her lover sails away, is somewhat like Aegeus,
committing suicide after his son forgets his loving command

---

144) and to Odysseus (*Od.* 5.203-213), but the tone and words are surely
different.

and returns with black sails (Cat. 64.241-245). Is he too in-
genious in suggesting that Iris freeing Dido from her wounded
life (*Aen.* 4.693-705) resembles Dionysus visiting Ariadne
(Cat. 64.251-264)? Perhaps; and yet each is an unexpected
deus ex machina liberating a suffering woman from her agony.

To return to the speeches: both Dido and Ariadne begin
with an energetic couplet in the form of a denunciatory ques-
tion (*Aen.* 4.305-306 ≈ Cat. 64.132-133). Dido, upbraiding her
lover for keeping silent about his plans, also resembles Medea
reproaching Jason (Eur. *Med.* 586-587): "ἀλλὰ μὴ σιγῆι
φίλων." Both Ariadne and Dido twice address their lovers as
"perfide" (*Aen.* 4.305, 366 ≈ Cat. 64.132, 133) and once de-
scribe them as "perfidus" (*Aen.* 4.421 ≈ Cat. 64.174). Dido
reminds Aeneas of the handfast pledge she says they ex-
changed, "data dextera" (*Aen.* 4.307, cf. 314) as Euripides'
Medea does in 488-498, φεῦ δεξιὰ χείρ! But Medea, both in
Euripides and in Apollonius, mentions the oath which Jason
swore to her (*Med.* 492-495, *Argon.* 4.358-359); while Dido
cannot say that Aeneas ever took a vow of fidelity to her. All
that she can say is "per conubia nostra, per inceptos hymen-
aeos" (*Aen.* 4.316). This does not mean that the marriage was
concluded (see p. 136)—rather, it echoes Ariadne's plea to
Theseus, who deserted her without marrying her:

> sed conubia laeta, sed optatos hymenaeos,
> quae cuncta aerii discerpunt irrita uenti.
>
> (Cat. 64.141-142)

Then Dido speaks of herself as "moritura . . . crudeli funere
Dido" (*Aen.* 4.308). Here Vergil is recalling his own poetic
treatments of unhappy love and premature death: Hero dying
on the body of Leander, *moritura super crudeli funere uirgo*
(*Georg.* 3.263), and the handsome boy mourned by the
nymphs, *exstinctum . . . crudeli funere Daphnin* (Buc. 5.20).
Dido next quotes Aeneas's own narrative, to remind him that,
as his new home is distant, his former home has disappeared:

"Troia antiqua maneret" (*Aen.* 4.312) echoes one of Aeneas's most passionate outcries (*Aen.* 2.56):

Troiaque nunc staret, Priamique arx alta maneres!

She then begs him to have pity and to change his mind (*Aen.* 4.318-319)—"miserere . . . et istam / . . . exue mentem"—as Ariadne asks (Cat. 64.136-138)

> nullane res potuit crudelis flectere *mentis*
> consilium? tibi nulla fuit clementia praesto
> immite ut nostri uellet *miserescere* pectus?

Speaking of the loneliness to which Aeneas is abandoning her (*Aen.* 4.320-330), she resembles Medea (Eur. *Med.* 499-515, Ap. Rhod. 4.360-363 + 370-372) as well as Tecmessa pleading with her self-doomed love and lord in Sophocles' *Ajax* 514-524. At last, when she says with the utmost delicacy that she would have been less unhappy if she had had a son by Aeneas, she distantly resembles Hypsipyle[42] saying farewell to Jason and asking for his commands as a father in case heaven grants her motherhood (*Argon.* 1.897-898).

One of the most touching of all Vergil's echoes of earlier poetry occurs in this passage. It is little more than a word, the word "paruulus" (*Aen.* 4.328). Diminutives such as this are beneath the grand style of epic poetry.[43] Vergil uses them very

---

[42] See p. 186 above.

[43] See the discussion by B. Axelson on pp. 38-45 of *Unpoetische Wörter* (Lund, 1945) and a list of Vergil's diminutives by A.S.F. Gow in *CQ* 26 (1932) 150-157. The other occurrences of *paruulus* in poetry of Vergil's era are: Lucr. 4.193 (*paruula causa*), Lucr. 4.1162 (in the satiric passage on lovers' blindness), Cat. 61.209, and Horace, *Serm.* 1.1.33 (*paruula formica*), *Ep.* 1.15.42 (*tuta et paruula laudo*), and *Ep.* 1.18.29 ("tibi paruula res est"). In his speeches Cicero very rarely uses the word. L. Laurand, *Études sur le style des discours de Cicéron* (Paris, 1936-1938⁴, repr. Amsterdam, 1965) pp. 265-268, lists the diminutives in his oratorical works: the only occurrences of *paruulus* are: *Quinct.* 53 (*in paruula re*); *Rosc. Com.* 23 (*illa pecunia immanis, haec paruula*); *Verr.* 2.2.99 (*paruulo nauigio*); and *Clu.* 137 (*pueri paruuli lacrimis*). In *Verr.* 2.4.95 and 96 he speaks of Verres' men stealing *sigilla perparuula* and *unum perparuulum signum*. *Paruulus* here is the only diminutive adjective in the entire *Aeneid*.

rarely in the *Aeneid*, and when he does, he always evokes tenderness and sympathy: e.g. *puellae* of the doomed Trojan girls in 2.238 and the unhappy ghosts in 6.307, and *papilla* of the maiden Camilla's wounded breast in 11.803 (note *bibit* in 804).[44] Here Vergil is thinking of one of Catullus's poems introducing the happiness of married love, the wedding song, 61. As the bridegroom goes to join his bride, Catullus tells them to enjoy their love and have children soon. Then, in an enchanting stanza (61.209-213), he imagines the first baby in its mother's arms, a little son named after the father:

> Torquatus uolo paruulus
> matris e gremio suae
> porrigens teneras manus
> dulce rideat ad patrem
> semihiante labello.

By employing the word "paruulus," so unusual in an epic context, and linking it with the name of Aeneas (as Catullus links it with the name of the husband and future father), Vergil conjures up a dream of wedded happiness, the happiness Dido had hoped for in vain.

In her second speech (*Aen.* 4.365-387), after listening to Aeneas's exculpation of his conduct, Dido is far more violent. He is not human, she cries, but a monster (365-367). This idea goes back to Patroclus reproaching Achilles in *Il.* 16.33-35, emerges again in Eur. *Bacch.* 987-990, and then appears in Vergil's own *Bucolic* 8.43-45. She declares that he was suckled by tigresses (*Aen.* 4.367) as Ariadne says that Theseus was littered by a lioness (Cat. 64.154). Her trust in the sure indignation of the gods (*Aen.* 4.371-372) alludes to a passage in

---

[44] *Exserta papilla* in 803, when Camilla is wounded to the death; while she was in combat she was *unum exserta latus pugnae* (11.649). The same word is used of the archer nymph who avenges her, without any trace of tenderness, but perhaps suggested by Camilla's wounding (11.862). It is employed in an erotic context by Catullus (66.81), but is uncommon in serious poetry.

Accius's tragedy *Antigona* (frg. V Ribbeck) although the sentiment is reversed:

iam iam neque di regunt
neque profecto deum supremus rex <iam>
curat hominibus.[45]

"Nusquam tuta fides," cries Dido (*Aen.* 4.373), Medea "ὅρκων δὲ φρούδη πίςτις" (Eur. *Med.* 492) and "ποῦ τοι Διὸς Ἱκεςίοιο / ὅρκια;" (Ap. Rhod. 4.358-359), and Ariadne "femina . . . / nulla uiri speret sermones esse fideles" (Cat. 64.143-144). As Medea says "ἔςωιςα c'" (Eur. *Med.* 476) and Ariadne "eripui" (Cat. 64.150), so Dido says "excepi" of her hospitality to Aeneas after the tempest. She recounts her services to him (*Aen.* 4.373-375) as Medea does with Jason (Eur. *Med.* 476-487, Ap. Rhod. 4.364-367) and Calypso speaking of Odysseus (*Od.* 5.130-136). Then, after scornfully quoting, distorting, and discarding Aeneas's own assertions (*Aen.* 4.376-380, see p. 151), she dismisses him (380-381). The incomparable imperative "i," followed by "sequere" and "pete," resembles Medea's congé to Jason (Eur. *Med.* 623 + 625), "χώρει . . . νύμφευ'."[46] It is followed by a curse (*Aen.* 4.382-387) which is mainly inspired by the curses of Apollonius's Medea directed against Jason (*Argon.* 4.382-390). However, there are other models for the curse pronounced against an enemy departing on a sea voyage. Poems of regret and blessing addressed to friends at embarkation were composed in both Greek and Latin, although they cannot be certainly traced until the Hellenistic period: the most famous is Horace's little poem for Vergil, *Carm.* 1.3.[47] But the reverse, a poem of ill wishes addressed to a departing enemy, is also known. Horace wrote such a poem, *Epode* 10; the

---

[45] iam *add. Keil*; res *Buecheler.* A similar thought is voiced by Medea in Eur. *Med.* 492-494.

[46] More distantly it recalls Calypso's words to Hermes, "ἐρρέτω . . . πόντον ἐπ' ἀτρύγετον" (*Od.* 5.139-140).

[47] A historical survey, with analyses, is given by F. Jäger in *Das antike Propemptikon und das 17. Gedicht des Paulinus von Nola* (Rosenheim, 1913).

Epodes are largely modelled on Archilochus; and there is a sizable fragment of a poem by Archilochus himself, expressing the hope that an enemy of his will be shipwrecked on the Thracian coast, shivering and seaweed-covered, and be enslaved by the barbarous natives.[48] Such poems also are among Vergil's models for Dido's first curse on Aeneas.[49] Finally, foreseeing her own death, she promises that her ghost will haunt Aeneas everywhere to punish him for his treachery (*Aen.* 4.384-386). This vow resembles the *Thyesteas preces* uttered by the boy doomed to be sacrificed by witches in Horace: "nocturnus occurram Furor / petamque uultus umbra curuis unguibus" (*Epod.* 5.92-93).[50]

With this Dido leaves Aeneas, never to see him again alive. Their parting is designed by Vergil to recall the separation of Aeneas and Creusa and the loss of Eurydice to Orpheus. In each case the beloved woman vanishes in silence; and the lover, deserted, is pathetic and less than heroic. So Dido

> aegra fugit seque ex oculis auertit et aufert,
> linquens multa metu *cunctantem et multa parantem*
> *dicere.*

The translated spirit of Creusa

> *lacrimantem et multa uolentem*
> *dicere* deseruit, tenuisque recessit in auras.
>
> (*Aen.* 2.790-791)

---

[48] This is the first "Strasbourg epode," which is probably, although not quite certainly, by Archilochus. The text appears in E. Diehl, *Anthologia Lyrica Graeca* 3 (ed. R. Beutler, Leipzig, 1952³) pp. 34-35. M. Treu, *Archilochos* (Berlin, 1959), has the text on p. 76 and valuable notes on pp. 224-228. C. M. Bowra on pp. 58-59 of the third series of *New Chapters in Greek Literature* (ed. J. U. Powell, Oxford, 1933) discusses the poem briefly and points to the analogy with Dido's speech. E. Fraenkel, *Horace* (Oxford, 1957) pp. 24-36, analyzes the two malevolent *propemptica*.

[49] Her first curse (*Aen.* 4.382-387) relates only to Aeneas's voyage; her second (607-621) extends the imprecation to his arrival and sojourn in Italy.

[50] This parallel is touched by G. Luck, *Hexen und Zauberei in der römi-*

226

The lost soul of Eurydice

> fugit diuersa, neque illum
> *prensantem* nequiquam umbras *et multa uolentem*
> *dicere* praeterea uidit.
>
> *(Georg.* 4.500-502)

Dido's plaintive appeal conveyed through Anna the confidante (*Aen.* 4.416-436) seems to have no extant model. Her willingness to abandon the idea of marriage (4.431) recalls Ariadne's readiness to serve Theseus, if not as a wife, then as a slave (Cat. 64.158-163); and her plea for a last mark of favor, to be repaid with her own death as interest (4.433-436) restates the dying words of Vergil's own Damon (*Buc.* 8.58-60; see p. 138 above). Her deceptive account of the magical rites she intends (4.478-498) has something in common with the spells of Alphesiboeus in the same poem (*Buc.* 8.90-99), although the whole picture is not pastoral, but heroic and tragic.[51] The witch herself (*Aen.* 4.487-491) resembles Apollonius's Medea (*Argon.* 3.528-533).

Awake in agony while the rest of the world sleeps, Dido broods on her love (*Aen.* 4.522-552) like Medea (*Argon.* 3.744-824); and like her she contemplates suicide (*Aen.* 4.547 ≈ *Argon.* 3.798-801). She is locked into a dilemma (534-546) like that of Ajax resolving to kill himself (Soph. *Aj.* 457-470), Medea denouncing Jason (Eur. *Med.* 499-508 and Ennius, *Medea Exul* frg. X), and Ariadne deserted (Cat. 64.177-187). The younger Gracchus had adapted this dilemma in a speech which brought tears even to the eyes of his enemies:

> Quo me miser conferam? quo uortam? in Capitoliumne?
> at fratris sanguine redundat. an domum? matremne ut
> miseram lamentantem uideam et abiectam?[52]

---

schen *Dichtung* (Zurich, 1962) p. 17, although he rather undervalues its force, saying that Dido "wünscht keine Rache an den Mann, den sie bis zuletzt liebt."

[51] G. Luck on p. 18 (with note 29) of his book cited above, n. 50.

[52] Cicero, *De Or.* 3.214; E. Malcovati, *Oratorum Romanorum Fragmenta*

Homeric heroes never speak to themselves in the second person.[53] But in Euripides' tragedy, when Medea strengthens her resolution, she addresses herself by name and gives herself stern commands in the second person (Eur. *Med.* 401-409). That is the first extant monologue in which a character speaks directly to himself or herself as though to another individual.[54] Here, at a moment of comparable intensity, Vergil makes Dido do the same (*Aen.* 4.541-542, 547; cf. also 596-597).[55]

Her reference to the deceitfulness of the race of Laomedon (542) is taken from a passage of Vergil's own poetry: an evocation of the horrors of civil strife and general war as punishment for the ancestral sin (*Georg.* 1.502: *Laomedonteae luimus periuria Troiae*). At the end, her reproach to Anna (4.548-549) may be a reminiscence of Phaedra's fury against her nurse (Eur. *Hipp.* 682-694), but it is less fierce, more plaintive.

Dido's final tirade of rage (4.590-629) is based upon no single model, but—like the best pages of Vergil elsewhere—takes up many different strengths and beauties, molding them into one. The first section, in which she feels herself going mad (590-606), sounds like a scene of insanity from a drama—something comparable to Euripides' *Orestes* 253-279; yet it is a monologue, and no such speech is extant.[56] In the reported speech

---

(Turin, 1955²) p. 196. Cicero himself adapted the dilemma several times: *Verr.* 2.5.126, *Mur.* 88-89, *Flacc.* 4. See also Perseus' speech in Livy 40. 10.3-10. Ennius, *Andromacha Aechmalotis* frg. IX and Cic. *Scaur.* 19, adduced by E. Lindholm, *Stilistische Studien* (Lund, 1931) p. 56, do not quite follow the same pattern.

[53] See H. Otter, *De soliloquiis quae in litteris Graecorum et Romanorum occurrunt obseruationes* (Marburg, 1914) c. 1. "Τέτλαθι δή, κραδίη" in *Od.* 20.18 is exceptional: a rebuke addressed by Odysseus to his unquiet heart almost as though it were a restive dog or horse: see lines 22-24.

[54] Medea however uses only the first person in 872-883.

[55] This is pointed out by O. Maar (p. 63). He notes that Ovid uses this dramatic device even more freely in Medea's soliloquy (*Met.* 7.11-71), which, by the way, contains several explicit allusions to the passion of Dido.

[56] It is unlikely that Dido's "ferte citi flammas" (4.594) is suggested by Hector's οἴσετε πῦρ in *Il.* 15.718, since the situations are so different and the

228

of Hercules in Eur. *HF* 936-946 the delusions of mania are complete: Dido knows where she is and what she is doing. The second section, her solemn prayer and curse (607-621), contains echoes from the imprecations of the blinded Polyphemus in *Od.* 9.528-535; of Ajax in Sophocles' *Ajax* 835-844; and of Medea in *Argon.* 4.382-390. Apollonius after reporting Medea's denunciation adds: "She spoke boiling with violent rage: she longed to set the ship ablaze and hew it all in pieces, and to throw herself into the fierce flames" (*Argon.* 4.391-393). But this longing is simply part of the poet's narrative. Vergil makes it more forcible by giving it directly as the thoughts of Dido, who in her soliloquy wishes that she had done all that to Aeneas's fleet, and killed the Trojans as well (*Aen.* 4.604-606). Hecate, invoked by Dido in *Aen.* 4.609, is called to witness Medea's oath of vengeance in Eur. *Med.* 395-400; and Catullus's Ariadne closes her speech with an appeal to the snaky-haired Eumenides (64.192-201) which Vergil adapts in Dido's call to the "Dirae ultrices" (*Aen.* 4.610). The striking hypermeter at the end of Dido's speech, "pugnent ipsique nepotesque," is clearly inspired by Ariadne's final phrase, "funestet seque suosque."

Dido's soliloquy bears some resemblance to the closing words of Cassandra in Aesch. *Agam.* 1313-1320 + 1322-1330, spoken in the expectation of immediate death. Fraenkel on *Agam.* 1322 points to the prayer for vengeance which is often part of a lament for the dead, and cites E. Reiner, *Die rituelle Totenklage der Griechen* (Stuttgart, 1938), p. 21. There is, however, an important difference. Dido is no Cassandra, κωκύcουc' ἐμὴν . . . μοῖραν. She utters no lamentation. In her words there is no sorrow for her people or for herself, save in the word "infelix," 596, which is part of a reproach. Rage, rage even against herself, linked with a solemn curse and a command

---

words in themselves unremarkable; and her invocation of the sun in 607 has quite a different context from Agamemnon's in *Il.* 3.277.

laid on her subjects, is the entire substance of the speech. It is therefore best understood as a suicide's call for vengeance on those responsible for her death—an imprecation which the act of self-murder was believed to make effective.[57]

The ominous line 625

exoriare aliquis nostris ex ossibus ultor

is modelled on Cassandra's prophecy of the coming of Orestes the avenger (*Agam.* 1280):

ἥξει γὰρ ἡμῶν ἄλλος αὖ τιμάορος.

As so often, Vergil has elaborated on his model. In both poets, the verb begins the line and the word "avenger" closes it, with the personal pronoun between; but "nostris ex *ossibus*" is more drastic than Aeschylus's ἡμῶν and the jussive subjunctive "exoriare" more striking than the plain future ἥξει. It is in the second person singular, as though Dido were addressing someone whom she saw standing before her. It is remarkable to find the second person singular associated with "aliquis";[58] no doubt the pronoun was suggested by Aeschylus's ἄλλος, but it is more strange: the rise of the avenger Hannibal is still centuries distant in the future.

Now Dido prepares to die. First, she sends her husband's old nurse to fetch her sister Anna (*Aen.* 4.634-640). Why? To help her in completing the magic ritual, she says: that is false. "To comfort her as she dies," says Austin in his edition of Book Four; but surely Dido expects and hopes to die instantly like Ajax (Soph. *Aj.* 831-834). "Vt sola et sine arbitro esset," says Heyne; but a queen can always dismiss her attendants without giving an elaborate reason. She sends for Anna so that

[57] See M. Delcourt, "La Suicide par vengeance dans la Grèce ancienne," *RHR* 119 (1939) 154-171, and compare the curse before suicide in Soph. *Ajax* 835-844.

[58] W. Havers, *Handbuch der erklärenden Syntax* (Heidelberg, 1931) para. 76, notes that such a mixture of grammatical persons appears in commands, and cites Plaut. *Epid.* 399, "exite huc aliquis!"

her next of kin may be the first to reach her dead body, compose it, and prepare it for decent burial. Thus Ajax prays Zeus to send a messenger for Teucer, who will be the first to lift his body off the sword and protect it from dishonor (Soph. *Aj.* 823-830).[59] In its formality, Dido's suicide resembles that of Ajax more than that of Deianira (Soph. *Trach.* 912-931) or Jocasta (Soph. *O.T.* 1237-1264). Ajax is the only figure in extant Greek tragedy who commits suicide on stage; and Vergil represents Dido's last actions as though she were a tragic heroine killing herself before our watching eyes. For the death-thrust Ajax uses the sword of his foe Hector, and Dido the sword of Aeneas, the beloved enemy.

Dido's farewell to life (4.651-662) contains some sentences which might have come from the *elogium* of a Roman statesman (653-656; see above, p. 182), and looks back to the happier days of proud achievement before she met Aeneas: "urbem praeclaram statui" (4.655) recalls "urbem quam statuo" (1.573). Then (4.657-658) it moves into the famous might-have-been thought from Euripides' *Medea* 1-8, which reappears in *Argon.* 4.32-33 and in Ariadne's monologue (Cat. 64.171-176): a thought of irremediable regret. Kissing her bed (*Aen.* 4.659) she makes the gesture of Medea in the *Argon.* (4.26) bidding good-bye to maidenhood and home; but she is a figure of tragedy rather than romance. Her kisses and her tears are more like those of the grief-stricken Deianira (Soph. *Trach.* 912-931) and the doomed Alcestis (Eur. *Alc.* 175-184); and indeed her earlier words to her sister, "lectum iugalem / quo perii" (4.496-497), closely resemble the farewell of Alcestis, "᾽Ω λέκτρον, . . . ἀπώλεσας δ᾽ ἐμέ."

Anchises

Vergil's affectionate interest in the character of Anchises is shown in many ways: not least by the fact that he models

---

[59] This suggestion comes from Penquitt.

Anchises' speeches on a wide variety of memorable passages from earlier poetry and philosophy.

Although a cripple, Anchises is brave and resolute, determined to perish in his home rather than flee (*Aen.* 2.638-649), like the old Roman senators awaiting the Gauls.[60] Of Jupiter he speaks reverently in a phrase coined by Ennius (*Ann.* 175) as "diuum pater atque hominum rex" (648).[61] As Priam, before quitting Troy on the perilous journey to Achilles' camp, prays Zeus for help and a favorable omen (*Il.* 24.308-313), so does Anchises before deciding to leave Troy under the guidance of the gods (*Aen.* 2.689-691).

Later he interprets the oracular utterance of Phoebus, "antiquam exquirite matrem," as pointing to Crete (*Aen.* 3.103-117). His explanation recalls the Homeric Aeneas's account of the first settlement before Troy was built (*Aen.* 3.106-110 ≈ *Il.* 20.215-218) but names Teucer rather than his son-in-law Dardanus as the founder. Island Crete with its many cities is described by Odysseus to Penelope in terms similar to those of Anchises (*Aen.* 3.104-106 ≈ *Od.* 19.172-174).[62] "Audite, o proceres" (*Aen.* 3.103) is like Agamemnon's "Κλῦτε, φίλοι" (*Il.* 2.56), both in a supernatural context; "cultrix Cybeli" (*Aen.* 3.111) recalls Catullus 64.300, and the yoked lions (*Aen.* 3.113) Catullus 63.76. Subsequently Anchises remembers a prophecy heard but not credited (*Aen.* 3.182-188) as the Cyclops remembers an unheeded warning about Odysseus (*Od.* 9.507-516); he interprets an omen involving horses (*Aen.* 3.539-543) as Peleus does in *Argon.* 4.1370-1379; and when he sights Scylla and Charybdis he sounds briefly like Odysseus encouraging his crew (*Aen.* 3.558-560 ≈ *Od.* 12.208-221).

In the fifth book his utterance as an admonitory phantom (*Aen.* 5.724-739) is introduced by words of loving affection

---

[60] See p. 123.

[61] The phrase is used seriously by Vergil himself in 10.2; with a semblance of awe by Juno in 1.65; with sneering irony by Mezentius in 10.743.

[62] But ἐννήκοντα πόληεc in the *Odyssey*, "centum urbes" in the *Aeneid* and in *Il.* 2.649.

232

modelled on those spoken to Theseus by his father in Catullus 64.215, and a reassurance like that of Iris to Priam (*Il.* 24.173-174); then it goes on to instructions similar to those which Circe gives Odysseus in *Od.* 10.490-495 + 526-540. In one of those graceful and unobtrusive, but touching, echoes of his own poetry, Vergil makes Anchises leave Aeneas by saying "iamque uale"—the same phrase, at the same place in the line, as was spoken by the ghost of Creusa to Aeneas (2.789) and by the doomed Eurydice to Orpheus (*Georg.* 4.497).

In the world of the dead, Anchises' welcome to Aeneas (*Aen.* 6.687-694) begins "uenisti tandem" like the fatherly greeting of Eumaeus to Telemachus, "ἦλθες," but without the tender phrase "γλυκερὸν φάος" (*Od.* 16.23). The remainder is like the speech of Odysseus' mother Anticleia in *Od.* 11.155-162; but her naive remark that the Ocean cannot be crossed on foot (158-159) is replaced by an adaptation of Catullus's address to his dead brother, "multas per gentes et multa per aequora uectus" (101.1).

Then Anchises unfolds a grand doctrine (*Aen.* 6.713-751). Human souls, he tells his son, never die. On the extinction of the body, they enter the other world, to be purged by air, water, and fire of the taints which they acquired from the body and its passions during their earthly life. Then, a thousand years after their prior existence, they drink the water of Lethe and are reborn in new bodies. (Sinners who are incurably evil go to a hell of eternal punishment; but Anchises does not mention them: their fate has been described to Aeneas by the Sibyl in *Aen.* 6.562-627; see p. 244.) A few souls have earned the happiness of heaven by their benefactions to mankind. Their purgation is brief—Anchises is one of them and has been dead for only a few months—and thereafter they inhabit Elysium forever (*Aen.* 6.637-665). It is a world of the blessed, with its own sky and sun and stars. Being immortal and immortally happy, they are like gods.

Various versions of this doctrine are expounded as myths by

233

the Socrates of Plato: rather simply in *Phaedo* 113d1-114c8, with more complexity in *Gorgias* 523a1-526d2, and infused with much vivid detail in *Republic* 614b2-621a9. It is alluded to in Pindar (frg. 114 Bowra).[63] This is the doctrine of the mystical sect now called Orphics.[64] They held that the musician Orpheus, one of the few human beings who had ever journeyed to the world of death and returned, had described the post-mortem rewards and punishments of human souls and had explained how his followers, by living according to strict rules of purity, might avoid hell and find salvation.[65] Neither Plato nor Vergil cared anything for the Orphic rituals of purification; but both respected the Orphic visions of the afterlife—or, as the Orphics might call it, the life of the soul after liberation from the body. In 1893 Eduard Norden conjectured that one of Vergil's chief sources for this eschatology was a description of the other world, either in poetry or in highly poetic prose, embodying Orphic doctrine and certain Pythagorean themes together with Stoic mysticism.[66] In his edition of *Aeneid* 6 he modified but maintained this theory, pointing to Posidonius as the probable author of the vision: it was also, he thought, the source of Cicero's *Dream of Scipio*, which contains many of the same exalted ideas as the apocalypse of Anchises.

No such book is now extant, although many were read in antiquity. Quite recently, however, fragments of an apparently Orphic poem were found, written in Greek hexameters. It is in a papyrus codex dated to the third or fourth century A.D., now

---

[63] Aristophanes, *Frogs* 137-163, 273-459, gives a similar picture of the afterworld, but makes its dominant figures Dionysus and Demeter, who do not occur here.

[64] See W.K.C. Guthrie's admirable *Orpheus and Greek Religion* (London, 1935, revised 1952).

[65] Vergil treats Orpheus with reverence, relating his story at length in *Georg.* 4.453-527, making Aeneas cite him as a precedent in *Aen.* 6.119-120, and giving him a prominent place in Elysium (*Aen.* 6.645-647).

[66] E. Norden, "Vergilstudien. I. Die Nekyia; ihre Composition und Quellen," *Hermes* 28 (1893) 360-406.

in Bologna. Although badly broken, it is consecutive, and has yielded good results to analysis.[67] Scholars are reluctant to date it exactly, but agree that it can scarcely have been composed before the second century of our era. Vergil could not have read it; but it shows us the kind of thing which he did read. The poem classifies virtues to be rewarded and sins to be punished, as Vergil does in the sixth book. There are some remarkable coincidences of phrasing. Thus, in Vergil's Elysium, among the eternally blessed are those *qui uitam excoluere per artes* (*Aen.* 6.663); in the Orphic poem, among the saved are οἳ . . . βίον coφίηιcιν ἐκόcμεον. And there are poets, who ἀοιδὰc / θεcπεcίαc ἐφύτευcαν ἐν Ἀπόλλωνοc <ἀλωῆι> ≈ *Phoebo digna locuti* (*Aen.* 6.662). Purification by water is mentioned in the poem (as in *Aen.* 6.741, "sub gurgite uasto"), while Vergil's "terreni artus moribundaque membra" are easy to recognize in θνητῶν μελέων cκιόεντα χιτῶνα. Some of the sinners listed in this strange little work appear in Vergil's hell, as described by the Sibyl (see p. 245).

Fragments of a similar doctrine are written on golden plates found in graves in southern Italy and elsewhere: evidently quotations from mystical poetry in Greek intended to guide and comfort the soul of the dead on entering the afterworld.[68] One of these warns the spirit to "go to the right"—like the Sibyl in *Aen.* 6.540-543. On several of them, however, the souls are told to ask in the underworld for a drink of water from the Lake of Memory, which will make them immortal. The reverse of this appears in Anchises' speech: just as in Plato (*Rep.* 620e6-621a9), the souls which are to be sent back to earthly life drink of the water of Forgetfulness (*Aen.* 6.748-751).

[67] Published by R. Merkelbach, *MH* 8 (1951) 1-11; discussed by A. Vogliano, "Il papiro Bolognese Nr. 3," *Acme* 5 (1952) 385-417; M. Treu, "Die neue 'orphische' Unterweltsbeschreibung und Vergil," *Hermes* 82 (1954) 24-51; and R. Turcan, "La Catabase orphique du papyrus de Bologne," *RHR* 150 (1956) 136-172.

[68] See Guthrie (cited above, n. 64), pp. 171-182.

The didactic style of this eschatological passage is, in the main, Lucretian; and it shows how greatly Vergil's views had changed from the Epicureanism of his youth that he should select Lucretian phrases in which to expound a doctrine that would have profoundly shocked Lucretius. A. K. Michels, "Lucretius and the sixth book of the *Aeneid*," *AJP* 65 (1944) 135-148, indicates some useful parallels, but she is surely mistaken in suggesting that Vergil, while writing the epic, was still an orthodox Epicurean, because "it would have been difficult for him to continue living in the *hortulus Cecropius*[69] in Naples on any other terms." Heinze (p. 475) succinctly says "Die Aeneis ist ein positiver Antilukrez." Vergil's hostility to Epicureanism has been explained and exemplified by B. Farrington,[70] who brings out resemblances between several pairs of passages where Vergil is clearly echoing, and not less clearly correcting, his Epicurean predecessor. Such are the two divine love-scenes. Lulled by Lucretius's Venus, *aeterno deuictus uulnere amoris* (1.34), Mars will cease from war. Charmed by Vergil's Venus, *aeterno . . . deuinctus amore* (*Aen.* 8.394), Vulcan will make weapons for a righteous war. (The god of war is *deuictus*; the complaisant husband is *deuinctus*.) Another of Vergil's alterations is intended to be amusing. Lucretius declares it is pleasant *magnum alterius spectare laborem* (2.2); but Vergil tells the farmer, "unless you work hard to conquer weeds and marauding birds,

heu magnum alterius frustra spectabis aceruum."

(*Georg.* 1.158)

This little parody was pointed out earlier, on p. 34 of a sensitive article by C. Bailey on Vergil and Lucretius.[71] He

[69] The phrase comes from *Ciris* 3.

[70] "Polemical allusions to the *De Rerum Natura* of Lucretius in the works of Vergil," *Acta Vniversitatis Carolinae Phil. et Hist.* 1 (1963), *Graecolatina Pragensia* II, pp. 87-94.

[71] *PCA* 28 (1931) pp. 21-39. Some of the borrowings pointed out in this essay are noted here in the appropriate places.

started by considering W. A. Merrill's *Parallels and Coincidences in Lucretius and Vergil* (Berkeley, 1918). The 1,635 passages in Lucretius to which Merrill detected resemblances in Vergil, he reduced to "well over a thousand," most of the others being trivial coincidences or far-fetched similarities. But among the thousand-plus he found many beautiful and significant borrowings by the younger from the elder poet. For example, Lucretius's contemplation of death (3.895-896)

> nec dulces occurrent oscula nati
>
> praeripere

is changed by Vergil into a detail of the farmer's happy life (*Georg.* 2.523):

> interea dulces pendent circum oscula nati.

To most thoughtful critics, Vergil's use of Lucretian terms to expound a doctrine far removed from Lucretius's theories appears to be a skillful poetic stratagem. But one Vergilian scholar, Augustin Cartault, considered it to be a fault of technique. In his *L'Art de Virgile dans l'Énéide* (Paris, 1926) he described Vergil's exposition of the doctrine of metempsychosis as "lofty philosophical poetry," but went on (p. 474): "Il est à regretter que Virgile l'ait fait avec la phraséologie de Lucrèce, qui était pour lui le créateur de la langue de la poésie scientifique, qu'il n'ait pas vu que pour développer des idees stoïciennes tout à fait divergentes des idées épicuriennes, il fallait d'autres termes que ceux dont s'était servi Lucrèce et qu'il n'ait pas rivalisé avec lui d'invention." This implies that Vergil did not possess enough talent to create a new vocabulary in which to describe these metaphysical conceptions in poetic terms. Yet Stoic doctrines are more moving to the imagination (particularly when intermingled with Pythagorean ideas) than those of Epicurus; and Vergil was a lord of language. He could most certainly have written of Stoicism in new wording and imagery suited to the grandeur of the creed. But evidently

237

he wished to emphasize the view that Epicureanism (once so attractive to him and some of his friends) was a false and evil doctrine, by using the vocabulary of the great Epicurean poet to describe a higher and nobler set of beliefs. One particular phrase in an important position confirms this. Lucretius speaks of the growing complexity of civilization and the increasing greed for wealth and power (5.1105-1135). He describes the folly of those who struggle up the narrow pathway of ambition, and says the struggle is vain (1129-1130)

> ut satius multo iam sit parere quietum
> quam *regere imperio* res uelle et regna tenere.

But Anchises solemnly exhorts his son and his descendants not to cultivate Epicurean quietism: rather (*Aen.* 6.851)

> tu *regere imperio* populos, Romane, memento.

There are other significant reminiscences of *De Rerum Natura*. The tranquil skies of Elysium in *Aen.* 6.640-641 are like the *sedes quietae* of Lucretius 3.18-22. Lucretius says that they are ever peaceful

> semperque innubilus aether
> integit, et large diffuso lumine rident.

In Vergil's Elysium

> largior hic campos aether et lumine uestit
> purpureo.

The doctrinal difference here is that the remote and tranquil heaven of Lucretius is the abode of the gods, who have nothing whatever to do with mankind; while the Elysium of Vergil is the eternal dwelling-place of the purest souls of men. Before starting his exposition of metempsychosis Anchises says

> dicam equidem, nec te suspensum, nate, tenebo
>
> (6.722)

—on the model of Lucretius explaining the force of lightning:

expediam, neque te in promissis plura morabor.
(6.245)

"Principio" at the opening of his revelation (6.724) is one of Lucretius's customary beginnings for an important chain of arguments.[72] The impressive opening

Principio caelum ac terras camposque liquentis
lucentemque globum lunae

combines Lucr. 5.68-69

terram caelum mare sidera solem
lunaique globum

with Lucr. 5.92

principio maria ac terras caelumque tuere

and Lucr. 6.405

liquidam molem camposque natantis.

The living beings on the earth are described in *Aen.* 6.728-729:

hominum pecudumque genus uitaeque uolantum
et quae marmoreo fert monstra sub aequore pontus.

Lucretius had already written (2.1082-1083, cf. 2.342-346)

sic hominum genitam prolem, sic denique mutas
squamigerum pecudes et corpora cuncta uolantum.

Vergil drew the phrase "caelestis origo / seminibus" (*Aen.* 6.730-731) from the noble sentence in Lucr. 2.991:

caelesti sumus omnes semine oriundi.

---

[72] Norden (*Aeneis VI*) p. 309, who states that Lucretius uses it thirty-seven times. Many of the above parallels come from Norden.

239

The "moribunda membra" of *Aen.* 6.732 are adapted from Lucretius's description of physical death (3.129); and Anchises' solemn

quin et supremo cum lumine uita reliquit   (6.735)

recalls Lucretius 5.63

cernere cum uideamur eum quem uita reliquit.

Even the hexameter close "funditus omnes" (*Aen.* 6.736) is suggested by Lucretius (1.956), and the beautiful phrase "purumque reliquit" (*Aen.* 6.746) echoes part of a declaration of Lucretius on the fear of death and hell (3.40).

It has, however, been conjectured that Vergil in the opening of Anchises' speech, Lucretius in Book One and elsewhere, and Cicero in part of his poem *De Consulatu Suo* were all three indebted to an important passage of Ennius's *Annals*: the opening scene, in which the ghost or *eidolon* of Homer appeared to Ennius and expounded to him much mystical lore, including the doctrine of metempsychosis. W. H. Friedrich[73] points out the similarity between the speech of Anchises and the paraphrase of Ennius in Lucr. 1.120-126. Further, he notes that the speech of the Muse Urania in Cicero's poem (quoted in *De Diu.* 1.17-22) resembles Lucretius 2.991-1001 both in style and in theme, and proposes that both were inspired by part of Homer's speech in Ennius, from which one significant line survives, about the upward journey of the souls after death (*Ann.* 9):

quae caua corpore caeruleo cortina receptat.

---

[73] "Ennius-Erklärungen," *Phil.* 97 (1948) 277-288. Homer's appearance in Ennius was sad and tearful because he died wretchedly, and his *eidolon* resembled him at the moment of death. Vergil adapted this vision in his account of the appearance of Hector's ghost to Aeneas. So "maestissimus Hector / uisus adesse mihi" (*Aen.* 2.270-271) ≈ *uisus Homerus adesse poeta* (*Ann.* 6); "largosque effundere fletus" (*Aen.* 2.271) ≈ *lacrimas effundere salsas* (Lucr. 1.125); and "ei mihi, qualis erat!" (Aen. 2.274) ≈ *Ann.* 7.

He suggests therefore that Ennius is the common source for all
three passages of philosophical poetry, even to such details as
"principio," "modis miris," and *singula pandit* (cf. Lucr. 1.126,
expandere dictis).

The procession of the unborn souls described and com-
mented on by Anchises (*Aen.* 6.756-859) has two clear models
in Homer: Odysseus's account of the dead heroines and heroes
he saw in the underworld (*Od.* 11.225-330 + 385-635; see
Knauer, pp. 123-129) and Helen's naming of the Greek pala-
dins (*Il.* 3.161-244). To these may be added the muster of the
Argonauts coming to fit and launch their ship (Ap. Rhod.
1.23-227). In the Nekuia the phantoms, eager to drink the
blood, flock together without order, in the Teichoskopia the
chieftains stand still or move among their men, but in the
Argonautica the heroes walk into view one by one or in pairs—
ἤλυθε, ἵκανεν, βῆ, ὦρσεν, εἵπετο—as some at least of the
heroic souls do in the *Aeneid: uenientum discere uultus*
(6.755), "sequitur" (6.815), "ingreditur" (6.856), *una ire*
(6.860), "comitatur" (6.863).

Three further prototypes have been suggested, from the life
of Rome. Several of the old kings are described as though they
were seen in lifelike painting or statuary: "pura iuuenis qui
nititur hasta" (6.760), "umbrata gerunt ciuili tempora quercu"
(6.772), "geminae stant uertice cristae" (6.779), "crinis inca-
naque menta" (6.809). L. Delaruelle therefore proposes that
Vergil was thinking of the archaic statues which stood on the
Capitol and elsewhere (e.g. Camillus at the Rostra, Pliny, *N.H.*
34.11.22-23).[74] H. T. Rowell goes further, and conjectures that

[74] "Souvenirs d'oeuvres plastiques dans la revue des héros au livre VI de
l'Énéide," *RA*, 4ᵉ série, 21 (1913) 153-170. On p. 154 Delaruelle corrects
Norden's note on 6.760 that Silvius is leaning on his spear of honor "beim
Gehen." Aeneas in 12.386—like Diomede and Odysseus in *Il.* 19.47-49—sup-
ports himself with his spear while walking because he is wounded; but
Silvius the warrior king stands leaning on his spear in an attitude of triumph.
On p. 157 he adds that the double-crested helmet of Romulus (6.779) which
has puzzled some commentators is a type favored in Italy: Mars appears with

this scene evokes the statues of great Romans and of the ancestors and kinsmen of the Princeps which were to stand in the new forum planned by Augustus.[75] Although Vergil died some time before the forum was finished and dedicated, he would certainly have known about this important aspect of its decoration, and may well have taken pleasure in paying it an anticipatory compliment. And finally, E. Skard points to Polybius's description of the funeral of a Roman statesman, at which all his important ancestors appeared walking in the procession and wearing their insignia, their portrait-busts being carried or even worn by mourners (Polyb. 6.53-54).[76] He suggests that this passage in the *Aeneid* reproduces the effect of the funeral of young Marcellus. It is not easy to conceive of images of Pompey, Fabius Maximus, the Scipios, and the Tarquins being carried at that ceremony; but Skard's central point is well taken—that Anchises' speech surveys much of Roman history presented as a procession of famous men, and is itself a mighty eulogy inspired by the *laudationes* spoken in honor of dead Roman nobles.

In his speech to Caesar and Pompey entreating them not to make civil war (*Aen.* 6.832-835) Anchises echoes the sentences with which the herald stops the duel between Hector and Ajax (*Il.* 7.279-281) but fills them with more intense feeling.[77] Once he recalls a phrase from an important speech made by

it on some Republican coins and in a vision described by Val. Max. 1.8.6. Apropos, F. Weege, "Virgilio e l'arte figurativa," *Conferenze Virgiliane, Pubb. della Università Cattolica del Sacro Cuore* 12 (1931), believes that the depiction of Cleopatra on the shield (*Aen.* 8.696-713) is modelled on the paintings carried in triumphal processions—specifically, no doubt, in the triumph of Augustus in 29 B.C. He points to the vividness of the details: *geminos a tergo . . . anguis* (8.697), *pallentem morte futura* (8.709), with which compare Dido, *pallida morte futura* (4.644).

[75] "Vergil and the Forum of Augustus," *AJP* 62 (1941) 261-276.

[76] "Die Heldenschau in Vergils Aeneis," *SO* 40 (1965) 53-65.

[77] Vergil's "ualidas . . . uiris" comes from Ennius, *Ann.* 300. Lucan in his exordium adapted Vergil's thought: *populumque potentem / in sua uictrici conuersum uiscera dextra.*

his own son at a crisis: "metus Ausonia prohibet consistere terra?" (*Aen.* 6.807) closely resembles the question of Aeneas to Dido (4.349-350):

> quae tandem Ausonia Teucros considere terra
> inuidia est?

Echoes of Ennius also appear. Speaking of Romulus and preparing to speak of Augustus, Anchises says "huius . . . auspiciis illa incluta Roma" (*Aen.* 6.781), with a resonance from the great line (*Ann.* 502)

> *augusto* augurio postquam inclita condita Roma est.

"Bella mouentis" in 6.820 is a cadence suggested by *Ann.* 410; the famous verse about the Delayer in 6.846 comes from *Ann.* 370, and the phrase "rem Romanam" in the tribute to Marcellus (6.857) from *Ann.* 466.

Even here there are some memories of Lucretius. The fasces and the cruel axes of *Aen.* 6.818-819 come from Lucr. 3.996 ($\approx$ 5.1234) and the Scipios, thunderbolts of war (*Aen.* 6.842-843) from Lucr. 3.1034; but Vergil remodelled Lucretius's "Carthaginis horror" into the briefer and more dramatic "cladam Libyae."

At the end of this scene there is a sentence full of echoes (6.884-885). Pitying the fate of his doomed descendant, the handsome young Marcellus, Anchises says

> manibus date lilia plenis
> purpureos spargam flores.[78]

In this, one cadence comes from Vergil's youthful poem of passionate love for a handsome boy (*Buc.* 2.45-46):

> huc ades, o formose puer: tibi lilia plenis
> ecce ferunt Nymphae calathis.

[78] Sabbadini notes what some readers have overlooked, that "spargam" is subordinate to "date," as in Anna's outcry in 4.683-684, "date uulnera lymphis / abluam." He credits Wagner with pointing out the syntactical parallel.

The other comes from Aeneas's mourning for his father, where (5. 79) he scatters *purpureos . . . flores* over the tomb.[79]

Minor Characters

Of the other speeches in the *Aeneid* (apart from those of the gods) the most notable are made by Latinus, Evander, Sinon, and Drances; and there is one important descriptive speech, the Sibyl's account of hell.

The Sibyl

This speech (*Aen.* 6.562-627) combines two different conceptions of hell. One of them is Homeric. In the world of death Odysseus saw certain famous malefactors being punished: individuals, whom he recognized and named (*Od.* 11.576-600). Vergil's Sibyl saw several of the sinners mentioned by Odysseus: Tityus (*Aen.* 6.595-600, explicitly contradicting Lucr. 3.984-991); Theseus and Pirithous (*Aen.* 6.618 + 601); and surely the punishment of the hanging stone implies Tantalus (*Aen.* 6.602-603 ≈ Lucr. 3.980-981).[80] Other such evildoers, not in Homer, appear in her account: the Titans of *Aen.* 6.580-581 come from Hesiod, *Theog.* 729-730; and the blasphemy of Salmoneus (*Aen.* 6.585-594) is not Homeric either (cf. *Od.* 11.236) but later:

$$θεοῦ\ μανεὶς\ ἔρριψε\ Cαλμωνεὺς\ φλόγα.$$
(Eur. *Aeolus* frg. 14 Nauck)

The abyss of hell is like Homer's but twice as deep (*Aen.* 6.577-579 ≈ *Il.* 8.13-16).

The other conception of hell in this speech belongs to a later period, with more rigid ethical standards. In this inferno no individuals appear. Instead, entire classes and types of sinners

---

[79] *Purpureus flos* also appears in a simile at the death of Euryalus (9.435).

[80] F. Weege (cited in n. 74 above) believes Vergil is here following Polygnotus, who was the first to portray Tantalus suffering two different punishments at once, the hanging rock as well as hunger and thirst.

are punished for different classes of sin. The Sibyl refuses to specify their penalties, saying merely that some roll huge stones or are tied to wheels—like Sisyphus and Ixion (*Aen.* 6.616-617), as though Vergil were trying to blend the two different notions of eternal punishment. The "Orphic" apocalypse which shows some parallels with his description of Elysium[81] also embodies several resemblances both to his narrative account of the sad underworld and to the description of hell which he attributes to Deiphobe. Among the damned the Sibyl saw those who hated their brothers (*Aen.* 6.608) and those who found treasure but kept it for themselves ("quae maxima turba est," 6.611). Damnation in the Orphic poem falls on those sinners who, for the love of gain, killed their brothers, sold their wives, or brought their sons to shame. (Two different sins, pollution of the family and avarice, are here confused: Vergil distinguishes them.) Last among the typical sinners in the Sibyl's account is one who committed incest with his daughter. Incest with a mother is punished in the Orphic hell. Yet the wording is curiously similar: "thalamum *inuasit* natae" (*Aen.* 6.623) and ὃς δὲ παρέδραθε μητρί . . . καὶ ἀρούραν ἐπέδραμεν. Even the structure of this part of Vergil's hell, with each class marked off by "hic . . . hic . . . hic," reappears in the Orphic apocalypse as ὁ δὲ . . . τοῦ δὲ . . . ὃς δὲ. . . .

Quotations, more than we can now detect, appear in this eloquent passage. The graphic phrase describing the vulture's activity, "rimatur epulis" (*Aen.* 6.599), was created by Maecenas (Sen. *Ep.* 114.5)—unless perhaps Maecenas borrowed it from Vergil. The description of the corrupt statesman (6.621-622)—

uendidit hic auro patriam dominumque potentem
imposuit; fixit leges pretio atque refixit

—is inspired by two lines in a poem of Vergil's friend Varius.[82]

[81] See pp. 234-235 above, and note 67.
[82] Macrobius 6.1.39; Varius Rufus frg. 1 Morel.

Even the final sentence, in which the Sibyl says she could not describe the infinite variety of sins and punishments in hell even if she had a hundred tongues and mouths and a voice of iron, shows how Vergil adopted, improved, and transmitted the ideas of earlier poets.[83] The poet of the *Iliad* begins the catalogue of the ships by asking the Muses to name the captains; but says that without their help he could not possibly list the ordinary soldiers even if he had ten tongues and ten mouths and an "unbreakable" voice and a heart of bronze (*Il.* 2.484-493). Later Greek poets did not adopt this curious conception, but the Romans took it up: first Ennius (*Ann.* 561-562):

> non si lingua loqui saperet, acsi ora decem sint,
> immensum, ferro cor sit pectusque reuinctum.[84]

It must often have been repeated,[85] but the next extant occurrence comes from a Roman epic on the Dalmatian wars, where the poet says he could not describe the full wealth of events unless he had a *hundred* tongues.[86] Vergil employs it in the *Georgics* (2.42-44), declaring that he could not describe all the farmer's lore if he had a hundred tongues and mouths and a voice of iron; and then he uses the concept to its fullest effect at the end of the speech of the Sibyl.[87]

[83] See P. Courcelle, "Histoire du cliché virgilien des cent bouches," *REL* 33 (1955) 231-240, tracing later appearances of the formula down to John of Salisbury; and G. Pascucci, "Ennio, *Ann.*, 561-62 V² e un tipico procedimento di αὔξηϲιϲ nella poesia latina," *SIFC* 31 (1959) 79-99.

[84] The suggested text is Pascucci's, which scarcely solves all the problems, but is preferable to Vahlen's: fortunately the meaning is clear.

[85] "Si linguas decem / habeam" turns up in Caecilius Statius (frg. 126-127 Ribbeck).

[86] Macrobius 6.3.6; Hostius, Bellum Histricum frg. 3 Morel.

[87] On the passage in the *Georgics* Servius says that the verse is by Lucretius, but that he wrote "*aenea* uox"; on the passage in the *Aeneid* he repeats the assertion with "*aerea* uox." It does not appear in our manuscripts of *De Rerum Natura*. H. D. Jocelyn, "Ancient Scholarship and Virgil's Use of Republican Latin Poetry. II," *CQ* 15 (1965) 140-141, gives this as an instance of Servius's unreliability, and appears not to believe that Vergil's source here is Lucretius.

Sinon

For the speech of Sinon (*Aen.* 2.69-72 + 77-104 + 108-144 + 154-194) Vergil's models are lost. Doubtless they included passages from the *Little Iliad*[88] and from Arctinus's *Sack of Troy*[89] as well as tragedy. Sophocles wrote a *Sinon* and each of the three great playwrights wrote a *Palamedes*. The closest parallel to the behavior of Sinon among the Trojans and to the falsehood he tells comes from the opening of the lost *Philoctetes* of Euripides, paraphrased by Dio Chrysostom 59.6-10. There Odysseus (disguised) claims to be a friend of Palamedes and declares that, when Palamedes was destroyed by Odysseus' slanders, he himself had to flee or be put to death. Sinon's exclamation of feigned despair (*Aen.* 2.69-72) is partly modelled on those of Odysseus in and after the storm that wrecked his raft (*Od.* 5.299 and 465): in the tradition Sinon was Odysseus' cousin. Also, it is very much in the Odyssean manner for Sinon to begin a narrative which is a tissue of lies with the assurance that he will tell the whole truth and nothing but the truth (*Aen.* 2.77-78). He declares "Cuncta equidem tibi, rex, fuerit quodcumque, fatebor / uera" just as Odysseus, ψεύδεα πολλὰ λέγων ἐτύμοιϲιν ὁμοῖα, sets out to deceive Eumaeus (*Od.* 14.192) and his own father (*Od.* 24.303). His lofty antithesis of misery and honesty (*Aen.* 2.79-80) is likened by Macrobius (6.1.57) to a boast of the beggar-king in Accius's tragedy *Telephus* (frg. VI):

> nam si a me regnum Fortuna atque opes
> eripere quiuit, at uirtutem nec quiit.[90]

The curious phrase "cassum lumine" (*Aen.* 2.85) comes from Lucretius 5.719; as so often, Vergil improves what he borrows,

---

[88] See Ar. *Poet.* 23.1459b7.

[89] In *Homeri Opera* vol. 5, ed. T. W. Allen (Oxford, 1912, often reprinted), p. 107, lines 26-27.

[90] nequit, nequiit *MSS*; nec quiit *ci. Ribbeck*. H. D. Jocelyn, on pp. 128-129 of the article cited above, n. 87, suggests that the sentence and the drama were by Ennius, not Accius.

changing *cassum lumine fertur* to "cassum *lu*mine *lu*gent."
(Later, in 12.935, he alters the phrase again, to the more drastic
"spoliatum lumine.") And "hinc mihi prima labes" (*Aen.* 2.97)
may well be an adaptation of a phrase in Homer's narrative,
κακοῦ δ᾽ ἄρα οἱ πέλεν ἀρχή, used of Patroclus in *Il.* 11.604.
Sinon ennobles himself by quoting Homeric heroes. His pa-
thetic reference to home and children (*Aen.* 2.137-138) echoes
Sarpedon lying grievously wounded (*Il.* 5.687-688); while the
last sentence in his acceptance of death, "hoc Ithacus uelit et
magno mercentur Atridae" (*Aen.* 2.104), inverts Nestor's re-
proach to Agamemnon and Achilles (*Il.* 1.255-256), perhaps
also echoes the Sophoclean chorus imagining the glee of Odys-
seus and the Atridae at the death of their enemy (Soph. *Aj.*
955-960).

Drances

In his oration at the council (*Aen.* 11.343-375) Drances be-
gins—after a compliment to old Latinus devised to place all the
Latins on his side—by reproaching Turnus. His tone some-
what resembles that of Thersites' attack on Agamemnon (*Il.*
2.225-242) but is more polished. Thersites upbraids the king to
his face, addressing him directly in the first line and the last
as Ἀτρείδη; Drances does not at first name Turnus or even
speak to him in the second person, but counts on Turnus's
quick reactions and hasty temper to betray him. On the other
hand, Thersites does not accuse Agamemnon of anything
worse than greed for loot, while Drances charges Turnus with
poor leadership and cowardice.[91] Turning back to king Lati-
nus, Drances proposes that Lavinia be espoused to Aeneas, as
Antenor recommends the return of Helen in *Il.* 7.348-353.
Then, for the first time, he faces Turnus, and begs him on be-
half of all the Latins to make peace. (Thersites calls on all the
Greeks to leave Agamemnon and sail home, that is, to aban-

[91] Thersites in *Il.* 2.241 calls Achilles a slacker.

don the war: *Il.* 2.235-240.) Finally he endeavors to shame Turnus into fighting a decisive duel with Aeneas (*Aen.* 11.368-375) as Hector shames Paris into duelling with Menelaus (*Il.* 3.39-57); but Hector as the elder brother is bitter and abusive, while Drances is more circumspect, making Turnus a haughty warrior sacrificing helpless commoners to his pride (as Hector says of Paris in *Il.* 6.326-331). Drances' phrase "inhumata infletaque turba" (*Aen.* 11.372) is tragic: Antigone speaks of her brother's corpse as "ἄκλαυτον ἄταφον" (Soph. *Ant.* 29; cf. Eur. *Hec.* 30 and *Aen.* 6.325). Yet it is a rhetorical distortion of the facts: the dead were all buried or cremated, and duly mourned by their families (*Aen.* 11.203-217).

The Drances episode shows how Vergil borrowed from Homer, what he omitted, and what he changed.

The intervention of Thersites in the debate of the chiefs is, so to speak, detachable from the fabric of the poem. After Agamemnon's disastrous speech, the entire army, rushing to the beach, prepares to launch the ships and return home (*Il.* 2.142-154). Only a miracle, together with the wisdom of the wisest prince, can save the expedition. So, prompted by Hera, Athena descends and encourages Odysseus to restore order. By persuasion and rebuke he drives the mob back to the assembly (*Il.* 2.155-210). Thersites alone attacks Agamemnon; Odysseus beats him into silence, and the folk approve (2.211-277). Then Odysseus, supported by Athena in the guise of a herald, makes a statesmanlike speech: Nestor and Agamemnon also speak, and the assembly dissolves (2.278-399). It is the activity of Odysseus and Athena which saves the situation; and that could (perhaps once did) run continuously from the marshalling (155-210) into the speechmaking (278-399). The interruption of Thersites is emotionally justified. The common soldiers were eager to go home. Some of them shouted protests: Odysseus had to drive them back with blows and rebukes (2.198-199): Thersites personifies their mutinous spirit. But dramatically his speech has no result whatever.

249

The speech of Drances, on the other hand, has been prepared for. He was part of the Latin delegation asking for a burial truce (*Aen.* 11.100-132). Then he welcomed Aeneas's pacific words, promised to re-establish his association with king Latinus, and dismissed Turnus with a brief contemptuous sentence. When the final debate opens, Drances is consistent: supporting and strengthening Latinus's peace proposal and endeavoring to isolate Turnus (*Aen.* 11.336-375). In his reply, Turnus ends by accepting the suggestion that he should fight a duel with Aeneas (11.434-444); and the meeting might well have resolved that he should—but it was thrown into disorder by the news of Aeneas's advance, and Turnus left before a vote could be taken (11.445-467).

The speeches of Thersites and Drances obviously differ in tone, although not in motivation: both men hate their opponents. Thersites does not argue. He simply upbraids Agamemnon for his greed and for injuring Achilles' honor, and although he does propose to abandon the enterprise, he gives no solid reason to support this (as Agamemnon did in *Il.* 2.130-138 and as Odysseus does in 291-297), but spitefully says, "Let us go home and leave him here." Drances speaks nearly twice as long as Thersites: his speech is a little masterpiece of diplomatic skill, supporting feeble Latinus and exasperating violent Turnus. Thersites contrives to insult everyone—Agamemnon, the army, and Achilles. Drances insults only his one enemy, and that eloquently. Thersites pictures Agamemnon making love to a captive girl (*Il.* 2.232). Drances depreciates Turnus's suit for Lavinia by saying he wants her dowry (*Aen.* 11.369). Thersites screams and shouts. Drances speaks with earnest pathos ("miserere," "animae uiles"). Thersites is ridiculously ugly. Drances is not described, but he is wealthy and on one side nobly born. After speaking, Thersites is beaten and humiliated (*Il.* 2.265-269). Drances is threatened by a gesture of Turnus's sword-arm (*Aen.* 11.408, see p. 61) but not touched.

So, in taking over the Thersites episode, Vergil has made it more dignified, more intellectual, and more effectively incorporated into the poem.

Yet why is it that everyone knows Thersites, while only a few know Drances? In the *Iliad* Thersites is a rootless character, who appears for a few minutes and then vanishes. But the Greeks after Homer eagerly invented stories about him. They gave him noble ancestry, making him a kinsman of Diomede; they had him crippled by Meleager, killed by Achilles, and sent to the underworld. He lived on in paintings and proverbs and fantasies. After many centuries he was reborn in Shakespeare's *Troilus and Cressida*, railing at Greeks and Trojans and even himself, "bastard in mind, bastard in valour." But Drances? Why did he never win such fame?

Vergil could not create minor characters who came alive. The name Drances sounds unpleasant, suggesting *draco* and *rancens*, but Thersites, Bragson, is more vivid and apt. Of Drances we can form no clear picture: we know his mind and emotions, not his face and form. Thersites is pictured with incomparable clarity; and while Drances merely *aggerat iras*, Thersites can actually be heard ὀξέα κεκληγώς. Nothing happens to Drances, who fades into the background with the ineffectual elders; but Thersites is publicly thrashed with a golden scepter, and sits wiping away his tears. Drances and Turnus are enemies, but almost equals. Thersites makes a superb contrast with Achilles the bravest, with Agamemnon the royallest, and with Odysseus the wisest of the Achaeans. Exaggerated though he is, he is the first impressive comic figure in literature; Drances, like so many of Vergil's people, is a voice without a body. Drances makes a better speech; Thersites is a more vital and memorable character.

Latinus

Latinus is a Homeric monarch. His first speech, to the Trojan embassy (*Aen.* 7.195-211), opens with a question resembling that of Nestor to Telemachus in *Od.* 3.71-74—although

251

he does not (like Nestor) assume that they might easily be pirates. After listening to the oration of Ilioneus, he offers the Trojan prince his daughter, like Alcinous to Odysseus in *Od.* 7.311-315.[92] Before he makes the grand refusal and retires behind closed doors, he warns the Latins and Turnus of their future sufferings, and implies he has not long to live (*Aen.* 7.594-599)—as Priam does with the Trojans, although in a much harsher and more masterful tone (*Il.* 24.239-246). Later, when he emerges from seclusion, his speech to the Latins stresses the fact that their resistance is ill-starred and that they should make important concessions to the Trojans: two themes which appear in Antenor's proposal with reference to Helen and the breaking of the oath (*Il.* 7.348-353) but which are expressed much more fully by Latinus. When he attempts to persuade Turnus to abandon his claim to Lavinia and avoid the duel with Aeneas (*Aen.* 12.19-45), Latinus speaks like Priam to Hector in *Il.* 22.38-76, but with more tact.[93] He would never say outright, as Priam does, that the young hero's opponent was stronger and more likely to win (*Il.* 22.39-40). Instead, he mentions death twice, guardedly (*Aen.* 12.38 + 41), and warns Turnus that all war is uncertain (12.43). Priam beseeches Hector to have pity on him, and dilates on his own sufferings past and future (*Il.* 22.44-55 + 59-76). More calmly, Latinus refers to his own mistakes in diplomacy and the defeats of his people (*Aen.* 12.29-36) and reminds Turnus of his old father Daunus (*Aen.* 12.43-45). And yet Priam, although he foresees his own death and the destruction of his city, never suggests a surrender, while Latinus is willing to contemplate a compromise (*Aen.* 12.39). The war between the

[92] Agamemnon's offer to Achilles made through the envoys (*Il.* 9.144-148) occurs in a totally different situation.

[93] The opening lines of his speech (*Aen.* 12.19-21) are adapted from a Roman tragedy: perhaps the words of Ismene to her strong-willed sister:

> quanto magis te isti modi esse intellego,
> tanto, Antigona, magis me par est tibi consulere et parcere.
>
> (Accius, *Antigona* frg. II Ribbeck)

Trojans and the Achaeans was irreconcilable, while Vergil wished to show the Trojans as peaceful immigrants who would eventually merge with the Italians.

In the oath-taking ceremony before the duel (*Aen.* 12.197-211) Latinus invokes Jupiter and the powers of the underworld as Agamemnon does in his two great pledges (*Il.* 3.276-291 and 19.258-265). He strengthens his oath with two ἀδύνατα—one about the world's destruction, adapted from Lucretius 3.842, the other about the burgeoning of a dry wooden scepter, like Achilles in *Il.* 1.233-239. Thereafter he speaks no more. He is last seen befouling his grey hair with dust (*Aen.* 12.611) like old Aegeus in Catullus 64.224, and watching the fatal duel (*Aen.* 12.707) like Priam in *Il.* 22.25-35 + 408.

Evander

In the second book of Apollonius's *Argonautica* the adventurers pass between the Dark Rocks and reach the land of the Mariandyni on the south coast of the Euxine. There they are welcomed and feasted by king Lycus, who sends his son to accompany them (2.752-814). This is the closest parallel for Evander's festive welcome to the Trojans (*Aen.* 8.152-183), his entertainment of Aeneas (184-369), and his speech entrusting his son Pallas to Aeneas (470-519). Details emphasize the parallelism. Both Lycus and Evander have suffered grievous losses from aggression by their neighbors.[94] Lycus relates how, when he was a youth, Hercules (until recently an Argonaut) visited his father's court; Evander recalls how, when he was a youth, Anchises visited his father's court.[95] Shortly before their visit, the Argonauts, after seeing an epiphany of Apollo, built a special altar for him, and praised one of his heroic exploits, the killing of the monster Typhon, with song and dance (*Argon.* 2.694-719). The Arcadians are celebrating the festival of Her-

---

[94] *Argon.* 2.757-758 + 792-795 ≈ *Aen.* 8.474 + 569-571.
[95] *Argon.* 2.774-791 ≈ *Aen.* 8.157-168: "ἐμὲ ... νέον χνοάοντα παρειάϛ" ≈ "mihi prima genas uestibat flore iuuentas."

cules at his special altar; Evander relates one of his heroic exploits, the killing of the monster Cacus; and a double chorus sings a hymn praising his deeds of valor (*Aen.* 8.184-305).[96] Vergil adds a delicate allusion to Catullus's poem mentioning the Argonauts. There (64.4) they are *lecti iuuenes, Argiuae robora pubis*; Evander declares in *Aen.* 8.518-519 that he will give Aeneas "equites bis centum, robora pubis / lecta." There is also an echo from an earlier part of the *Aeneid*. Evander's generous phrase "auxilio laetos dimittam opibusque iuuabo" (8.171) is the statement made by Dido in 1.571 to the Trojan delegation—with one word altered, as so often in Vergil's adaptations of his own verses.

Something of the *Odyssey* too appears in Aeneas's visit to Pallanteum. Evander's welcome to the sacrificial feast (*Aen.* 8.172-183) recalls Pisistratus's courteous reception of Athena and Telemachus in *Od.* 3.31-66; and Evander remarks on Aeneas's resemblance to his father (*Aen.* 8.154-156) as Nestor does with Telemachus (*Od.* 3.122-125).

Apart from the paean sung by the Argonauts no extant Greek prototype has been suggested for Evander's tale of Hercules' victory over Cacus (*Aen.* 8.185-275)[97] and none for his description of the site of Rome (306-358). But Farrington (cited on p. 236 above) proposes plausibly enough that here again Vergil has inserted a little propaganda for heroism as opposed to Epicurean quietism. Evander declares that the festival his people are celebrating is not a custom imposed by "uana superstitio" (*Aen.* 8.187)—which is Lucretius's view of

[96] The Arcadians are not explicitly described as dancing; but the hymn is sung by the Salii, whose name means "dancers" and who dance on the shield in *Aen.* 8.663. They were usually priests of Mars; but Hercules had Salii at Tibur, so this may be "a piece of antiquarian lore": so C. Bailey, *Religion in Virgil* (Oxford, 1935) p. 57.

[97] One detail: the blow with which Hercules unroofs the cave of Cacus is comparable to Poseidon's earthquake, which makes Aidoneus tremble in his subterranean realm (*Aen.* 8.233-246 ≈ *Il.* 20.57-65): note "dis inuisa" (*Aen.* 8.245) and τά τε στυγέουσι θεοί περ (*Il.* 20.65).

religion;[98] and he says that Hercules through superhuman effort saved the Arcadians from oppression. By implication this is a retort to Lucretius, who in 5.1-54 claims that Epicurus deserves the title of god more than Ceres and Bacchus and Hercules. When describing the aboriginal wood-folk to whom Saturn brought civilization (*Aen.* 8.314-318), Evander combines a quaint proverbial saying from Homer (*Od.* 19.163) with several ideas and phrases from Lucretius (4.580-581, 5.933-942 + 953-959).

Evander's farewell to his son (*Aen.* 8.560-583) begins in the tone of Nestor regretting his youth (560-571 ≈ *Il.* 7.132-158; cf. *Il.* 11.670f., 23.629f.). It contains an echo of Priam's plea to Hector,[99] and then, more clearly, an adaptation of the prayer of Achilles sending forth Patroclus (*Aen.* 8.572-583 ≈ *Il.* 16.233-248).[100] For Evander's lament over the dead Pallas (*Aen.* 11.152-181) there is no model in extant Greek epic: neither Priam nor Laertes speaks thus about his son.[101] It is reminiscent of some of the θρῆνοι of Greek tragedy. Such, although more lyrical and less orderly in the disposition of its thoughts, is the lament of Peleus over Neoptolemus in Euripides' *Andromache* (1173-1183). Evander's opening words, "non haec . . . dederas promissa parenti," echo the deserted Ariadne (Cat. 64.139-140), "at non haec quondam blanda promissa dedisti / uoce mihi." Exculpating the Trojans, he says (*Aen.* 11.165)

[98] The word *superstitio* is not found in Latin before Cicero; but Bailey in his edition of Lucretius (Oxford, 1947) suggests on 1.63 that Lucretius may have been hinting at it in the sentence where religion appears "horribili *super* aspectu mortalibus *instans*" (1.65).

[99] Knauer, n. 4 on pp. 254-255, points to the repeated "if"—a good example of his sharp eye for structural detail.

[100] The intense pathos of the end of Evander's farewell resembles the speech of Aegeus in Catullus 64.215-237, and the alternatives of life and death are described by both fathers, but there are no verbal similarities.

[101] G. R. Manton in *AUMLA* 17 (1962) 5-17, following up a suggestion of E. Fraenkel in *Phil.* 87 (1932) 242-248, suggests that Evander grieving for the dead Pallas resembles Nestor grieving for Antilochus in the *Aethiopis* of Arctinus: cf. Prop. 2.13.45-50.

"iunximus hospitio dextras," in words used by Aeneas of another friendly monarch (3.83). It is a noble speech.

Helenus

The prophecy of Helenus in *Aen*. 3.374-462 covers several different topics and has several different models. A curious discourse, it alternates, paragraph by paragraph, fairly exact sailing directions with counsels about the supernatural. Helenus advises Aeneas to approach Italy from the *west* by circumnavigating Sicily (381-387), to avoid Calabria, the Gulf, and Bruttium, all populated by "bad Greeks" (396-402), and not to attempt the Sicilian strait imperiled by Scylla and Charybdis (410-432). This itinerary is suggested by Circe's injunctions to Odysseus in *Od*. 12.37-110 + 116-141 and by Phineus's forecast to the Argonauts in Ap. Rhod. 2.311-425.[102] But also, like Odysseus in the underworld, Aeneas is given a description of the omen which will mark the end of his long journey (*Aen*. 3.388-395 ≈ *Od*. 11.119-129) and directed to placate a hostile divinity (*Aen*. 3.433-440 ≈ *Od*. 11.130-134; cf. *Argon*. 2.423-425). Odysseus is told by Circe to consult the dead seer Tiresias (*Od*. 10.508-540) and Aeneas is told by Helenus to consult the "mad seer" Deiphobe (*Aen*. 3.441-460), with special precautions to be taken in each case. Only the prescription to cover the head while sacrificing (*Aen*. 3.403-409)—a prescription which Aeneas is never stated to observe, but which was carried back to his lifetime in Roman mythology—has no parallel in Homer or Apollonius: it is another of Vergil's antiquarian touches, designed to connect Italic usage with the earlier world of Greece and Troy.[103]

The farewell of Helenus and Andromache to Anchises and

---

[102] Note *Aen*. 3.377-380 ≈ *Argon*. 2.311-312.

[103] In the oath-taking Aeneas appears to wear a helmet (*Aen*. 12.167), which he throws off when the disorder breaks out (12.312). R. D. Williams in his edition of Book Three (line 405) quotes Festus for the aetiological story that Aeneas after reaching Italy was sacrificing, and covered his head in order not to be recognized by Odysseus.

Ascanius (*Aen.* 3.475-481 + 486-491) is parallel to that of Menelaus and Helen to Telemachus (*Od.* 15.111-119 + 125-129); but Helenus is far more respectful, revering the man beloved by Venus and favored by Apollo, while Andromache is far more affectionate, seeing in young Ascanius the image of her lost son:

> et nunc aequali tecum pubesceret aeuo.

Numanus

The flyting addressed by Numanus to the besieged Trojans (*Aen.* 9.598-620) has a number of good models. His scorn for the pent-up enemy (598-600) echoes the rebuke of Hector to Polydamas (*Il.* 18.285-287) and also resembles the challenges of the Etruscans to the Romans in their camp (Livy 2.45.3-4). We know no prototype for the fine description of the primitive Italians' rugged life (603-613) except Vergil's own account of the tough Aequi in the catalogue (7.746-749). There he says *armati terram exercent*; here he elaborates the idea, "uersaque iuuencum / terga fatigamus hasta."[104] There he writes *semperque recentis / conuectare iuuat praedas et uiuere rapto*; here he repeats the sentence, changing one word, the rare "conuectare" to the more usual "comportare." The youth of the tribe, boasts Numanus, is "patiens operum paruoque adsueta iuuentus"—a description taken, with one word changed, from the eulogy of Italian farmers in *Georg.* 2.472. The insult to the soft Trojans distantly recalls a remark of king Alcinous, who tells Odysseus that his people love dances and changes of clothes and bed (*Aen.* 9.614-616 ≈ *Od.* 8.248-249).[105] The final four lines (617-620) contain some of Vergil's most brilliant adaptations. Ridiculing the Phrygian worship of Cybele, they incorporate allusions to the monologue of her votary Attis in Catullus's sixty-third poem. There (12-13 + 20-22) Attis, self-

---

[104] Note the effortful lengthening in "fatigamūs."
[105] On the allusion to *Il.* 13.636-639 see p. 185 above.

THE SPEECHES IN VERGIL'S *AENEID*

castrated and surrounded by other eunuchs, beats his tambourine and sings:

agite *ite ad alta, Gallae,* Cybeles nemora simul,
simul *ite, Dindymenae* dominae uaga pecora, . . .
Phrygiam ad domum Cybebes, *Phrygia* ad nemora deae,
ubi cymbalum sonat uox, ubi *tympana* reboant,
tibicen ubi *canit* Phryx curuo graue calamo.

And so Numanus shouts:

o uere *Phrygiae,* neque enim Phryges, *ite per alta
Dindyma, ubi* adsuetis biforem dat *tibia cantum.
tympana* uos buxusque uocat Berecyntia Matris.

Catullus makes Attis describe his unmanned companions as "Gallae," not "Galli." Vergil synthesizes this with an abusive phrase of Thersites, who calls his fellow-soldiers women of Achaea, not men (*Il.* 2.235). The line about the Trojans' effeminate costume has a special sneering rhythm (9.616; see p. 90 above):

et tunicae manicas et habent redimicula mitrae.

It has recently been pointed out that the rhythm of this line is modelled on a verse of Lucretius which describes a menstruous woman fainting (6.795):

et manibus nitidum teneris opus effluit ei.[106]

Vergil's ingenuity is remarkable. The last six words of Numanus, "sinite arma uiris et cedite ferro," echo a famous speech in the *Iliad* (6.490-493), adapted by Vergil once before, in 7.444: a line addressed in Homer by a warrior to a woman, but in the *Aeneid* spoken with ill-advised contempt by Turnus to the Fury, and to the Trojans by Numanus, who will soon die.

---

[106] H. Jacobson, "Nonnulla Lucretiana," *CP* 61 (1966) 156.

258

Ilioneus

The first speech of Ilioneus, made to Dido, resembles the plea addressed to the Argonauts by the sons of Phrixus (*Aen.* 1.522-558 ≈ *Argon.* 2.1123-1133). Both parties are shipwrecked, both ask for help, both invoke the gods as defenders of morality. However, the speech of Ilioneus is calmer (*placido pectore, Aen.* 1.521), longer, and less humble. His reference to Italy (1.530, quoted from the Penates, 3.163), so old-fashioned in phrasing (asyndetic parataxis),

> est locus, Hesperiam Grai cognomine dicunt

would remind Roman readers of the account of Aeneas's voyage early in the *Annals* of Ennius (23):

> est locus, Hesperiam quam mortales perhibebant.

His indignant question, "quod genus hoc hominum?" (*Aen.* 1.539), comes from Furius Bibaculus's epic on the Gallic wars (frg. 11 Morel)—according to Macrobius 6.1.32 (*si credere dignum est*). Speaking of his lost leader (*Aen.* 1.546-547), he resembles Eumaeus in his first greeting to Odysseus (*Od.* 14.42-44); but the strange phrase "uescitur aura" comes from Lucretius 5.857.

The second speech of Ilioneus, addressed to Latinus (*Aen.* 7.213-248), begins with a reverse of the plea of the Argonaut hero Euphemus to Triton in Ap. Rhod. 4.1566-1570, and goes on to persuasive diplomatic argument. As he declares that the destiny of the gods led the Trojans to Italy, "imperiis egere suis" (7.239-240), he is echoing the declaration which his leader Aeneas addressed to Dido, "me iussa deum . . . / imperiis egere suis" (*Aen.* 6.461-463), and with no less conviction.

The Gods

Jupiter

Vergil's Jupiter speaks with less bluster and more majesty than the Zeus of the *Iliad*. There Zeus bullies the other gods, boasting of his strength, until the thing becomes ridiculous. He threatens Hera in 1.565-567 and 15.14-33, Athena (and Hera) in 8.399-408 and 447-456, Poseidon in 15.162-167 and 221-228, and all the Olympians as a body in 8.10-27; and this is not a new trait, for Sleep remembers how, when angered by Hera's persecution of Hercules, he was furious, ῥιπτάζων κατὰ δῶμα θεούς (14.257). Vergil's Jupiter is above such conduct. He makes no physical threats. He bids, and forbids, and is obeyed.

His first pronouncement (*Aen.* 1.257-296) and his last (12.830-840) are both modelled on and expanded from the speech in which the Homeric Zeus foretells the end of the war (*Il.* 15.49-77) together with his promise to bring Odysseus home (*Od.* 1.64-79) and Poseidon's forecast of the future greatness of Aeneas and his house (*Il.* 20.293-308). Both these speeches are introduced by similar lines, which have the ring of Ennius (1.254, cf. 12.829):

olli subridens hominum sator atque deorum.[107]

Jupiter's opening words, "parce metu, Cytherea," resemble the reassurance of Zeus to Athena at a time when she too is anxious about those she is protecting, in *Il.* 8.39, "θάρσει, Τριτογένεια." In Ennius's *Annals* (65-66) Jupiter made a speech promising the deification of Romulus, which is echoed here in lines 259-260. One phrase is anticipated in Vergil's early eulogy of Varus, whose name *cantantes sublime ferent ad sidera cycni* (*Buc.* 9.29 ≈ *Aen.* 1.259). The description of the Romans, "gentem togatam," was (if we believe Macrobius, *Sat.* 6.5.15) coined by the mime-writer Laberius (*Ephebus*, frg. II Ribbeck).

In this interview Jupiter reverts to a thought he expressed

---

[107] Cf. Enn. *Ann.* 33 and 119. F. Gloeckner, "Zum Gebrauch von olli bei Vergil," *ALL* 14 (1906) 185-188, corrects Servius's explanation of *olli* here as "then," and shows that *olli . . . natae* is a hyperbaton like 2.146-147, 5.609-610, and 12.901-902.

in his first. Reproaching Juno and preparing to prohibit her from further hostile actions, he says "terris agitare uel undis / Troianos potuisti" (12.803-804) as he said to Venus in 1.279-280 "Iuno, / quae mare nunc terrasque metu caelumque fatigat."[108] But when talking to Venus he says "*aspera Iuno*"; when speaking directly to his consort, he says "tuo *dulci* . . . ex ore."[109]

Jove's command sent through Mercury that Aeneas shall set sail at once (*Aen.* 4.223-237) resembles Zeus's message sent through Hermes to Calypso (*Od.* 5.29-42 + 105-115) in that it dispatches the hero on his way after a long pause. But Zeus does not rebuke Odysseus as Jove rebukes Aeneas. A more earnest reproach in a similar situation is voiced by Hercules when he scolds the Argonauts for dallying in Lemnos (Ap. Rhod. 1.865-874), reminding them of their ancestry ("πάτρης ἐμφύλιον αἷμ' " ≈ "genus alto a sanguine Teucri") and quest for fame ("οὐ μάλ' εὐκλεεῖς . . . ἐccόμεθ' " ≈ "si nulla accendit . . . gloria"). Although effective, that denunciation is naturally less peremptory and imperious in tone than the terrifying reprimand of Jupiter.

Twice Jupiter tells a divinity that the bounds of mortality cannot be overpassed: Cybele anxious for the ships (*Aen.* 9.94-103) and Hercules weeping for Pallas (10.467-472). This is a reversal of the Homeric situation. There, when Zeus would save his son Sarpedon, Hera tells him it would be wrong to do so, and suggests a consolatory solution (*Il.* 16.440-457; cf. Athena on Hector, *Il.* 22.178-181). Vergil emphasizes his higher conception of godhead by making Jupiter, while comforting Hercules, allude to the inevitability of Sarpedon's death, which in the *Iliad* he had not wished to admit.

In the Olympian council he warns the gods to assist neither

---

[108] The strong phrase "caelum fatigat" comes from Lucretius's description of the gloomy farmers in 2.1169. Another phrase from the same paragraph, *caput quassans*, is also applied to Juno in *Aen.* 7.292.

[109] Noted by Cartault, p. 157.

261

side, as Zeus does early in the *Iliad* (*Aen.* 10.6-15 + 104-113 ≈ *Il.* 8.5-27). He understands the necessity for warfare; but unlike Zeus (*Il.* 20.22-23, 21.385-390) he does not enjoy it as a spectacle. For him it is the painful but necessary precondition for a state of peace.

The council is modelled partly on Homer, and partly on the assembly of the gods called to discuss the fate of Rome in the Hannibalic war, as described by Ennius, *Annals* 7.[110] Both Jupiter's opening and his closing speech contain verbal Ennian reminiscences. "Caelicolae" was coined by Ennius (*Ann.* 491), and the first sentence is a variation of *Annals* 259:

<di,> quianam dictis nostris sententia flexa est?[111]

The curious phrase "res rapuisse" (*Aen.* 10.14) comes from Roman thought about the legal declaration of war, according to Servius ad loc. First the fetial priests *res repetunt* (Livy 1.32.5-14; cf. Enn. *Ann.* 273); if satisfaction is not forthcoming, war is declared: *et iam sic licebat more belli res rapere.*[112] There are also at least two echoes of earlier speeches in the *Aeneid* itself. "Nullo discrimine habebo" (10.108) recalls Dido's offer to treat Trojans and Tyrians alike (1.574); while "fata uiam inuenient" (10.113) has become weightier since it first appeared in Helenus's reassurance to Aeneas (3.395).

Once Jupiter teases Juno (*Aen.* 10.607-610) as Zeus teases Hera and Athena (*Il.* 4.7-19): in each case Aphrodite/Venus is assisting a Trojan hero in battle. When Juno protests, he gives her permission to save Turnus (*Aen.* 10.622-627) as Zeus does with "ἔρξον ὅπως ἐθέλεις" (*Il.* 4.37), permitting Hera to initiate counter-measures against Troy. Jupiter's final warning that Juno has gone far enough (*Aen.* 12.793-806) is as firm

---

[110] See an imaginative reconstruction of Ennius's council of the gods in E. Norden, *Ennius und Vergilius* (Leipzig, 1915) c. 2.

[111] <di,> added by Norden (n. 110, above) p. 47, who compares *Aen.* 3.265, 6.264, 9.247, etc., and notes the assonance "*di . . . dictis*." Vergil makes Aeneas quote from the adjoining line, *Ann.* 258, in 12.565.

[112] See Norden, cited above, n. 110; p. 51 n. 2.

as Zeus's threats to Hera after his beguiling (*Il.* 15.14-33) but more calm, more serious, more dignified. Finally Jupiter agrees to the concessions urged on him by Juno (*Aen.* 12.830-840), accepting terms more unequal than those he imposed on the combatants at the end of the *Odyssey* (*Od.* 24.478-486).[113] In addition, Norden makes it seem probable that Vergil is here adapting a crucial scene from the *Annals* of Ennius.[114] Norden argues that during the second Punic war Ennius made Juno exercise her full hostility on the Romans, and made Jupiter either side with her or (as in *Aen.* 10) declare himself neutral. But after Cannae, when Hannibal failed to march on Rome, the favor of heaven shifted. In the eighth book of the *Annals*, not in a divine council but during a conversation alone with Juno as in *Aeneid* 12, Jupiter persuaded her to relent. He addressed her in terms of warmth—perhaps in the line

> optima caelicolum, Saturnia, magna dearum
>
> (*Ann.* 491)

of which Vergil's ruefully affectionate line 12.830 is reminiscent. Juno was placated: as Jupiter in *Aen.* 1.279-282 forecast that she would be.

Neptune

In tones of rage recalling those of Homer's Zeus after the beguiling (*Il.* 15.14-33) Neptune rebukes the winds and bids them carry his reprimand to Aeolus (*Aen.* 1.132-141). His manner, however, is haughtier. His remark that winds and Aeolus alike are beings inferior to himself (*Aen.* 1.132-134) contrasts with the epithets employed by the Homeric Zeus; and where Zeus describes a humiliating punishment he once inflicted on

---

[113] See Knauer, pp. 323-325. He also cites the conversation of Athena and Zeus in *Il.* 22.177-185, and (p. 431) the speech of Zeus to Hera in *Il.* 15.49-77; but both these speeches forward war, not peace—although it is true, as he remarks, that by making these concessions Zeus and Jupiter permit the killing of Hector and Turnus.

[114] Pp. 167-169.

his consort (*Il.* 15.18-24) Neptune is content with a menacing gesture and a warning (*Aen.* 1.135-136). The resemblance and difference between the two speeches are strengthened by the fact that both allude to tempests stirred up by Hera/Juno against heroes destined for heaven: Hercules and Aeneas.

Later, Neptune grants Venus's plea for her son's safe voyage (*Aen.* 5.800-815), but pointedly reminds her that he saved Aeneas at Troy by wrapping him in cloud and carrying him away from Achilles (*Il.* 20.288-339). The phrase "nec dis nec uiribus aequis" (*Aen.* 5.809) is diplomatically adapted from Poseidon's description of Achilles spoken as a warning to Aeneas in *Il.* 20.334: ὃς ϲεῦ ἅμα κρείϲϲων καὶ φίλτεροϲ ἀθανάτοιϲιν. Neptune places his rescue of Aeneas at the time when the river Xanthus was clogged with Trojan corpses (*Aen.* 5.806-808); but in fact it was *before* Achilles in his fiery progress reached the river banks (*Il.* 21.1-16). Vergil's speakers are seldom wholly accurate.

Juno

For the speech of Juno in the council of the gods (*Aen.* 10.63-95) there is no close Homeric parallel. In vehemence, though not in eloquence, one utterance of Homer's Hera resembles it: the short flyting she addresses to Artemis before she beats her about the head with her own bow (*Il.* 21.481-492). But Vergil's Juno does not smile as she speaks. The final sentence contains, in "tum decuit" (*Aen.* 10.94) an echo of Dido's self-reproach in *Aen.* 4.597: that was another defeat for Juno.

The words with which she tries to cajole and circumvent Jupiter in *Aen.* 10.611-620 and 628-632 are the reverse of Hera's defiance in *Il.* 4.25-29, but are no less effective in gaining the point. Her remark in *Aen.* 10.617 about Turnus, "Teucrisque pio det sanguine poenas," is typically malicious. It applies to Turnus the adjective so often used of Aeneas, "pius"; and it

264

contains a concealed reference to the future murder of Remus by Romulus: as he killed his brother, Romulus was to cry "calido dabis sanguine poenas" (Enn. *Ann.* 100).

Juno moves three subordinate deities to execute her will: Aeolus, Allecto, Juturna.

Vergil always paints Juno in the darkest colors—sometimes by contrasting her words and actions in the *Aeneid* with her behavior in earlier poems. Toward the end of the *Argonautica* (4.764-769) Hera through Iris bids Aeolus to smooth the sea and send a western breeze to waft the Argonauts to Phaeacia. At the opening of the *Aeneid* (1.65-75) Juno personally induces Aeolus to destroy the fleet of Aeneas. She begins by mentioning Jupiter in terms of respectful awe: he is, as Ennius described him (*Ann.* 175), "diuum pater atque hominum rex." Her hatred for Troy breaks out in line 68, "*Ilium in Italiam portans uictosque penates,*" which looks like part of a chorus in Euripides' *Orestes* (1364-1365):

> διὰ τὸν ὀλόμενον ὀλόμενον Ἰδαῖον
> Πάριν, ὃς ἄγαγ' Ἑλλάδ' εἰς Ἴλιον.[115]

Then she speaks to Aeolus in soft persuasive tones, like Hera to Sleep, and similarly promises him a beautiful wife (*Aen.* 1.71-75 ≈ *Il.* 14.267-268). In Homer there is no fiendish figure like Allecto. Hera's pacific summons to Athena in *Il.* 2.157-165 only superficially resembles Juno's speech to Allecto in *Aen.* 7.331-340, the closest extant prototype of which is the invocation of Madness by Iris in Euripides' *Hercules* 833-842: "uirgo sata Nocte" ≈ "Νυκτὸς . . . παρθένε." In her final intrigue, encouraging Juturna to aid Turnus (*Aen.* 12.142-153), Juno speaks like Hera to Thetis in Apollonius's *Argon.* 4.783-832— except that her bitter reference to Jupiter's many Latin mistresses is the reverse of what Hera says to Thetis in *Argon.*

---

[115] *Manet alta mente repostum* / *iudicium Paridis* (*Aen.* 1.26-27). Aeneas is identified with Paris by Iarbas in *Aen.* 4.215 and by Juno in 7.321.

4.790-797, and is a distant echo of the catalogue of conquests which the Homeric Zeus deploys in *Il.* 14.315-328. The line in which Juno says that she cannot bear to watch Turnus fighting Aeneas (*Aen.* 12.151) restates the genuine emotion expressed by Priam before the duel of Paris and Menelaus (*Il.* 3.306-307); but as we can see from *Aen.* 12.791-792, it is a lie.[116]

When intriguing with Venus to effect the union of Aeneas and Dido (*Aen.* 4.93-104 + 115-127), Juno speaks condescendingly, like Hera to Aphrodite before the beguiling of Zeus (*Il.* 14.190-192 + 198-210); and the two conspire together like Hera and Aphrodite in *Argon.* 3.56-110. Juno's cold litotes, "nec me adeo fallit" (4.96), may have been unconsciously remembered by Vergil from an earnest assertion in Lucretius (1.136). Her suggestion that the Trojans and the Carthaginians should become one people "paribus auspiciis" (*Aen.* 4.102-103) is adverse to the will of destiny, which is expressed, in the same words, about the Latins and the Trojans in *Aen.* 7.256-257.

More brilliantly than any other of her speeches, the two great soliloquies expose the depths of Juno's anger, hatred, and determination. The first (*Aen.* 1.37-49) is introduced by the phrase *aeternum seruans sub pectore uulnus*, adapted from Lucretius's description of the fear of Cybele that her husband Saturn might devour the new-born Jove (2.639). It has several Homeric models, all less passionate. For its opening (37-38) there is Poseidon's cry at the sight of Odysseus (*Od.* 5.286-290). Juno's

---

[116] Cartault (p. 885) comments "Il y a une contradiction entre XII, 792 et ce que dit Junon 151, Non *pugnam* aspicere hanc . . . possum; elle paraît résulter de la composition fragmentaire de l'*Enéide*; les commentateurs qui ne tiennent pas compte de ce mode de rédaction et qui prétendent sauver l'honneur de l'écrivain qu'ils commentent, alors même qu'il n'est pas compromis, diront que Junon, malgré sa répugnance à assister au dénouement fatal, n'a pas pu se décider à quitter le champ de bataille; c'est un mouvement psychologique que Virgile aurait traité κατὰ τὸ σιωπώμενον." But see p. 285 on the difference between what Vergil's characters say and what the facts are. Even here, contrast Juno's two declarations, one to the soft-hearted Juturna (12.151), the other to the stern Jove (12.808-812).

266

reference to the burning of the Argive fleet (39-40) echoes Hector's oath to burn the enemy ships, reported by Agamemnon in *Il.* 14.44-47: "classem / . . . atque ipsos" ≈ νῆας . . . καὶ αὐτούς. Her description of the fate of Ajax (42-45) is more gruesome than Proteus's narrative in *Od.* 4.499-511. It is enhanced by reminiscences of the dialogue of Athena and Poseidon in Euripides' *Troades* (especially lines 80-84 and 92-94) and by phrasing adapted from Lucretius. Juno says (*Aen.* 1.44-45)

> illum *exspirantem transfixo pectore flammas*
> *turbine corripuit.*

Lucretius denies the possibility of monsters:

> *flammam* taetro *spirantis* ore Chimaeras (2.705)

and declares (6.387-395) that thunderbolts ought, if the gods hurled them, to strike the guilty—

> icti *flammas* ut fulguris halent
> *pectore perfixo*

so that the innocent should not suffer—

> *turbine* caelesti subito *correptus* et igni.

Juno's boast of her own lofty rank (*Aen.* 1.46-47) repeats those of Hera addressed to Zeus in *Il.* 4.58-61 and 18.364-366.

Her second monologue (*Aen.* 7.293-322) also begins with an echo of Poseidon's speech in *Od.* 5.286-290; but where Poseidon speaks of the gods' change of purpose (286-287), Juno adduces a more durable and impressive concept, the conflict of destinies, "fatis contraria nostris / fata Phrygum" (*Aen.* 7.293-294). This concept has appeared once before, in an equally important speech, where Venus tells Jupiter of her long-frustrated hopes (*Aen.* 1.238-239): "occasum Troiae . . . solabar fatis contraria fata rependens." Now, dwelling on the miraculous survival of

267

the Trojans (*Aen.* 7.294-296), Juno uses an Ennian paradox about Pergama, which

> neque Dardaniis campis potuere perire
> nec cum capta capi nec cum combusta cremari.
>
> (*Ann.* 358-359)

In her angry question (*Aen.* 7.302-303)

> quid Syrtes aut Scylla mihi, quid uasta Charybdis profuit?

there are two echoes. Line 302 is derived from a passage of hatred in the monologue of Ariadne, asking what monster spawned Theseus (Cat. 64.156):

> quae Syrtis, quae Scylla rapax, quae uasta Charybdis?

But the phrase *uasta Charybdis* also appears in Lucretius (1.722) who may have coined it. In *Aen.* 7.314 "immota . . . fatis" is a bitter acknowledgment of Jupiter's reassurance to Venus ("immota tuorum / fata") in 1.257-258. Turning away from heaven toward hell in *Aen.* 7.312, Juno speaks strangely like the suppliants of Aeschylus (*Suppl.* 154-161); and then, forecasting disaster for the betrothal of Aeneas and Lavinia (317-322), she echoes the oath of Medea discarded and humiliated (Eur. *Med.* 395-400). As Medea, after determining to kill her victims, says "εἶέν" (*Med.* 385-386), so Juno (313) says "esto."

The last speech made by Juno (*Aen.* 12.808-828) is the most important: in that it shows her yielding ("cedo equidem," 12.818) and then, out of the jaws of defeat, snatching a victory by persuading Jupiter to acquiesce in the total disappearance of the Trojan people.[117] There are Homeric models. Ostensibly

---

[117] Fraenkel scarcely does justice to this περιπέτεια by remarking on p. 268 of his *Horace* (above, n. 48) "When a proud goddess makes an important concession, she must at least be permitted to score a modest point." The "modest point" was described by Venus in *Aen.* 5.787-788: "cineres atque ossa peremptae / insequitur [Troiae]."

submissive, inwardly triumphant, Juno pretends to resemble the intimidated Hera of *Il.* 15.36-46—both swear by the Styx that they do not bear full responsibility for the warlike acts of another deity—but in fact she lays down firm conditions for peace, like Zeus himself at the end of the *Odyssey* (24.478-486): "cum iam leges et foedera iungent" ≈ "ὅρκια πιστὰ ταμόντες"; "esto" ≈ "ἔστω."[118] But she does not suggest (as Zeus does) that both sides should live together and love each other. She proposes that the Trojans be absorbed into the native population and disappear. Jupiter agrees (12.834-837): "faciam omnis . . . Latinos."

The third of Horace's "Roman odes" (*Carm.* 3.3) contains a long oration by Juno about the deification of Romulus.[119] The subject was discussed at the council of the gods in the first book of Ennius's *Annals* (frgs. 60-65) before the founding of Rome; Horace sets it after the establishment of the city, at the death of Romulus, possibly because (like Vergil) he wishes to emphasize the long-enduring implacability of Juno. As given by Horace, Juno's speech embodies two themes of her final speech in the *Aeneid*: her willingness to accept the existence of Rome, and her hatred of Troy. Furthermore, Vergil's Jupiter reminds his spouse that Aeneas is destined to become a god (*Aen.* 12.794-795) and Horace's Juno declares she will permit Romulus to be deified as Quirinus (*Carm.* 3.3.30-36). On the other hand, in Vergil Juno asks Jove not to allow the Trojans to dominate the Latins in such a way that Troy may survive *in Italy*. In Horace, Juno does not ask. She states her will ("redonabo," "patiar," "regnanto," "fata dico"); and her chief resolve is that Troy shall not be rebuilt *in Asia*.

There are no apparent verbal coincidences between these two speeches. But it is remarkable how many words and phrases in Horace's poem appear in telling positions elsewhere in the

[118] This is discussed by Knauer, p. 32.
[119] See the analyses of the poem by E. Fraenkel (above, n. 48) pp. 265-272 and S. Commager, *The Odes of Horace* (New Haven, 1962) pp. 209-225.

Aeneid. Helen is described in the ode as "Lacaena adultera" (25); twice in the *Aeneid* she is "Lacaena" (2.601 and 6.511) and Paris in Juno's speech is "adulter" (10.92). The deceit of Laomedon and "Priami domus / periura" are mentioned by Horace's Juno (21-22 + 26-27)—recalling "Laomedonteae . . . periuria gentis" from *Aen.* 4.542. The adjective "Hectoreus" (line 28 of the ode) appears in *Aen.* 2.543 and elsewhere.[120] Horace makes Juno say she will abandon her "grauis iras" (30-31), while Vergil's Venus declares that "Iunonis grauis ira" compels her to ask for help (*Aen.* 5.781). Horace's Juno calls Romulus "inuisum nepotem" in *Carm.* 3.3.31; Vergil's Juno calls the Trojans "stirpem inuisam" in *Aen.* 7.293 (cf. *genus inuisum* in *Aen.* 1.28, also in Juno's mind). Above all else, Vergil's Aeneas is *pius*, the Trojans are *pii* (*Aen.* 3.266), and Jupiter foretells that the Romans will outdo both gods and men in *pietas* (*Aen.* 12.839); but in Horace, Juno warns the Romans that they must not rebuild Troy, "nimium pii" (*Carm.* 3.3.58). She adds that, if revived, "Troiae fortuna" will again be disastrous (61-62); on arriving in Italy, Vergil's Aeneas prays

> hac Troiana tenus fuerit fortuna secuta.

> (*Aen.* 6.62)

Horace's Juno says the attack on a new Troy will be resumed by her, "coniuge . . . Iouis et sorore" (64), as Vergil's Juno boasts that she is "Iouis . . . / et soror et coniunx" (*Aen.* 1.46-47). The goddess's final warning in Horace, "ter si resurgat murus aeneus / . . . ter pereat meis / excisus Argiuis" (65-67), recalls "fas regna resurgere Troiae" (*Aen.* 1.206) and *excisa Troia* (2.637) together with *Iunoni Argiuae* (3.547).

It seems likely that Horace (like other friends) heard Vergil's *Aeneid* recited in sections, and felt impelled to produce something parallel to it in lyric form: one of the most ambi-

---

[120] J. Wackernagel, *Vorlesungen über Syntax* 2 (Basel, 1928²) p. 70, citing "coniugis Hectoreae" (*Aen.* 3.488), suggests Vergil modelled it on Ἑκτορέην ἄλοχον in the *Little Iliad* (frg. 19.2 Allen).

tious of his odes. In the same way Propertius (4.1) adapted some of the material of *Aeneid* 8 to the style of Callimachean elegy; and in the *Carmen Saeculare* (41-52) Horace touched on another Vergilian theme, the link between Aeneas and Augustus.

Venus

Venus in the *Aeneid* is not the goddess of sexual love so much as a protective guardian and mother. The chief Homeric divinities of whom she reminds us in her speeches are Thetis mother of Achilles and Athena protector of Odysseus.

Her initial supplication to Jupiter (*Aen.* 1.229-253) takes several themes from Athena's pleas to Zeus in *Od.* 1.45-62 and to Zeus and the Olympians in *Od.* 5.7-20. The *exordium*, in its rich elaboration, is even more respectful than those of Athena: it has an unexpected prototype in the prayer of the oppressed slave-woman in *Od.* 20.112-119: note "fulmine terres" ≈ "μεγάλ᾽ ἐβρόντηcαc." The query "how has Aeneas offended you?" (*Aen.* 1.231-233) resembles the punning question put by Athena to Zeus in *Od.* 1.60-62, "τί νύ οἱ τόcον ὠδύcαο, Ζεῦ;", with an echo of Zeus asking Hera about the Trojans in *Il.* 4.31-33, "τί νύ ce . . . τόcca κακὰ ῥέζουcιν;" Athena in the *Odyssey* goes into greater detail in describing the hero's sufferings and Zeus's neglect, while Venus in the *Aeneid* emphasizes Jupiter's promises and the successful escape of another Trojan prince. Both stress the piety of the heroes, and both end with a plaintive question. Macrobius (6.2.31) says the entire situation is based on a passage in the first book of Naevius's *Punic War*: there too the Trojans were smitten by a tempest, Venus complained to Jupiter, and he consoled her *spe futurorum*. But his report is very general, he does not quote any words, and he may have the information only at second- or third-hand. It is scarcely likely that he ever saw a copy of Naevius: see pp. 284-285 of H. D. Jocelyn's article (cited above, n. 12).

After encountering Aeneas in Libya, Venus tells him the history of the monarch he is to visit—like Athena describing Alcinous (*Aen.* 1.335-370 ≈ *Od.* 7.48-77). When she encourages him to enter Carthage, she speaks both like Nausicaa and like Athena, for she appears to him as a young girl (*Aen.* 1.387-401 ≈ *Od.* 6.187-197 and 7.48-52). Her first assurance, that he must surely be under divine protection, is like that given by Athena to Telemachus as the two approach Nestor's palace: *Aen.* 1.387-388 ≈ *Od.* 3.27-28. In each case the speaker is a protecting divinity; the hero is in a momentary fit of self-doubt; and he is about to visit a monarch who, although strange to him, will make him welcome. The curiously impressive phrase "auras / uitalis carpis" (*Aen.* 1.387-388) is adapted from Lucretius 3.405. Venus gives a hopeful interpretation of an omen involving birds (*Aen.* 1.390-400) like her favorite Helen at the departure of Telemachus (*Od.* 15.160-178). One phrase in her interpretation is an elaboration of a few words in the *Iliad*: "*pu*ppesque *tu*ae *pu*besque *tu*orum" (*Aen.* 1.399) ≈ "*cὺν νηυcί τε cῆιc καὶ coῖc ἑτάροιcι*" (*Il.* 1.179). Vergil has added an echo-effect, doubtless because oracular utterances often contain strange-sounding assonances like Helenus's

longa procul longis uia diuidit inuia terris. (3.383)

When Aeneas rages alone on the roof of Priam's palace, Venus restrains him, in terms like those used by Athena to Achilles (*Aen.* 2.594-595 ≈ *Il.* 1.207-210).[121] Athena reinforces her persuasion by a glimpse of the future atonement to be paid to Achilles (*Il.* 1.211-214); but Venus (*Aen.* 2.601-618) vouchsafes Aeneas a superb and terrible vision of the gods destroying his city, all the ruins "with dreadful faces thronged and fiery arms." For this scene the closest Homeric parallels are

[121] Knauer (p. 381) also compares Thetis comforting Achilles in *Il.* 1.362-363 and 18.73-77, but there is a difference between Achilles' tears of frustration and Aeneas's vengeful fury.

272

not speeches, but portions of the Homeric narrative telling how Poseidon wielding his trident overthrew the Greek wall (*Aen.* 2.608-612 ≈ *Il.* 12.27-33) and how Hera and Pallas and the other gods fought in person, encouraged by Zeus (*Aen.* 2.612-618 ≈ *Il.* 21.385-513). Smaller motifs come from other Homeric scenes. "Not hateful Helen, but the harsh gods" (*Aen.* 2.601-603) is a grim variation on Priam's words to Helen on the wall (*Il.* 3.164-165); and Venus removes the cloud from her son's vision (*Aen.* 2.604-607) as Athena does for Diomede in a similar situation (*Il.* 5.127-128). Her phrase "sternitque a culmine Troiam" (*Aen.* 2.603) restates the revelation made by Hector's phantom, "ruit alto a culmine Troia" (2.290), and echoes (more solemnly) a rebuke of Hector to Paris (*Il.* 13. 772-773).

Venus's part in the plot with Juno against Dido (*Aen.* 4.107-114) is confined to promising co-operation and expressing respect for the consort of Jupiter—like Aphrodite with Hera in *Il.* 14.194-196 + 212-213 + 219-221, and like Aphrodite with Hera and Athena in *Argon.* 3.36-110. But she makes one reservation. Dido had prayed for Jupiter's favor to both peoples together "Tyriis . . . Troiaque profectis" (*Aen.* 1.732). Here Venus, repeating the phrase (4.111), expresses emphatic doubt that the peoples can ever be united.

Her plea to Neptune for Aeneas's safe passage (*Aen.* 5.781-798) is justified by her description of Juno's hatred for Troy. The leading phrase, "Iunonis grauis ira," reflects *saeuae memorem Iunonis ob iram* in *Aen.* 1.4. Then comes an example of Vergil's tact. In the *Iliad* (4.31-36) Zeus taunts Hera with her cruelty in the presence of the other gods. Your anger will not be glutted, he says, until you can enter Troy and eat the Trojans raw. Vergil's divinities do not gibe at one another so brutally. Yet even if their words are nobler their emotions are no less violent: so Venus alludes to Juno's devouring hatred:

273

non media de gente Phrygum *exedisse* nefandis
urbem odiis satis est.   (*Aen.* 5.785-786)

Then she reminds Neptune of his own words spoken during
the tempest. She says of Juno

> quam *molem* subito excierit: maria omnia *caelo*
> *miscuit.*[122]   (*Aen.* 5.790-791)

Neptune had said (1.133-134):

> iam *caelum* terramque meo sine numine, uenti,
> *miscere* et tantas audetis tollere *moles*?

Venus's "in regnis hoc ausa tuis" (5.792) makes the same point
as Neptune's "imperium pelagi" (*Aen.* 1.138). In the *Aeneid*
it is a god's prerogative to know the words of another without
being present when they are uttered.

As she asks her husband Vulcan to make weapons for
Aeneas (*Aen.* 8.374-386), Venus resembles Thetis pleading
with Hephaestus (*Il.* 18.429-461). Both divinities emphasize
the sorrows of motherhood and the bitterness of war. As Vul-
can's wife Venus adds a personal appeal: with feminine pride,
she reminds him that he has already done similar favors for
Thetis and Aurora. Her final picture of fortified cities sharpen-
ing swords for the destruction of her and her people (*Aen.*
8.385-386) comes from Vergil's own narrative:

> quinque adeo magnae positis incudibus urbes
> tela nouant.   (*Aen.* 7.629-630)

Naturally, when she brings the finished armor to her son in
Aen. 8.612-614, she speaks like Thetis to Achilles in *Il.*
19.8-11;[123] yet there may be a slightly sinister overtone about
her first words, "en perfecta," for they echo the triumphant
boast of the Fury to Juno in 7.545.

---

[122] Cf. Lucretius 3.842: *non si terra mari miscebitur et mare caelo.*

[123] Knauer (p. 258 n. 1) also points to Menelaus and Helen giving presents
to Telemachus (*Od.* 15.110-129); but the situations are scarcely comparable.

In her speech at the divine council (*Aen.* 10.18-62) Venus reverts to some of the themes she treated in her first speech: for in both she addresses Jupiter. She elaborates them with the emotion of Thetis imploring Zeus on behalf of Achilles (*Il.* 1.503-510 + 514-516), and speaks of his long wanderings as Athena of Odysseus' long exile (*Od.* 1.45-62 + 5.7-20). Smaller and remoter echoes from Homer appear in Knauer's comprehensive lists. Triumphant Turnus (*Aen.* 10.20-22) is like Hector on the floodtide of victory (*Il.* 9.237-239). The protective ditch of the Trojan fort is deluged with blood (*Aen.* 10.24) like the towers and battlements of the Greek camp in *Il.* 12.430-431. Venus recalls how Diomede wounded her in the hand (*Aen.* 10.29-30 ≈ *Il.* 5.330-342); and her sad concession, "uincant quos uincere mauis" (*Aen.* 10.43) resembles Hera's submission to Zeus in *Il.* 8.429-431. Several times Venus echoes phrases from the opening of Aeneas's narrative of his wanderings. Feigning to resign all hopes of a Trojan realm in Italy, she says "sperauimus ista / dum fortuna fuit" (10.42-43); her son says the Thracian king Lycurgus had been a friend of Troy "dum fortuna fuit" (3.16). The same pathetic verb appears both in her "solum quo Troia fuit" (10.60) and in Aeneas's "campos ubi Troia fuit" (3.11). And her invocation "per euersae . . . fumantia Troiae / excidia" (10.45-46) has the resonance of Aeneas's phrase, "omnis humo fumat Neptunia Troia" (3.3).

Once only does she appear as *Vénus toute entière à sa proie attachée.*[124] This is in her speech to Amor (*Aen.* 1.664-688). Its chief model is Aphrodite's persuasion of Eros in Apollonius's *Argon.* 3.129-153. But there Eros is described as a boy: he must be coaxed with the offer of a plaything. In the *Aeneid* Venus treats her son as more mature. She stresses his all-conquering power.[125] She reminds him of his sympathy for his persecuted

---

[124] *Toute entière* and not *tout entière* in all seventeenth-century editions.

[125] So does Hera speaking to Aphrodite in *Il.* 14.198-199. Cartault (p. 170) points to the deft flattery of "patris summi qui tela Typhoea temnis" (*Aen.*

brother Aeneas (667-669); but she deftly aligns him with
young Ascanius, whom she calls "mea maxima cura" (678), a
phrase comparable to her address to Amor himself, "mea
magna potentia" (664); then she merges the two in the magi-
cal sentence "notos pueri puer indue uultus" (684). As for
Dido, Venus regards her without a trace of sympathy. She
describes Dido's welcome to the Trojans as cunning flattery,
"blandisque moratur / uocibus" (*Aen.* 1.670-671)—an echo of
Athena's remark about Calypso, "αἰεὶ δὲ μαλακοῖcι καὶ
αἰμυλίοιcι λόγοιcι / θέλγει" (*Od.* 1.56-57).[126] She forecasts that
Dido, when holding the boy in her arms, "dabit amplexus
atque oscula dulcia figet" (*Aen.* 1.687). Dido will believe this
is motherly affection, but the overtones show that it will (as
Venus intends) awaken her sexual passion. To Venus herself,
her desirous husband *optatos dedit amplexus* (*Aen.* 8.405); and
the wooer in Lucretius 4.1179 *foribus miser oscula figit*. In
this speech Venus appears no less cunning and cruel than her
opponent Juno. For her, Dido is a victim to be captured "dolis
et flamma" (1.673); and her last injunction to Amor is pitiless:

occultum inspires ignem fallasque ueneno.

1.665) as overmatching Venus's address to her father, "qui res . . . fulmine
terres" (1.229-230).

[126] "Blandis" also contains a possible echo of Naevius: see p. 219 above.

CHAPTER SIX

VERGILIVS ORATOR
AN POETA

IT IS POSSIBLE to treat Vergil as an orator, or as a poet whose chief aim was to produce rhetorical effects. This was done by Tiberius Claudius Donatus, among others. Thus, when Dido requests Aeneas to describe the fate of Troy and his wanderings in exile, he replies that although it is a heartbreaking tale, he will, since she wishes to hear it in brief, relate it (*Aen.* 2.3-13). He sorrows for the fate of his countrymen, he has toiled and suffered for seven years, and he is reluctant to renew the agonies he has endured by evoking them in detail; but, with an effort, he says "incipiam." This is a powerful opening to his narrative, like ten slow heavy minor chords ushering in a tragic symphony; and it is full of fine sounds and rhythms.[1] But Donatus treats it as that part of a formal speech which introduces the recital of the facts of the case, and explains the tactical reasons why Aeneas says he will make his story short: "hoc loco supra artis praecepta Vergilius docet quid in talibus causis [!] obseruandum sit; nam cum omnis narratio debeat breuitate succingi, tum magis colligenda est cum propria mala narrantur. nullus enim haec refert, nisi fuerit aliqua, ut Aeneas, necessitate compulsus." For such a man, as for certain speakers in Macrobius's *Saturnalia*, Vergil's epic poem was neither epic nor a poem, but a formal oration or a collection of orations, and even Vergil's

---

[1] R. G. Austin in his edition of Book Two points out such touches as "lamentabile" (a coinage of Vergil's) and the alliteration and assonance in "*suadent*que ca*dent*ia *s*idera *s*omno*s*"; to which add the cadence of "et quorum pars magna fui" and the rare rhythm of "infandum, regina, iubes renouare dolorem" (R. Lucot, "Sur un type latin d'hexamètre," *Hommages à L. Herrmann, Latomus* 3, 1944, pp. 492-498).

own narrative was treated as though it had been oratorically conceived.

No one is likely to make such a mistake today, any more than to seek in the Homeric epics for arcane philosophical doctrines. But since so much of the *Aeneid* is devoted to speeches of many different types, it is necessary to inquire how important the techniques and ideals of oratory were in the mind of Vergil, as he composed his masterwork.

First, we observe that the poem contains relatively few formal speeches employing the structural plans developed by generations of orators and analysts. There are only two debates. Beyond them, there are six diplomatic speeches (two delivered in private); only two speeches which could be called legalistic in manner; a few addresses by commanding officers to their men; and one elaborate piece of vituperation. As against these, there are several important narratives, prophecies, and descriptive statements, which are indeed orderly in their arrangement, but follow no rhetorical rules. The most impressive piece of speech in the epic is the narrative of Aeneas in Books Two and Three; the next is surely the prophecy of Anchises in Book Six. Although they contain many powerful and graceful devices of style, neither of them can properly be described as oratory: it is a waste of effort to dissect them on traditional lines, dividing them into *exordium, narratio,* and so forth. The same applies to the numerous emotional speeches—the apostrophes, soliloquies, and addresses of farewell, most of them so different from one another.[2] None of these is incoherent. It is possible to analyze them, every one; but rather by tracing the various currents of emotion (e.g. in Dido's five-part soliloquy, 4.590-629; see p. 177) than by attempting to impose any tradi-

---

[2] Juno's soliloquies in the first and seventh books do resemble each other, because the situation and the speaker are the same; the second, however, is longer and more intense.

tional rhetorical schemata upon them. Even the smaller utter-ances, the persuasions and responses, commands and prayers, all seem perfectly spontaneous, each of them rooted in its con-text and the character of its speaker. Rarely, in such a speech, are we aware that some devices which an orator might use are present.

For example, after hearing the oracle pronounced by Dei-phobe, Aeneas waits until the transports of her possession have subsided. Then he asks her for permission to visit his father in the realm of the dead, and for her guidance on the journey (6.103-123). His first words are not the *exordium* of a formal speech, but a response to her somber forecast of the future (103-105). Then, simply introduced by "unum oro," comes his request (106-109). The rest is persuasion, a series of reasons to convince the Sibyl to grant what he asks. First, three statements about the mutual love of father and son: I saved him from burning Troy; he endured the long sea-wandering with me; he commanded me to visit you (110-116). These statements are orderly, and their order gives them emphasis: "illum . . . ille . . . idem"; but this is the order of logical argument strongly colored by personal emotion, the kind of thing which is seen in Greek tragedy.[3] Next, an argument of a different type: Dei-phobe is feminine and gracious ("alma")[4] and ought to pity the separated father and son; and she has the power to grant the request (116-118). Lastly, precedents, set out, like the state-ments about Anchises, in three sections: "si . . . si . . . quid?" First, Orpheus, who means so much to Vergil; then Pollux, who visits the underworld regularly on a mission of familial love; and then Theseus and Hercules, brought in through the first trick which could be called obviously rhetorical, a *prae-*

---

[3] E.g., Soph. *Trach.* 436-469, Eur. *Helen* 894-943.

[4] Vergil uses *alma* once of Juturna (as Turnus's sister, 10.439), twice of Cybele (10.220 and 252), thrice of Diana (7.774, 10.215, 11.557), and four times of Venus (1.618, 2.591, 2.664, 10.332); of the Sibyl in Aeneas's two entreaties, here and 6.74. *Alma Venus*, Lucr. 1.2.

279

teritio: "quid Thesea magnum, / quid memorem Alciden?"[5] (The reason for passing over these latter names so rapidly is that—although the heroes did visit the underworld—they went on sinister missions, one to carry off Proserpina, the other to carry off Cerberus: *Aen.* 6.392-397.) Aeneas gives his persuasion no elaborate close: merely the proud phrase (part of which he has once before used, to his disguised mother in 1.380) "et mi genus ab Ioue summo." This is not, in any real sense, formal oratory.

The same is true of all the informal speeches in the *Aeneid*. It is only in the important formal addresses that we can see Vergil arranging the thoughts of his characters in accordance with traditional patterns of rhetoric.

Figures of speech and figures of thought appear in all kinds of sophisticated writing, whether prose or poetry. In oratorical technique they were held to be highly important: Quintilian devotes much space to discussing them (8.6-9.3). Some orators used them rarely and unobtrusively: for instance, Lysias. Others sowed with the full sack, and gloried in the power and fecundity of the figures which they so openly deployed: such was Cicero. Such, in poetry, was Ovid. As Butler says of Hudibras, he could not ope his mouth, but out there flew a trope.[6] On every page of the *Metamorphoses* there are neat but never invisible, never quite unstudied figures of speech. Thus, Midas

tollit humo saxum; saxum quoque palluit auro.

(11.110)

The daughters of Pelias are told to let his blood:

his, ut quaeque pia est, hortatibus impia prima est.

(7.339)

---

[5] Compare, in formal orations, Venus's "quid repetam exustas Erycino in litore classes?" (10.36) and Diomede's "regna Neoptolemi referam?" (11.264).
[6] S. Butler, *Hudibras* 1.1.81-82.

Figures of thought are common too. Most of them could have come from the practice of quasi-legal display speaking in the rhetorical schools and recital halls. Achelous, for instance, challenges Hercules:

nam quo te iactas, Alcmena nate, creatum,
Iuppiter aut falsus pater est aut crimine uerus.
matris adulterio patrem petis: elige, fictum
esse Iouem malis, an te per dedecus ortum.[7]

(9.23-26)

In what is little more than metrical prose, the poet praises Julius Caesar for being the adoptive father of Augustus:

neque enim de Caesaris actis
ullum maius opus quam quod pater exstitit huius.

(15.750-751)

This is the type of poetry which developed in the generation after Vergil, the generation in which rhetoric ceased to be a training for the melees of the political platform, and became, like musical studies developing technical dexterity on one instrument, an end in itself, aiming not at victory but at the display of versatility and ingenuity, blended with extreme, often excessive, psychological subtlety.[8] But Vergil was trained in a simpler type of school, and he had better taste than his successors. Therefore he did not stud every page with glittering epigrams and fill every speech with arabesques of figured style. The reader often feels that the characters of Ovid and Lucan talk for the sake of talking. Most of Vergil's men and women and divinities say less than they could, and usually speak only when they must.

[7] Fit ex duobus (quorum necesse est <esse> alterum uerum) *eligendi* aduersario potestas, efficiturque ut, utrum elegerit, noceat (Quint. 5.10.69).

[8] R. Heinze, *Ovids elegische Erzählung, SB Leipzig* 71 (1919) 7, pp. 70-72, emphasizes Ovid's interest in complex, perverse, and labile emotions, adds that the "declamations" of his time developed this interest, and remarks it is a pity that such a wealth of observation did not pour into an important psychological novel.

281

The examination of the models which Vergil used confirms this view. The survey in Chapter Five makes it clear that he borrowed little from orators, whether Greek or Roman, and much from poets, both Greek and Roman. It is difficult for us to imagine him doing as Ovid was to do later: taking a clever idea out of a contemporary speech and giving it to one of his own characters.[9]

Although Vergil knows the power of oratory, he has little praise for it. The Homeric ideal, μύθων τε ῥητῆρ' ἔμεναι πρηκτῆρά τε ἔργων (*Il.* 9.443), was also the ideal of Julius Caesar and of Augustus and of many other Romans; but it was not Vergil's. Early in the *Iliad* Antenor remembers hearing Menelaus and Odysseus make diplomatic speeches (*Il.* 3.203-224). Menelaus spoke briefly, clearly, and sensibly. When Odysseus stood up, he looked like a fool; but when his great voice came out, with words like the winter snowflakes, he was invincible. There is no such praise of eloquence in the *Aeneid*. On the Trojan side there is one orator, Ilioneus, who is wise and patriotic; his speeches are skillful, effective, and at least in part sincere. On the other side there is one orator, Drances, who is wise and patriotic. He does not make the worse cause appear the better. On the contrary, his policies are right. He eulogizes Aeneas for his magnanimity and promises to help in building the new Trojan city (11.124-131); and the Latin embassy agrees with him. He proposes that king Latinus should make peace with the Trojans and give his daughter to Aeneas; and that, if Turnus wants glory and a princess's dowry, he should fight a decisive duel (11.343-375). This is a development of Latinus's own proposals at the same debate (11.316-334) and is clearly wisest in the critical situation. Yet Vergil

---

[9] Seneca the elder says (*Controu.* 2.2[10].8) that Ovid heard Porcius Latro declaim Ajax's speech in the contest for the arms of Achilles, and lifted one of his *sententiae*, "mittamus arma in hostis, et petamus," changing it into

> arma uiri fortis medios mittantur in hostes:
> inde iubete peti!   (*Met.* 13.121-122)

explicitly states that his speech was dictated not by wisdom, but by spite and hatred. In one phrase, not very warm, he says Drances was *consiliis habitus non futtilis auctor* (11.339).[10] In another, even less warm, he calls him *largus opum et lingua melior* (11.338). All the rest of Vergil's characterization makes Drances an objectionable figure who is urged on to speak, not by positive statesmanship but by his skill in revolutionary tactics (*seditione potens*), not by wisdom but by a bitter sense of social inferiority (*genus huic materna superbum / nobilitas dabat, incertum de patre ferebat*), not by love of his country but by personal hatred for Turnus (*stimulis . . . amaris*). The oration which he delivers at the council is eloquent and thoughtful—but, according to Vergil, dictated by evil motives. On the other hand, the speech made by Turnus is even more eloquent, and quite as persuasive. The policy which it recommends is wrong. Yet, because of the emotional energy of the speaker and his youthful earnestness, it is more attractive. The tirade of Drances ends with a mean-spirited challenge, "illum aspice contra / qui uocat."[11] The reply of Turnus ends with a resounding piece of bravado, or even bravery:

> nec Drances potius, siue est haec ira deorum,
> morte luat, siue est uirtus et gloria, tollat.

Like Plato, Vergil distrusted oratory; although, like Aristotle, he accepted the fact that it is sometimes necessary, or at least useful.[12] Once and once only does he praise it in the *Aeneid*: even then his praise is limited. When Neptune calms the tempest (1.142-156) Vergil compares the sudden change to the repression of a riot by the appearance of a single man (= Cato?) known for his rectitude and service to his country.

---

[10] This is far less laudatory than the possible Homeric parallel mentioned by Knauer (p. 422): 'Οδυσσεὺς . . . Διὶ μῆτιν ἀτάλαντος (*Il.* 2.636).

[11] Admittedly the speech is unfinished; yet Vergil stopped on a characteristic note.

[12] Ar. *Rhet.* 1.1.1355a19-b7.

283

The *ignobile uulgus* becomes silent and attentive *before* he speaks; and then

ille regit dictis animos et pectora mulcet.

Thus, like Aristotle, Vergil believed that for a public speaker character mattered as much as eloquence; or more.[13]

Many readers have been surprised by his description of the achievements of Greek genius, compared with the mission of Rome, in *Aen.* 6.847-853. First comes Greek sculpture in bronze and marble. Painting, apparently as a subordinate art, is not mentioned; while architecture (linked with sculpture) has been splendidly praised in *Georg.* 3.13-39, and Greek music and dancing are marked by implication as a high art in *Aen.* 6.644-647. Next comes oratory—*forensic* oratory: "orabunt causas melius." The great political speeches of Demosthenes are not mentioned; nor is Greek historical writing, with its many elaborate orations. Nor is Greek philosophy, either here or in the abode of the blessed (*Aen.* 6.660-665), although Greek science, in particular astronomy, is highly esteemed (*Aen.* 6.849-850).[14] Apart from the legendary Orpheus and Musaeus there is no mention whatever of Greek poetry. Homer may be one of the throng of blessed souls, *pii uates et Phoebo digna locuti* (*Aen.* 6.662), along with Hesiod and Aeschylus and many others; but he is not named; nor are the works of these poets mentioned as part of the Greek contribution to civilization. In this peculiar list the only mention of Greek prose artistry is "orabunt causas melius." Cicero's admirers, including himself, would have considered this to be quite wrongheaded, and would have compared the *Verrines* with Demosthenes' *Crown*, or the *Philippics* against Antony with the

---

[13] Ar. *Rhet.* 1.2.1356a1-13. Cicero passes rapidly over τὸ ἠθικόν, to describe his own specialty, τὸ παθητικόν (*Or.* 128-133).

[14] Philosophy and science (although the Greeks would not so distinguish them) are eulogized together in *Georg.* 2.475-492.

284

Philippics against Philip; but Vergil never mentions Cicero by name, here or elsewhere.[15]

That Vergil distrusted oratory is shown by another curious fact. In formal speeches and in persuasions and other types of emotional discourse almost all his speakers distort the truth. So do characters in the Homeric epics, but not nearly so often or so subtly. This is hard to believe: at least, many intelligent readers have failed to understand it. Much discussion has been wasted on the problem of μαχόμενα, *pugnantia*, contradictions or inconsistencies in the epics of Homer and Vergil, by earnest critics who started by assuming that, if a character made a statement, his statement ought to be in complete agreement with the facts related in the poet's own narrative. (The elaborate stories told by Odysseus during his scenes of homecoming were so obviously big strategic falsehoods that the critics seldom went further, to detect small tactical falsehoods.) The most surprising case of this blindness is Plato. In the *Symposium* (174a-c) Socrates urges Aristodemus to go with him to Agathon's banquet, although uninvited. He adds that Menelaus went uninvited to a feast given by Agamemnon (sc. *Il.* 2.408-409) although he was a "timid spearman," inferior to his brother. But the injurious phrase "μαλθακὸς αἰχμητής" is not in the passage describing Agamemnon's feast. It comes from the second half of the poem, thousands of lines away; and it is not even part of the poet's narrative. In the narrative Menelaus is usually called ἀρηΐφιλος or (as in the passage about the feast) βοὴν ἀγαθός. The phrase "timid spearman" comes from a speech made to Hector by Apollo, who is masquerading as a friend of Hector and urging him to attack (*Il.* 17.588).

Such apparent inconsistencies needlessly perplexed some Greek commentators on Homer. In *Iliad* 1.184-185 Agamemnon declares that he personally, "αὐτός," will take Briseis away

from Achilles' hut; yet in 1.299 Achilles complains that an un-
specified group (evidently meaning the Achaeans as a whole)
took the girl: "ἐπεί μ' ἀφέλεσθέ γε δόντες." He is angry, and
hostile to everybody; but Zenodotus endeavored to remove the
seeming inconsistency by writing the singular, "ἐπεί ῥ' ἐθέλεις
ἀφελέσθαι." So in other passages of Homer, e.g. *Il.* 18.176-177,
Od. 3.228.

It was Aristarchus of Samothrace who worked out the solu-
tion for this type of difficulty: the λύσις ἐκ τοῦ προσώπου.[16] In
fact, the speeches of Homer's (and Vergil's) characters are not
objective statements, but subjective utterances. A man says
what he feels, or what he believes at the time, or what he
wishes his hearers to believe. He may, like the disguised Apollo
in *Il.* 17.588, speak εἰς διαβολήν. He may, like Hector politely
contradicting his mother in *Il.* 6.265 X 261, simply wish to win
a little argument. Those scholiasts on Homer who understand
this usually comment on such a speech: ἔχει ἦθος ὁ λόγος.
Plato's misapprehension is discussed by Athenaeus 5.178 and
corrected, possibly in the very words of Aristarchus: οὐ γὰρ εἴ
τι λέγεται παρ' Ὁμήρωι, τοῦθ' Ὅμηρος λέγει (178d).

Nevertheless, the misapprehension persisted. It still persists.
C. Robert[17] athetized *Il.* 9.650-655 because Achilles' statement
made to Ajax there is different from 9.356-363, spoken to an-
other man, Odysseus, at an earlier stage of the discussion. In
scholiasts on Vergil there are traces of the same perplexity;
and Augustin Cartault in particular delighted in pointing out
"inconsistencies" which he considered due to the poet's habit
of composing piecemeal and the poem's lack of revision. Of
such inconsistencies there are indeed several in the narrative
itself; but apparent disharmonies between narrative and speech

---

[16] This discussion, as far as concerns Homer, is based on H. Dachs' Erlangen
dissertation of 1913, *Die λύσις ἐκ τοῦ προσώπου*. From Goethe's conversations
with Eckermann, Dachs quotes a disquisition on the same topic with reference
to the "inconsistencies" in *Macbeth*, 18th April 1827. See also G. M. Grube,
The Greek and Roman Critics (Toronto, 1965) pp. 130-131.

[17] *Studien zur Ilias* (Berlin, 1901), p. 497.

always deserve careful and sympathetic analysis, to discover whether the poet did not create them deliberately. Very often he did.[18]

It would be feasible to maintain that, in every important speech of the *Aeneid* which is intended to persuade, there is at least one lie. Just after war breaks out, when the Trojans are isolated, with no friends or allies in the entire Italian peninsula, Turnus and Latinus send an embassy to ask Diomede for assistance. The chief ambassador, Venulus, is instructed to state that many tribes are joining Aeneas (*Aen.* 8.13-14). Servius says that this is a lie, as indeed it is; and Donatus comments "haec non fuerant facta, sed idcirco ueris admixta sunt, ut pro certis acciperentur." Touching on the passage, Heinze (p. 423 n. 2) compares it with another "deliberate exaggeration," the claim by Ilioneus in 7.236-238 that many nations and tribes had invited the wandering Trojans to join them—when in the narrative only Dido is recorded as having done so (1.572-574). In diplomatic speeches we should expect facts to be altered. It may not be necessary. Talleyrand pointed this out in his comparison of Mazarin and Metternich. "Le Cardinal trompait; mais il ne mentait pas. Or, M. de Metternich ment toujours, et ne trompe jamais."[19] Nevertheless, it is customary. Hence it is no surprise when Drances declares that the bold Turnus "trusts in flight" (11.351), or when Turnus says, *after* a serious battle, that his side trembles *before* hearing the trumpet (11.424), or when Juno speaks of the loyalty and peacefulness of the rebellious Etruscans (10.71). There is no sign that Aeneas ever thought of Evander before father Tiber directed him to Pallanteum (8.49-58); yet he declares that Evander's widespread renown brought him to seek his friendship (8.132-133). Even in a prayer to Jupiter, Iarbas asserts that

---

[18] See Heinze, pp. 421-424, on distortions of fact in the speeches of the *Aeneid*.

[19] G. O. Trevelyan, *The Life and Letters of Lord Macaulay* (Oxford, 1961), vol. 1, p. 215 (July 1831).

he gave Dido "the shore to plough" and imposed "loci leges" upon her—as though she were not an independent monarch but one of his vassals (4.212-213). He goes on (4.215-217) to characterize Aeneas as an effeminate Phrygian, and, instead of admitting that Dido loves Aeneas, uses the phrase "ille . . . / . . . rapto potitur."[20]

So also in speeches of attack and defense the facts are often treated as flexible. Dido declares she recovered Aeneas's fleet after it was lost, and brought his comrades back from death (4.375). Amata complains that Aeneas—although he is fated, and known to be fated, to settle down in Italy—is a pirate resolved on carrying off her daughter as soon as the north wind blows (7.361-362).[21] Even the noblest characters depart from the truth in order to make an impression on their hearers. This subject is touched upon in a Würzburg dissertation by V. Henselmanns called *Die Widersprüche in Vergils Aeneis* (Aschaffenburg, 1913). It is a curious little book, which looks as though it had been started under one adviser and completed under one or two others.[22] It begins by listing apparent contradictions within the poem (some of them trivial, e.g. clouds in 5.10-20 and stars in 5.25) as though they were irreconcilable and inexplicable; then, much later, on pp. 111-127, it explains many of them intelligently and sympathetically "aus rhetorisch-pathetischen Tendenzen." Thus, in 1.200-201 Aeneas speaks as though he and his men had actually braved the dangers of Scylla and Charybdis, whereas the narrative shows that they avoided them by sailing southward along the Sicilian coast (3.554-567 + 684-686; see p. 34). But this (Henselmanns points out, pp. 114-115) is said in order to praise the valor of Aeneas's men and to encourage them—and also to make

[20] Servius points out the inexactitude of the phrase: "proprie raptus est inlicitus coitus: nec enim hic rapuerat."

[21] On p. 422 Heinze bluntly calls Amata's speech "eine grosse Lüge."

[22] The names of Stangl, Stählin, and Hosius are given by the author. He deals only with Books One to Six, asserting that the latter six books are "im allgemeinen widerspruchsfrei."

Aeneas more like Odysseus (*Od.* 12.201-259). Juno also mentions Scylla and Charybdis (7.302) because her anger causes her to exaggerate. Again, Aeneas declares that he carried his father out of Troy "per . . . mille sequentia tela" (6.110), whereas the narrative does not show that a single shot was aimed at them (2.721-744). Henselmanns considers this to be an insoluble contradiction (p. 127); yet Aeneas is trying to persuade the Sibyl and therefore stresses his love for his father.

Henselmanns does not deal with several of the most striking inconsistencies between narrative and speech, but they are to be explained in the same manner. The boldest comes in Aeneas's self-defense addressed to Dido, where he makes a deliberate misstatement of fact (4.337-338):

> neque ego hanc abscondere furto
> speraui (ne finge) fugam.[23]

In Book Ten Jupiter asserts that he had forbidden Italy to make war on the Trojans and forbidden the gods to join in (10.8-9); yet in Book One he tells Venus that Aeneas is to wage a great war in Italy (1.263-264). Possibly this is an inconsistency between two of Vergil's plans. (Jupiter can scarcely have issued a prohibition while foreknowing that it would be transgressed.) But when he permits Juno to extricate Turnus from the battle (10.622-625) and prompts Mezentius to attack the Trojan and Etruscan forces (10.689-690), how can this be reconciled with his grand pronouncement (10.108 + 112)?

> Tros Rutulusne fuat, nullo discrimine habebo. . . .
> rex Iuppiter omnibus idem.

Vergil, it seems, held that powerful oratory was incompatible with pure truth, and that every speaker presented his or her own case by misrepresenting the facts. He might have agreed with Plato that rhetoric was a part of flattery (*Gorg.* 463a6-

---

[23] See p. 75.

289

466a6)—although he would certainly not have accepted the further Platonic deduction that high poetry also was no more than flattering rhetoric (*Gorg.* 502b1-d8). Truth, for Vergil as for Plato, resided in the other world, the world of immortal souls freed from the body and of immutable incorruptible ideals. Oratory, with all its energy and charm and suppleness, was part of this world, the world of disorder and conflict and pain, inhabited by false dreams.

APPENDIX 1

The Speeches in the *Aeneid* Listed in Sequence

For the classification, see Appendix 2. In the following list, the various types of speech are identified by these abbreviations:

A=Apostrophe to one unable or unwilling to hear or reply
C=Command from a superior to an inferior or inferiors
D=Diplomatic or political speech
E=Encouragement or *cohortatio*, a speech by a commander to his men
F=Farewell
G=Greeting
L=Legalistic speech of self-defense or rebuttal
N=Narrative, explanation, description
O=Oracle, prophecy, or interpretation of omen or oracle
P=Persuasion
Pra=Prayer
Q=Question
R=Response to persuasion, question, or command
S=Soliloquy either thought or spoken
T=Taunt, challenge, threat
V=Vituperation

To assist those who may wish to study particular types of speech, the numbers after these abbreviations indicate the position of each speech within its class. Thus, the first soliloquy in the poem (1.37-49) is marked S1, and the eighth and last (7.293-322) S8.

BOOK ONE

(1)	Iuno	37-49	$12\frac{3}{4}$ lines	S1
(2)	Iuno	65-75	11 lines	P1
(3)	Aeolus	76-80	$4\frac{7}{12}$ lines	R1
(4)	Aeneas	94-101	$7\frac{7}{12}$ lines	S2
(5)	Neptunus	132-141	10 lines	C1
(6)	Aeneas	198-207	10 lines	E1
(7)	Venus	229-253	$24\frac{2}{3}$ lines	P2
(8)	Iuppiter	257-296	40 lines	O1
(9)	Venus	321-324	$3\frac{2}{3}$ lines	C2
(10)	Aeneas	326-334	9 lines	Pra1

(11)	Venus	335-370	$35\frac{1}{4}$ lines	N1
(12)	Aeneas	372-385	$13\frac{7}{12}$ lines	N2
(13)	Venus	387-401	15 lines	O2
(14)	Aeneas	407-409	3 lines	Q1
(15)	Aeneas	437	1 line	S3
(16)	Aeneas	459-463	$4\frac{1}{2}$ lines	P3
(17)	Ilioneus	522-558	37 lines	D1
(18)	Dido	562-578	17 lines	R2
(19)	Achates	582-585	4 lines	P4
(20)	Aeneas	595-610	$15\frac{1}{6}$ lines	G1
(21)	Dido	615-630	16 lines	G2
(22)	Venus	664-688	25 lines	P5
(23)	Dido	731-735	5 lines	Pra2
(24)	Dido	753-756	$3\frac{5}{6}$ lines	Q2

Total for Book One: twenty-four speeches; $328\frac{7}{12}$ lines of direct speech. Nine different characters speak, five being divinities.

BOOK TWO

The narrative of Aeneas runs from 2.3 to 3.715 $= 801 + 715$ lines $= 1,516$ lines; line 2.76 is omitted as misplaced.

(1)	Laocoon	42-49	$7\frac{5}{6}$ lines	P6
(2)	Sinon 69-72 $+$ 77-104 $+$ 108-144 $+$ 154-194		$109\frac{7}{12}$ lines	N3
(3)	Apollo[1]	116-119	$3\frac{1}{4}$ lines	O3
(4)	Priamus	148-151	4 lines	Q3
(5)	Aeneas	281-286	6 lines	Q4
(6)	Hector	289-295	$6\frac{11}{12}$ lines	C3
(7)	Aeneas	322	1 line	Q5
(8)	Panthus	324-335	12 lines	N4
(9)	Aeneas	348-354	$6\frac{7}{12}$ lines	E2
(10)	Androgeos	373-375	3 lines	C4
(11)	Coroebus	387-391	$4\frac{1}{4}$ lines	P7
(12)	Hecuba	519-524	5 lines	P8
(13)	Priamus	535-543	$8\frac{3}{4}$ lines	T1
(14)	Pyrrhus	547-550	$2\frac{11}{12}$ lines	T2
(15)	Aeneas	577-587[2]	11 lines	S4
(16)	Venus	594-620	27 lines	N5

[1] Reported in Sinon's speech.
[2] This speech is accepted as being genuine: see pp. 164-176.

(17)	Anchises	638-649	$11\frac{1}{2}$ lines	C5
(18)	Aeneas	657-670	14 lines	R3
(19)	Creusa	675-678	4 lines	P9
(20)	Anchises	689-691	3 lines	Pra3
(21)	Anchises	701-704	4 lines	Pra4
(22)	Aeneas	707-720	14 lines	C6
(23)	Anchises	733-734	$1\frac{1}{2}$ lines	C7
(24)	Creusa	776-789	14 lines	O4

Total for Book Two: twenty-four speeches; $281\frac{5}{6}$ lines of direct speech (a count excluding the short speech 2.116-119 attributed to Apollo within Sinon's narrative). Fourteen different characters speak, only two being deities.

BOOK THREE

Aeneas's narrative continues to line 715.

(1)	Polydorus	41-46	6 lines	C8
(2)	Aeneas	85-89	5 lines	Pra5
(3)	Apollo	94-98	5 lines	O5
(4)	Anchises	103-117	$14\frac{11}{12}$ lines	O6
(5)	Penates	154-171	18 lines	O7
(6)	Anchises	182-188	$6\frac{3}{4}$ lines	C9
(7)	Celaeno	247-257	11 lines	O8
(8)	Anchises	265-266	$1\frac{7}{12}$ lines	Pra6
(9)	Andromache	310-312	$2\frac{1}{4}$ lines	Q6
(10)	Aeneas	315-319	5 lines	Q7
(11)	Andromache	321-343	23 lines	N6
(12)	Aeneas	359-368	10 lines	Q8
(13)	Helenus	374-462	89 lines	O9
(14)	Helenus	475-481	$6\frac{11}{12}$ lines	F1
(15)	Andromache	486-491	6 lines	F2
(16)	Aeneas	493-505	13 lines	F3
(17)	Anchises	528-529	2 lines	Pra7
(18)	Anchises	539-543	$3\frac{5}{6}$ lines	O10
(19)	Anchises	558-560	$2\frac{7}{12}$ lines	C10
(20)	Achaemenides	599-606		
		+ 613-654	$49\frac{5}{12}$ lines	N7

Total for Book Three: twenty speeches; $281\frac{1}{4}$ lines of direct speech. Nine different characters speak, among whom Apollo, the Penates, and Celaeno are superhuman.

293

BOOK FOUR

(1)	Dido	9-29	21 lines	N8
(2)	Anna	31-53	22¾ lines	D2
(3)	Iuno	93-104	12 lines	P10
(4)	Venus	107-114	6⅔ lines	R4
(5)	Iuno	115-127	12⁵⁄₁₂ lines	P11
(6)	Iarbas	206-218	13 lines	Pra8
(7)	Iuppiter	223-237	15 lines	C11
(8)	Mercurius	265-276³	9⅚ lines	C12
(9)	Dido	305-330	26 lines	P12
(10)	Aeneas	333-361	28⁷⁄₁₂ lines	L1
(11)	Dido	365-387	23 lines	R5
(12)	Dido	416-436	21 lines	P13
(13)	Dido	478-498	21 lines	C13
(14)	Dido	534-552	19 lines	S5
(15)	Mercurius (?)	560-570	10⅙ lines	C14
(16)	Aeneas	573-579	6 lines	C15
(17)	Dido	590-629	39⅓ lines	S6
(18)	Dido	634-640	7 lines	C16
(19)	Dido 651-658 +	659-662	11⅓ lines	S7
(20)	Anna	675-685	10¼ lines	A1
(21)	Iris	702-703	1⅓ lines	N9

Total for Book Four: twenty-one speeches; 336⅔ lines of direct speech. Nine different personages speak, five of them being gods.

BOOK FIVE

(1)	Palinurus	13-14	1⁷⁄₁₂ lines	A2
(2)	Palinurus	17-25	9 lines	P14
(3)	Aeneas	26-31	5⁷⁄₁₂ lines	C17
(4)	Aeneas	45-71	27 lines	C18
(5)	Aeneas	80-83	4 lines	G3
(6)	Gyas 162-164 +	166	3¼ lines	C19
(7)	Mnestheus	189-197	8 lines	C20
(8)	Cloanthus	235-238	4 lines	Pra9
(9)	Aeneas	304-314	11 lines	C21
(10)	Aeneas	348-350	2⁵⁄₁₂ lines	R6
(11)	Nisus	353-356	3⁷⁄₁₂ lines	Q9
(12)	Aeneas	363-364	2 lines	C22

³ Omitting 4.273.

(13)	Dares	383-385	$2\frac{5}{12}$ lines	P15
(14)	Acestes	389-393	5 lines	P16
(15)	Entellus	394-400	$6\frac{1}{3}$ lines	R7
(16)	Entellus	410-420	11 lines	P17
(17)	Aeneas	465-467	$2\frac{1}{4}$ lines	C23
(18)	Entellus	474-476	$2\frac{5}{6}$ lines	C24
(19)	Entellus	483-484	2 lines	Pra10
(20)	Aeneas	533-538	6 lines	C25
(21)	Aeneas	548-551	$3\frac{1}{12}$ lines	C26
(22)	Iris	623-640	$17\frac{5}{6}$ lines	P18
(23)	Cassandra[4]	637-638	$\frac{5}{6}$ line	O11
(24)	Pyrgo	646-652	7 lines	N10
(25)	Ascanius	670-673	$3\frac{1}{12}$ lines	C27
(26)	Aeneas	687-692	6 lines	Pra11
(27)	Nautes	709-718	10 lines	P19
(28)	Anchises	724-739	16 lines	C28
(29)	Aeneas	741-742	$1\frac{7}{12}$ lines	Q10
(30)	Venus	781-798	18 lines	P20
(31)	Neptunus	800-815	16 lines	R8
(32)	Somnus	843-846	4 lines	P21
(33)	Palinurus	848-851	4 lines	R9
(34)	Aeneas	870-871	2 lines	A3

Total for Book Five: thirty-four speeches; $227\frac{5}{6}$ lines of direct speech (excluding the short speech 5.637-638 attributed to Cassandra by Iris). Eighteen different characters (including Cassandra) speak: among them are four divinities and the ghost of Anchises.

BOOK SIX

(1)	Deiphobe	37-39	3 lines	C29
(2)	Deiphobe	45-46	$\frac{3}{4}$ line	C30
(3)	Deiphobe	51-53	$2\frac{1}{12}$ lines	C31
(4)	Aeneas	56-76	$20\frac{5}{12}$ lines	Pra12
(5)	Deiphobe	83-97	15 lines	O12
(6)	Aeneas	103-123	$20\frac{5}{12}$ lines	P22
(7)	Deiphobe	125-155	$29\frac{2}{3}$ lines	C32
(8)	Aeneas	187-189	3 lines	Pra13
(9)	Aeneas	194-197	$3\frac{1}{4}$ lines	Pra14
(10)	Deiphobe	258-261	$3\frac{1}{6}$ lines	C33

[4] Reported in the speech of Iris disguised as Beroe.

(11)	Aeneas	318-320	$2^{11}\!/_{12}$ lines	Q11
(12)	Deiphobe	322-330	9 lines	N11
(13)	Aeneas	341-346	$5^{7}\!/_{12}$ lines	Q12
(14)	Palinurus	347-371	$24^{3}\!/_{4}$ lines	N12
(15)	Deiphobe	373-381	9 lines	C34
(16)	Charon	388-397	10 lines	C35
(17)	Deiphobe	399-407	$7^{1}\!/_{2}$ lines	P23
(18)	Aeneas	456-466	11 lines	P24
(19)	Aeneas	500-508	9 lines	Q13
(20)	Deiphobus	509-534	$25^{7}\!/_{12}$ lines	N13
(21)	Deiphobe	539-543	5 lines	C36
(22)	Deiphobus	544-546	$2^{7}\!/_{12}$ lines	F4
(23)	Aeneas	560-561	2 lines	Q14
(24)	Deiphobe	562-627	$65^{5}\!/_{12}$ lines	N14
(25)	Phlegyas[5]	620	1 line	C37
(26)	Deiphobe	629-632	$3^{11}\!/_{12}$ lines	C38
(27)	Deiphobe	669-671	3 lines	Q15
(28)	Musaeus	673-676	4 lines	R10
(29)	Anchises	687-694	8 lines	G4
(30)	Aeneas	695-698	$3^{3}\!/_{4}$ lines	G5
(31)	Anchises	713-718	$5^{7}\!/_{12}$ lines	N15
(32)	Aeneas	719-721	3 lines	Q16
(33)	Anchises 722 +	724-751	29 lines	N16
(34)	Anchises	756-853		
		+ 855-859	103 lines	O13
(35)	Aeneas	863-866	4 lines	Q17
(36)	Anchises	868-886	$18^{1}\!/_{6}$ lines	O14

Total for Book Six: thirty-six speeches; $475^{1}\!/_{2}$ lines of direct speech (not counting the utterance of Phlegyas reported by Deiphobe, 6.620). Eight different personages speak: Aeneas, two superhuman beings, and five spirits of the dead.

BOOK SEVEN

(1)	Vates Latinorum	68-70	$2^{5}\!/_{12}$ lines	O15
(2)	Faunus	96-101	6 lines	O16
(3)	Ascanius	116	$2\!/_{3}$ line	N17
(4)	Aeneas	120-134	$14^{2}\!/_{3}$ lines	O17
(5)	Anchises[6]	124-127	4 lines	O18

[5] Reported in the Sibyl's account of hell.
[6] Reported by Aeneas.

(6)	Latinus	195-211	17 lines	Q18
(7)	Ilioneus	213-248	36 lines	D3
(8)	Latinus	259-273	$14\frac{7}{12}$ lines	R11
(9)	Iuno	293-322	30 lines	S8
(10)	Iuno	331-340	10 lines	P25
(11)	Amata	359-372	14 lines	P26
(12)	Amata	400-403	$3\frac{11}{12}$ lines	C39
(13)	Allecto	421-434	14 lines	P27
(14)	Turnus	436-444	$8\frac{3}{4}$ lines	R12
(15)	Allecto	452-455	4 lines	T3
(16)	Allecto	545-551	7 lines	P28
(17)	Iuno	552-560	$7\frac{5}{6}$ lines	R13
(18)	Latinus	594-599	$5\frac{5}{12}$ lines	O19

Total for Book Seven: eighteen speeches; $196\frac{1}{4}$ lines of direct speech (excluding the short speech of Anchises reported by Aeneas, 7.124-127). Eleven characters speak, three of them super-human.

BOOK EIGHT

(1)	Tiberinus	36-65[7]	29 lines	O20
(2)	Aeneas	71-78	8 lines	Pra15
(3)	Pallas	112-114	$2\frac{5}{12}$ lines	Q19
(4)	Aeneas	117-120	4 lines	C40
(5)	Pallas	122-123	$1\frac{11}{12}$ lines	C41
(6)	Aeneas	127-151	25 lines	D4
(7)	Euandrus	154-174	$20\frac{7}{12}$ lines	R14
(8)	Euandrus	185-275	$90\frac{7}{12}$ lines	N18
(9)	Salii	293-302	$9\frac{3}{4}$ lines	Pra16
(10)	Euandrus	314-336	23 lines	N19
(11)	Euandrus	351-358	$7\frac{5}{6}$ lines	N20
(12)	Euandrus	362-365	$3\frac{5}{12}$ lines	P29
(13)	Venus	374-386	13 lines	P30
(14)	Vulcanus	395-404	$9\frac{7}{12}$ lines	R15
(15)	Vulcanus	439-443	$4\frac{1}{4}$ lines	C42
(16)	Euandrus	470-519	50 lines	N21
(17)	Haruspex Etruscorum[8]	499-503	$4\frac{1}{3}$ lines	O21
(18)	Aeneas	532-540	$8\frac{3}{4}$ lines	O22

[7] Omitting 8.46.
[8] Reported by Euandrus.

(19)	Euandrus	560-583	23⅙ lines	F5
(20)	Venus	612-614	3 lines	P31

Total for Book Eight: twenty speeches; 337¼ lines of direct speech (not counting the speech of the Haruspex Etruscorum reported by Evander). Eight characters or groups speak, three being gods.

BOOK NINE

(1)	Iris	6-13	8 lines	C43
(2)	Turnus	18-22	4⁵⁄₁₂ lines	Pra17
(3)	Caicus	36-38	2⁵⁄₁₂ lines	C44
(4)	Turnus	51-52	1¹⁄₁₂ lines	C45
(5)	Cybele	83-92	9⁵⁄₁₂ lines	P32
(6)	Iuppiter	94-103	10 lines	R16
(7)	Cybele	114-117	3⅔ lines	C46
(8)	Turnus	128-158	31 lines	E3
(9)	Nisus	184-196	12¾ lines	P33
(10)	Euryalus	199-206	8 lines	R17
(11)	Nisus	207-218	11¾ lines	P34
(12)	Euryalus	219-221	2 lines	R18
(13)	Nisus	234-245	11⁷⁄₁₂ lines	P35
(14)	Aletes 247-250 +	252-256	8⅙ lines	R19
(15)	Ascanius	257-280	23 lines	R20
(16)	Euryalus	281-292	11⅙ lines	P36
(17)	Ascanius	296-302	7 lines	R21
(18)	Nisus	320-323	4 lines	C47
(19)	Nisus	355-356	1¹¹⁄₁₂ lines	C48
(20)	Volcens	376-377	1⁵⁄₁₂ lines	C49
(21)	Nisus	390-391	1¼ lines	A4
(22)	Nisus	404-409	6 lines	Pra18
(23)	Volcens	422-423	1⁵⁄₁₂ lines	T4
(24)	Nisus	427-430	4 lines	P37
(25)	Euryali mater	481-497	17 lines	A5
(26)	Turnus	560-561	1⅙ lines	T5
(27)	Numanus	598-620	23 lines	V1
(28)	Ascanius	625-629	5 lines	Pra19
(29)	Ascanius	634-635	1⅚ lines	T6
(30)	Apollo	641-644	3⁵⁄₁₂ lines	O23
(31)	Apollo	653-656	3⁷⁄₁₂ lines	C50
(32)	Pandarus	737-739	2¾ lines	T7

(33)	Turnus	741-742	2 lines	T8
(34)	Turnus	747-748	2 lines	T9
(35)	Mnestheus	781-787	$6\frac{7}{12}$ lines	E4

Total for Book Nine: thirty-five speeches; $253\frac{3}{4}$ lines of direct speech. Fifteen personages speak, four of them being deities.

BOOK TEN

(1)	Iuppiter	6-15	10 lines	C51
(2)	Venus	18-62	$44\frac{7}{12}$ lines	D5
(3)	Iuno	63-95	$32\frac{7}{12}$ lines	L2
(4)	Iuppiter	104-113	$9\frac{5}{12}$ lines	C52
(5)	Cymodocea	228-245	$17\frac{5}{12}$ lines	N22
(6)	Aeneas	252-255	4 lines	Pra20
(7)	Turnus	279-284	6 lines	E5
(8)	Tarchon	294-298	$4\frac{7}{12}$ lines	C53
(9)	Aeneas	333-335	$2\frac{5}{12}$ lines	C54
(10)	Pallas	369-378	10 lines	E6
(11)	Pallas	421-423	3 lines	Pra21
(12)	Turnus	441-443	$2\frac{7}{12}$ lines	C55
(13)	Pallas	449-451	$2\frac{1}{4}$ lines	T10
(14)	Pallas	460-463	4 lines	Pra22
(15)	Iuppiter	467-472	6 lines	P38
(16)	Turnus	481	1 line	T11
(17)	Turnus	491-495	$4\frac{1}{12}$ lines	T12
(18)	Magus	524-529	6 lines	P39
(19)	Aeneas	531-534	4 lines	R22
(20)	Aeneas	557-560	4 lines	T13
(21)	Liger	581-583	$2\frac{5}{12}$ lines	T14
(22)	Aeneas	592-594	$2\frac{2}{3}$ lines	T15
(23)	Liger	597-598	2 lines	P40
(24)	Aeneas	599-600	$1\frac{5}{12}$ lines	T16
(25)	Iuppiter	607-610	4 lines	T17
(26)	Iuno	611-620	$9\frac{7}{12}$ lines	P41
(27)	Iuppiter	622-627	6 lines	R23
(28)	Iuno	628-632	$4\frac{7}{12}$ lines	P42
(29)	Turnus	649-650	2 lines	T18
(30)	Turnus	668-679	12 lines	A6
(31)	Mezentius	737	1 line	T19
(32)	Orodes	739-741	$2\frac{7}{12}$ lines	O24
(33)	Mezentius	743-744	$1\frac{1}{6}$ lines	T20

(34)	Mezentius	773-776	$3\frac{1}{4}$ lines	Pra23
(35)	Aeneas	811-812	$1\frac{2}{3}$ lines	T21
(36)	Aeneas	825-830	$5\frac{2}{3}$ lines	A7
(37)	Mezentius	846-856	$10\frac{1}{4}$ lines	A8
(38)	Mezentius	861-866	6 lines	A9
(39)	Aeneas	875-876	2 lines	T22
(40)	Mezentius	878-882	4 lines	T23
(41)	Aeneas	897-898	$1\frac{1}{6}$ lines	T24
(42)	Mezentius	900-906	7 lines	P43

Total for Book Ten: forty-two speeches; $270\frac{1}{3}$ lines of direct speech. Twelve characters speak, of whom four are superhuman.

BOOK ELEVEN

(1)	Aeneas	14-28	$14\frac{11}{12}$ lines	C56
(2)	Aeneas	42-58	$16\frac{5}{6}$ lines	A10
(3)	Aeneas	96-98	$2\frac{5}{12}$ lines	F6
(4)	Aeneas	108-119	12 lines	R24
(5)	Drances	124-131	$7\frac{3}{4}$ lines	R25
(6)	Euandrus	152-181	30 lines	A11
(7)	Venulus	243-295	53 lines	N23
(8)	Diomedes[9]	252-293	42 lines	D6
(9)	Latinus	302-335	34 lines	D7
(10)	Drances	343-375	33 lines	D8
(11)	Turnus	378-444[10]	66 lines	D9
(12)	Turnus	459-461	$1\frac{11}{12}$ lines	T25
(13)	Turnus	463-467	$4\frac{11}{12}$ lines	C57
(14)	Matres Latinae	483-485	3 lines	Pra24
(15)	Camilla	502-506	5 lines	P44
(16)	Turnus	508-519	12 lines	C58
(17)	Diana	535-594	$59\frac{3}{4}$ lines	N24
(18)	Amasenus[11]	557-560	4 lines	Pra25
(19)	Camilla	686-689	4 lines	T26
(20)	Auni filius	705-708	$3\frac{3}{4}$ lines	T27
(21)	Camilla	715-717	3 lines	T28
(22)	Tarchon	732-740	9 lines	E7
(23)	Arruns	785-793	9 lines	Pra26
(24)	Camilla	823-827	$4\frac{1}{4}$ lines	F7

[9] Reported by Venulus.
[10] Omitting 11.404 as misplaced.
[11] Reported by Diana.

(25)	Opis	841-849	8⁵⁄₁₂ lines	A12
(26)	Opis	855-857	2⁵⁄₆ lines	T29

Total for Book Eleven: twenty-six speeches; 400¾ lines of
direct speech (excluding the speech of Diomede reported by
Venulus and the speech of Amasenus reported by Diana). Four-
teen personages and one group speak: two speakers are super-
human.

BOOK TWELVE

(1)	Turnus		11-17	7 lines	C59
(2)	Latinus		19-45	26⅙ lines	D10
(3)	Turnus		48-53	6 lines	R26
(4)	Amata		56-63	8 lines	P45
(5)	Turnus		72-80	9 lines	R27
(6)	Turnus		95-100	5¾ lines	A13
(7)	Iuno		142-153	12 lines	P46
(8)	Iuno		156-159	2⅚ lines	C60
(9)	Aeneas		176-194	19 lines	Pra27
(10)	Latinus		197-211	14¼ lines	Pra28
(11)	Iuturna		229-237	9 lines	E8
(12)	Tolumnius		259-265	6⅚ lines	E9
(13)	Messapus		296	1 line	T30
(14)	Aeneas		313-317	5 lines	C61
(15)	Turnus		359-361	3 lines	T31
(16)	Iapyx	425 +	427-429	3¾ lines	C62
(17)	Aeneas		435-440	6 lines	F8
(18)	Aeneas		565-573	9 lines	C63
(19)	Turnus		620-621	2 lines	Q20
(20)	Iuturna		625-630	5⁵⁄₁₂ lines	P47
(21)	Turnus		632-649	18 lines	R28
(22)	Saces		653-664	12 lines	N25
(23)	Turnus		676-680	5 lines	P48
(24)	Turnus		693-695	3 lines	C64
(25)	Turnus		777-779	2⅚ lines	Pra29
(26)	Iuppiter		793-806	13⁷⁄₁₂ lines	C65
(27)	Iuno		808-828	21 lines	P49
(28)	Iuppiter		830-840	11 lines	O25
(29)	Iuturna		872-884	13 lines	A14
(30)	Aeneas		889-893	5 lines	T32
(31)	Turnus		894-895	1⁷⁄₁₂ lines	T33

| (32) | Turnus | 931-938 | $7\frac{1}{8}$ lines | P50 |
| (33) | Aeneas | 947-949 | $2\frac{3}{4}$ lines | R29 |

Total for Book Twelve: thirty-three speeches; $276\frac{11}{12}$ lines of direct speech. Eleven characters speak, three of them immortals.

SUMMARY

Book	Speeches		Lines of direct speech
1		24	$328\frac{7}{12}$
2 }	I { or	24	801 or $281\frac{5}{6}$ [12]
3 }	{ or	20	715 or $281\frac{1}{4}$ [12]
4		21	$336\frac{2}{3}$
5		34	$227\frac{5}{6}$
6		36	$475\frac{1}{2}$
7		18	$196\frac{1}{4}$
8		20	$337\frac{1}{4}$
9		35	$253\frac{3}{4}$
10		42	$270\frac{1}{3}$
11		26	$400\frac{3}{4}$
12		33	$276\frac{11}{12}$
		290 or 333[12]	4,619$\frac{5}{6}$ or 3,666$\frac{11}{12}$ [12]

There are two possible methods of calculating the number of lines in the *Aeneid* which are occupied by direct speech.

One is to treat the narrative of Aeneas as one long continuous speech, and to ignore the many smaller speeches within it. If we do this, there are in the poem 290 speeches, covering 4,619$\frac{5}{6}$ lines of direct speech. In the *Aeneid* as it stands there are 9,883 lines—considering each part-line (e.g. 3.218) as equivalent to one full line, and excising forged and displaced lines.[13] Therefore nearly half of the epic is devoted to direct speech: 46.75%. This may at first seem surprising, but is understandable when we remember that Aeneas occupies one-sixth of the poem with one speech and utters nearly two thousand lines altogether; and that several of the most important scenes are given over to speech with relatively little narrative: Dido's despair and suicide, the journey through

[12] The first figure, if Aeneas's narrative is counted as one speech; the second, if it is not, and if only the speeches within it are counted.

[13] The following lines should be excised: 2.76, 4.273, 4.528, 6.242, 8.46, 9.29, 9.121, 9.529, 10.278, 11.404, and 12.612-613.

the afterworld, the council of the gods, and the debate of the Latins.

The other method is to treat Aeneas's narrative as though it were not direct speech, but Vergil's narrative, and to count only the individual speeches inside it, including Aeneas's own short utterances such as 2.281-286. On this method, there are 333 speeches, covering 3,666$11\frac{1}{12}$ lines of direct speech.

As explained on p. 15, I believe that the poet intends us to hear Aeneas's voice all through his account of Troy's fall and his own wanderings: therefore I prefer the former method of counting. But some scholars may choose the second. In *Paradise Lost* (5.563-6.892) Raphael relates to Adam the rebellion of Satan and his overthrow. The narrative is introduced with the angel's words

> High matter thou enjoin'st me, O prime of Men—
> Sad task and hard

—a clear adaptation of *Aen.* 2.3; and it is closed by a paragraph in which Raphael personally warns Adam against disobedience: "remember, and fear to transgress." Nevertheless, within it we seldom if ever hear Raphael's voice or think of him as telling the tale: the narrative style exactly resembles that of the rest of the epic, and indeed events which Raphael could not have witnessed, such as the rebels' council (6.413-523), are described in detail. Those who wish to distinguish long retrospective narratives, such as those of Raphael, Odysseus, and Aeneas, from shorter speeches more closely set within the poem, will prefer this latter method of calculation.

With different definitions and limits for the speeches, different totals can be reached. Thus M. Schneidewin, "Statistisches zu Homeros und Vergilius," *NJbb* 129 (1884) 129-134, says there are 337 speeches in the *Aeneid*. But his definitions are loose: "als 'rede' habe ich jedes von einer person der dichtung gesprochene wort verstanden" (p. 130); and he excludes the narratives of Odysseus and Aeneas, on the ground that they are only disguises for the poets' own narratives—in spite of the intense personal feeling which infuses such episodes as *Od.* 11.541-564 and *Aen.* 2.431-434 and 2.559-563. His statistics are careless: he says that he himself worked out the figures for the speeches in Homer, but that the figures for Vergil were put together by "einige fleissige obersecundaner" (p. 130). Apparently he did not check the Vergilian statistics, for *Aeneid* 12, with all the relevant figures, is omitted

303

from the list on pp. 132-133; it is impossible to account for his datum of 487 lines of speeches in *Aeneid* 8 (pp. 131, 132) even by adding the description of the shield to the real speeches; and his figure of 354 lines for the eleventh book is off in the other direction.

J. Kvíčala, *Neue Beitraege zur Erklaerung der Aeneis* (Prague, 1881), lists 336 speeches on pp. 266-268 and (with a trifling subtraction) on pp. 272-274. However, he entirely omits some short speeches: 5.166, 6.620, 6.722, 7.116, 10.737, and 10.739-741. Also he treats some interrupted speeches as two or more, instead of single units: thus, he takes Sinon's speech (2.69-194) as four distinct addresses, the speech of Achaemenides (3.599-654) as two, Dido's farewell (4.651-662) as two, and Anchises' review of his descendants (6.756-859) as two speeches. There are one or two displacements and mistaken references, less important.

Kvíčala's calculations are questioned by H. P. Lipscomb on pp. 15 and 37 of his *Aspects of the Speech in the Later Roman Epic* (Baltimore, 1909), who says there are 331 speeches in the *Aeneid* but gives no catalogue of them. He points out some of the discrepancies in Schneidewin's article (pp. 6-7 n. 9), and gives the total number of lines of direct speech in the poem as 3,757 (pp. 7, 15), but does not record the numbers of lines in individual books. J. R. Gjerløw, "Bemerkungen über einige Einleitungen zur direkten Rede in Vergils Aeneis," *SO* 32 (1956) 53, also notes some of Kvíčala's omissions and modifies some of his definitions. He proposes a total of 343 direct speeches, but gives no list of his own. O. Maar, on p. 76 of his Vienna dissertation, *Pathos und Pathosrede in dem Didobuch von Vergils Aeneis* (1953, microfilm), gives the following line-counts for passages of direct speech in five books of the poem—which differ, sometimes by a considerable amount, from those given in this study: Book One, 315 rather than 329; Book Four, 346 rather than 337; Book Nine, 257 rather than 254; Book Ten, 275 rather than 270; Book Eleven, 353 rather than 401.

Readers who take different views of the nature and boundaries of certain speeches in the *Aeneid* will wish to modify the figures and definitions given here. I hope that the data given are sufficiently clear and copious to allow them to do so without difficulty.

APPENDIX 2

Classification of the Speeches

Nearly every speech in the *Aeneid* has one chief purpose. This makes most of the speeches easy to classify. They fall into sixteen main groups.

There are apostrophes to persons absent, dying, or dead; to divinities who may not hear or reply; or to things which cannot answer. There are commands, given by superiors to inferiors. Here delicate distinctions must sometimes be made. Camilla's position does not permit her to give a command to Turnus, so that her speech in 11.502-506 should, in spite of its bluff imperatives, be styled a persuasion. Turnus is the commander-in-chief: his reply to her (11.508-519), although polite, is essentially an order—like his tactical directions in 11.463-467. There are also speeches of encouragement or reproach by chieftains to their men in battle, known as *cohortationes*. The formal speeches include a few important orations of the class technically called deliberative, intended to mold policy on a matter of state; two speeches of the forensic type, similar to rebuttals in a court of law; and one elaborate speech of vituperation. Further, there are farewells and greetings; narratives which explain to the hearer what has happened or is happening; oracles, prophecies, and interpretations of oracles or of omens; persuasions—which are less peremptory than commands and less formal than deliberative orations; prayers; questions; responses to questions, to various types of persuasion, or (rarely) to commands; soliloquies spoken or thought; and, as in any poem dealing with war, a number of taunts, threats, and challenges. In Appendix 1 each speech is identified under one of these heads.

Some speeches contain two or even more themes. For instance, Diana's long utterance in 11.535-594 is both a narrative of Camilla's strange upbringing and of her service to Diana (535-586) and a command that Opis shall avenge her death (587-594); while Juno's final speech (12.808-828) begins as a response to Jupiter's command (808-818) and then moves into a persuasion (819-828). Such speeches are classified under what appears to be the essential purpose of the speech or its weightiest theme. Thus, although Diana tells the story in order to explain to Opis the reason for her command, Vergil's poetic purpose in introducing it was evidently

305

to allow him to insert a romantic narrative (as with that of Achaemenides in 3.599-606 + 613-654): therefore the speech is listed as a narrative; and both Juno and Vergil care much more about the persuasion, "delenda est Troia," than about Juno's initial response to Jupiter's command, so that her speech is classified as a persuasion.

APOSTROPHES (A)

(1)	4.675-685	Anna to Dido
(2)	5.13-14	Palinurus to Neptune
(3)	5.870-871	Aeneas to Palinurus[1]
(4)	9.390-391	Nisus to Euryalus
(5)	9.481-497	Euryalus's mother to his corpse
(6)	10.668-679	Turnus to Jupiter and the winds[2]
(7)	10.825-830	Aeneas to Lausus
(8)	10.846-856	Mezentius to Lausus
(9)	10.861-866	Mezentius to Rhaebus
(10)	11.42-58	Aeneas to Pallas
(11)	11.152-181	Evander to Pallas
(12)	11.841-849	Opis to Camilla
(13)	12.95-100	Turnus to his spear
(14)	12.872-884	Juturna to Turnus

COMMANDS (C)

(1)	1.132-141	Neptune to the winds
(2)	1.321-324	Venus to the Trojans[3]
(3)	2.289-295	Hector to Aeneas
(4)	2.373-375	Androgeos to his "comrades"
(5)	2.638-649	Anchises to Aeneas and the family
(6)	2.707-720	Aeneas to Anchises and the family
(7)	2.733-734	Anchises to Aeneas
(8)	3.41-46	Polydorus to Aeneas
(9)	3.182-188	Anchises to Aeneas
(10)	3.558-560	Anchises to the Trojans

[1] The two apostrophes frame Book Five.

[2] In his excitement, Turnus first addresses Jupiter, then asks a series of desperate questions addressed to no special hearer, and finally prays to the winds to wreck his ship.

[3] In substance Venus's speech is a question, but her bold "monstrate" marks it as a command in form.

(11)	4.223-237	Jupiter to Mercury
(12)	4.265-276	Mercury to Aeneas
(13)	4.478-498	Dido to Anna
(14)	4.560-570	Mercury (?) to Aeneas
(15)	4.573-579	Aeneas to the Trojans[4]
(16)	4.634-640	Dido to Barce
(17)	5.26-31	Aeneas to Palinurus
(18)	5.45-71	Aeneas to the Trojans
(19)	5.162-166	Gyas to Menoetes
(20)	5.189-197	Mnestheus to his crew
(21)	5.304-314	Aeneas to the competitors
(22)	5.363-364	Aeneas to the competitors
(23)	5.465-467	Aeneas to Dares
(24)	5.474-476	Entellus to Aeneas and the Trojans[5]
(25)	5.533-538	Aeneas to Acestes
(26)	5.548-551	Aeneas to Epytides
(27)	5.670-673	Ascanius to the Trojan women[6]
(28)	5.724-739	Anchises to Aeneas
(29)	6.37-39	The Sibyl (Deiphobe) to Aeneas
(30)	6.45-46	Deiphobe to Aeneas
(31)	6.51-53	Deiphobe to Aeneas
(32)	6.125-155	Deiphobe to Aeneas
(33)	6.258-261	Deiphobe to the *profani* and to Aeneas
(34)	6.373-381	Deiphobe to Palinurus
(35)	6.388-397	Charon to Aeneas
(36)	6.539-543	Deiphobe to Aeneas
(37)	6.620	Phlegyas to all
(38)	6.629-632	Deiphobe to Aeneas
(39)	7.400-403	Amata to the Latin matrons
(40)	8.117-120	Aeneas to Pallas
(41)	8.122-123	Pallas to Aeneas
(42)	8.439-443	Vulcan to the Cyclopes
(43)	9.6-13	Iris to Turnus

[4] The speech ends with a prayer, but the important thing is his command "soluite uela citi!"

[5] It is a little odd for a Sicilian to address a Trojan prince and his followers in a tone of command, "cognoscite," but Entellus is *superans animis tauroque superbus.*

[6] The vehement questions of Ascanius and his rebuke are equivalent to a command, "Stop!"

(44)	9.36-38	Caicus to the Trojans
(45)	9.51-52	Turnus to the Rutulians
(46)	9.114-117	Cybele to the Trojans and the Trojan ships
(47)	9.320-323	Nisus to Euryalus
(48)	9.355-356	Nisus to Euryalus
(49)	9.376-377	Volcens to Nisus and Euryalus
(50)	9.653-656	Apollo to Ascanius
(51)	10.6-15	Jupiter to the gods[7]
(52)	10.104-113	Jupiter to the gods
(53)	10.294-298	Tarchon to his crew
(54)	10.333-335	Aeneas to Achates
(55)	10.441-443	Turnus to the Rutulians
(56)	11.14-28	Aeneas to his officers
(57)	11.463-467	Turnus to his officers
(58)	11.508-519	Turnus to Camilla
(59)	12.11-17	Turnus to Latinus[8]
(60)	12.156-159	Juno to Juturna[9]
(61)	12.313-317	Aeneas to the Trojans
(62)	12.425-429	Iapyx to the attendants
(63)	12.565-573	Aeneas to his officers
(64)	12.693-695	Turnus to the Rutulians and Latins
(65)	12.793-806	Jupiter to Juno

DIPLOMATIC OR POLITICAL SPEECHES (D)

(1)	1.522-558	Ilioneus to Dido
(2)	4.31-53	Anna to Dido
(3)	7.213-248	Ilioneus to Latinus
(4)	8.127-151	Aeneas to Evander
(5)	10.18-62	Venus to Jupiter
(6)	11.252-293	Diomede to the Latin mission
(7)	11.302-335	Latinus to the Latins
(8)	11.343-375	Drances to Latinus and Turnus

[7] Although Jupiter begins with questions, his speech is equivalent to a command, and ends with imperatives.

[8] It is quite inappropriate for Turnus to give commands to Latinus, but the imperatives "fer . . . et concipe" are uncompromising.

[9] *Sic exhortata* in the narrative (12.159); but the tone is imperative, and the peremptory beginning "non lacrimis hoc tempus" resembles Deiphobe's imperious reprimand to Aeneas, "non hoc ista sibi tempus spectacula poscit" (6.37).

(9) 11.378-444   Turnus to Drances and Latinus
(10) 12.19-45   Latinus to Turnus

ENCOURAGEMENTS (Cohortationes) (E)

(1) 1.198-207   Aeneas to the Trojans
(2) 2.348-354   Aeneas to the Trojans
(3) 9.128-158   Turnus to the Rutulians
(4) 9.781-787   Mnestheus to the Trojans
(5) 10.279-284   Turnus to the Rutulians
(6) 10.369-378   Pallas to the Arcadians
(7) 11.732-740   Tarchon to the Etruscans[10]
(8) 12.229-237   Juturna to the Rutulians[11]
(9) 12.259-265   Tolumnius to the Rutulians

FAREWELLS (F)

(1) 3.475-481   Helenus to Anchises
(2) 3.486-491   Andromache to Ascanius
(3) 3.493-505   Aeneas to Helenus and his people
(4) 6.544-546   Deiphobus to Aeneas[12]
(5) 8.560-583   Evander to Pallas
(6) 11.96-98   Aeneas to the dead Pallas
(7) 11.823-827   Camilla to Acca
(8) 12.435-440   Aeneas to Ascanius[13]

GREETINGS (G)

(1) 1.595-610   Aeneas to Dido
(2) 1.615-630   Dido to Aeneas
(3) 5.80-83   Aeneas to Anchises

[10] Although his words and tone are vituperative—lines 736-740 are like Numanus's flyting of the Trojans in 9.614-620—the purpose of his speech is to encourage his disheartened army. Tarchon, *nomine quemque uocans* (731), is like Agamemnon in *Il.* 4.223-421: *reficit in proelia.*

[11] This encouragement in 12.233 echoes a thought voiced by Agamemnon, *Il.* 2.123-128.

[12] This speech starts as an acknowledgement of the Sibyl's implied command, but the last line, the most beautiful and powerful, is a farewell.

[13] Although this is a protreptic address, it may be described as a farewell. Aeneas is going to face possible death (cf. 12.183-186); and in the closing lines (438-440) he looks forward to the time when he, like Hector, will be dead, and only his memory and example will live.

(4)   6.687-694   Anchises to Aeneas
(5)   6.695-698   Aeneas to Anchises

LEGALISTIC SPEECHES (L)

(1)   4.333-361   Aeneas to Dido
(2)   10.63-95   Juno to Venus

NARRATIVES, EXPLANATIONS, DESCRIPTIONS (N)

(1)   1.335-370   Venus to Aeneas
(2)   2.372-385   Aeneas to Venus
Aeneas's narrative in Books Two and Three
(3)   2.69-194   Sinon to Priam and the Trojans
(4)   2.324-335   Panthus to Aeneas
(5)   2.594-620   Venus to Aeneas
(6)   3.321-343   Andromache to Aeneas[14]
(7)   3.599-654   Achaemenides to the Trojans[15]
(8)   4.9-29   Dido to Anna[16]
(9)   4.702-703   Iris to Dido[17]
(10) 5.646-652   Pyrgo to the Trojan women[18]
(11) 6.322-330   Deiphobe to Aeneas
(12) 6.347-371   Palinurus to Aeneas[19]
(13) 6.509-534   Deiphobus to Aeneas
(14) 6.562-627   Deiphobe to Aeneas
(15) 6.713-718   Anchises to Aeneas
(16) 6.722-751   Anchises to Aeneas

[14] The initial apostrophe to Polyxena (321-324) is part of Andromache's pathetic narrative (death would have been better than my slavery). At 336 she concludes her narrative and turns to questioning (337-343, ending with the beloved name).

[15] Vergil sometimes makes a narrative pass into a persuasion (e.g. 6.347-362 + 363-371). Here Achaemenides begins and ends with persuasions (599-606 + 652-654) which are justified by the horrible narrative.

[16] Dido's speech is essentially a description of a profound change in her character and view of life.

[17] Iris explains what she is doing and why: hence the classification of her words as descriptive or narrative.

[18] What Pyrgo says is not a persuasion, but a straightforward description, casting light on a strange nexus of facts. A persuasion might have been more effective.

[19] Palinurus's narrative (347-362) answers Aeneas's question; then he turns to persuasion (363-371).

(17)	7.116	Ascanius to Aeneas and the Trojans
(18)	8.185-275	Evander to Aeneas
(19)	8.314-336	Evander to Aeneas
(20)	8.351-358	Evander to Aeneas
(21)	8.470-519	Evander to Aeneas[20]
(22)	10.228-245	Cymodocea to Aeneas[21]
(23)	11.243-295	Venulus to the Latins and Latinus[22]
(24)	11.535-594	Diana to Opis[23]
(25)	12.653-664	Saces to Turnus

ORACLES, PROPHECIES, INTERPRETATIONS OF OMENS AND ORACLES (O)

(1)	1.257-296 (prophecy)	Jupiter to Venus[24]
(2)	1.387-401 (interpretation)	Venus to Aeneas
(3)	2.116-119 (oracle)	Apollo to the Greeks[25]
(4)	2.776-789 (prophecy)	Creusa to Aeneas[26]
(5)	3.94-98 (oracle)	Apollo to the Trojans
(6)	3.103-117 (interpretation)	Anchises to the Trojans[27]
(7)	3.154-171 (oracle)	Apollo (through the Penates) to the Trojans

[20] Again the narrative (470-511) passes into a persuasion.

[21] Cymodocea's address contains several commands and a forecast, but the explanatory parts of her speech are more important; Vergil shows that its main purpose is informative by introducing the speech with *ignarum adloquitur* and closing with *stupet inscius*.

[22] He begins "o ciues," and addresses the king only at the end (11.294).

[23] Here the narrative leads into an injunction (587-594).

[24] Jupiter begins by responding to Venus's persuasion (257-260, note 260 ≈ 237), and then continues with a weighty oracular pronouncement.

[25] In Sinon's story.

[26] Creusa's words are also a farewell; their chief importance, however, lies in their revelation of the future.

[27] There are commands in this speech, but its essence is the interpretation of an obscure oracle.

311

(8) 3.247-257   Celaeno to the Trojans
     (prophecy)
(9) 3.374-462   Helenus to Aeneas
     (prophecy)
(10) 3.539-543   Anchises to the Trojans
     (interpretation)
(11) 5.637-638   Cassandra to "Beroe"
     (prophecy)
(12) 6.83-97   Deiphobe to Aeneas
     (prophecy)
(13) 6.756-859   Anchises to Aeneas
     (prophecy)
(14) 6.868-886   Anchises to Aeneas
     (prophecy)
(15) 7.68-70   Latin soothsayer to Latinus
     (interpretation)
(16) 7.96-101   Faunus to Latinus
     (oracle)
(17) 7.120-134   Aeneas to the Trojans[28]
     (interpretation)
(18) 7.124-127   Anchises to Aeneas[29]
     (prophecy)
(19) 7.594-599   Latinus to the Latins and Turnus
     (prophecy)
(20) 8.36-65   Tiber to Aeneas[30]
     (oracle)
(21) 8.499-503   Etruscan diviner to the Etruscans
     (oracle)
(22) 8.532-540   Aeneas to Evander
     (interpretation)
(23) 9.641-644   Apollo to Ascanius
     (oracle)
(24) 10.739-741   Orodes to Mezentius
     (prophecy)

---

[28] The most important part of this speech is Aeneas's interpretation of the grisly prophecy as fulfilled (120-129): the commands which follow arise out of it.

[29] Within Aeneas's speech.

[30] The prediction of the white sow ("haud incerta cano," 8.49) is the essential part of Tiber's speech.

312

(25) 12.830-840   Jupiter to Juno[31]
      (prophecy)
(Six interpretations, seven oracles, twelve prophecies)

PERSUASIONS (P)

(1)	1.65-75	Juno to Aeolus
(2)	1.229-253	Venus to Jupiter
(3)	1.459-463	Aeneas to Achates[32]
(4)	1.582-585	Achates to Aeneas
(5)	1.664-688	Venus to Love
(6)	2.42-49	Laocoon to the Trojans
(7)	2.387-391	Coroebus to the Trojans
(8)	2.519-524	Hecuba to Priam
(9)	2.675-678	Creusa to Aeneas
(10)	4.93-104	Juno to Venus
(11)	4.115-127	Juno to Venus[33]
(12)	4.305-330	Dido to Aeneas
(13)	4.416-436	Dido through Anna to Aeneas
(14)	5.17-25	Palinurus to Aeneas
(15)	5.383-385	Dares to Aeneas
(16)	5.389-393	Acestes to Entellus
(17)	5.410-420	Entellus to Dares
(18)	5.623-640	"Beroe" to the Trojan women
(19)	5.709-718	Nautes to Aeneas
(20)	5.781-798	Venus to Neptune
(21)	5.843-846	Sleep to Palinurus
(22)	6.103-123	Aeneas to Deiphobe
(23)	6.399-407	Deiphobe to Charon
(24)	6.456-466	Aeneas to Dido[34]
(25)	7.331-340	Juno to Allecto[35]

[31] The initial and final prophecies of Jupiter frame the poem.

[32] This famous little speech of encouragement is, in form, a persuasion. Aeneas says "Since the Trojan war in which we fought is known here, we have not fallen among ignorant savages: therefore you need not despair." Compare Athena's encouragement in *Od.* 7.50-52.

[33] That this, in spite of its haughty tone, is a persuasion is shown by *petenti / adnuit* (4.127-128).

[34] Aeneas attempts to persuade Dido to soften her resentment (*lenibat dictis animum*).

[35] Juno's rank would enable her to command Allecto, but she gives rea

(26)	7.359-372	Amata to Latinus
(27)	7.421-434	Allecto as Calybe to Turnus
(28)	7.545-551	Allecto to Juno
(29)	8.362-365	Evander to Aeneas[36]
(30)	8.374-386	Venus to Vulcan
(31)	8.612-614	Venus to Aeneas[37]
(32)	9.83-92	Cybele to Jupiter
(33)	9.184-196	Nisus to Euryalus
(34)	9.207-218	Nisus to Euryalus
(35)	9.234-245	Nisus to Ascanius and the Trojan chiefs
(36)	9.281-292	Euryalus to Ascanius
(37)	9.427-430	Nisus to the Rutulians
(38)	10.467-472	Jupiter to Hercules[38]
(39)	10.524-529	Magus to Aeneas
(40)	10.597-598	Liger to Aeneas
(41)	10.611-620	Juno to Jupiter
(42)	10.628-632	Juno to Jupiter
(43)	10.900-906	Mezentius to Aeneas
(44)	11.502-506	Camilla to Turnus
(45)	12.56-63	Amata to Turnus
(46)	12.142-153	Juno to Juturna
(47)	12.625-630	Juturna to Turnus
(48)	12.676-680	Turnus to Juturna
(49)	12.808-828	Juno to Jupiter[39]
(50)	12.931-938	Turnus to Aeneas

PRAYERS (Pra)

| (1) | 1.326-334 | Aeneas to Venus[40] |
| (2) | 1.731-735 | Dido to Jupiter |

---

sons for her wish (7.332-334) and praises Allecto's special powers (335-338), so that her speech is persuasive rather than jussive.

[36] A modest and charming speech of persuasion: note the argument "Alcides . . . te quoque."

[37] The Homeric model of this speech, spoken by Thetis to Achilles (*Il.* 19.8-11 + 29-36), is a persuasion; and compare Venus's "ne mox . . . dubites" with Anchises' protreptic "et dubitamus adhuc?" (6.806).

[38] In effect, a consolation.

[39] Juno begins with a meek response (808-818), and then goes on to a powerful persuasion (819-828), which is essential to her purpose and to the design of the *Aeneid*.

[40] Aeneas's address is a question in substance, but it is framed as a prayer.

(3)	2.689-691	Anchises to Jupiter
(4)	2.701-704	Anchises to the gods[41]
(5)	3.85-89	Aeneas to Apollo
(6)	3.265-266	Anchises to the gods
(7)	3.528-529	Anchises to the gods of sea, land, and weather
(8)	4.206-218	Iarbas to Jupiter
(9)	5.235-238	Cloanthus to the sea-gods
(10)	5.483-484	Entellus to Eryx
(11)	5.687-692	Aeneas to Jupiter
(12)	6.56-76	Aeneas to Apollo, the gods hostile to Troy, and the Sibyl[42]
(13)	6.187-189	Aeneas to no particular deity
(14)	6.194-197	Aeneas to Venus and her doves
(15)	8.71-78	Aeneas to the Nymphs and Tiber
(16)	8.293-302	The Salii to Hercules
(17)	9.18-22	Turnus to Iris
(18)	9.404-409	Nisus to the Moon
(19)	9.625-629	Ascanius to Jupiter
(20)	10.252-255	Aeneas to Cybele
(21)	10.421-423	Pallas to the Tiber
(22)	10.460-463	Pallas to Hercules
(23)	10.773-776	Mezentius to his right hand and spear
(24)	11.483-485	Latin matrons to Minerva
(25)	11.557-560[43]	Amasenus to Diana
(26)	11.785-793	Arruns to Apollo
(27)	12.176-194	The oath of Aeneas
(28)	12.197-211	The oath of Latinus
(29)	12.777-779	Turnus to Faunus and Earth

QUESTIONS (Q)

(1)	1.407-409	Aeneas to Venus
(2)	1.753-756	Dido to Aeneas
(3)	2.148-151	Priam to Sinon

[41] Anchises' words combine a prayer to the gods with a response to his son, but the prayer—beginning with the grave "iam iam" and ending "uestroque in numine Troia est"—dominates the speech.

[42] Strictly speaking, Aeneas addresses prayers to Apollo and the inimical deities (56-65) and a persuasion to the Sibyl (65-76).

[43] Within Diana's narrative.

(4)	2.281-286	Aeneas to Hector
(5)	2.322	Aeneas to Panthus
(6)	3.310-312	Andromache to Aeneas
(7)	3.315-319	Aeneas to Andromache
(8)	3.359-368	Aeneas to Helenus
(9)	5.353-356	Nisus to Aeneas
(10)	5.741-742	Aeneas to Anchises[44]
(11)	6.318-320	Aeneas to the Sibyl
(12)	6.341-346	Aeneas to Palinurus
(13)	6.500-508	Aeneas to Deiphobus
(14)	6.560-561	Aeneas to the Sibyl
(15)	6.669-671	The Sibyl to Musaeus
(16)	6.719-721	Aeneas to Anchises
(17)	6.863-866	Aeneas to Anchises
(18)	7.195-211	Latinus to the Trojans[45]
(19)	8.112-114	Pallas to the Trojans
(20)	12.620-621	Turnus to himself

RESPONSES TO QUESTIONS, COMMANDS, AND VARIOUS TYPES OF PERSUASION (R)

(1)	1.76-80	Aeolus to Juno
(2)	1.562-578	Dido to Ilioneus and the Trojans
(3)	2.657-670	Aeneas to Anchises[46]
(4)	4.107-114	Venus to Juno
(5)	4.365-387	Dido to Aeneas
(6)	5.348-350	Aeneas to Salius and Diores
(7)	5.394-400	Entellus to Acestes
(8)	5.800-815	Neptune to Venus
(9)	5.848-851	Palinurus to Sleep
(10)	6.673-676	Musaeus to Deiphobe
(11)	7.259-273	Latinus to Ilioneus and the Trojans
(12)	7.436-444	Turnus to Allecto as Calybe

[44] This question resembles that which Aeneas addresses to his mother in 1.407-409.

[45] After his questions, Latinus extends to the Trojans a generous greeting (199-211); but it is the questions to which Ilioneus pays attention first in his reply (213-215 ≈ 197-201).

[46] This is a confused and highly emotional speech, containing a command and an apostrophe; but in essence it is the only response Aeneas feels he can make to his father's order to depart from Troy and leave him.

316

(13)	7.552-560	Juno to Allecto
(14)	8.154-174	Evander to Aeneas[47]
(15)	8.395-404	Vulcan to Venus
(16)	9.94-103	Jupiter to Cybele
(17)	9.199-206	Euryalus to Nisus
(18)	9.219-221	Euryalus to Nisus
(19)	9.247-256	Aletes to Nisus and Euryalus[48]
(20)	9.257-280	Ascanius to Nisus and Euryalus
(21)	9.296-302	Ascanius to Euryalus
(22)	10.531-534	Aeneas to Magus
(23)	10.622-627	Jupiter to Juno
(24)	11.108-119	Aeneas to the Latins[49]
(25)	11.124-131	Drances to Aeneas
(26)	12.48-53	Turnus to Latinus
(27)	12.72-80	Turnus to Amata[50]
(28)	12.632-649	Turnus to Juturna[51]
(29)	12.947-949	Aeneas to Turnus

SOLILOQUIES (S)

(1)	1.37-49	Juno
(2)	1.94-101	Aeneas
(3)	1.437	Aeneas[52]
(4)	2.577-587	Aeneas[53]
(5)	4.534-552	Dido

[47] This address contains both an affirmative reply to Aeneas's proposal (169-171) and a warm greeting.

[48] The apostrophe to the ancestral gods (247-250) is part of his response, and is equivalent to heartfelt praise of the two young warriors.

[49] The first sentence strongly resembles the magnanimous *exordium* of Diomede replying to another Latin embassy (11.252-254) and thus emphasizes the sympathy of the Greek for the Trojan hero.

[50] Turnus dismisses Amata with twenty-two words; the rest of his speech is a command to his herald, which is indirectly a reply, and a snub, to the queen.

[51] Turnus moves away from Juturna, and ends by invoking the Manes (646-649)—as, in an earlier emotional speech, he turned from Jupiter to the winds (10.668-679).

[52] This little exclamation is a soliloquy comparable to 1.94-101: both begin "o" with a vocative adjective connoting happiness, and both reflect Aeneas's misery.

[53] See pp. 164-176.

317

(6)   4.590-629   Dido[54]
(7)   4.651-662   Dido
(8)   7.293-322   Juno

TAUNTS, THREATS, CHALLENGES (T)

(1)   2.535-543   Priam to Pyrrhus
(2)   2.547-550   Pyrrhus to Priam
(3)   7.452-455   Allecto to Turnus
(4)   9.422-423   Volcens to Euryalus
(5)   9.560-561   Turnus to Lycus
(6)   9.634-635   Ascanius to Numanus
(7)   9.737-739   Pandarus to Turnus
(8)   9.741-742   Turnus to Pandarus
(9)   9.747-748   Turnus to Pandarus
(10)   10.449-451   Pallas to Turnus
(11)   10.481   Turnus to Pallas
(12)   10.491-495   Turnus to the Arcadians[55]
(13)   10.557-560   Aeneas to Tarquitus
(14)   10.581-583   Liger to Aeneas
(15)   10.592-594   Aeneas to Lucagus
(16)   10.599-600   Aeneas to Liger
(17)   10.607-610   Jupiter to Juno[56]
(18)   10.649-650   Turnus to the phantom Aeneas
(19)   10.737   Mezentius over Orodes
(20)   10.743-744   Mezentius to Orodes
(21)   10.811-812   Aeneas to Lausus[57]
(22)   10.875-876   Aeneas to Mezentius[58]
(23)   10.878-882   Mezentius to Aeneas
(24)   10.897-898   Aeneas to Mezentius
(25)   11.459-461   Turnus to the Latins and Rutulians
(26)   11.686-689   Camilla to Ornytus
(27)   11.705-708   The son of Aunus to Camilla
(28)   11.715-717   Camilla to the son of Aunus

[54] This soliloquy contains a prayer (607-621) and a command (622-629).
[55] More a taunt (judging by the tone) than a command.
[56] This is a taunt like its Homeric model, the speech of Zeus to Hera, κερτομίοις ἐπέεσσι (*Il.* 4.7-19).
[57] Although the words sound kindly, they are a threat of death, introduced by *minatur*.
[58] Aeneas seems to be praying, but Mezentius recognizes his words as a threatening challenge: "quid me . . . terres?"

318

(29)   11.855-857   Opis to Arruns
(30)   12.296   Messapus over Aulestes
(31)   12.359-361   Turnus to Eumedes
(32)   12.889-893   Aeneas to Turnus
(33)   12.894-895   Turnus to Aeneas

VITUPERATION (V)

(1)   9.598-620   Numanus to the Trojans

APPENDIX 3

Grouping of the Speeches

This is a list of the speeches in the *Aeneid* as they occur in isolation, in pairs, or in clusters. Only the first and last lines of each group of speeches are cited, and intermediate passages of narrative between grouped speeches are not given.

ONE SPEAKER: SOLILOQUY

(1) Juno	1.37-49	
(2) Aeneas	1.94-101	
(3) Aeneas	1.437	
(4) Aeneas	2.577-587	
(5) Dido	4.534-552	
(6) Dido	4.590-629	
(7) Dido	4.651-662	
(8) Juno	7.293-322	

ONE SPEAKER: NO ANSWER

Speaker		Addressee	Type of speech
(1) Neptune	1.132-141	Winds	C
(2) Aeneas	1.198-207	Trojans	E
(3) Aeneas	1.459-463	Achates	P
(4) Achates	1.582-585	Aeneas	P
(5) Venus	1.664-688	Amor	P
(6) Dido	1.731-735	Jupiter and others	Pra
(7) Laocoon	2.42-49	Trojans	P
(8) Apollo	2.116-119	Greeks	O reported
(9) Aeneas	2.348-354	Trojans	E
(10) Androgeos	2.373-375	Trojans as Greeks	C
(11) Coroebus	2.387-391	Trojans	P
(12) Hecuba	2.519-524	Priam	P
(13) Venus	2.594-620	Aeneas	N (+ C)
(14) Anchises	2.733-734	Aeneas	C
(15) Creusa	2.776-789	Aeneas	O
(16) Polydorus	3.41-46	Aeneas	C
(17) Penates	3.154-171	Aeneas	O
(18) Anchises	3.182-188	Aeneas and the Trojans	C
(19) Anchises	3.528-529	Gods	Pra
(20) Anchises	3.539-543	Trojans	O

320

Speaker		Addressee	Type of speech
(21) Anchises	3.558-560	Trojans	C
(22) Achaemenides	3.599-654	Trojans	N
(23) Mercury	4.265-276	Aeneas	C
(24) Dido	4.416-436	Aeneas and Anna	P + C
(25) Dido	4.478-498	Anna	C
(26) Mercury (?)	4.560-570	Aeneas	C
(27) Aeneas	4.573-579	Trojans + Mercury	C + Pra
(28) Dido	4.634-640	Barce	C
(29) Anna	4.675-685	Dido	A
(30) Iris	4.702-703	Dido	N
(31) Aeneas	5.45-71	Trojans	C
(32) Aeneas	5.80-83	Anchises	G
(33) Gyas	5.162-166	Menoetes	C
(34) Mnestheus	5.189-197	His crew	C
(35) Cloanthus	5.235-238	Sea-gods	Pra
(36) Aeneas	5.304-314	Competitors	C
(37) Aeneas	5.363-364	Competitors	C
(38) Aeneas	5.465-467	Dares	C
(39) Entellus	5.474-476	Aeneas and Trojans	C
(40) Entellus	5.483-484	Eryx	Pra
(41) Aeneas	5.533-538	Acestes	C
(42) Aeneas	5.548-551	Epytides	C
(43) Cassandra	5.637-638	"Beroe"	O reported
(44) Ascanius	5.670-673	Trojan women	C
(45) Aeneas	5.687-692	Jupiter	Pra
(46) Nautes	5.709-718	Aeneas	P
(47) Aeneas	5.870-871	Palinurus	A
(48) Deiphobe	6.37-39	Aeneas	C
(49) Aeneas	6.187-189	vague	Pra
(50) Aeneas	6.194-197	Doves and Venus	Pra
(51) Deiphobe	6.258-261	*Profani* and Aeneas	C
(52) Aeneas	6.456-466	Dido	P
(53) Phlegyas	6.620	All	C reported
(54) Deiphobe	6.629-632	Aeneas	C
(55) Vates Latinorum	7.68-70	Latinus	O
(56) Faunus	7.96-101	Latinus	O
(57) Anchises	7.124-127	Aeneas	O reported
(58) Juno	7.331-340	Allecto	P
(59) Amata	7.359-372	Latinus	P
(60) Amata	7.400-403	Latin women	C
(61) Latinus	7.594-599	Latins and Turnus	O
(62) Evander	8.185-275	Aeneas	N
(63) Salii	8.293-302	Hercules	Pra
(64) Evander	8.314-336	Aeneas	N

Speaker		Addressee	Type of speech
(65) Evander	8.351-358	Aeneas	N
(66) Evander	8.362-365	Aeneas	P
(67) Vulcan	8.439-443	Cyclopes	C
(68) Evander	8.470-519	Aeneas	N
(69) Haruspex Etruscorum	8.499-503	Etruscans	O reported
(70) Aeneas	8.532-540	Evander	O
(71) Evander	8.560-583	Pallas	F
(72) Venus	8.612-614	Aeneas	P
(73) Caicus	9.36-38	Trojans	C
(74) Turnus	9.51-52	Rutulians	C
(75) Cybele	9.114-117	Trojans and ships	C
(76) Turnus	9.128-158	Rutulians and Latins	E
(77) Nisus	9.320-323	Euryalus	C
(78) Nisus	9.355-356	Euryalus	C
(79) Volcens	9.376-377	Nisus and Euryalus	C
(80) Nisus	9.390-391	Euryalus	A
(81) Nisus	9.404-409	Moon	Pra
(82) Euryali mater	9.481-497	Euryalus	A
(83) Turnus	9.560-561	Lycus	T
(84) Mnestheus	9.781-787	Trojans	E
(85) Turnus	10.279-284	Rutulians and Latins	E
(86) Tarchon	10.294-298	His crew	C
(87) Aeneas	10.333-335	Achates	C
(88) Pallas	10.369-378	Arcadians	E
(89) Pallas	10.421-423	Tiber	Pra
(90) Aeneas	10.557-560	Tarquitus	T
(91) Turnus	10.649-650	Phantom Aeneas	T
(92) Turnus	10.668-679	Jupiter and winds	A
(93) Mezentius	10.773-776	Right hand and spear	Pra
(94) Aeneas	10.811-812	Lausus	T
(95) Aeneas	10.825-830	Lausus	A
(96) Mezentius	10.846-856	Lausus	A
(97) Mezentius	10.861-866	Rhaebus his horse	A
(98) Aeneas	11.14-28	His officers	C
(99) Aeneas	11.42-58	Pallas	A
(100) Aeneas	11.96-98	Pallas	F
(101) Evander	11.152-181	Pallas	A
(102) Turnus	11.463-467	Volusus and other officers	C
(103) Matres Latinae	11.483-485	Minerva	Pra
(104) Diana	11.535-594	Opis	N
(105) Amasenus	11.557-560	Diana	Pra reported
(106) Camilla	11.686-689	Ornytus	T

Speaker			Addressee	Type of speech
(107)	Tarchon	11.732-740	Etruscans	E
(108)	Arruns	11.785-793	Apollo	Pra
(109)	Camilla	11.823-827	Acca	F
(110)	Opis	11.841-849	Camilla	A
(111)	Opis	11.855-857	Arruns	T
(112)	Turnus	12.95-100	His spear	A
(113)	Juno	12.142-153	Juturna	P
(114)	Juno	12.156-159	Juturna	C
(115)	Juturna	12.229-237	Rutulians	E
(116)	Tolumnius	12.259-265	Rutulians	E
(117)	Messapus	12.296	Aulestes	T
(118)	Aeneas	12.313-317	Trojans	C
(119)	Turnus	12.359-361	Eumedes	T
(120)	Iapyx	12.425-429	Attendants	C
(121)	Aeneas	12.435-440	Ascanius	F
(122)	Aeneas	12.565-573	Trojans	C
(123)	Saces	12.653-664	Turnus	N
(124)	Turnus	12.676-680	Juturna	P
(125)	Turnus	12.693-695	Rutulians and Latins	C
(126)	Turnus	12.777-779	Faunus and Earth	Pra
(127)	Juturna	12.872-884	Turnus	A

TWO SPEAKERS: TWO SPEECHES

(1)	Juno and Aeolus	1.65-80	P + R
(2)	Venus and Jupiter	1.229-296	P + O
(3)	Ilioneus and Dido	1.522-578	D + R
(4)	Aeneas and Dido	1.595-630	G + G
(5)	Dido and Aeneas	1.753-3.715	Q + N
(6)	Sinon and Trojans (Priam)	2.69-194	N + Q
(7)	Aeneas and Hector	2.281-295	Q + C
(8)	Aeneas and Panthus	2.322-335	Q + N
(9)	Priam and Pyrrhus	2.535-550	T + T
(10)	Aeneas and Helenus	3.359-462	Q + O
(11)	Dido and Anna	4.9-53	N + D
(12)	Aeneas and Nisus	5.348-356	R + Q
(13)	Anchises and Aeneas	5.724-742	C + Q
(14)	Venus and Neptune	5.781-815	P + R
(15)	Somnus and Palinurus	5.843-851	P + R
(16)	Aeneas and Deiphobe	6.318-330	Q + N
(17)	Charon and Deiphobe	6.388-407	C + P
(18)	Aeneas and Deiphobe	6.560-627	Q + N

(19) Deiphobe and Musaeus	6.669-676	Q + R
(20) Ascanius and Aeneas	7.116-134	N + O
(21) Allecto and Juno	7.545-560	P + R
(22) Tiber and Aeneas	8.36-78	O + Pra
(23) Aeneas and Evander	8.127-174	D + R
(24) Venus and Vulcan	8.374-404	P + R
(25) Iris and Turnus	9.6-22	C + Pra
(26) Cybele and Jupiter	9.83-103	P + R
(27) Magus and Aeneas	10.524-534	P + R
(28) Aeneas and Drances	11.108-131	R (P) + R
(29) Camilla and Turnus	11.502-519	P + C
(30) Auni filius and Camilla	11.705-717	T + T
(31) Aeneas and Turnus	12.889-895	T + T
(32) Turnus and Aeneas	12.931-949	P + R

TWO SPEAKERS: TWO SPEECHES INDEPENDENT BUT ON SAME OCCASION

(1) Celaeno and Anchises	3.247-257, 265-266	O and Pra
(2) Iarbas and Jupiter	4.206-218, 223-237	Pra and C
(3) Iris and Pyrgo	5.623-640, 646-652	P and N
(4) Volcens and Nisus	9.422-423, 427-430	T and P
(5) Cymodocea and Aeneas	10.228-245, 252-255	N and Pra
(6) Aeneas and Latinus	12.176-194, 197-211	Pra and Pra

TWO SPEAKERS: THREE SPEECHES

(1) Andromache, Aeneas, Andromache	3.310-343
(2) Juno, Venus, Juno	4.93-127
(3) Dido, Aeneas, Dido	4.305-387
(4) Palinurus, Palinurus, Aeneas	5.13-31
(5) Latinus, Ilioneus, Latinus	7.195-273
(6) Allecto, Turnus, Allecto	7.421-455
(7) Pallas, Aeneas, Pallas	8.112-123
(8) Pandarus, Turnus, Turnus	9.737-748
(9) Mezentius, Orodes, Mezentius	10.737-744
(10) Turnus, Juturna, Turnus	12.620-649
(11) Jupiter, Juno, Jupiter	12.793-840

TWO SPEAKERS: FOUR SPEECHES

(1) Nisus, Euryalus, Nisus, Euryalus   9.184-221
(2) Liger, Aeneas, Liger, Aeneas   10.581-600
(3) Jupiter, Juno, Jupiter, Juno   10.607-632
(4) Aeneas, Mezentius, Aeneas, Mezentius   10.875-906

TWO SPEAKERS: SIX SPEECHES

(1) Venus, Aeneas, Venus, Aeneas, Venus, Aeneas   1.321-409
(2) Deiphobe, Deiphobe, Aeneas, Deiphobe,
    Aeneas, Deiphobe   6.45-155

TWO SPEAKERS: EIGHT SPEECHES

(1) Anchises, Aeneas, Anchises, Aeneas,
    Anchises, Anchises, Aeneas, Anchises   6.687-886

THREE SPEAKERS: THREE SPEECHES

(1) Aeneas, Apollo, Anchises   3.85-117
(2) Helenus, Andromache, Aeneas   3.475-505
(3) Aeneas, Palinurus, Deiphobe   6.341-381

THREE SPEAKERS: FOUR SPEECHES

(1) Dares, Acestes, Entellus, Entellus   5.383-420
(2) Aeneas, Deiphobus, Deiphobe, Deiphobus   6.500-546
(3) Jupiter, Venus, Juno, Jupiter   10.6-113

THREE SPEAKERS: FIVE SPEECHES

(1) Numanus, Ascanius, Ascanius, Apollo, Apollo   9.598-656
(2) Turnus, Latinus, Turnus, Amata, Turnus   12.11-80

THREE SPEAKERS: SIX SPEECHES

(1) Anchises, Aeneas, Creusa, Anchises,
    Anchises, Aeneas   2.638-720
(2) Turnus, Pallas, Pallas, Jupiter, Turnus, Turnus   10.441-495

FOUR SPEAKERS: FIVE SPEECHES

(1) Nisus, Aletes, Ascanius, Euryalus, Ascanius   9.234-302

FIVE SPEAKERS: SIX SPEECHES

(1) Venulus, (Diomede), Latinus, Drances, Turnus,
    Turnus   11.243-461
        (Turnus leaves the meeting at 11.462;
        his next speech is made elsewhere.)

The Speeches listed by
Names of Characters

(All speeches within Book Two and Book Three are reported by Aeneas, addressing Dido; but to make the tabulation clearer and simpler, they have not been so signalized here. For a complete list see Appendix 6.)

(1) Acestes		5.389-393	5 lines
(2) Achaemenides		3.599-606 + 613-654	49 5/12 lines
(3) Achates		1.582-585	4 lines
(4) Aeneas	(1)	1.94-101	7 7/12 lines
	(2)	1.198-207	10 lines
	(3)	1.326-334	9 lines
	(4)	1.372-385	13 7/12 lines
	(5)	1.407-409	3 lines
	(6)	1.437	1 line
	(7)	1.459-463	4 1/2 lines
	(8)	1.595-610	15 1/6 lines

Book 1: 8 speeches by Aeneas, 63 5/6 lines

Narrative of Aeneas: 2.3–3.715 = 1,516 lines[1]

	(9)	2.281-286	6 lines
	(10)	2.322	1 line
	(11)	2.348-354	6 7/12 lines
	(12)	2.577-587[2]	11 lines
	(13)	2.657-670	14 lines
	(14)	2.707-720	14 lines

Book 2: 6 speeches by Aeneas, excluding the narrative, 52 7/12 lines

	(15)	3.85-89	5 lines
	(16)	3.315-319	5 lines
	(17)	3.359-368	10 lines
	(18)	3.493-505	13 lines

Book 3: 4 speeches by Aeneas, excluding the narrative, 33 lines

[1] Line 2.76 is omitted as spurious.   [2] See pp. 164-176.

(19) 4.333-361 $28\frac{7}{12}$ lines
(20) 4.573-579   6 lines

Book 4: 2 speeches by Aeneas, $34\frac{7}{12}$ lines

(21) 5.26-31 $5\frac{7}{12}$ lines
(22) 5.45-71   27 lines
(23) 5.80-83   4 lines
(24) 5.304-314   11 lines
(25) 5.348-350 $2\frac{5}{12}$ lines
(26) 5.363-364   2 lines
(27) 5.465-467 $2\frac{1}{4}$ lines
(28) 5.533-538   6 lines
(29) 5.548-551 $3\frac{1}{12}$ lines
(30) 5.687-692   6 lines
(31) 5.741-742 $1\frac{7}{12}$ lines
(32) 5.870-871   2 lines

Book 5: 12 speeches by Aeneas, $72\frac{11}{12}$ lines

(33) 6.56-76 $20\frac{5}{12}$ lines
(34) 6.103-123 $20\frac{5}{12}$ lines
(35) 6.187-189   3 lines
(36) 6.194-197 $3\frac{1}{4}$ lines
(37) 6.318-320 $2\frac{11}{12}$ lines
(38) 6.341-346 $5\frac{7}{12}$ lines
(39) 6.456-466   11 lines
(40) 6.500-508   9 lines
(41) 6.560-561   2 lines
(42) 6.695-698 $3\frac{3}{4}$ lines
(43) 6.719-721   3 lines
(44) 6.863-866   4 lines

Book 6: 12 speeches by Aeneas, $88\frac{1}{3}$ lines

(45) 7.120-134 $14\frac{2}{3}$ lines

Book 7: 1 speech by Aeneas, $14\frac{2}{3}$ lines

(46) 8.71-78   8 lines
(47) 8.117-120   4 lines
(48) 8.127-151   25 lines
(49) 8.532-540 $8\frac{3}{4}$ lines

Book 8: 4 speeches by Aeneas, $45\frac{3}{4}$ lines

Book 9: Aeneas does not speak

328

(50)	10.252-255	4 lines
(51)	10.333-335	$2\frac{5}{12}$ lines
(52)	10.531-534	4 lines
(53)	10.557-560	4 lines
(54)	10.592-594	$2\frac{2}{3}$ lines
(55)	10.599-600	$1\frac{5}{12}$ lines
(56)	10.811-812	$1\frac{2}{3}$ lines
(57)	10.825-830	$5\frac{2}{3}$ lines
(58)	10.875-876	2 lines
(59)	10.897-898	$1\frac{1}{6}$ lines

Book 10: 10 speeches by Aeneas, 29 lines

(60)	11.14-28	$14\frac{11}{12}$ lines
(61)	11.42-58	$16\frac{5}{6}$ lines
(62)	11.96-98	$2\frac{5}{12}$ lines
(63)	11.108-119	12 lines

Book 11: 4 speeches by Aeneas, $46\frac{1}{6}$ lines

(64)	12.176-194	19 lines
(65)	12.313-317	5 lines
(66)	12.435-440	6 lines
(67)	12.565-573	9 lines
(68)	12.889-893	5 lines
(69)	12.947-949	$2\frac{3}{4}$ lines

Book 12: 6 speeches by Aeneas, $46\frac{3}{4}$ lines

In all, Aeneas utters 69 separate speeches, covering $527\frac{7}{12}$ lines: this figure excludes the narrative in Book Two and Book Three, but includes the speeches made by Aeneas within it and reported by him. Or, if we consider the narrative as one long speech and omit Aeneas's shorter speeches within it, the total is 60 speeches = 1,958 lines.

(5) Aeolus		1.76-80	$4\frac{7}{12}$ lines
(6) Aletes		9.247-250 + 252-256	$8\frac{1}{6}$ lines
(7) Allecto	(1)	7.421-434	14 lines
	(2)	7.452-455	4 lines
	(3)	7.545-551	7 lines
		Total: 25 lines	
(8) Amasenus[3]		11.557-560	4 lines
(9) Amata	(1)	7.359-372	14 lines

[3] Reported by Diana.

329

	(2)	7.400-403	$3\frac{11}{12}$ lines
	(3)	12.56-63	8 lines

Total: $25\frac{11}{12}$ lines

(10) Anchises	(1)	2.638-649	$11\frac{1}{2}$ lines
	(2)	2.689-691	3 lines
	(3)	2.701-704	4 lines
	(4)	2.733-734	$1\frac{1}{2}$ lines

Book 2: 4 speeches by Anchises, 20 lines

	(5)	3.103-117	$14\frac{11}{12}$ lines
	(6)	3.182-188	$6\frac{3}{4}$ lines
	(7)	3.265-266	$1\frac{7}{12}$ lines
	(8)	3.528-529	2 lines
	(9)	3.539-543	$3\frac{5}{6}$ lines
	(10)	3.558-560	$2\frac{7}{12}$ lines

Book 3: 6 speeches by Anchises, $31\frac{2}{3}$ lines

	(11)	5.724-739	16 lines

Book 5: 1 speech by Anchises, 16 lines

	(12)	6.687-694	8 lines
	(13)	6.713-718	$5\frac{7}{12}$ lines
	(14)	6.722 + 724-751	29 lines
	(15)	6.756-853 + 855-859	103 lines
	(16)	6.868-886	$18\frac{1}{6}$ lines

Book 6: 5 speeches by Anchises, $163\frac{3}{4}$ lines

	(17)	7.124-127[4]	4 lines

Book 7: 1 speech by Anchises, 4 lines

In all, Anchises utters 17 speeches, covering $235\frac{5}{12}$ lines.

(11) Androgeos		2.373-375	3 lines
(12) Andromache	(1)	3.310-312	$2\frac{1}{4}$ lines
	(2)	3.321-343	23 lines
	(3)	3.486-491	6 lines

Total: $31\frac{1}{4}$ lines

(13) Anna	(1)	4.31-53	$22\frac{3}{4}$ lines
	(2)	4.675-685	$10\frac{1}{4}$ lines

Total: 33 lines

(14) Apollo	(1)	2.116-119[5]	$3\frac{1}{4}$ lines

[4] Reported by Aeneas.   [5] Reported by Sinon.

	(2)	3.94-98	5 lines
	(3)	9.641-644	$3\frac{5}{12}$ lines
	(4)	9.653-656	$3\frac{7}{12}$ lines
		Total: $15\frac{1}{4}$ lines	
(15) Arruns		11.785-793	9 lines
(16) Ascanius	(1)	5.670-673	$3\frac{7}{12}$ lines
	(2)	7.116	$\frac{2}{3}$ line
	(3)	9.257-280	23 lines
	(4)	9.296-302	7 lines
	(5)	9.625-629	5 lines
	(6)	9.634-635	$1\frac{5}{6}$ lines
		Total: $40\frac{7}{12}$ lines	
(17) Auni filius		11.705-708	$3\frac{3}{4}$ lines
Beroe: see Iris			
Butes: see Apollo			
(18) Caicus		9.36-38	$2\frac{5}{12}$ lines
Camers: see Iuturna			
(19) Camilla	(1)	11.502-506	5 lines
	(2)	11.686-689	4 lines
	(3)	11.715-717	3 lines
	(4)	11.823-827	$4\frac{1}{4}$ lines
		Total: $16\frac{1}{4}$ lines	
Calybe: see Allecto			
(20) Cassandra[6]		5.637-638	$\frac{5}{6}$ line
(21) Celaeno		3.247-257	11 lines
(22) Charon		6.388-397	10 lines
(23) Cloanthus		5.235-238	4 lines
(24) Coroebus		2.387-391	$4\frac{1}{4}$ lines
(25) Creusa	(1)	2.675-678	4 lines
	(2)	2.776-789	14 lines
		Total: 18 lines	
(26) Cybele	(1)	9.83-92	$9\frac{5}{12}$ lines
	(2)	9.114-117	$3\frac{2}{3}$ lines
		Total: $13\frac{1}{12}$ lines	
(27) Cymodocea		10.228-245	$17\frac{5}{12}$ lines
(28) Dares		5.383-385	$2\frac{5}{12}$ lines
(29) Deiphobe	(1)	6.37-39	3 lines
	(2)	6.45-46	$\frac{3}{4}$ line
	(3)	6.51-53	$2\frac{1}{12}$ lines
	(4)	6.83-97	15 lines

[6] Reported by Iris disguised as Beroe.

331

(5)	6.125-155	$29\frac{2}{3}$ lines
(6)	6.258-261	$3\frac{1}{6}$ lines
(7)	6.322-330	9 lines
(8)	6.373-381	9 lines
(9)	6.399-407	$7\frac{1}{2}$ lines
(10)	6.539-543	5 lines
(11)	6.562-627	$65\frac{5}{12}$ lines
(12)	6.629-632	$3\frac{11}{12}$ lines
(13)	6.669-671	3 lines

Total: $156\frac{1}{2}$ lines

(30) Deiphobus	(1)	6.509-534	$25\frac{7}{12}$ lines
	(2)	6.544-546	$2\frac{7}{12}$ lines

Total: $28\frac{1}{6}$ lines

(31) Diana		11.535-594	$59\frac{3}{4}$ lines
(32) Dido	(1)	1.562-578	17 lines
	(2)	1.615-630	16 lines
	(3)	1.731-735	5 lines
	(4)	1.753-756	$3\frac{5}{6}$ lines

Book 1: 4 speeches by Dido, $41\frac{5}{6}$ lines

(5)	4.9-29	21 lines
(6)	4.305-330	26 lines
(7)	4.365-387	23 lines
(8)	4.416-436	21 lines
(9)	4.478-498	21 lines
(10)	4.534-552	19 lines
(11)	4.590-629	$39\frac{1}{3}$ lines
(12)	4.634-640	7 lines
(13)	4.651-658 + 659-662	$11\frac{1}{3}$ lines

Book 4: 9 speeches by Dido, $188\frac{2}{3}$ lines

In all, Dido utters 13 speeches, covering $230\frac{1}{2}$ lines.

(33) Diomedes[7]		11.252-293	42 lines
(34) Drances	(1)	11.124-131	$7\frac{3}{4}$ lines
	(2)	11.343-375	33 lines

Total: $40\frac{3}{4}$ lines

(35) Entellus	(1)	5.394-400	$6\frac{1}{3}$ lines
	(2)	5.410-420	11 lines
	(3)	5.474-476	$2\frac{5}{6}$ lines
	(4)	5.483-484	2 lines

Total: $22\frac{1}{6}$ lines

[7] Reported by Venulus.

(36) Euandrus   (1)   8.154-174 $20\frac{7}{12}$ lines

                   (2)   8.185-275 $90\frac{7}{12}$ lines

                   (3)   8.314-336   23 lines

                   (4)   8.351-358 $7\frac{5}{6}$ lines

                   (5)   8.362-365 $3\frac{5}{12}$ lines

                   (6)   8.470-519   50 lines

                   (7)   8.560-583 $23\frac{1}{6}$ lines

Book 8: 7 speeches by Evander, $218\frac{7}{12}$ lines

                   (8)   11.152-181   30 lines

In all, Evander utters 8 speeches, covering $248\frac{7}{12}$ lines

(37) Euryalus   (1)   9.199-206   8 lines

                   (2)   9.219-221   2 lines

                   (3)   9.281-292 $11\frac{1}{6}$ lines

                      Total: $21\frac{1}{6}$ lines

(38) Euryali mater   9.481-497   17 lines

(39) Faunus   7.96-101   6 lines

(40) Gyas   5.162-164 + 166 $3\frac{1}{4}$ lines

(41) Haruspex

    Etruscorum[8]   8.499-503 $4\frac{1}{3}$ lines

(42) Hector   2.289-295 $6\frac{11}{12}$ lines

(43) Hecuba   2.519-524   5 lines

(44) Helenus   (1)   3.374-462   89 lines

                   (2)   3.475-481 $6\frac{11}{12}$ lines

                      Total: $95\frac{11}{12}$ lines

(45) Iapyx   12.425 + 427-429 $3\frac{3}{4}$ lines

(46) Iarbas   4.206-218   13 lines

(47) Ilioneus   (1)   1.522-558   37 lines

                   (2)   7.213-248   36 lines

                      Total: 73 lines

(48) Iris   (1)   4.702-703 $1\frac{1}{3}$ lines

                   (2)   5.623-640 $17\frac{5}{6}$ lines

                   (3)   9.6-13   8 lines

                      Total: $26\frac{1}{6}$ lines

Iulus: *see* Ascanius

(49) Iuno   (1)   1.37-49 $12\frac{3}{4}$ lines

                   (2)   1.65-75   11 lines

Book 1: 2 speeches by Juno, $23\frac{3}{4}$ lines

[8] Reported by Euandrus.

(3)	4.93-104	12 lines
(4)	4.115-127	12$\frac{5}{12}$ lines

Book 4: 2 speeches by Juno, 24$\frac{5}{12}$ lines

(5)	7.293-322	30 lines
(6)	7.331-340	10 lines
(7)	7.552-560	7$\frac{5}{6}$ lines

Book 7: 3 speeches by Juno, 47$\frac{5}{6}$ lines

(8)	10.63-95	32$\frac{7}{12}$ lines
(9)	10.611-620	9$\frac{7}{12}$ lines
(10)	10.628-632	4$\frac{7}{12}$ lines

Book 10: 3 speeches by Juno, 46$\frac{3}{4}$ lines

(11)	12.142-153	12 lines
(12)	12.156-159	2$\frac{5}{6}$ lines
(13)	12.808-828	21 lines

Book 12: 3 speeches by Juno, 35$\frac{5}{6}$ lines

In all, Juno utters 13 speeches, covering 178$\frac{7}{12}$ lines.

(50) Iuppiter	(1)	1.257-296	40 lines
	(2)	4.223-237	15 lines
	(3)	9.94-103	10 lines
	(4)	10.6-15	10 lines
	(5)	10.104-113	9$\frac{5}{12}$ lines
	(6)	10.467-472	6 lines
	(7)	10.607-610	4 lines
	(8)	10.622-627	6 lines

Book 10: 5 speeches by Jupiter, 35$\frac{5}{12}$ lines

(9)	12.793-806	13$\frac{7}{12}$ lines
(10)	12.830-840	11 lines

Book 12: 2 speeches by Jupiter, 24$\frac{7}{12}$ lines

In all, Jupiter utters 10 speeches, covering 125 lines.

(51) Iuturna	(1)	12.229-237	9 lines
	(2)	12.625-630	5$\frac{5}{12}$ lines
	(3)	12.872-884	13 lines
		Total: 27$\frac{5}{12}$ lines	
(52) Laocoon		2.42-49	7$\frac{5}{6}$ lines
(53) Latinus	(1)	7.195-211	17 lines

(2)	7.259-273	$14\frac{7}{12}$ lines
(3)	7.594-599	$5\frac{5}{12}$ lines

Book 7: 3 speeches by Latinus, 37 lines

(4)	11.302-335	34 lines

Book 11: 1 speech by Latinus, 34 lines

(5)	12.19-45	$26\frac{1}{6}$ lines
(6)	12.197-211	$14\frac{1}{4}$ lines

Book 12: 2 speeches by Latinus, $40\frac{5}{12}$ lines
In all, Latinus utters 6 speeches, covering $111\frac{5}{12}$ lines.

(54) Liger	(1)	10.581-583	$2\frac{5}{12}$ lines
	(2)	10.597-598	2 lines
		Total: $4\frac{5}{12}$ lines	
(55) Magus		10.524-529	6 lines
(56) Matres Latinae		11.483-485	3 lines
(57) Mercurius	(1)	4.265-276[9]	$9\frac{5}{6}$ lines
	(2)	4.560-570	$10\frac{1}{6}$ lines
		Total: 20 lines	
(58) Messapus		12.296	1 line
Metiscus: *see* Iuturna			
(59) Mezentius	(1)	10.737	1 line
	(2)	10.743-744	$1\frac{1}{6}$ lines
	(3)	10.773-776	$3\frac{1}{4}$ lines
	(4)	10.846-856	$10\frac{1}{4}$ lines
	(5)	10.861-866	6 lines
	(6)	10.878-882	4 lines
	(7)	10.900-906	7 lines
		Total: $32\frac{2}{3}$ lines	
(60) Mnestheus	(1)	5.189-197	8 lines
	(2)	9.781-787	$6\frac{7}{12}$ lines
		Total: $14\frac{7}{12}$ lines	
(61) Musaeus		6.673-676	4 lines
(62) Nautes		5.709-718	10 lines
(63) Neptunus	(1)	1.132-141	10 lines
	(2)	5.800-815	16 lines
		Total: 26 lines	
(64) Nisus	(1)	5.353-356	$3\frac{7}{12}$ lines
	(2)	9.184-196	$12\frac{3}{4}$ lines

[9] Omitting 4.273.

(3)	9.207-218	$11\frac{3}{4}$ lines
(4)	9.234-245	$11\frac{7}{12}$ lines
(5)	9.320-323	4 lines
(6)	9.355-356	$1\frac{11}{12}$ lines
(7)	9.390-391	$1\frac{1}{4}$ lines
(8)	9.404-409	6 lines
(9)	9.427-430	4 lines

Nisus utters one speech in Book Five and eight in Book Nine: $56\frac{5}{6}$ lines.

(65) Numanus		9.598-620	23 lines
(66) Opis	(1)	11.841-849	$8\frac{5}{12}$ lines
	(2)	11.855-857	$2\frac{5}{6}$ lines
		Total: $11\frac{1}{4}$ lines	
(67) Orodes		10.739-741	$2\frac{7}{12}$ lines
(68) Palinurus	(1)	5.13-14	$1\frac{7}{12}$ lines
	(2)	5.17-25	9 lines
	(3)	5.848-851	4 lines
	(4)	6.347-371	$24\frac{3}{4}$ lines
		Total: $39\frac{1}{3}$ lines	
(69) Pallas	(1)	8.112-114	$2\frac{5}{12}$ lines
	(2)	8.122-123	$1\frac{11}{12}$ lines

Book 8: 2 speeches by Pallas, $4\frac{1}{3}$ lines

(3)	10.369-378	10 lines
(4)	10.421-423	3 lines
(5)	10.449-451	$2\frac{1}{4}$ lines
(6)	10.460-463	4 lines

Book 10: 4 speeches by Pallas, $19\frac{1}{4}$ lines

In all, Pallas utters 6 speeches, $23\frac{7}{12}$ lines.

(70) Pandarus		9.737-739	$2\frac{3}{4}$ lines
(71) Panthus		2.324-335	12 lines
(72) Penates		3.154-171	18 lines
(73) Phlegyas[10]		6.620	1 line
(74) Polydorus		3.41-46	6 lines
(75) Priamus	(1)	2.148-151	4 lines
	(2)	2.535-543	$8\frac{3}{4}$ lines
		Total: $12\frac{3}{4}$ lines	

[10] Reported by Deiphobe.

(76) Pyrgo	5.646-652	7 lines
(77) Pyrrhus	2.547-550	$2^{11}\!/_{12}$ lines

Remulus: *see* Numanus

(78) Saces	12.653-664	12 lines
(79) Salii	8.293-302	$9\frac{3}{4}$ lines
(80) Sinon	2.69-72 + 77-104 + 108-144 + 154-194	$109^{7}\!/_{12}$ lines
(81) Somnus	5.843-846	4 lines
(82) Tarchon (1)	10.294-298	$4^{7}\!/_{12}$ lines
(2)	11.732-740	9 lines

Total: $13^{7}\!/_{12}$ lines

(83) Tiberinus	8.36-65[11]	29 lines
(84) Tolumnius	12.259-265	$6\frac{5}{6}$ lines
(85) Turnus (1)	7.436-444	$8\frac{3}{4}$ lines
(2)	9.18-22	$4^{5}\!/_{12}$ lines
(3)	9.51-52	$1^{1}\!/_{12}$ lines
(4)	9.128-158	31 lines
(5)	9.560-561	$1\frac{1}{6}$ lines
(6)	9.741-742	2 lines
(7)	9.747-748	2 lines

Book 9: 6 speeches by Turnus, $41\frac{2}{3}$ lines

(8)	10.279-284	6 lines
(9)	10.441-443	$2^{7}\!/_{12}$ lines
(10)	10.481	1 line
(11)	10.491-495	$4\frac{1}{2}$ lines
(12)	10.649-650	2 lines
(13)	10.668-679	12 lines

Book 10: 6 speeches by Turnus, $27\frac{2}{3}$ lines

(14)	11.378-444[12]	66 lines
(15)	11.459-461	$1^{11}\!/_{12}$ lines
(16)	11.463-467	$4^{11}\!/_{12}$ lines
(17)	11.508-519	12 lines

Book 11: 4 speeches by Turnus, $84\frac{5}{6}$ lines

(18)	12.11-17	7 lines
(19)	12.48-53	6 lines

[11] Omitting 8.46.   [12] Omitting 11.404.

337

(20)	12.72-80	9 lines
(21)	12.95-100	$5\frac{3}{4}$ lines
(22)	12.359-361	3 lines
(23)	12.620-621	2 lines
(24)	12.632-649	18 lines
(25)	12.676-680	5 lines
(26)	12.693-695	3 lines
(27)	12.777-779	$2\frac{5}{6}$ lines
(28)	12.894-895	$1\frac{7}{12}$ lines
(29)	12.931-938	$7\frac{1}{6}$ lines

Book 12: 12 speeches by Turnus, $70\frac{1}{3}$ lines

In all, Turnus utters 29 speeches, covering $233\frac{1}{4}$ lines.

Vates Etruscorum: *see* Haruspex Etruscorum

(86)	Vates Latinorum	7.68-70	$2\frac{5}{12}$ lines
(87)	Venulus	11.243-295	53 lines
(88)	Venus	(1) 1.229-253	$24\frac{2}{3}$ lines
		(2) 1.321-324	$3\frac{2}{3}$ lines
		(3) 1.335-370	$35\frac{1}{4}$ lines
		(4) 1.387-401	15 lines
		(5) 1.664-688	25 lines

Book 1: 5 speeches by Venus, $103\frac{7}{12}$ lines

(6)	2.594-620	27 lines

Book 2: 1 speech by Venus, 27 lines

(7)	4.107-114	$6\frac{2}{3}$ lines

Book 4: 1 speech by Venus, $6\frac{2}{3}$ lines

(8)	5.781-798	18 lines

Book 5: 1 speech by Venus, 18 lines

(9)	8.374-386	13 lines
(10)	8.612-614	3 lines

Book 8: 2 speeches by Venus, 16 lines

(11)	10.18-62	$44\frac{7}{12}$ lines

Book 10: speech by Venus, $44\frac{7}{12}$ lines

In all, Venus utters 11 speeches, covering $215\frac{5}{6}$ lines.

(89) Volcens   (1) 9.376-377 $1\frac{5}{12}$ lines

                        (2) 9.422-423 $1\frac{5}{12}$ lines

                        Total: $2\frac{5}{6}$ lines

(90) Vulcanus   (1) 8.395-404 $9\frac{7}{12}$ lines

                        (2) 8.439-443 $4\frac{1}{4}$ lines

                        Total: $13\frac{5}{6}$ lines

339

APPENDIX 5

Speeches by Disguised Characters

The following characters deliver speeches under assumed identities.

Allecto as Calybe: 7.421-434
Apollo as Butes: 9.653-656
Iris as Beroe: 5.623-640
Iuturna as Camers:
   12.229-237

Iuturna as Metiscus:
   12.625-630
Somnus as Phorbas: 5.843-846
Venus as a Carthaginian
   maiden: 1.321-334, 335-370,
   387-401

Speeches Within Speeches

This is a list of the speeches in the *Aeneid* which occur within larger speeches. Most naturally belong to Aeneas's narrative in Books Two and Three. Occasionally a speaker will quote a few words from a speech made by an opponent (e.g. 10.85, 11.399, 11.442), but these are not complete speeches reported by a hearer.

Achaemenides: 3.599-606, 613-654
Aeneas: 2.281-286, 322, 348-354, 577-587, 657-670, 707-720; 3.85-89, 315-319, 359-368, 493-505
Amasenus: 11.557-560
Anchises: 2.638-649, 689-691, 701-704, 733-734; 3.103-117, 182-188, 265-266, 528-529, 539-543, 558-560; 7.124-127
Androgeos: 2.373-375
Andromache: 3.310-312, 321-343, 486-491
Apollo: 2.116-119; 3.94-98
Cassandra: 5.637-638
Celaeno: 3.247-257
Coroebus: 2.387-391
Creusa: 2.675-678, 776-789
Diomedes: 11.252-293
Haruspex Etruscorum: 8.499-503
Hector: 2.289-295
Hecuba: 2.519-524
Helenus: 3.374-462, 475-481
Laocoon: 2.42-49
Panthus: 2.324-335
Penates: 3.154-171
Phlegyas: 6.620
Polydorus: 3.41-46
Priamus: 2.148-151, 535-543
Pyrrhus: 2.547-550
Sinon: 2.69-72, 77-104, 108-144, 154-194
Venus: 2.594-620

APPENDIX 7

Speeches and Thoughts in Oratio Obliqua

Sometimes Vergil reports the words or reflections of his characters not directly, but in oratio obliqua. When he does so, he abbreviates them tightly, in order to speed up the pace of his narrative: so tightly that it is not difficult for readers to overlook an important piece of information, as in 11.898-900. Sometimes, on the other hand, Vergil intends us to use our imagination to fill in his outline: as with the song of Iopas (1.743-746) and the ravings of Amata (7.389-391).

It is possible that during his revision Vergil would have turned at least some of these passages into direct speech. For example, Turnus's orders to his officers in 7.467-469 are closely compressed, and the boast which follows them is put into indirect speech: *se satis ambobus Teucrisque uenire Latinisque.* Yet it is followed by *haec ubi dicta dedit.* Elsewhere in the *Aeneid,* this phrase closes a passage—usually an important passage—of direct speech.[1] (The other instances are 2.790, 6.628, 7.323, 8.541, 10.633, 12.81, and 12.441; *dicta dabat* and *dicta dabas* also refer to direct speech in 5.852 and 10.600.) Therefore Vergil may have intended to convert Turnus's briefly reported vaunt into a warlike speech directly uttered.

The most important examples of speech, song, and thought reported in oratio obliqua are the following.

1.743-746: the song of Iopas
1.751-752: Dido's questions
2.229-233: the shouts of the Trojans about Laocoon's death
4.191-194: the report of Fama about Aeneas and Dido
4.229-231: Venus's promise to Jupiter about Aeneas
4.283-284: Aeneas's self-interrogation
4.289-294: Aeneas's orders to his officers
4.598-599: reports about Aeneas's escape from Troy
5.615-616: complaints of the Trojan women

---

[1] This shows that line 9.430, "tantum infelicem nimium dilexit amicum," which a few editors have taken to be a comment by the poet, is in fact part of Nisus' speech, since it is immediately followed by *talia dicta dabat.* Confirmation is given by G. E. Duckworth, "The significance of Nisus and Euryalus," *AJP* 88 (1967) 139 n. 42.

6.161-162: Aeneas and Achates discuss the Sibyl's warning
6.892:   Anchises' advice
7.79-80:   interpretation of the omen of Lavinia's flaming head
7.150-151: results of the Trojans' exploration
7.255-258: Faunus's prophecy
7.389-391: Amata's ravings
7.470:   Turnus's boast
8.10-17:   the diplomatic message carried by Venulus to Diomede
8.288-293: part of the hymn to Hercules
9.41-43:   Aeneas's instructions to his officers
9.67-68:   Turnus's self-interrogation
9.399-401: Nisus' self-interrogation
9.804-805: Jupiter's message to Juno
10.149-153: Aeneas's diplomatic speech to Tarchon
11.102-105: the plea of the Latin envoys
11.227-230: the report of the Latin embassy
11.449-450: the news of Aeneas's offensive
11.898-900: the news of the Volscian defeat and Aeneas's advance
12.76-80:   Turnus's message to Aeneas
12.486:   Aeneas's doubt
12.600:   Amata's self-accusation

The brief message from Jupiter to Juno summarized in 9.804-805 shows how Vergil always works for τάχος. In Homer such a message would have been given twice, once by the originator Zeus and once in the same words by his messenger, both times in direct speech. On this see J. Endt, "Botenberichte bei Vergil und Ovid," *WS* 25 (1903) 293-307.

Aeneas's announcements of contests in 5.291-292 and 5.485-486 are not (as Lipscomb says on p. 21, quoting Heinze p. 409) true instances of speeches reported in oratio obliqua. Lipscomb adds that "it is estimated" that the speeches in oratio obliqua amount to "not over 140 lines"; yet those listed above scarcely reach 85 lines. No such estimate is useful unless it is supported by lists which allow readers to verify the assertion for themselves.

SELECT BIBLIOGRAPHY

TEXTS

The text of Vergil used is that edited by R.A.B. Mynors (Oxford, 1969); there are also some references to the text of R. Sabbadini (Turin, 1930, ed. L. Castiglioni, Turin, 1964). Citations from Ennius's *Annals* come from J. Vahlen's edition (Leipzig, 1928², repr. Amsterdam, 1963). The tragedies of Ennius and other Roman playwrights are quoted from O. Ribbeck's edition (Leipzig, 1897³).

WORKS OF REFERENCE

Ernesti, *Graec.* = Io. Christ. Theoph. Ernesti, *Lexicon Technologiae Graecorum Rhetoricae* (Leipzig, 1795, repr. Hildesheim, 1962). List of the Greek technical terms used in discussing oratory and literary style in general, with definitions, illustrations, and explanations.

Ernesti, *Lat.* = Io. Christ. Theoph. Ernesti, *Lexicon Technologiae Latinorum Rhetoricae* (Leipzig, 1797, repr. Hildesheim, 1962). Similar list for Latin technical terms.

Halm = C. Halm, *Rhetores Latini Minores* (Leipzig, 1863, repr. Frankfurt am Main, 1964). The standard edition of the minor Latin rhetorical manuals.

Lausberg = H. Lausberg, *Handbuch der literarischen Rhetorik* (2 vols., Munich, 1960). Handbook of rhetorical terms, carefully arranged, explained, and indexed, with many examples from Greek, Latin, and French literature.

Marouzeau = J. Marouzeau, *Traité de Stylistique latine* (Paris, 1962⁴). A perceptive analysis of many types of Latin style: it reads with deceptive ease, but is full of learning.

Spengel 1 = *Rhetores Graeci ex recognitione Leonardi Spengel*, ed. C. Hammer, vol. 1 (Leipzig, 1894).

Spengel 2 = *Rhetores Graeci ex recognitione Leonardi Spengel* II (Leipzig, 1854).

Spengel 3 = *Rhetores Graeci ex recognitione Leonardi Spengel* III (Leipzig, 1856).

These three volumes bring together almost all the post-Aristotelian Greek writers on rhetorical technique.

Szantyr = *Lateinische Syntax und Stilistik, von J. B. Hofmann,*

neubearbeitet von Anton Szantyr (Munich, 1965). Indispensable: the best of all books on the Latin language.
Volkmann = R. Volkmann, *Die Rhetorik der Griechen und Römer* (Leipzig, 1885²). The best book on rhetorical theory as taught by the Greek and Roman technicians, with examples from Greek and Roman oratory. The technical terms are nearly all there, but Volkmann does not over-emphasize them, and works always toward explaining real speeches on important issues.

GENERAL WORKS ON VERGIL

Büchner = K. Büchner, "P. Vergilius Maro," *RE* VIII A, 1 (1955) 1021-1264 and VIII A, 2 (1958) 1265-1486; published separately as *P. Vergilius Maro, der Dichter der Römer* (Stuttgart, 1959). The basic modern treatise on Vergil.
Cartault = A. Cartault, *L'Art de Virgile dans l'Énéide* (2 vols., Paris, 1926). Interpretation of the poem paragraph by paragraph: intelligent, but harsh and hypercritical.
Heinze = R. Heinze, *Vergils epische Technik* (Leipzig, 1915³). This book brought Vergil back into serious consideration in Germany as a poet, after his eclipse as an "imitator" in the nineteenth century. Part two, chapter three, section III, deals with the speeches. Heinze was against the idea that Vergil's poetry, and in particular the speeches, should be interpreted through the application of rhetorical rules: he said so emphatically in a lecture to a group of scholars, "Die römische Poesie und die Rhetorik," *Humanistisches Gymnasium* 38 (1924) 181. There is much interest in his comparison of Ovid's speeches with those of Vergil in "Ovids elegische Erzählung," *SB Leipzig* 71 (1919) 7.
Heyne = P. *Virgilius Maro ed. C. G. Heyne* (fourth edition by G.P.E. Wagner: *Aen.* 1-6, Leipzig and London, 1832; 7-12, 1833): obsolete as far as the textual tradition is concerned, but full of wisdom and common sense, with instructive essays on Vergiliana.
Kvíčala = J. Kvíčala, *Neue Beitraege zur Erklaerung der Aeneis* (Prague, 1881). Analyses by a Vergilian who knew the poem by heart and detected many hitherto-unseen subtleties.
Norden = E. Norden, P. *Vergilius Maro, Aeneis Buch VI* (Leipzig, 1915², repr. Stuttgart, 1957). A remarkable display of learn-

ing on almost every conceivable topic suggested by the sixth book of the *Aeneid*, illuminating not only the poem but much else in classical antiquity.

Otis = B. Otis, *Virgil, a study in civilized poetry* (Oxford, 1963). A clever and occasionally over-ingenious analysis of Vergil's ideals and techniques in building a new poem on old foundations.

Pöschl = V. Pöschl, *The art of Vergil; image and symbol in the Aeneid* (tr. G. Seligson, Ann Arbor, 1962). Thoughtful evocation of the symbols behind the actions and the imagery.

SPECIAL STUDIES

Austin 2 = R. G. Austin, *Aeneidos liber secundus* (Oxford, 1964).

Austin 4 = R. G. Austin, *Aeneidos liber quartus* (Oxford, 1955). Perceptive line-by-line commentaries.

Bassett = S. E. Bassett, *The Poetry of Homer* (Berkeley, 1938). A simple straightforward book on the two epics, written by a convinced Unitarian.

Conrad = E. Conrad, *Untersuchungen zu der Technik der Reden in Vergils Aeneis* (Tübingen dissertation, 1923, unpublished). Sensitive analysis of twelve important speeches.

Eichhoff = F. G. Eichhoff, *Etudes grecques sur Virgile* (3 vols., Paris, 1825). List of passages of Greek poetry adapted by Vergil: valuable.

Fingerle = A. Fingerle, *Typik der homerischen Reden* (Munich, 1939, microfilm). This unpublished work reached me only after I had completed the last draft of the present book. It classifies all the speeches in the *Iliad* and the *Odyssey* (apart from a small group of questions), dividing them into types along lines roughly the same as those used here for the *Aeneid*: requests, taunts and threats, jests, etc. It eschews rhetorical analysis, and seems to aim chiefly at showing how repetitive many Homeric speeches are. It contains many statistical data which I have not seen elsewhere, and deserves to be made more widely available to students of epic poetry.

F. Gladow, *De Vergilio ipsius imitatore* (Greifswald, 1921). A list of the passages (more than one would imagine) in which Vergil echoes his own poetry: useful as an enumeration but devoid of critical comment.

347

Halter = T. Halter, *Form und Gehalt in Vergils Aeneis* (Munich, 1963). An intelligent study of responsions within the poem, and of structural principles underlying certain important passages.

Hügi = M. Hügi, *Vergils Aeneis und die hellenistische Dichtung* (Berne, 1952). Parallels between extant Hellenistic poems and the work of Vergil.

Knauer = G. N. Knauer, *Die Aeneis und Homer* (*Hypomnemata* 7, Göttingen, 1964). By minute analysis of the three epics Knauer shows how Vergil embodied many essential elements of the Homeric poems within his own.

Maar = O. Maar, *Pathos und Pathosrede in dem Didobuch von Vergils Aeneis* (Vienna, 1953, microfilm). Detailed investigation of Vergil's techniques in conveying extreme emotion through speech in Book Four.

Penquitt = E. Penquitt, *De Didonis Vergilianae exitu* (Königsberg, 1910). Careful discussion of problems in Book Four.

Williams 3 = R. D. Williams, *Aeneidos liber tertius* (Oxford, 1962).

Williams 5 = R. D. Williams, *Aeneidos liber quintus* (Oxford, 1960).

Two line-by-line commentaries resembling R. G. Austin's, equally useful.

Wlosok = A. Wlosok, *Die Göttin Venus in Vergils Aeneis* (Heidelberg, 1967). Lively discussion not only of Venus and her role in the epic but of many structural and rhetorical problems of much interest.

Indexes

Figures within parentheses, (123), show that the subject of the note is alluded to, but not actually named, in the passage cited.

INDEX LOCORVM

351

INDEX NOMINVM ET RERVM

INDEX

Saturn, 106, 120, 161, 255, 266;
 Saturnian peace, 56, 145-146 n. 87,
 255; *Saturnia (Iuno)*, 120, 145,
 161
sceleratus, 192 n. 8
cχῆμα, 66, 147
scilicet, 31, 152, 175
Scipio: P. Cornelius (d. 211), 85;
 P. Cornelius (Aemilianus, d. 129),
 42; Q. Caecilius Metellus Pius
 (d. 46), 182; the Scipios, 111,
 242, 243
Scylla, 34 n. 27, 188, 232, 256,
 288, 289
Seneca the younger, 47
sermocinatio, 136-137 n. 76
Servius, 5, 7-8, 197 n. 12, 246 n. 87
Shakespeare, 56
Sibyl: *see* Deiphobe
Silvius, Aeneas, 17, 241 n. 74
Sinon, 10 n. 14, 16-17, 27, 28,
 28-29 n. 20, 107, 174, 244,
 247-248
Sisyphus, 245
Sleep, 260, 265
Socrates, 48 n. 4, 234, 285
soliloquies, 4 and n. 2, 11, 15-16,
 20, 24, 36, 39, 48, 50, 112, 147,
 157-184, 188, 189-191, 198,
 226-231, 266-268, 278, 305,
 317-318
sound-effects, 29 n. 22, 31, 70-71,
 75 n. 50, 99, 124, 133 n. 72, 134,
 137, 147, 151 n. 96, 153, 161,
 162, 171, 175, 178, 189; *and see*
 alliteration, rhyme
spolia opima, 18, 101 n. 10
"stage-directions" in speeches, 17
Statius, 11
Stoicism, 43, 73, 234, 237
suasoria, 7, 8, 82
suicide, 230-231
superstitio, 254-255
Sychaeus, 111-112, 177
cύγκρισιс, 61, (90)
Symmachus, Q. Aurelius, 4

Talleyrand, 287
Tantalus, 244
Tarchon, 39, 114, 309 n. 10
Tarquins, 242
taunts, 5, 116-117, 193, 205, 209,
 216, 217, 248-249, 250, 262, 305,
 318
Tecmessa, 223
Telemachus, 23, 28, 31, 141, 199,
 204, 212 n. 29, 233, 251, 254,
 257, 272, 274 n. 123
τελικὰ κεφάλαια, 51 n. 8, 80 n. 58
Teucer: ancestor of Trojan kings,
 232; half-brother of Ajax, 115,
 169, 195, 231
Thersites, 210-211, 248-251, 258
Theseus, 219, (220), 221, 222, 227,
 244, 268, 279-280
Thetis, 22, 126, 265, 271, 272 n. 121,
 274, 275, 314 n. 37
threats, 48, 116-117, 209, 211, 216,
 305, 318
θρῆνοι, 255
Thucydides, 25, 84-85
Tiber: god, 21, 67, 102-103, 118 n.
 40, 120, 200, 204, 287, 312 n. 30;
 name, 108; river, 21
Tiberius, 95
Tiresias, 201 n. 15, 256
Titans, 143, 244
Titianus, Julius, 7 n. 7
Tityus, 244
tractatio, 51
tragedy: generally, 18, 45, 186, 187,
 228; Greek, 16-17, 40, 158 n. 106,
 163-164, 174, 191 n. 7, 255, 279;
 Roman, 209; *and see individual
 playwrights*
translatio, 70
transmigration: *see* metempsychosis
Trebatius Testa, C., 142 n. 85
tricolon, 57, 150
Triton, 259
Trojans: *see* Greece and Troy
Tucca, Plotius, 165, 169 n. 122, 173

379